T0320445

Low Carbon Mobility Transitions

Edited by

Debbie Hopkins and James Higham

(G) **Goodfellow Publishers Ltd**

(G) Published by Goodfellow Publishers Limited,
26 Home Close, Wolvercote, Oxford OX2 8PS
http://www.goodfellowpublishers.com

British Library Cataloguing in Publication Data: a catalogue record for this title is available from the British Library.

Library of Congress Catalog Card Number: on file.

ISBN: 978-1-910158-64-7

 Design and typesetting by P.K. McBride, www.macbride.org.uk

Printed by Baker & Taylor, www.baker-taylor.com

Cover design by Cylinder

Contents

Part 3: Innovations for Low Carbon Mobility

Conclusion

Biographies

Editors

Debbie Hopkins is a Research Fellow at the Transport Studies Unit, School of Geography and the Environment, and a Junior Research Fellow in Geography at Mansfield College, both at the University of Oxford (UK), where she works with the Centre on Innovation and Energy Demand (CIED). Debbie is an environmental social scientist and human geographer with research interests relating to climate change mitigation and adaptation, mobility cultures, and low carbon mobility practices and innovations. A comprehensive summary of Debbie's publication record can be viewed on Google Scholar at: http://tinyurl.com/jl8k4y2. Email: debbie.hopkins@ouce.ox.ac.uk

James Higham is a Professor at the University of Otago (New Zealand), Visiting Professor, University of Stavanger (Norway) and co-editor or the Journal of Sustainable Tourism. His research addresses tourism and environmental change across the spectrum of spatial scales. A comprehensive summary of James's publication record can be viewed on Google Scholar at: http://tinyurl.com/j9ksq7u. Email: james.higham@otago.ac.nz

Contributing authors

Stewart Barr is Professor of Geography at the University of Exeter, UK. His research focuses on the social science of behavioural change for sustainability. He has worked on a wide range of projects that seek to understand how publics engage with contemporary environmental issues and undertakes teaching at the undergraduate and postgraduate levels on sustainability, risk and the geographies of transport and mobility. Email: s.w.barr@exeter.ac.uk

David Beeton is Managing Director of Urban Foresight, a consulting think tank focused on strategies and solutions for future cities. He is also Director of E-cosse, a government-backed partnership to advance electric vehicle adoption in Scotland, and led the development of Transport Scotland's *Switched on Scotland* roadmap to Widespread Adoption of Plug-in Vehicles. David holds Master's degrees in Civil and Environmental Engineering, an MBA and a PhD in Technology Management from University of Cambridge. Email: david.beeton@urbanforesight.org

Rob Bongáerts is a Lecturer at NHTV Breda University of Applied Sciences (Breda, Netherlands), where he also researches for the Centre for Sustainable Tourism and Transport. Rob focuses on business and airline economics, aviation management, tour operating and sustainable tourism. Email: bongaerts.r@nhtv.nl

Vivek Chandran is a Research Associate at the Centre for Urban Equity and visiting faculty at the Faculty of Planning, CEPT University. He has been working on sustainable land use and transport issues for more than three years. His research interests lie in land use transport integration and parking policy in the Indian context. Email: vivek.chandran@cept.ac.in

Scott A. Cohen is Head of the Department of Tourism and Events and Deputy Director of Research for the School of Hospitality and Tourism Management at the University of Surrey (United Kingdom). Scott primarily researches sociological and consumer behaviour issues in tourism, transport and leisure contexts, with particular interests in sustainable mobility, hypermobility and in lifestyle travel. Email: s.cohen@surrey.ac.uk

Alexa Delbosc is a Lecturer in the Institute of Transport Studies in the Monash University Department of Civil Engineering. She draws from her research-based Master's in social psychology from Harvard University to study the changing travel habits of young people, transport and psychological well-being, travel behaviour and human factors in public transport. In 2016 she was awarded a Discovery Early Career Research Award by the Australian Research Council to conduct a three-year study of the travel and life transitions of Australian millennials. Email: alexa.delbosc@monash.edu

Eke Eijgelaar is Senior Researcher at the Centre for Sustainable Tourism and Transport of NHTV Breda University of Applied Sciences, the Netherlands. His main research interest concerns the monitoring and mitigation of tourism's carbon footprint, and related topics like carbon management and low- as well as high-carbon tourism such as cycle and cruise tourism. Eke has co-authored articles in the *Journal of Sustainable Tourism* and *Tourism Management*, amongst others, and published several book chapters in edited volumes. Email: eijgelaar.e@nhtv.nl

Stefan Gössling is a Professor at Lund and Linnaeus Universities, both Sweden. He is also the research co-ordinator at the Western Norway Research Institute's Centre for Sustainable Tourism. He studies interrelationships of tourism, transport and sustainability. Email: sgo@vestforsk.no

C. Michael Hall is Professor at the University of Canterbury, New Zealand and a Docent, University of Oulu, Finland. He also holds positions at Linneaus University, Sweden; the University of Eastern Finland; and the University of Johannesberg, South Africa. Current research focuses on global environmental change, regional development and World Heritage in Denmark, Germany, Mauritius and Sweden. Further details on Michael's work can be found here: http://tinyurl.com/h5tuw7j

Muhammad Imran is an Associate Professor and teaches transport and urban planning at Massey University, New Zealand. His current research explores how institutions can promote sustainable transport in cities in developing and developed countries. His research argues for a greater recognition of the role of politics and the influence of discourse on transport decision-making and reveals the limitations of technical methodologies. Imran is an author of a book, *Institutional Barriers to Sustainable Urban Transport in Pakistan* published by Oxford University Press in 2010. Imran has received research grants from the Royal Society of NZ Marsden Fund (2013-2016) and, the NZ Transport Agency (2008) and has acted as a consultant for the World Bank (2010). Email: m.imran@massey.ac.nz

Yogi Joseph is a Research Associate at the Centre for Urban Equity, CEPT University, Ahmedabad, India. He is keenly interested in accessibility studies, especially from the perspective of vulnerable groups including women, children and the differently-abled. Email: yogi.joseph@cept.ac.in

Rutul Joshi teaches at the Faculty of Planning, CEPT University and is a founding member of Centre for Urban Equity at CEPT University, Ahmedabad, India. His research interests consist of issues of sustainable mobility and transport equity in the cities of Global South. Rutul teaches subjects related to land use and transport planning along with urban history. Email: rutul.joshi@cept.ac.in

Shigemi Kagawa obtained his BA in Civil Engineering, MA in Information Sciences, and Ph.D. from Tohoku University, Japan, in 2001. Since 2016, he has been a Professor of environmental and economic statistics at Kyushu University, Japan. His research interests include integrated industrial ecology modelling techniques and sustainability research. Email: kagawa@econ.kyushu-u.ac.jp

Lisa Kane is an engineer-sociologist with a special research interest in how ways of valuing circulate in road engineering practices. She has advised on several low carbon transport transition projects in South Africa and has consulted to various NGOs, including the World Wildlife Fund. She is co-founder of the Centre for Transport Studies at the University of Cape Town, where she is currently an Honorary Research Associate. She is also co-founder and board member of the NGO Open Streets Cape Town. Email: lisa@lisakane.co.za

Sophie-May Kerr is a PhD student in the School of Geography and Sustainable Communities at the University of Wollongong. Her research interests include ethnic diversity and low carbon mobilities and the experiences of families with children living in apartments, sharing materials and space. Through her research, Sophie-May seeks to explore social and environmental transformations that address high-carbon and space intensive urban lifestyles. Email: smk534@uowmail.edu.au

Paula Kivimaa is a Senior Research Fellow at Science Policy Research Unit, University of Sussex, and a Senior Researcher in the Finnish Environment Institute SYKE. She obtained a PhD in organisations and management from Helsinki School of Economics in 2008, focusing on the innovation effects of environmental policies on the Nordic forest industry. Her more recent research links to the interface between public policies and sustainability transitions, covering a range of empirical topics from innovations and policies related to transport and mobility to bioenergy and energy efficiency of buildings. Email: p.kivimaa@sussex.ac.uk

Natascha Klocker is a Senior Lecturer in the School of Geography and Sustainable Communities, at the University of Wollongong, Australia. Natascha's research seeks to foreground the contributions of diverse migrant groups to environmental thinking – and practice – in Australia. Her central argument is that environmental thinking urgently needs to be more open to the diverse cultural resources that migrants bring. Email: natascha@uow.edu.au

Tobias Kuhnimhof heads the department for passenger transport at the Institute for Transport Research of the German Aerospace Center (DLR) in Berlin since 2014. From 2002 to 2010 he worked at KIT's (Karlsruhe Institute of Technology) Institute for Transport Studies; from 2009 to 2010 he was director of statistics and modelling for STRATA GmbH, a consultancy specializing in travel and tourism; from 2010 to 2014 he worked for ifmo, a research establishment of BMW. He holds a diploma in civil engineering and a doctorate degree in transportation engineering. Email: tobias.kuhnimhof@dlr.de

Hamish Mackie leads a small consultancy (Mackie Research and Consulting) and has 20 years of research and consultancy experience in various areas of human factors and ergonomics, with the last ten years spent mostly in the transport sector. The design of transport environments and the associated influence on people's behaviour is Hamish's major area of focus and much of his work in this area involves demonstration projects or trials. The associated uptake of sound transport design processes and outcomes by stakeholders is also an active area of Hamish's work. Email: hamish@mackieresearch.co.nz

Alex Macmillan is a public health physician and Senior Lecturer in Environmental Health at the Department of Preventive and Social Medicine, University of Otago. Her main interests are in translating evidence linking environmental sustainability and health into policy knowledge using participatory modelling. Her particular areas of focus are climate change, transport and housing. Alex is also involved in community based epidemiological research to understand the impacts of changing urban environments on health, equity and environmental sustainability. Email: alex.macmillan@otago.ac.nz

Craig Morton is a Research Fellow in the Institute for Transport Studies at the University of Leeds where he investigates the uptake of low carbon technologies in the transport and household energy sectors. His interests primarily involve the factors which motivate the adoption of low carbon technologies and how the adoption of these technologies varies across space and time. Craig holds a bachelor's degree in Economics from the University of Stirling, a Master's degree in Ecological Economics from the University of Edinburgh and PhD in Human Geography from the University of Aberdeen. Email: c.l.morton@leeds.ac.uk

Yuya Nakamoto obtained his BA in Economics from Kyushu University, Japan, in 2016. Yuya is currently a Ph.D. candidate at Kyushu University, Japan, with research interests including product lifetime analysis and climate policy analysis. Email: y.nakamoto0527@gmail.com

Jeroen Nawijn is Senior Researcher at the Centre for Sustainable Tourism and Transport of NHTV Breda University of Applied Sciences, the Netherlands. His publications cover many aspects of the tourist experience, such as subjective well-being, sustainable behaviour, and emotional experiences at dark tourism sites. Jeroen's academic publications are often featured in popular media. Email: nawijn.j@nhtv.nl

Peter Newman is Professor of Sustainability at Curtin University in Australia. He served on the Board of Infrastructure Australia and was lead author for Transport on the IPCC. He was awarded an Order of Australia for his contribution to urban design and sustainable transport. Email: p.newman@curtin.edu.au

Daisuke Nishijima obtained his BA in Economics, and MA in Economics from Kyushu University, Japan, in 2016. Daisuke is currently a Ph.D. candidate at Kyushu University, Japan. His research interests include product lifetime analysis and climate policy analysis. Email: nishijindaiko@gmail.com

Jane Pearce is a PhD candidate at the University of Canterbury in New Zealand. Her research focuses on the potential of the alternative type of cycles to increase cycling rates among women. She is interested in women and marginal communities research area, and its link to complex issues of social exclusion and ecological sustainability. Email: jane.pearce@pg.canterbury.ac.nz

Paul Peeters is Associate Professor at the Centre for Sustainable Tourism and Transport of NHTV Breda University of Applied Sciences, the Netherlands. Paul is specialized in the impacts of tourism on the environment and specifically on climate change. His publications cover a wide range of topics like global and regional tourism and climate scenario's, system dynamic approaches to tourism, tourism transport mode choice and modal shift, policy making and transport technological developments. Email: peeters.p@nhtv.nl

Tim Schwanen is Associate Professor of Transport Studies and Director of the Transport Studies Unit in the School of Geography and the Environment at the University of Oxford (UK). He is a geographer whose research addresses a range of themes and concerns, including mobilities, cities, socio-technical transitions, social and spatial inequalities, well-being, and the conceptualisation of temporality in geography. Email: tim.schwanen@ouce.ox.ac.uk

Leanne Seeliger is a Research Associate of the University of Stellenbosch's Unit for Environmental Ethics. She has lectured environmental philosophy at several tertiary institutions and her research interests are the green economy, adaptive governance and environmental ethics. She is also passionate about doing environmental education among children living in underprivileged communities. Email: seeliger@sun.ac.za

Melanie Stroebel is a Research Associate at the University of Koblenz-Landau in Germany, where she is part of a cluster to set up a research network that engages with the governance of sustainable growth. She is particularly interested in climate change and approaches the challenge with an interdisciplinary perspective that draws on tourism management, corporate environmental management and global environmental governance. Her doctoral research at the University of Manchester explored how tour operators address and communicate carbon management as well as the context in which they do so. Email: melanie_stroebel@gmx.de

Gareth Shaw is Professor of Retail and Tourism Management in the Business School and was formally Professor of Human Geography at Exeter. He is currently working on Tourism, ecosystem services and wellbeing based on a 4 year EU grant. This involves aspects of social marketing and behaviour change. In addition he has worked on a number of projects relating innovations and behaviour change in consumers. Email: g.shaw@exeter.ac.uk

Armi Temmes is Professor of Practice at Aalto University, School of Business. Trained originally as a microbiologist she has long experience on paper industry, industrial R&D, and especially environmental and corporate responsibility management. At the moment she is involved in teaching of corporate responsibility and research on strategy and sustainable innovation journeys in transport, energy and circular economy. Email: armi.temmes@aalto.fi

David Tyfield is a Reader in Environmental Innovation & Sociology at the Lancaster Environment Centre, Lancaster University. He is Director of the International Research and Innovation Centre for the Environment (I-RICE), Guangzhou and Co-Director of the Centre for Mobilities Research (CeMoRe), Lancaster University. His research focuses on the interaction of political economy, social change and developments in science, technology and innovation, with a particular focus on issues of low carbon transition in China, especially urban e-mobility. He is currently Principal Investigator for a UK Economic and Social Research Council-funded project (2013-17) with colleagues at CeMoRe, Sussex, SOAS, Tsinghua and CAS on 'Low Carbon Innovation in China: Practice, Politics & Prospects', in which he is also leading the research package on urban e-mobility. Email: d.tyfield@lancaster.ac.uk

Gordon Waitt is Head of School and a Professor in the School of Geography and Sustainable Communities at the University of Wollongong, Australia. His research draws upon critical human geography perspective to address social inequalities. His current projects address the inequalities of domestic energy, everyday mobilities and regional cities. Email: gwaitt@uow.edu.au

Christine Weiss works as a research assistant at the Institute for Transport Studies at Karlsruhe Institute of Technology (KIT) since 2012, after concluding her studies in economics engineering at KIT. She is currently preparing her PhD thesis on modelling of car use during longer periods of time. Her main field of research includes surveys on travel behaviour, especially the German Mobility Panel (MOP) and various other topics in travel behaviour research. Email: christine.weiss@kit.edu

Dennis Zuev is a Researcher at CIES-ISCTE, Portugal and vice-president (research) of ISA WG03 Visual Sociology. He participated in the ECPR project Low Carbon Innovation in China at Lancaster University (2014-2016). His current research interests are urban mobility, circumpolar mobilities, visual sociology, and China. Email: tungus66@gmail.com

Acknowledgments

During the course of this book project we have accumulated various debts of favour that we must acknowledge. We are very grateful to Sally North (Goodfellow Publishers, Oxford) who has provided constant support throughout this project. It is very gratifying to work with high quality researchers and we are very grateful for the original empirical and theoretical contributions of all of the authors whose work appears in this volume. This book was inspired initially by collaborations with various scholars at the University of Otago (New Zealand), including our colleagues at the Otago Climate Change Network; Colin Campbell-Hunt, Ben Wooliscroft, Ceri Warnock, Chris Rosin, Hilary Phipps, Sara Walton and Bob Lloyd.

We are also grateful for the collegiality of colleagues and collaborators including Janet Stephenson, Michelle Scott, Jane Khan, Caroline Orchiston, Alaric McCarthy, Sandra Mandic, Sebastian Filep, Tara Duncan, Liz Slotten, Diana Kutzner, Sarah Tapp, Wiebke Finkler, Hassan Kamrul, Abbas Alizadeh, Abrar Faisal, Ismail Shaheer, Arif Hoque, Madda Fumagalli, Sam Spector (University of Otago), Tim Schwanen, Denver Nixon, Anna Plyushteva, Julio Soria-Lara (University of Oxford), Ezra Markowitz (University of Massachusetts Amherst), Graham Miller, Scott Cohen, Paul Hanna (University of Surrey), Tom Hinch (University of Alberta), Lars Bejder (Murdoch University), Ghazali Musa (University of Malaya), Michael Hall (University of Canterbury), Susanne Becken, Brent Moyle (Griffith University), Stefan Gössling (Linnaeus University and Western Norway Research Institute), Truls Engstrøm, Åsa Grahn (University of Stavanger), David Simmons (Lincoln University), Paul Peeters, Eke Eijgelaar (NHTV Breda), Arianne Reis (Western Sydney University), Martin Young (Southern Cross University), Francis Markham (The Australian National University), Brent Ritchie, Lisa Ruhanen, Gabby Walters, Andy Lee (University of Queensland), Bernard Lane (Leeds Beckett University), Bill Bramwell (Sheffield Hallam University), Jan Vidar Haukeland (Norwegian University of Life Sciences and Institute of Transport Economics), Christina Cavaliere (Stockton University), Trudie Walters (University of the Sunshine Coast) and Kelsey Johansen (University of Manitoba).

During the writing of this book, Debbie moved from the Centre for Sustainability (University of Otago) to the Transport Studies Unit (University of Oxford), and would like to acknowledge her colleagues at the Universities of Oxford, Sussex and Manchester, and funding from the Centre for Innovation and Energy Demand (CIED) part of the RCUK's Energy Programme; grant number EP/KO11790/1. James acknowledges with gratitude the University of Stavanger (Norway) and the University of Queensland Jim Whyte Fellowship.

Our greatest debts are to our *whānau*; Mitchell Hopping, Greg and Sue Hopkins, Kaye, Kevin, Joey and Sam Heseltine, and Linda Buxton, Alexandra, Katie and George, Polly and Charles Higham, Tom Higham, Katerina Douka (and Angelos), Caroline Orchiston (and Henry), and Emma Holt.

Debbie Hopkins, Oxford, United Kingdom
James Higham, Dunedin, New Zealand

1 Transitioning to Low Carbon Mobility

Debbie Hopkins

Transport Studies Unit, School of Geography and the Environment, University of Oxford, UK.

James Higham

Department of Tourism, University of Otago, NZ and University of Stavanger, Norway.

'The essence of Transition is in its name. It describes the era of change we are all living in'' (www.transitiontowntotnes.org)

Whether we are living in an era of change, or through the change of an era, since the turn of the century the world has experienced unprecedented economic, political, social and environmental transformation. The 21st Century has seen the rate and intensity of global environmental change surpass all but the most dire of expectations. Climatic events around the world have resulted in the loss of lives, livelihoods and habitats, and strained economies. And each year surpasses the last as 'the hottest year on record' (NOAA, 2016). The 'inconvenient truth' of climate change is now undeniable. At the same time, we[1] are becoming more mobile both domestically, and internationally (Sims *et al.*, 2014). The pace and frequency of corporeal travel is increasing, in order to reach everyday locations for employment, socialisation, recreation and education (Viry & Kaufmann, 2015; Cohen *et al.*, 2015), as well as international tourism destinations (UNWTO, 2016). These mobilities are often dependent on high carbon modes of transport, representing a substantial contribution to global greenhouse gas (GHG) emissions, the underlying cause of anthropogenic climate change.

Automobility is the dominant system of contemporary mobility (Urry, 2004; 2007); a system that supports, prioritises and rewards the hegemony of private, motorised transport. Automobility puts speed, privacy and autonomy at centre stage, and reinforces carbon-dependence (Urry, 2004). High-carbon practices of mobility, along with the technologies, policies, infrastructures and cultures that

---

1   Mobility is increasing, but it is important to note that it is a highly mobile minority.

facilitate them (Geels, 2012), are at odds with the pressing need for deep GHG emissions reductions in order to prevent the wide ranging impacts of unfettered climate change (Sims *et al.*, 2014) and this has led some to refer to transport as the 'road-block to climate change mitigation' (Creutzig *et al.*, 2015: 912). As time has passed, the discourse has become more emphatic, with calls for 'deep decarbonisation' and 'radical emissions reductions' increasing in volume and intensity (e.g. Anderson *et al.*, 2014; Capstick *et al.*, 2014). Tackling the carbon-intensity of current systems of mobility is of critical importance to attaining low carbon economies and societies, and accomplishing meaningful reductions in GHG emissions on a global scale.

A weight of expectation fell on the 2015 climate negotiations to gain new global commitments to extend beyond 2020, in order to limit GHG emissions and global average temperature increase. The Paris Agreement may not have gone far enough for some (Clémençon, 2016), but it *was* successful in elevating global climate policy goals. The Paris negotiations exceeded the previously conceived target of limiting global temperature increases to 'well below 2°C above pre-industrial levels', and instead called for actions to limit increases to *1.5°C* above pre-industrial levels (UN, 2016, Article 2: 22), in order to prevent the more extreme projections of a 2°C warmer world. In any scenario to achieve less than 2°C of warming, transport will play a critical role (ITDP, 2015), and decarbonisation will need to occur in a world of relatively abundant fossil fuels (McGlade & Ekins, 2015). This sentiment was echoed by Sheikh Ahmed Zaki Yamani, former Oil Minister of Saudi Arabia who, in an interview in 2000, stated that: *'The stone age came to an end, not because we had a lack of stones, and the oil age will come to an end not because we have a lack of oil'* (Fagan, 2000). In order to enact a process of meaningful and long-lasting systemic change, engagement with a wide range of actors, across a range of spatial scales, is required. And this must include transport.

With growing demand and rising emissions, the transport sector has a critical role to play in achieving GHG emissions reductions, and stabilising the global climate. Transport-related GHG emissions have more than doubled since 1970 (Sims *et al.*, 2014). The majority of GHG emissions from transport are carbon dioxide (CO_2), and together with the generation of electricity and heat, transport accounts for nearly two-thirds of global CO_2 emissions (IEA, 2015). Alone, transport accounts for 23% of global CO_2 emissions, or just under 7.4 billion tonnes of CO_2 in 2013 (IEA, 2015). Emissions from the road sector account for three quarters of transport-related CO_2 emissions, and have increased by 68% since 1990 (IEA, 2015). Emissions are projected to double by 2050, as are the number of light-duty vehicles (Sperling & Gordon, 2009; Creutzig *et al.*, 2015) as demand for private mobility grows in emerging economies including China, India and Brazil (Sperling & Gordon, 2009; Jetin, 2015). Freight transport demand is also forecast to increase, albeit at a slower pace than passenger transport (Sims *et al.*, 2014) and passenger aviation is projected to grow at a rate of 5% per annum to the 2030s (Airbus, 2013; Boeing, 2013). Thus transport represents a growing concern in efforts to mitigate climate change. Opportunities to reduce direct GHG emissions include: (i) continuing and extending efforts to increase vehicle efficiency, thereby lowering the energy intensity of travel, (ii) shifting to low carbon fuels, (iii) changing travel behaviour including the adoption of travel substitution, low carbon modal choice and purchasing behaviours (Sims *et al.*, 2014; Creutzig *et al.*, 2015). Individually, these efforts are unlikely to result in the required depth of reductions; a low carbon mobility transition requires multi-sectoral, multi-disciplinary efforts across scales.

(Mobility) transitions

The 21st Century has also seen a 'mobility-turn' across the social sciences (Sheller & Urry, 2006), through which processes and practices of mobility and immobility have been foregrounded. In a step away from traditional transport studies, mobilities scholars have highlighted the *'fragile entanglement of physical, movement, representations, and practices'* that constitute mobility (Cresswell, 2010: 18). Thus mobilities research has contributed new insights to traditional understandings of transport and travel, not least of which has been the centring of human experiences of travel. And while distinctions have been made between transport and mobilities studies, the complementarity of these lenses is now coming to the fore, with opportunities for the *'mobilising of transportation and transporting of mobilities'* (Sheller, 2015: 12).

Transport is a vast and complex socio-technical system (Rees *et al.*, 2016). The study of systemic transformations emerges from a range of academic traditions, which include: integrated assessment models, socio-technical transitions analysis and practice-based action research (Geels *et al.*, 2016). A socio-technical system denotes the range of technologies, markets, infrastructures, consumer practices, cultural meanings, policies and regulations, and scientific knowledges that come together to stabilise a particular [socio-technical] regime (Geels, 2004; Schwanen, 2013). Large-scale, complex change has been discussed in terms of 'transition', defined by the Oxford Dictionary as *'the process or a period of changing from one state or condition to another'*, and by socio-technical transitions scholars as *'changes from one sociotechnical regime to another'* (Geels & Schot, 2007: 399). The concept of transition provides a conceptual lens through which to examine change across temporal and spatial scales and from wide-ranging inter- and post-disciplinary positions. In its most basic sense, transition is the process of change from one state to another. This focus thereby calls for examinations of the processes of change; which can happen gradually, rapidly, or cumulatively. Transition studies also imply drastic changes to the technical, societal and cultural dimensions of the system of mobility (Elzen *et al.*, 2004), thus low carbon transitions need to incorporate behavioural, technological and policy approaches. Moreover, there is increasing evidence of the need to consider the specific, localised geographic contexts of transition, in which transition will be experienced. The value of adopting a transition lens is its focus on the procedural and systemic nature of the required change, thus it is specifically interested on the interactions between different (groups of) actors, and other aspects of the system.

The academic study of transitions parallels the development of a range of theoretical approaches and frameworks, arising from academic traditions including innovation studies, evolutionary economics, sociology, and science, technology and society (STS). The multi-level perspective (Rip & Kemp, 1998, Geels, 2002), along with strategic niche management (Kemp *et al.*, 1998, Schot & Geels, 2008) and transitions management (Rotman *et al.*, 2001), have been central to efforts to theoretically ground empirical understandings of transition. Through the multi-level perspective (MLP), transition is understood as the interplay between processes across three levels: niche-innovation, sociotechnical regime, and sociotechnical landscape. In short, three key processes lead to transition: internal momentum from the niche-innovations; landscape changes put pressure on the regime; and a unstable regime creates 'windows of opportunity' that allow the innovations to break through to mainstream markets (Geels & Schot, 2007). Strategic niche management focuses on the processes through which niche spaces can foster and facilitate sustainable innovation journeys (Schot & Geels, 2008). Transition management, on the other hand, presents a model for governance, through which social change is viewed '*as the result of the interactions between all relevant actors on different societal levels within the context of a changing societal landscape*' (Kemp *et al.*, 2007: 80). The contributions within this book draw from these, and other, theories of transition, socio-technical systems, and behaviour change.

The language of 'transition' has also gained traction beyond academia, and this is exemplified in a policy context by the UK government's national strategy for climate and energy, titled *The UK Low Carbon Transition Plan* (2009), which speaks to the need for transition to a low carbon economy and sets forth '*the UK's transition plan for becoming a low carbon country*' (p.5). It is also seen in a grassroots community context through the Transition Towns movement, which began in Kinsale, Ireland in 2005, with Totnes (UK) declared the first Transition Town in 2006 (Connors & McDonald, 2011), before the concept rapidly dispersed across the UK, and globally. There are now transitions initiatives across the globe, including: Australasia (e.g. Australia and New Zealand), North America (e.g. USA and Canada), South America (e.g. Argentina), Asia (e.g. Iran, South Korea, Indonesia,) and Europe (e.g. Hungary, England, Germany) (TransitionNetwork.org, 2013b). The organisation focuses on empowering communities around sustainable, low carbon objectives. In this way, the Transition Town movement can be viewed as transition-in-action, occurring at a local scale.

Climate change mitigation

In December 2015, 195 countries reached an unprecedented consensus on '*a global action plan to put the world on track to avoid dangerous climate change by limiting global warming to well below 2°C*' (European Commission, 2016: np). As the first major multilateral deal of the 21st Century, the Paris Agreement was signed by 177 countries on 22nd April 2016. In contrast to its predecessor, the Kyoto Protocol, the

Paris Agreement adopted a bottom-up approach by inviting Intended Nationally Determined Contributions (INDCs) from all nations, to state voluntary ambitions to reduce their national emissions. This agreement enters into international law in 2020, or when at least 55 countries, accounting for at least 55% of global GHG emissions have *'deposited their instruments of ratification, acceptance, approval or accession with the Depositary'* (UNFCCC, 2016). And whilst there have been questions around the ability of the Paris Agreement to achieve radical emissions reductions, it may indicate a growing consensus for a transition towards a low carbon world (Scott *et al.*, 2016).

Transport was not explicitly included in the Paris Agreement. Yet the importance of transportation on a national scale was signalled by the inclusion of proposed actions to mitigate transport-sector emissions in more than 61% of countries' INDCs (WRI, 2015). Transport was also explicitly mentioned in the Conference of Parties (COP21) opening statements from countries including China, Israel, Canada, Pakistan and Kenya (PPMC, 2015). These statements spoke of electrification of the private vehicle fleet and investment in public transport as dominant approaches to responding to transport-related CO_2 emissions (PPMC, 2015). Yet there are no emission reduction strategies for international aviation or shipping, two of the most carbon-intense transport subsectors (IPCC, 2014). Nor are there any official independent sector-specific assessments for aviation and shipping. Thus while the Paris Agreement may signify progress towards a low carbon, climate-stabilised world, it will not be achieved by the INDCs alone (Scott *et al.*, 2016). Analyses have shown that the pledged efforts are unlikely achieve 1.5- 2°C climate stabilisation by 2100 (Boyd *et al.*, 2015), and could result in up to 2.7°C of warming, *if* all pledged targets are met (Climate Action Tracker, 2015).

It has been argued that we need to *'focus on transport as a key part of the solution to climate change'* (Pierre Guislain, Senior Director, World Bank Group, 2015) yet the continued growth in demand for passenger travel is overwhelming mitigation efforts, and increasing the difficulty in reducing global transport GHG emissions (Sims *et al.*, 2014). The Paris-Lima Action Agenda (LPAA) presented 15 transport initiatives during COP21 in Paris. The Paris Process on Mobility and Climate [PPMC] (2015) recognised the importance of 'Avoid' and 'Shift' measures to complement the traditional technocentric 'Improve' measures centred on efficiency gains, which may signify a discursive shift towards a more socio-technical approach to low carbon mobility transitions.

Low carbon mobility transitions

Responding to climate change demands a fundamental, systemic transformation, moving away from the current high-carbon ways of moving people and goods. In this book we seek to engage in critical discussions of opportunities for radical and system-wide change to low carbon systems of mobility, examining place- and context-specific examples of the complexities of low carbon transition, as well as examples of transition-in-process. Here we depict a patchwork of responses, with contributing authors frequently noting the assemblages of material and immaterial, along with human and non-human actors that will be required to achieve a systemic transition. We also draw upon a range of academic disciplines and practical examples to focus on processes of change.

In this book, we specifically refer to the process of change from the current carbon-dependent systems of mobility characterised by private car dependence, towards a low carbon system. The chapters largely draw from socio-technical perspectives, which refer to the co-evolution of social and technological relationships and the dynamics by which fundamental change in these relationships will occur. *Low Carbon Mobility Transitions* examines the flows of people, and related ideas for private daily, business, and tourism travel. The opportunities for low carbon mobilities through the substitution of corporeal mobility with information communication technologies are also considered. Freight, whilst acknowledged as a critical part of any sustainability transition (e.g. Hopkins & McCarthy, 2016), is beyond the scope of the current text, but warrants critical attention in the future.

Low Carbon Mobility Transitions is also explicit in its focus on climate change mitigation: opportunities to reduce the carbon-intensity of the current systems of mobility. In this way, it considers how, why and where transitions to low carbon mobility could take place, or are already occurring. In this book we present 15 chapters and 6 shorter 'case studies' covering a diversity of themes and geographic contexts across three thematic sections: *People and Place, Structures in Transition,* and *Innovations for Low Carbon Mobility.* The three sections are highly interrelated, and with themes often overlapping, complementing, and challenging one another; the case studies provide an additional opportunity to think across the three overarching themes. *Low Carbon Mobility Transitions* presents critical, often neglected insights into low carbon mobility transitions across the world. In doing so, it sheds light on the place- and context-specific nature of mobility in a climate constrained world.

Part 1, *People and Place,* presents a series of chapters concerned with the intersection between people, place, and mobility. The section acknowledges the importance of human behaviour in processes of low carbon transition, and draws empirical examples from the UK, Australia, New Zealand and South Africa. *People and Place* examines themes including: attitude and behaviour change (Chapter 2); mobilities through the life course (Chapter 3); the opportunities to harness health and equity co-benefits (Chapter 4); and applying a discourse of well-being to stimulate low carbon behaviour changes (Chapter 5).

Part 2, *Structures in Transition,* examines the inertia, path dependency and structural constraints that can act to reinforce incumbent regime actors, and the hegemony of a high-carbon mobility regime. With examples from New Zealand, India, and Finland, it examines change trends, and the conditions or landscape alternations that are contributing to emergent mobility behaviour. This includes: the challenges of changing paradigms, regimes and structures (Chapter 6); institutions and path dependency in urban public transport (Chapter 7); infrastructural lock-in to high-carbon mobility practices across scales (Chapter 8); the co-existence of drivers and barriers to low carbon mobility (Chapter 9); and structures that lock in, or enable new mobility trends (Chapter 10).

Part 3, *Innovations for Low Carbon Mobility*, recognises the importance of both industry and innovation in transitioning to systems of low carbon mobility. However, they are not seen to be discrete elements, removed from their social and/ or regulatory context, but rather intertwined with a range of questions relating to governance, policy, and user behaviour. Chapters examine: policy and governance support for innovations in low carbon and socially just forms of mobility (Chapter 11 and Chapter 12); travel substitution through the uptake and integration of information communication technologies (Chapter 13); and opportunities to reduce the carbon intensity of the aviation industry (Chapter 14).

Across six case studies, people, place, policy and innovation intersect with unique socio-cultural, economic, and political contexts to highlight both complexities and opportunities for low carbon mobility transitions. The six case studies are geographically diverse, exploring low carbon mobility in Australia, South Africa, Brazil, the UK, China and Japan. Themes include: the low carbon mobility practices of Chinese migrant communities in Sydney (Case Study 1); overcoming historical and socio-cultural barriers to the uptake of low carbon mobility in South Africa (Case Study 2); the role of the car in Brazil's mobility future (Case Study 3); opportunities for tourism industry operators to achieve low carbon mobility transition (Case Study 4); technological innovation and the role of electric vehicles in China's low carbon mobility transition (Case Study 5); and the implications of Japanese government transport policy around vehicle disposal and retention through the lens of motor vehicle lifetime (Case Study 6).

The need for a low carbon mobility transition is clear, the pathways to achieve transition are less so. Transition demands action from a range of actors, across a range of scales. The spaces and geographies of transition are interwoven with specific culturally determined ways of practicing mobility, norms and values, policies and regulations, and funding regimes. Thus in this book, we shed light on, and critically engage with, some of the drivers and barriers, and opportunities and threats to a low carbon mobility transition, with the aim of providing the reader with new understandings of how, where, and why transition may occur, in order to move towards a low carbon future.

Acknowledgments

Debbie Hopkins is employed by the Centre on Innovation and Energy Demand (CIED) grant number EP/KO11790/1, one of six Research Centres on End Use Energy Demand funded by the RCUK Energy Programme.

References

Airbus (2013). Future Journeys. *Global Market Forecast 2013 – 2032*. Blagnac Cedex, France: Airbus.

Anderson, K., Le Quéré, C. & Mclachlan, C. (2014). Radical emission reductions: the role of demand reductions in accelerating full decarbonisation, *Carbon Management*, **5**(4), 321-323.

Boeing (2013). *Current Market Outlook 2013 – 2032*. Seattle: Boeing.

Boyd, R., Carnston Turner, J. & Ward, B. (2015). Tracking intended nationally determined contributions: what are the implications for greenhouse gas emissions in 2013? Policy paper. London: Grantham Research Institute on Climate Change and the Environment.

Capstick, S., Lorenzoni, I., Corner, A. & Whitmarsh, L. (2014). Prospects for radical emissions reduction through behaviour and lifestyle change, *Carbon Management*, **5**(4), 429-445.

Clémençon, R. (2016). The two sides of the Paris climate agreement: Dismal failure or historic breakthrough? *Journal of Environment & Development*, **25**(1), 3-24.

Climate Action Tracker (2015). Climate pledges will bring 2.7°C of warming, potential for more action, 8th Dec 2015. Available from: http://climateactiontracker.org/news/253/Climate-pledges-will-bring-2.7C-of-warming-potential-for-more-action.html

Cohen, S.A., Duncan, T. & Thulemark, M. (2015). Lifestyle mobilities: The crossroads of travel, leisure and migration, *Mobilities*, **10**(1), 155-172.

Connors, P. & McDonald, P. (2011). Transitioning communities: Community, participation and the Transition Town movement, *Community Development Journal*, **46** (4), 558-572.

Creutzig, F., Jochem, P., Edelenbosch, O.Y., Mattauch, L., van Vuuren, D.P., McCollum, D. & Minx, J. (2015). Transport: A roadblock to climate change mitigation? *Science* **350**, 911.

European Commission (2016). Climate Action: Paris Agreement. Available from: http://ec.europa.eu/clima/policies/international/negotiations/paris/index_en.htm

Fagan, M. (2000). Sheikh Yamani predicts price crash as age of oil ends. *The Telegraph*. 25 June.

Geels, F.W. (2002). Technological transitions as evolutionary reconfiguration processes: a multi-level perspective and a case-study, *Research Policy*, **31**(8), 1257-1274.

Geels, F.W. (2004). From sectoral systems of innovation to socio-technical systems: insights about dynamics and change from sociology and institutional theory, *Research Policy*, **33**, 897-920.

Geels, F.W. (2010). Ontologies, socio-technical transitions (to sustainability), and the multi-level perspective, *Research Policy*, **39**, 495-510.

Geels, F.W. (2012). A socio-technical analysis of low carbon transitions: introducing the multi-level perspective into transport studies, *Journal of Transport Geography*, **24**, 471-482.

Geels, F.W. & Schot, J. (2007). Typology of sociotechnical transition pathways, *Research Policy*, **36**(3), 399-417.

Geels, F.W., Berkhout, F. & van Vuuren, D.P. (2016). Bridging analytical approaches for low carbon transitions, *Nature Climate Change*, **6**(6), 576-583.

Haustein, S. & Nielsen, T.A.S. (2016). European mobility cultures: a survey-based cluster analysis across 28 European countries, *Journal of Transport Geography*, **54**, 173-180.

Hopkins, D. & McCarthy, A. (2016). Change trends in urban freight delivery: A qualitative inquiry, *Geoforum*, **74**, 158-170.

Institute for Transportation & Development Policy [ITDP]. (2015). The Paris Agreement What's Right and What's Next, December 17, 2015. Available from: https://www.itdp.org/the-paris-agreement-whats-right-and-whats-next/

Intergovernmental Panel on Climate Change (IPCC). (2014). Climate Change 2014: Mitigation of Climate Change. Contribution of Working Group III to the Fifth Assessment Report of the Intergovernmental Panel on Climate Change, in O. Edenhofer, R. Pichs-Madruga, Y. Sokona, E. Farahani, S. Kadner, K., Seyboth, J. Minx, (Eds.), *Climate Change 2014: Mitigation of Climate Change.* Cambridge: Cambridge University Press.

International Energy Agency [IEA] (2015). CO_2 Emissions from Fuel Combustion: Highlights, 2015 Edition. Paris: IEA. Available from: www.iea.org/ publications/free publications/publication/CO2EmissionsFromFuelCombustionHighlights2015.pdf

Jetin, B. (2015). Introduction. In: Jetin, B. (Eds.) *Global Automobile Demand: Major Trends in Emerging Economies Volume 2*. London: Palgrave Macmillan, 1-11.

Kemp, R., Geels, K.W. & Dudley, G. (2012). Introduction: Sustainability transitions in the automobility regime and the need for a new perspective, in: Geels, F.W., Kemp, R., Dudley, G. & Lyons, G. (Eds.). *Automobility in Transition? A Socio-Technical Analysis of Sustainable Transport*, Abingdon: Routledge.

Kemp, R., Loorbach, D. & Rotmans, J. (2007). Transition management as a model for managing processes of co-evolution towards sustainable development, *International Journal of Sustainable Development and World Ecology*, **14**(1), 78-91.

Kemp, R., Schot, J. & Hoogma, R. (1998). Regime shifts to sustainability through processes of niche formation: The approach of strategic niche management, *Technology Analysis & Strategic Management*, **10** (2), 175-198.

Manolas, E. (2016). The Paris climate change agreement. International Journal of Environmental Studies, **73**(2), 167-169.

McGlade, C. & Ekins, P. (2015). The geographical distribution of fossil fuels unused when limiting global warming to 2°C, *Nature*, **517**, 187-190.

Morgan, M.G. (2016b). Opinion: Climate policy needs more than muddling. *Proceedings of the National Academy of Sciences*, **113**(9), 2322-2324.

National Centers for Environmental Information [NOAA] (2016). State of the Climate: Global Analysis for Annual 2015, published online January 2016. Available from: http://www.ncdc.noaa.gov

Paris Process on Mobility and Climate (PPMC). (2015). Transport @ COP21 Paris: Preliminary Final Report, 15 December. Available from: www.ppmc-cop21.org

Rees, D., Stephenson, J., Hopkins, D. & Doering, A. (2016). Exploring stability and change in transport systems: combining Delphi and system dynamics approaches, *Transportation*, DOI: 10.1007/s11116-016-9677-7, Online First.

Rhodes, C.J. (2016). The 2015 Paris climate change conference: COP21. Science Progress, **99**(1), 97-104.

Rip, A. & Kemp, R. (1998). Technological change, In: Rayner, S. & Malone, L. (Eds.) *Human Choice and Climate Change, Vol. 2 Resources and Technology,* Washington D.C.: Batelle Press

Robbins, A. (2016). How to understand the results of the climate change summit: Conference of parties 21 (COP21) Paris 2015. *Journal of Public Health Policy*, **37**, 129-132.

Rotmans, J., Kemp, R. & van Asselt, M. (2001). More evolution than revolution: transition management in public policy, *Foresight*, **3**(1), 15 – 31.

Schot, J. & Geels, F.W. (2008). Strategic niche management and sustainable innovation journeys: theory, findings, research agenda, and policy, *Technology Analysis & Strategic Management*, **20**(5), 537-554.

Schwanen, T. (2013). Sociotechnical transition in the transport system, in: Givoni, M. & Banister, D. (Eds.). *Moving Towards Low Carbon Mobility*, Cheltenham: Edward Elgar.

Scott, D., Hall, C.M. & Gössling, S. (2016). A report on the Paris Climate Change Agreement and its implications for tourism: why we will always have Paris, *Journal of Sustainable Tourism*, **24**(7), 933-948.

Sheller, M. (2015). Foreword 2: Mobilizing transportation, transporting mobilities in: Cidell, J. & Prytherch, D. (Eds.). *Transport, Mobility and the Production of Urban Space*, Abingdon: Routledge.

Sheller, M. & Urry, J. (2006). The new mobilities paradigm, *Environment and Planning A*, **38**(2), 207-226.

Sims R., R. Schaeffer, F. Creutzig, X. Cruz-Núñez, M. D'Agosto, D. Dimitriu, M.J. Figueroa Meza, L. Fulton, S. Kobayashi, O. Lah, A. McKinnon, P. Newman, M. Ouyang, J.J. Schauer, D. Sperling, and G. Tiwari, (2014). Transport. In Edenhofer, O., R. Pichs-Madruga, Y. Sokona, E. Farahani, S. Kadner, K. Seyboth, A. Adler, I. Baum, S. Brunner, P. Eickemeier, B. Kriemann, J. Savolainen, S. Schlömer, C. von Stechow, T. Zwickel and J.C. Minx (Eds.) *Climate Change 2014: Mitigation of Climate Change. Contribution of Working Group III to the Fifth Assessment Report of the Intergovernmental Panel on Climate Change.* Cambridge University Press, Cambridge, United Kingdom and New York, NY, USA.

Sperling, D. & Gordon, D. (2009). *Two Billion Cars: Driving Towards Sustainability*. New York: Oxford University Press.

Transition Town Totnes (n.d.) What is Transition? Available from: http://www.transitiontowntotnes.org/about/what-is-transition/

TransitionNetwork.org. (2013a). About Transition Network. Available from: https://www.transitionnetwork.org/about

TransitionNetwork.org. (2013b). Transition project map. Available from: https://www.transitionnetwork.org/projects/map

UNFCCC, (2016). http://unfccc.int/paris_agreement/items/9444.php

UNWTO (2015). UNWTO Tourism Highlights 2015 Edition, Madrid, Spain: WTO. Available from: http://www.e-unwto.org/doi/pdf/10.18111/9789284416899

Urry, J. (2004). The 'system' of automobility, *Theory, Culture & Society*, **21**(4/5), 25-39.

Urry, J. (2007). *Mobilities*, Cambridge: Polity Press.

Viry, G. & Kaufmann (2015). *High Mobility in Europe: Work and Personal Life*, Basingstoke: Palgrave Macmillan.

World Resources Institute [WRI]. (2015). After COP21, Time to Use Sustainable Transport to Make Good on Climate Commitments, World Resources Institute, December 17 2015. Available from: http://www.wri.org/blog/2015/12/after-cop21-time-use-sustainable-transport-make-good-climate-commitments

Part 1: People and Place

2   Knowledge Co-production and Behavioural Change: Collaborative approaches for promoting low carbon mobility

Stewart Barr

Department of Geography, University of Exeter, UK.

Gareth Shaw

Business School, University of Exeter, UK.

Introduction: the behaviour change conundrum

If you've ever attended a policy seminar or workshop on how to promote sustainability amongst publics, it's likely that the conversation will focus on a discussion of three broad approaches. First, there is often the assertion that in some way people's attitudes are *wrong* and require *correction*: 'if only *we* could get people to see the problem *our* way; that would be a start'. Second, the means by which to achieve this shift in attitudes is often viewed as an issue of awareness-raising: 'communication is clearly the problem; *we* need to give people better *information*'. Finally, we arrive at what is often regarded as the golden bullet: 'if only *we* could get people to change *their* behaviour and make better choices'. These three logics of arriving at a behavioural change 'solution' (as it is so often framed) evidently have a number of conceptual and empirical problems, but we argue here that the most significant challenge posed by this seemingly compelling approach is really about how both

policy makers and many academic researchers have positioned themselves in relation to the publics whose behaviours they seek to influence and change.

In this chapter, we propose that for behavioural change to be both a meaningful
and useful approach for promoting sustainability, we need to contest embedded
assumptions about knowledge production and formations of 'expert' and 'lay' in
formulating campaigns for behavioural change. In other words, the binary that
exists between *us* and *them* needs to be questioned in a context where publics are
becoming ever more sceptical of science and experts (Owens, 2000; Lupton, 2013).
In this way, we draw on research from Science Technology Society (STS) studies in
the social sciences (Lupton, 2013; Whatmore *et al.*, 2009), to demonstrate how issues
of implementing attitude and behaviour change urgently need to be re-cast as ones
that are much more about co-identifying problems, co-researching approaches and
co-creating campaigns with consumers. In pursuing this approach, we argue for
a need to develop both new forms of engagement and innovative perspectives on
changing wider social practices for sustainability so that new possibilities for social
change can be developed and low carbon transitions realised.

The behaviour change 'problem'

As academic researchers, we are working in an environment where questioning
the logic of particular kinds of behavioural change and the political undercurrents
that have led to their enthusiastic adoption is often challenging and outside of the
mainstream (Shove, 2010). Yet we argue here that researchers need to recognise
that behavioural change, as it is currently formulated in most political discourse,
presents scholars with a major challenge on three levels. First, there are fundamental
and emergent debates surrounding the role and place of behavioural change as a
strategy for achieving the goals of sustainability, particularly when the 'wicked'
policy problem of low carbon mobility is concerned (Crompton & Thogersen, 2009).

As we have argued elsewhere (Barr *et al.*, 2011; Barr & Prillwitz, 2014), critical
questions surround the apparently compelling logic of promoting incremental
behavioural change as a strategy for dealing with mega-issues like anthropogenic
climate change. This concern is founded on our argument that particular kinds of
behavioural change have attained a privileged position in many policy contexts,
which has much to do with the underpinning logics of a shift towards a neo-liberal
way of governing that upholds the status of the free market and individual choice
(Giddens, 1991). As a result, policies for promoting behavioural change have
become focused on the choices of individuals that embody the 'citizen-consumer'
(Clarke *et al.*, 2007): an individual who simultaneously embodies the responsible
(ecological) citizen and also exercises full choice as a consumer. In this way, individuals are necessarily bounded in their choices, so that these are 'better' (DEFRA, 2005)
and more easily manipulated through a form of Libertarian Paternalism (Jones *et al.*,
2011). As such, through adopting particular forms of behavioural change, such as
behavioural economics, the state acts as arbiter over the 'right' choices to make. Such

approaches clearly crowd out alternative voices, opinions and logics that would prefer to see behavioural change as a component of wider strategies for achieving sustainability; ones that recognise the relationships between apparent individual choice and the broader economic and social structures within which individuals, households and communities act (Barr & Prillwitz, 2014; Shove *et al.*, 2012).

A second level on which behavioural change can be critiqued relates to the dominant ways in which we have come to understand and intellectually frame (un)sustainable behaviours. Shove (2010) has highlighted the particular kinds of research cultures and practices that have come to dominate the intellectual and policy landscape of behavioural change and without doubt, this has been characterised by a focus on the use of behavioural economics, insights from social-psychology and the use of psychological models to understand and influence behaviour. As seminal meta-analyses of pro-environmental behaviour research have demonstrated (Bamberg & Möser, 2007; Hines *et al.*, 1987; Oskamp, 2000), there is a vast body of scholarship that has sought to identify the key factors that determine participation in a range of pro-environmental behaviours.

The field of travel behaviour studies has until recently been dominated by the logics of psychological modelling of behaviours (e.g. De Groot & Steg, 2007; Heath & Gifford, 2002) using frameworks such as the Theory of Planned Behaviour (Ajzen, 1991) and the Theory of Reasoned Action (Fishbein & Ajzen, 1977). These and numerous other studies utilise the underpinning logic of rationalistic behaviour change (Owens, 2000) in which general models of behaviour can be used to predict particular outcomes. Yet the logics of such models have recently been questioned and heavily critiqued within other parts of the social sciences (Spaargaren & Mol, 2008) not least because they tend to focus on individual cognition and the quantification of 'factors'. This has enabled scholars from disciplines such as sociology and human geography to advocate an alternative approach for framing pro-environmental behaviours, as *practices* (Huddart *et al.*, 2015; Kasper, 2015; Reckwitz, 2002; Shove, 2003). In this way, researchers have argued for a deeper, contextually rich and holistic approach to the traditional behavioural problem by focusing on the intersections between individuals, technologies and practices (Barr, 2015; Kasper, 2015). In the field of travel behaviour research, this is marked by an increasing awareness of the challenges posed by research that does not place transport mode choice into a wider setting afforded by, for example, a mobilities perspective (Freudendal-Pedersen, 2009).

These two critiques of contemporary approaches to behavioural change are gaining traction in the social science community (Huddart *et al.*, 2015) and are being considered by a policy community that is frustrated with the inability of individualistic approaches to deliver change (Wilson & Chatterton, 2011). Yet there is a third challenge connected to these two critiques with which researchers and policy makers need to grapple if we are to realise our aspirations to deliver meaningful change for low carbon mobility, and to do so in ways that are engaged and long-lasting. This problem is one that *we* have, as an academic community, and one which is certainly present amongst many in policy and practitioner cultures, and it concerns the way we undertake research and promote change.

Let us dwell for a moment on the example of developing so-called low carbon 'smart cities' (Allwinkle & Cruickshank, 2011), where technological innovations will enable the more efficient use of infrastructure to reduce energy use and integrate 'big data' to aid decision making. The smart cities agenda is one that is emblematic of a traditional hierarchical approach to policy making and behavioural change that privileges 'expert' knowledge and expertise over 'lay' understandings and practices. In this way, smart cities are about delivering behavioural change through an expert-led model of policy deployment in which citizens almost take on the role of subjects in a technological experiment. In the following commentary on the smart city of Masdar in the United Arab Emirates, *Guardian* journalist John Vidal characterises the relationship between technology and citizenry as follows:

> 'Here, residents live with driverless electric cars, shaded streets cooled by a huge wind tower and a Big Brother-style 'green policeman' monitoring their energy use' (The Guardian, 26th April 2011).

Accordingly, much of what has come to characterise the smart cities agenda (and the associated discourses on 'big data') has made assumptions about how humans interact with technologies and the motivators and barriers for behaving in particular ways. In what we can define as a linear model of policy making and implementation, the concern is largely with developing and showcasing techno-logical innovations that will be used to promote behavioural change, which is often viewed as a given (and too often handed down to social scientists as 'their problem'). Yet research in the social sciences demonstrates how the emergence of smart technologies can be profoundly disrupting and dis-empowering to publics (Bickerstaff & Hinton, 2013: 362), representing a hierarchically driven approach to delivering change:

> '...we can also identify a more systemic, and technocratic, approach to delivering change, reflected in a suite of intervention-based programmes designed by national government, local governments, energy companies and civil society actors, aimed at materially and technologically re-engineering the domestic environment to ensure that reductions in GHG [greenhouse gas] emissions are achieved and to make participation 'easy''.

As Bickerstaff & Hinton (2013) go on to evidence, the imposition of particular kinds of technologies and the adjustments in practices required to utilise these 'assets' can lead to dis-engagement through a sense of powerlessness and material dissatisfaction. Metcalfe *et al.,* (2013) demonstrate how the roll-out of domestic recy-cling schemes in the UK has not been aligned with either the routines and rhythms of households nor the aesthetic characteristics of kitchen spaces. As a result, 'waste' conflicts directly with aesthetics and waste technologies, such as recycling bins, conflict with the multiple demands for space within the household.

This example highlights that in developing and implementing behavioural change strategies and campaigns, there has often been an assumption that behavioural change can be managed and targeted through discrete and bounded approaches that view practices as malleable, controllable and predictable.

Up-ending hierarchies: putting publics at the centre

To deal with the challenge of overcoming the 'expert-lay' divide in policy and practice for behavioural change requires us to recognise both the intellectual basis for current approaches and the opportunities afforded by an alternative. To start with the intellectual basis for our current practice, we might ask why, until recently, there has been such confidence in our ability to influence behaviour change through adopting a didactic approach? In large part, this has to do with a long tradition of 'expertisation' in national and local government (Lupton, 2013; Owens, 2000) and the desire for traditional forms of scientific practice to govern and mediate policy making, where specific kinds of knowledge are privileged over others (Whatmore *et al.*, 2009). Within the behavioural change policy community, this has entailed the adoption of particular kinds of social science approaches that can deliver the types of 'evidence' that are acceptable to policy makers, in the form of quantifiable, measureable and theoretically informed models of change (Whitehead *et al.*, 2011). As a result, in the UK, there has been huge investment in behavioural research (largely been founded on insights from behavioural economics and behavioural psychology), which has resulted in an almost industrial approach to researching behavioural change (Shove, 2010). In turn, this has led to particular forms of governing behaviour that emphasise the 'expert-lay' divide, illustrated by Jones *et al.* (2011: 15) as one that places the state in a position of patriarchal authority:

> '...using the new sciences of choice from psychology, economics and the neuro-sciences – as well as appealing to an improved understanding of decision-making and behaviour change – a libertarian paternalist mode of governing is being promoted in the UK'.

In the UK, the narrow intellectual focus on behavioural economics and psychology has meant that behavioural change policy has taken a necessarily dis-engaged pathway, as evidenced by the enthusiastic adoption of Nudge theory (Thaler & Sunstein, 2008) as a route for delivering change 'at a distance' (House of Lords, 2011). In what can be argued as a subversive form of practice (Whitehead *et al.*, 2011), Nudge does not seek to engage with citizens nor to have a dialogue with them directly about the merits and challenges of changing practices; rather, it is about an amendment to the 'choice architecture' that influences practices. What constitutes such architectures and the factors that might influence change are derived from the modelling outputs of behavioural scientists, rather than an engagement with publics. As such, in recent years, the behavioural change agenda in the UK has come under sustained scrutiny from both legislators (House of Lords,

2011) and those who argue for a different ethic to underpin 'influencing' behaviour – one that recognises the limitations and opportunities of behaviour change in the context of broader socio-economic structures (Barr & Prillwitz, 2014; Crompton & Thøgersen, 2009).

In considering alternatives to an expert-led approach to promoting behavioural change, we can look towards research in Science Technology and Society (STS) studies (Lupton, 2013). This research starts with the premise that there are underpinning and often unchallenged epistemic hegemonies (Hulme, 2009) that govern the ways in which knowledge is produced, and that implicit 'ways of seeing' are perpetuated by researchers from different disciplines (Demerit, 1996; 2001). Yet as Lupton (2013: 87) notes, a shift towards what Beck (1992) refers to as the new Risk Society leads publics to question the orthodoxies promoted by conventional science:

> *Lay people have become sceptical about science, because they are aware that science has produced many of the risks...People must therefore deal with constant insecurity and uncertainty.*

In this way, there are calls for a move towards a post-normal science, in which knowledge hierarchies are questioned and differentiated, and in which differently measured knowledges can be integrated to address complex problems (Whatmore *et al.*, 2009). Such a move promotes the up-ending of traditional scientific practice that is expert-led and creates a divide between apparently valuable, measurable and verifiable knowledge on the one hand and knowledge that is regarded as secondary, intangible and un-testable on the other. This move to a post-normal scientific approach directly challenges the assumptions made in conventional approaches to behavioural change research. Accordingly, we argue here for those working on behavioural change to look towards the field of STS studies to adopt the philosophy so ably presented over twenty years ago by Funtowitcz and Ravetz (1993: 739), who stated that:

> *...new styles of scientific activity are being developed. The reductionist, analytical worldview which divides systems into ever smaller elements, studied by ever more esoteric specialisms, is being replaced by a systemic, synthetic and humanistic approach. The old dichotomies of facts and values, and of knowledge and ignorance, are being transcended.*

We argue here that this flattening of knowledge hierarchies and up-ending of knowledge construction has much to offer the behavioural change debate. The principles of distributed knowledges and the benefits afforded by collaborative research and programme design are ones that not only offer the opportunity to deliver different outcomes, but they also provide a valuable and much needed challenge to academic researchers and policy makers on how they can develop integrative, inclusive and innovative methodologies for working *with* publics. As we will evidence in the next section, such an approach requires a 'letting go' for those who might exercise control over a process of campaign production so that they become co-producers rather than gatekeepers of knowledge. Moreover, such a process can also challenge our in-built assumptions about the potential for behavioural change to deliver the 'golden bullet'.

Co-creating behavioural change campaigns for low carbon mobility

The research on which this chapter is based stems from our long held interest in how academic research on sustainable lifestyles can lead to realistic policy interventions to promote change. Our previous research (Barr & Prillwitz, 2011; Barr et al., 2011) on promoting sustainable lifestyles and sustainable mobility had taken a conventional path and suggested that one segment of the population we had studied held very positive environmental attitudes and a willingness to change travel behaviours to reduce their carbon emissions and yet they tended to report very high levels of car use and were frequent flyers for short-haul breaks and holidays. These 'aspiring green travellers' exhibited what we might term a metropolitan and middle class set of characteristics; they tended to be either 'young professionals' who were often single, lived in shared properties, led high consumption lifestyles and had highly paid jobs, or were 'empty nesters' who were wealthy, retired couples whose children had left home and who had significant disposable income to spend on leisure and travel.

The dilemma we faced with these results was: how can we promote low carbon holiday travel amongst those groups who seem to be most wedded to carbon intensive travel practices, yet hold positive environmental attitudes? Our response to this question reflected our dissatisfaction with the limitations imposed by expert-led approaches to delivering behavioural change and a desire to explore some of the principles advocated by STS researchers. In identifying strategies to promote change amongst these aspiring green travellers, we therefore sought to move away from a dis-connected and didactic approach to behavioural change, to explore the potential for collaborative and co-creative strategies for engaging people in a conversation about change and potentially a campaign development. In doing so, we drew on research in marketing and management studies that has argued for what Vargo & Lusch (2008) have termed Service Dominant Logic, an approach where consumers become co-creators in the products that they buy and the services they use (French et al., 2009).

In seeking to develop a way of engaging publics in a conversation about high-consumption, mobility intensive lifestyles, our research engaged in a process of knowledge co-production that utilised a range of stages, which we outline in this section. Table 2.1 provides detail on each of these stages in our research and highlights the role and importance of relevant stakeholder engagement and knowledge co-production. This broadly followed the process developed by our lead partner organisation, Uscreates, who have argued for a circular and evolving model of knowledge co-production (Figure 2.1). During stage 1, we worked with Uscreates and three other UK social change organisations to collaboratively explore the findings of our academic research and the likely potential for promoting behavioural change amongst our key interest groups. This process revealed the importance of defining and refining our specific behavioural goal. This was supported during the second stage of work, in which we worked closely with Uscreates, who undertook a major desk study to identify the key characteristics of the 'aspiring green travellers'. However, it was the subsequent stages where the process of knowledge co-production was realised through two levels of activity.

Table 2.1: Stages adopted for knowledge co-production for a sustainable mobility behaviour change campaign.

Stage 1 Partner collaboration	Problem identification and developing relationships between researchers and social change practitioners
Stage 2 Market-based research	Identifying the key characteristics of the target audience and their mobility practices with social change partners
Stage 3 Consumer co-production workshop	Working with consumers to explore understandings of current practices and the barriers and motivations for future changes. Identifying ideas for behavioural change campaigns
Stage 4 Industry co-production workshop	Working with industry representatives to short-list ideas for a behavioural change campaign
Stage 5 Development and launch	Working with industry and social change partners to develop an app for promoting sustainable mobility

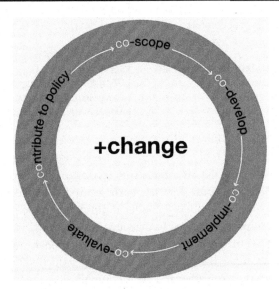

Figure 2.1: The approach to co-development utilised the process developed by Uscreates (Image reproduced with permission of Uscreates).

First, we worked with consumers representative of the two major constituencies of the 'aspiring green travellers' group (young professionals and empty nesters) to deeply appreciate both their motivations and barriers for participating in particular holiday travel practices, and also to explore their broader lifestyles and consumer aspirations. Recruited from retail locations in London boroughs, participants in these co-creation workshops were encouraged think freely and openly about their experiences of holiday travel and to contrast their current use of air travel with that of an alternative: continental holidays by rail. Unlike traditional focus group meetings, the workshops were inter-active, activity-based and involved the use of pictures, video and creative practices to engage participants in a conversation. Table 2.2 provides an overview of participant responses from the two groups concerning the positive and negative factors for the use of air travel versus rail travel for holidays. This highlighted both the major differences between the two groups, and also signified some of the perceptual barriers for moving from 'fast and cheap' air travel to 'slow and costly' rail travel.

Table 2.2: Positives and negatives identified by participants for air and rail travel for holidays.

	Positives	Negatives
Air travel	Cost Speed Choice of departure points Convenience Peace of mind Familiarity 'Starting the holiday at the airport'	Delays Poor food offering Waiting at airports Cramped conditions Luggage costs and constraints Greater carbon emissions
Rail travel	Higher quality of travel experience Greater level of comfort The train as part of the holiday experience Pleasant stations and facilities Better food More sociable Less waiting time	Cost Extra time involved in travelling to destination Perceived lack of personal safety and security Changing trains in unfamiliar cities Carrying luggage long distances Travel to London to get the Eurostar train

The data from the workshops also reveal some of the major opportunities that rail travel could deliver, notably, are transition from travel as lost time to mobility as valued experience, and the affordances of relaxation, better food and a more comfortable experience overall. This led each group to consider what changes would need to take place for them to consider shifting from air to rail travel for holidays. As Table 2.3 demonstrates, the two groups we worked with had contrasting views, although it is important to note that they aligned to similar categories, related to service changes, the booking process and associated benefits. Accordingly, those in the young professionals category highlighted the importance of easy online booking, clear comparisons with air travel costs and the role of marketing destinations as attractive places to visit. The empty nesters focused much more, in contrast, on service levels, the ease of changing trains and the importance of package deals that included all elements, without the need to book using multiple sites or agencies.

Table 2.3: Key changes required for each segment to shift behaviours.

	Empty Nesters	Young Professionals
Service changes	High speed rail links to more destinations (e.g. Madrid) No changes / seamless connections / baggage transfers / transfer assistance Train 'packages' from specialist providers - everything organised door-to-door Train miles / reward scheme Information about public transport at destination	Easy online booking A connection service such as a shuttle bus to the next train station A budget / 'slumming it' train option
Booking changes	Easy on-line booking Cost / time comparisons	Transparency: true costs and benefits of using train (door-to-door)
Fringe benefits / package benefits	Comfort extras such as a bottle of wine Better station facilities Comfortable seating Commentary on surroundings	Package stop off options, e.g. Paris-Venice-Rome Inspiring and customised routes

Table 2.4: Organisations and participants invited to the co-creation workshop in London, July 2012.

Organisation / Participant	Description
Seat 61	European rail travel advice website
Loco2	European rail travel booking site
Snowcarbon	Ski holidays by train
Travel Foundation	Independent UK charity promoting social and environmental benefits of tourism to host communities
Forum for the Future	Environmental lobbying organisation
Virgin Trains	UK rail operator
Green Traveller	UK promoter of sustainable travel
PricewaterhouseCoopers (PwC) Sustainability Unit	Professional services and major UK auditing company
DEFRA	UK Government Department for the Environment, Food and Rural Affairs
Sustainable tourism consultant	
Travel consultant and fast rail lobbyer	
Inn Travel	Specialist in walking and cycling holidays

The work on these co-creation workshops then fed into a second activity where the findings were presented to a range of industry representatives (Table 2.4), who were charged with the role of collaboratively identifying the key changes that could be developed.

Once again, an inter-active workshop was organised (Figure 2.2) that engaged stakeholders with what we termed 'walking in their shoes', through encouraging participants to explore the lifestyle and mobility aspirations of those from our two interest groups.

Figure 2.2: Invitation for co-creation workshop for industry stakeholders.

In so doing, we posed the question of what kinds of changes could be envisaged to promote a shift from air to rail travel for holidays. As the ideas in Table 2.5 highlight, emphasis was partly placed on the need for radical changes in service levels and the underlying infrastructures and technologies that could enable airline-style booking, most notably the integration of rail booking systems across Europe. However, many of the ideas focused on the importance of engaging consumers with the process of changing the social norms associated with air and rail travel and the technologies that could be used for this purpose. This involved the integration of destination marketing into the rail booking process and the production of different kinds of package products for different consumer segments. Notably, there was a focus on how a discourse should be created that focused not on the model of travel primarily, but the destination experience, after which a range of rail-based travel options could be offered.

Table 2.5: Potential social marketing interventions for changing holiday travel behaviours.

Intervention type	Examples
Service changes	Providing more services direct from London to destinations in continental Europe, to avoid the need to change trains in large urban centres, such as Paris Simpler booking systems to allow booking rail and holiday packages in one place Integration of European rail booking systems
Social advertising	Promoting destinations as part of rail holiday advertising Promoting the travel to and from a destination as part of the holiday experience Invoking romantic images / memories of rail travel as luxurious
Viral campaigns	Snowcarbon's approach to promoting ski holidays by train using video: http://www.snowcarbon.co.uk/
Incentives	Railcards or other frequent traveller discounts Integrated incentives for travelling on a range of rail companies to a holiday destination

The final part of the project involved linking the consumer-led and stakeholder-inspired ideas to a pragmatic output. The stated preference for the majority of stakeholders was the development of a prototype destination marketing and booking app. For this purpose, we worked with both Uscreates and Loco2, a rail booking company with expertise in app development. Taking the characteristics, ideas and factors into account from the two main collaborative parts of the project, a booking app called Trainaway was created (Figure 2.3). This app sought to combine a destination-based interface with booking functionality and was designed to meet many of the key requirements our two audiences had highlighted, such as the 'packaging' of holidays by train, guides to using European trains and an emphasis on the benefits and services available for holidays by rail. As such, the app was designed to be a tourism marketing tool, where the focus was on the experience, rather than simply a rail booking device.

Figure 2.3: Trainaway App.

The process we entered into that resulted in the app development was designed as an initial attempt to explore the benefits of knowledge co-production that could result in different and potentially more effective outcomes for behavioural change researchers and practitioners. In reflecting on the process, there are three major issues that our work highlighted.

- First, it is without question that working very closely alongside both consumers and industry partners enabled more challenging questions to be posed about the process of promoting a shift from air to rail travel for holidays. As the outcomes in Table 2.3 demonstrate, our consumer participants highlighted the many and varied changes that are required to make a shift from air to rail travel highly compelling. This often involves changes in infrastructures that are outside the remit of behaviour change advocates to influence and thus provides a vitally important 'reality check' for those who argue that behavioural change is the 'golden bullet'.

- Second, the research demonstrated that behavioural change is therefore likely to be part of, but not the whole story. As such, participants highlighted the important role of social norms and the underpinning incentives that lead to social practices evolving in particular ways. Embedded notions of speed, quality, time, cost and holiday experience all mediate how consumers view holiday travel modes and this points to a very real need to address underpinning conditions to facilitate change.

- Third, despite these formidable and significant challenges, the research did identify some key ways in which current systems of provision could be marketed and promoted through focusing on the positive, experiential and novel aspects of holidays by train. These aspects, as evidenced in the app, are ones that do not derive from a particular behavioural theory, but rather are the result of collaborative enquiry, where researchers were able to 'let go' and allow publics to voice their own concerns and ideas.

Conclusion: re-casting the behavioural change agenda

We face a significant problem when it comes to behavioural change as a strategy for tackling anthropogenic climate change and the challenge of promoting low carbon mobility. There is very little discussion about the appropriateness and value of using behavioural change to meet a whole series of climate targets. Questions of planning, infrastructure development, economic systems and the practice of everyday life are ignored in the hope that promoting incremental changes to lifestyles through behavioural shifts will be sufficient (Crompton & Thogersen, 2009). In contrast, we know that the current way we practice behavioural change does not work effectively (Shove, 2010). Numerous campaigns and messages have produced very little in the way of change and we continue to ask questions about how to promote specific changes in our practices (Barr, 2014). This failing needs to be realised and addressed through three fundamental shifts, which we propose here.

First, academic researchers need to fully take hold of the critiques from those who point out the danger of hierarchical and didactic approaches to 'communicating' risk through conventional methods (Lupton, 2013). This means being open to conversations about behavioural change at a number of levels. Most fundamentally, it does mean addressing the questions of 'whether and if' behavioural change is an appropriate strategy to adopt for promoting sustainable mobility (Barr & Prillwitz, 2014), when often the infrastructures and technologies contradict the sustainability imperative. It also means tackling the epistemic hegemony that exists in much of the research that informs behavioural campaigns (Whitehead *et al.*, 2011). Moreover, it requires academic researchers to use new methods of scholarship and engagement that take us away from our traditional scientific safe houses, and place us in a knowledge landscape that confronts us with knowledge controversies and previously dismissed sources of data and insight (Whatmore *et al.*, 2009). In so doing, we argue for an intellectual agenda that is constructively critical of behavioural change as a particular manifestation of the sustainability agenda and which is open to new ways of seeing the knowledges that can contribute to greater citizen engagement in the sustainable mobilities agenda.

Second, we argue that just as academia may have got stuck in a particular epistemic framework for promoting sustainable mobility through behavioural change, policy makers also need to recognise the limitations of behavioural change. As Shove (2010) has noted, an industry has sprung up that attends to the agendas of those seeking to utilise behavioural economics to promote behavioural shifts, and yet this is largely dominated by those who have promoted the 'citizen-consumer' agenda (Clarke *et al.*, 2007) that prescribes ecological responsibilities within a choice-based framework. This narrow framing ensures that a relatively small set of changes are deemed politically acceptable and emphasises the role nation states exercise over the potential to promote major shifts in mobility through much more ambitious changes in built environments and infrastructures. Accordingly, we argue that policy makers need to emerge from the silo of behavioural economics and consider how listening to and working with citizens can help them to recognise the place of behavioural change alongside other, more fundamental, interventions.

Finally, we argue that researchers and policy makers need to engage with and experience the role and value of knowledge co-production through a sustained relationship with publics (Lusch & Vargo, 2008; Whatmore et al., 2009). In the UK, the focus on highlighting the benefits of academic research to the wider society is leading researchers to think not only about the basic application of their research, but to consider how publics can become actively involved in framing research questions and collaborating in research projects. In this way, we argue that those who wish to promote sustainable mobility need to listen and be willing to react to those who have alternative views to their own. This means challenging ourselves to be willing to re-learn much of our trade and re-skill to work with, alongside and for publics. It also means being willing to play multiple roles, as academics, facilitators, negotiators, knowledge brokers and advocates. Accordingly, we argue for an approach to sustainable mobility that is deliberative and collaborative, where our stake in the research we conduct is as much about helping others to participate as it is about our own accumulation of knowledge.

Sustainable mobility is without doubt a wicked policy problem. However, in this chapter we have argued that both academic researchers and policy makers have made it just that little bit more wicked. We have boxed ourselves into an unambitious and often narrow intellectual agenda; we have gone along with a political approach that favours one particular kind of 'communication' strategy with citizens; and we have often believed that we, as the scientific community, have the answers. Yet we need to recognise that working collaboratively, however foreign, risky and unconventional it feels, offers us much more hope for promoting sustainable mobility, because we have not only engaged, consulted or surveyed, we have also come alongside and empathised with those whose behaviours we seek to change. And that may not only lead us to new ways of promoting behavioural change, it might also lead us to advocate for changes in places, infrastructures and technologies that foreground our ability to change. And thus we might come to see ourselves not only as passive researchers, but as active promoters of fundamental change.

Acknowledgements

The research reported in this chapter is based on work undertaken as part of a UK Economic and Social Research Council project entitled 'Social Marketing for Sustainability: developing a community of practice for co-creating behavioural change campaigns' (Grant reference: ES/J001007/1). The authors gratefully acknowledge the contributions of the project partners (Uscreates, CAG Marketing, Hyder Consulting and the Social Marketing Practice) and participants in the research.

References

Ajzen, I. (1991). The theory of planned behaviour, *Organisational Behaviour & Human Decision Processes*, **50**, 179-211.

Allwinkle, S. & Cruickshank, P. (2011). Creating smarter cities: an overview, *Journal of Urban Technology*, **18**, 1-16.

Anable, J. (2005). 'Complacent car addicts' or 'aspiring environmentalists'? Identifying travel behaviour segments using attitude theory, *Transport Policy*, **12**, 65–78.

Bamberg, S., Fujii, S., Friman, M. & Gärling, T. (2011). Behaviour theory and soft transport policy measures, *Transport Policy*, **18**, 228-235.

Bamberg, S. & Möser, G. (2007). Twenty years after Hines, Hungerford, and Tomera: A new meta-analysis of psycho-social determinants of pro-environmental behaviour, *Journal of Environmental Psychology*, **27**, 14-25.

Barr, S. (2014). Practicing the cultural green economy: where now for environmental social science?, *Geografiska Annaler: Series B, Human Geography* **96**, 231-243.

Barr, S. (2015). Beyond behaviour change: social practice theory and the search for sustainable mobility, in E. H. Kennedy, M. H. Cohen & N. T. Krogman (Eds) *Putting Sustainability into Practice: Applications & advances in research on sustainable consumption*, Edward Elgar: Cheltenham, 91-108.

Barr, S., Gilg, A. W. & Shaw, G. (2011). Citizens, consumers and sustainability: (re) framing environmental practice in an age of climate change, *Global Environmental Change* **21**, 1224-1233.

Barr, S. & Prillwitz, J. (2014). A smarter choice? Exploring the behaviour change agenda for environmentally sustainable mobility, *Environment & Planning C: Government & Policy* **32**, 1-19.

Beck, U. (1992). *Risk Society*, Sage: London.

Bickerstaff, K. & Hinton, E. (2013). Climate change, human security and the built environment, in M. R. Redclift & M. Grasso (Eds) *Handbook on Climate Change & Human Security*, Edward Elgar: Cheltehham, 361-381.

Clarke, J., Newman, J., Smith, N., Vidler, E. & Westmarland, L. (2007). *Creating Citizen— Consumers; Changing Publics and Changing Public Services*, Sage: London.

Crompton, T. & Thøgersen, J. (2009) *Simple and Painless? The limitations of spillover in environmental campaigning*, WWF UK: London.

Demeritt, D. (1996). Social theory & the reconstruction of science and geography, *Transactions of the Institute of British Geographers*, **21**, 484-503.

Demeritt, D. (2001). The construction of global warming & the politics of science , *Annals of the Association of Geographers*, **91**, 307–337.

Department of the Environment, Food and Rural Affairs (DEFRA) (2008) *Framework for Environmental Behaviours*, DEFRA: London.

Department of the Environment, Food and Rural Affairs (DEFRA). (2005) *Securing the Future*, Cm 6467 DEFRA: London.

Department for Transport (DfT) (2004) *Smarter Choices: changing the way we travel. Final report of the research project: the influence of 'soft' factor interventions on travel demand,* DfT: London.

Fishbein, M. & Ajzen, I. (1977). *Belief, Attitude, Intention, and Behaviour: An introduction to theory & research,* Addison-Wesley: Reading, MA.

French, J., Blair-Stevens, C., McVey, D. & Merritt, R. (2009) *Social Marketing & Public Health: Theory & Practice,* Oxford University Press: Oxford.

Freudendal-Pedersen, M. (2009) *Mobility in Daily Life,* Ashgate: Aldershot.

Funtowitz, S. & Ravetz, J. (1993). Science for the Postnormal Age, *Futures,* **25**, 739-755.

Giddens, A. (1991) *Modernity & Self-Identity,* Polity Press: Cambridge.

The Guardian (2011). *Masdar City – a glimpse of the future in the desert.* 26th April 2011

Heath, Y. & Gifford, R. (2002). Extending the theory of planned behaviour: Predicting the use of public transportation, *Journal of Applied Social Psychology,* **32**, 2154-2189.

Hines, J. M., Hungerford, H. R. & Tomera, A. N. (1987). Analysis and synthesis of research on responsible environmental behaviour: A meta-analysis, *Journal of Environmental Education,* **18**, 1-8.

House of Lords Science & Technology Committee (2011) *Behaviour Change Report,* HL Paper 179, The Stationary Office: London.

Hulme, M. (2009). *Why we disagree about climate change: Understanding controversy, inaction & opportunity,* Cambridge University Press: Cambridge UK.

Huddart, E. K., Cohen, M. J. & Krogman, N. T. (Eds). (2015). *Putting Sustainability into Practice: Applications and advances in research on sustainable consumption,* Edward Elgar: Cheltenham.

Jones, R., Pykett, J. & Whitehead, M. (2011). Governing temptation: Changing behaviour in an age of libertarian paternalism, *Progress in Human Geography,* **35**, 483-501.

Kasper, D. (2015). Contextualising social practices: insights into social change, in E. H. Kennedy, M. H. Cohen & N. T. Krogman (Eds) *Putting Sustainability into Practice: Applications and advances in research on sustainable consumption,* Edward Elgar: Cheltenham, 25-46.

Landström, C., Whatmore, S. J., Lane, S. N., Odoni, N., Ward, N. & Bradley, S. (2011) Coproducing flood risk knowledge: redistributing expertise in critical participatory modelling, *Environment & Planning A,* **43**, 1617-1633.

Lane, S. N., Odoni, N., Landström, C., Whatmore, S. J., Ward, N. & Bradley, S. (2011). Doing flood risk science differently: an experiment in radical scientific method, *Transactions of the Institute of British Geographers,* **36**, 15–36.

Lutpon, D. (2013). *Risk,* Routledge: London.

Metcalfe, A., Riley, M., Barr, S., Tudor, T., Robinson & G., Guilbert, S. (2012). Food waste bins: bridging infrastructures and practices, *The Sociological Review,* **60**, 135-155.

Oskamp, S. (2000). Psychology of promoting environmentalism: Psychological contributions to achieving an ecologically sustainable future for humanity, *Journal of Social Issues,* **56**, 373-390.

Owens, S. (2000). Engaging the public: information and deliberation in environmental policy, *Environment & Planning A*, **32**, 1141-1148.

Reckwitz, A. (2002). Toward a theory of social practices a development in culturalist theorizing, *European journal of social theory*, **5**, 243-263.

Shove, E. (2010). Beyond the ABC: climate change policy and theories of social change, *Environment & planning A*, **42**, 1273-1285.

Shove, E. (2003) *Comfort Cleanliness & Convenience: the social organisation of normality*, Berg, Oxford.

Shove, E., Pantzar, M. & Watson, M. (2012). *The Dynamics of Social Practice: Everyday Life & How It Changes*, Sage: London.

Steg, L. & Gifford, R. (2005). Sustainable transport and quality of life, *Journal of Transport Geography*, **13**, 59–69.

Steg, L. & Vlek, C. (2009). Encouraging pro-environmental behaviour: An integrative review & research agenda, *Journal of environmental psychology*, **29**, 309-317.

Stern, P. C., Kalof, L., Dietz, T. & Guagnano, G. A. (1995). Values, beliefs, and proenvironmental action: attitude formation toward emergent attitude objects, *Journal of Applied Social Psychology*, **25**, 1611-1636.

Spaargaren, G. & Mol, A. P. J. (2008). Greening global consumption: Redefining politics and authority, *Global Environmental Change*, **18**, 350-359.

Stern, P. (2000). New Environmental Theories: toward a coherent theory of environmentally significant behaviour, *Journal of Social Issues*, **56**, 407-424.

Sustrans (2011) *TravelSmart Initiative* (Sustrans, Bristol) www.sustrans.org.uk/what-we-do/travelsmart.

Thaler, R. H. & Sunstein, C. R. (2008) *Nudge: Improving Decisions about Health, Wealth and Happiness*, Yale University Press: New Haven, CT.

Vargo, S. L. & Lusch, R. F. (2008) Service-dominant logic: continuing the evolution, *Journal of the Academy of Marketing Science*, **36**, 1-10.

Whatmore, S. J. (2009). Mapping knowledge controversies: science, democracy and the redistribution of expertise, *Progress in Human Geography*, **33**, 587-598.

Whitehead, M., Jones, R. & Pykett, A. (2011). Governing irrationality, or a more than rational government? Reflections on the rescientisation of decision making in British public policy, *Environment & Planning A*, **43**, 2819-2837.

Wilson, C. & Chatterton, T. (2011). Multiple models to inform climate change policy: a pragmatic response to the 'beyond the ABC' debate, *Environment & Planning A*, **43**, 2781-2787.

3 Generational Mobilities: Transitions for the millennial generation

Alexa Delbosc

Institute of Transport Studies, Department of Civil Engineering, Monash University, Australia.

Auto-mobility through the life course

Mobility and accessibility plays a fundamental role throughout the life course. Accessibility enables participation in essential tasks such as work and education, as well as psychosocially important activities such as recreation, socialisation and intergenerational care (Metz, 2000; Social Exclusion Unit, 2003). Although some of these tasks can be undertaken in the home or through alternative means (such as online shopping or e-communication, see Chapter 13), evidence suggests that out-of-home mobility has its own benefits (Metz, 2000; Ettema *et al.*, 2010; Bergstad *et al.*, 2012). Indeed, an increasing body of research has demonstrated that restricted mobility and accessibility can result in a range of negative outcomes, from greater social exclusion (Delbosc & Currie, 2011a; Delbosc & Currie, 2011b; Stanley *et al.*, 2011), to poorer health outcomes (Frank *et al.*, 2006; Jones *et al.*, 2008), to reduced psychological well-being (Bergstad *et al.*, 2012; Delbosc, 2012; Reardon & Abdallah, 2013).

In most of the developed world, the majority of this mobility is provided directly or indirectly through the private car (Kenworthy, *et al.*, 1999; Lucas & Jones, 2009). Although this provides mobility benefits, it also results in a range of negative impacts on the environment, health and safety of the community. Road collisions globally cause 1.2 million deaths each year and are the eighth leading cause of death globally, as well as the leading cause of death for those aged 15-29 (WHO 2012). Globally, in 2010 transport was responsible for 14% of greenhouse gas emissions, or 6.9 gigatons per year. Decades of growth in car travel have worked against goals to improve the safety and sustainability of the transport system.

Yet our relationship with car travel varies significantly through the life course. Household car ownership follows a 'life cycle effect' (see Figure 3.1), increasing as young households form and peaking when the head of household reaches the mid-40s; from there, car ownership declines (Dargay & Vythoulkas, 1999). Part of this pattern is a reflection of household size (first as households form, then have children, then children move out), yet even car ownership *per adult* tends to follow a similar pattern (Klein & Smart, 2016). The reason for this is that the role of the car changes through the life cycle.

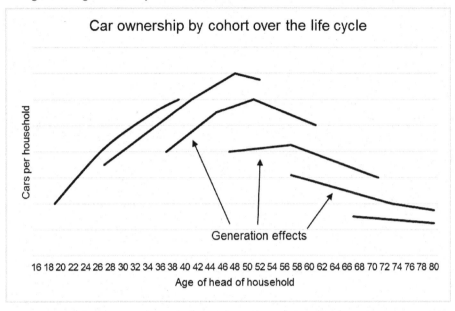

Figure 3.1: Car ownership by generation cohort across the life cycle. Adapted from Dargay and Vythoulkas (1999).

Babies and young children are entirely dependent on adults for their mobility and these trips are increasingly being conducted in cars rather than on foot or by bicycle (Fotel & Thomsen, 2002). In addition, as part of a greater shift toward supervised parenting, children have less freedom of movement than in the past (Fotel & Thomsen, 2002). Whereas in the past children were more likely to engage in unstructured, unsupervised play throughout the local neighbourhood, modern childhoods are characterised by scheduled and supervised activities, usually facili-tated by car travel (Hofferth & Sandberg, 2001). So too the journey to school has transitioned away from a walk or bike ride to the closest school and is more likely than in the past to take place in the back of the family car (Department for Transport, 2007; McDonald, 2007). This has potentially discouraging implications for the future of sustainable transport, as there is evidence that parental attitudes toward independent travel of children influence their travel habits through adolescence and young adulthood (Baslington, 2008; Driller & Handy, 2013; Thigpen & Handy, 2016).

In adolescence, teenagers seek and are granted greater freedom of movement. Their travel and activity needs – including after-school activities, sporting, visiting friends and part-time employment – become more complex and independent

(Currie, 2007). This is also the small window in the life course when the only way a young person can practice fully independent mobility is through 'alternative' transport modes – walking, cycling, skateboarding or taking public transport. There is a strong suggestion that adolescents would prefer to use these modes when they are feasible and available (Currie, 2007). The alternative, relying on getting lifts (generally from parents or other family members), can put significant time pressures on other household members (Bell & Currie, 2007).

For many young people, the chance to get a driving licence then becomes the ultimate expression of independent mobility (Nakanishi & Black, 2015). Especially for those teenagers who had to rely on parental lifts, getting a driving licence provides their first taste of freedom. In cities with an auto-centric transport system, access to a car broadens the potential pool of locations to work, study, shop and live, expanding economic opportunity (Cervero et al., 2002). However at the same time, young adults tend to have fewer economic resources to pay for a motor vehicle, forcing many young people to actively balance the trade-offs between the additional mobility and additional cost of a car. This is a time of life when young people are still exploring where to live, where to work, what to spend their money on and what to save money for.

These choices about where to live, where to work and how to travel tend to lock into place when people transition into the traditionally 'adult' life stages of full-time work, purchasing a home, cohabitation and raising a family (Nakanishi & Black, 2015; Schoenduwe et al., 2015). Each of these life stage transitions is associated with higher rates of drivers licensing (Delbosc & Currie, 2014a). Cohabitation usually requires a compromise between two different job locations, often balanced against the current or future need for family amenities. These compromises often require one or more household vehicles to manage these travel needs. This is only exacerbated in households with children, who in turn develop their own travel needs.

In the context of societal pressures to increase sustainable travel, this transition into 'adult' life stage, and the associated shifts in travel mode choice, is a crucial window of time. There is clear evidence that once driving has become a habitual behaviour it becomes ingrained in how households organise their daily lives (Gärling & Axhausen, 2003; Verplanken & Orbell, 2003). This tends to set up life-long travel habits that are difficult to change, even when people reach later life stages (Nakanishi & Black, 2015).

When households reach the 'empty nest' stage and retirement, travel needs change once again. Although work may become less central during this transition, work and home locations and travel habits are likely to be strongly entrenched. Once households have become accustomed to choosing their shopping, leisure and socialisation destinations based on the freedom provided by the private vehicle, it is not common for households to willingly forgo that mobility (Nakanishi & Black, 2015).

Eventually people do lose the physical ability to drive a motor vehicle, and where no alternative travel methods are available the loss of a driving licence is strongly associated with negative well-being (Fonda *et al.*, 2001). There is an increasing amount of work being undertaken to help older people manage this transition (e.g., NZ Transport Agency, 2015).

This overview of automobility through the life course highlights the importance of encouraging and supporting sustainable transport choices early in the life course. Children who are allowed less freedom of movement before they can drive are more likely to drive early and often (Baslington, 2008; Driller & Handy, 2013; Thigpen & Handy, 2016). Young adulthood is a time when many are exploring a range of travel options, due in part to lower incomes before full-time work is established. But when someone starts to shape their daily travel choices around the mobility provided by a car (often in association with 'adult' life transitions such as parenthood), car use becomes habitual (Gärling & Axhausen, 2003; Verplanken & Orbell, 2003). Changing habitual behaviour presents a much greater challenge to policy and planning.

Thus far, each generation has increased household car ownership across the life cycle, peaking earlier and holding onto their car for longer (note the 'generation effects' in Figure 3.1). This trend has discouraging implications for low carbon mobility transitions, creating an uphill battle for sustainable travel. Yet there is some hope that this trend may be slowing, providing an opportunity to encourage sustainable transport in the next generation.

At present, the millennial generation – also called generation Y – are starting to turn 30[1], which means they are in the middle of making this crucial transition into 'adulthood'. The next section explores whether this generation may provide an important opportunity to help the transport system transition to a lower-carbon future.

Millennial mobility – breaking new ground?

The baby boomer generation was the first to undertake their whole lifecycle facilitated by the mobility provided by the private car. They were, in a sense, the trail blazers that set these patterns in place for generation X that followed them. However there is emerging evidence that the millennial generation may be following a slightly different path (Kuhnimhof *et al.*, 2012; Blumenberg *et al.*, 2013; Delbosc & Currie, 2013; Ministry of Infrastructure and the Environment, 2014; McDonald, 2015; Rive *et al.*, 2015). Compared to previous generations, millennials are more likely to delay when they get a driving license, use public transport and active modes and take advantage of new ways to use the car such as car-sharing (e.g. ZipCar, GoGet) and ride-sharing (e.g. Uber, Lyft). Their propensity toward smartphones makes them a particularly suitable market for a range of apps that encourage different mobility patterns (see Chapter 13).

---

1 Although the exact cut-off for the millennial generation varies, they are generally considered to be born between the years 1980 and 2000.

An international review of driver licence rates found that young people (generally 18 to 30) were becoming less likely to get a driving licence in 9 out of 14 developed countries reviewed (Delbosc & Currie, 2013). In those countries showing a decline in licensing, the average decline was 0.6% per annum (Delbosc and Currie, 2013). It is not yet clear whether these declines reflect a generation that has truly turned its back on the car or are simply delaying getting a licence until later in life (Delbosc, 2016). It is also important to note that although licensing rates are declining, in most contexts the majority of millennials have a driving licence and use the car as their primary travel mode.

There is significant international variation in these patterns. In some developed countries, such as New Zealand, Germany and the Netherlands, youth driver licensing has not declined (Kuhnimhof *et al.*, 2012; Ministry of Infrastructure and the Environment, 2014; Rive *et al.*, 2015). Yet even in these countries there is evidence that young adults are driving less than in the past (Kuhnimhof *et al.*, 2012, Blumenberg *et al.*, 2013, Ministry of Infrastructure and the Environment 2014, McDonald 2015, Rive *et al.*, 2015). What modes are replacing driving also depends on the national and local context. Where alternatives are available, millennials are using public transport and active modes more (Rive *et al.*, 2015); in other contexts (most notably in the United States), young people are not using transit more and instead appear to be travelling less overall than in the past (McDonald, 2015). Transport choices are strongly context-dependent and there is also likely to be a great deal of sub-national variation (e.g. between urban and rural); however this has not yet been explored in the research literature. Even within a city, different populations will have very different relationships to the car (see Case Study 1). The discussion in this chapter should in no way preclude these subtleties and variations.

In addition, there is an assumption that millennials are more inclined to use 'shared mobility services' than older generations, although research in this area is still very nascent (Rayle *et al.*, 2016). Rather than opt for a traditional vehicle ownership arrangement, recently there has been a proliferation of car-sharing, bike-sharing, ride-sharing and ride-sourcing services to choose from. These services allow their users to enjoy many of the benefits of personal mobility at a reduced cost. Although these services are still considered relatively niche, they are more popular amongst millennials than other age groups, and have the potential to challenge the dominant automobility regime. For example a survey of ride-sourcing services (such as Uber and Lyft) in San Francisco found that 73% of respondents were millennials compared to only 32% of the population (Rayle *et al.*, 2016).

A number of explanations have been explored for this change in millennial mobility and can be broadly categorised under the following headings (Delbosc & Currie, 2013):

- Changes to driving licence regulations
- Affordability of car ownership and use
- Attitudes

- Use of information communication technology and smartphones
- Location and transport choices
- Life stage changes

The next section will review these explanations using the case study of Australian millennials; in particular those in Melbourne and the state of Victoria.

Melbourne millennials – a case study

In many ways Australian millennials have typified the changes seen in many developed countries. Australia is a highly urbanised population of over 23 million with over 75% living in the 20 largest cities (Department of Infrastructure and Regional Development, 2015). The larger capital cities vary in population between 1.8 and over 4 million residents. The larger cities tend to have a small and dense urban core surrounded by extremely dispersed suburban development, similar to North American cities. Although car travel is dominant, other modes are more common than in most American cities; in 2011, 66% of Australians drove or were driven to work, 10% used public transport and 4% walked (Australian Bureau of Statistics, 2011a). The larger cities have radial public transport systems made up of heavy rail, some light rail (particularly in Melbourne), bus and some ferries (particularly in Sydney). The evidence for this section is drawn primarily from Melbourne, Australia's second-largest city of over 4 million and the capital of the state of Victoria.

Driver licensing rates among young Victorians have dropped significantly since the turn of the century (see Figure 3.2), dropping 0.8% a year for those aged 18-23 and 0.6% for those aged 24-30.

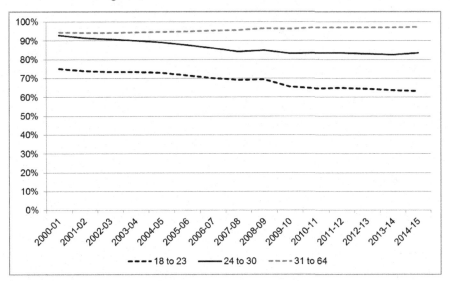

Figure 3.2: Driver licensing rate by age, Victoria, 2000-2015. Years given in Australian financial years (July to June). Source: Australian Bureau of Statistics (2015a), VicRoads (2015).

In addition, household travel survey data found that since 1994 young Victorians were less likely to use a car or walk but more likely to use public transport (Delbosc & Currie 2013), see Figure 3.3.

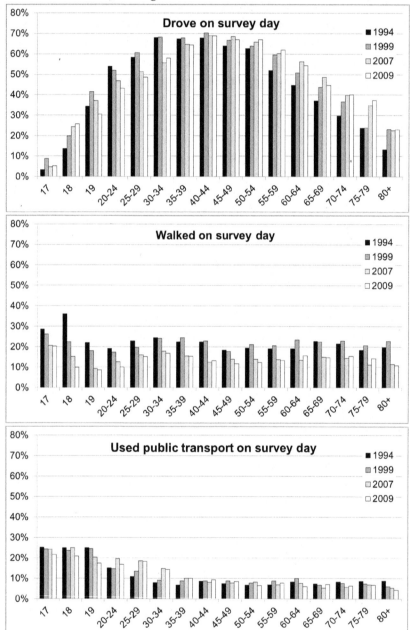

Figure 3.3: Mode use on day of travel survey by age, 1994-2009, Victoria. Note: Minimum legal age of unsupervised driving in Victoria is 18. Source: Author's analysis of VATS and VISTA travel surveys (Transport Research Centre, 2001; Department of Transport, 2009).

In Australia, as in almost every developed country, changes to driver licensing regulations have made it more difficult and time-consuming to get a licence in the first place. The state of Victoria has the strictest regulations in Australia, and possibly in the world; 120 supervised driving hours are required before young adults can apply for a provisional driver's licence and they cannot drive independently until they are 18. Yet these restrictions cannot be the only explanation for changes to millennial driving, as declines were noted some years before stricter regulations were put in place (Delbosc & Currie, 2014a).

Higher petrol prices and lower disposable income, due to youth unemployment rates and a shift toward part-time work (Delbosc & Currie, 2014a), mean that running a car is less affordable; some young people would rather prioritise their limited income to other pursuits (Delbosc & Currie, 2014b). There is also some evidence that attitudes toward the car have shifted since the days of the baby boomers. A qualitative study in Victoria found that the car was a symbol of adult responsibility, rather than an aspirational symbol of status (Delbosc & Currie, 2014c). However this may not be the case universally, as research in the Netherlands found that young people are just as likely as their parents to believe that a car gives them prestige (Steg 2005).

The role of new technology and its impact on the travel of millennials is still a very open question (see Chapter 13). Qualitative work in Melbourne suggests that although virtual contact can complement in-person social contact, it is unlikely fully replace it (Delbosc & Currie, 2014c). This is a complex and rapidly-changing area in great need of further research.

Another potential explanation for the change in mobility is that Australian millennials are more likely than previous generations to prefer living in accessible, inner-urban areas where a car is not always a necessity. Many car-oriented cities (especially in Australia and parts of North America) have been going through a period of 'urban rejuvenation', with an increase in inner-city housing; millennials are a major market for this trend (Belden Russonello & Stewart, 2011; Lachman & Brett, 2011; Davis et al., 2012). Figure 3.4 shows the proportion of the population aged 20-29 in the three largest capitals in Australia (Sydney, Melbourne and Brisbane). The maps clearly show the concentration of millennials within 5-10km of city centres. Most of the 'hotspots' outside of that ring correspond with major train stations or universities. One could argue that people in their 20s were always more likely to live in accessible inner areas, but there is evidence in Australia that millennials are increasingly concentrating there. As shown in Table 3.1, all three inner-city areas[2] have seen significant population growth between 2001 and 2011, reflecting an increase in housing density in these areas. Furthermore, the proportion of the population aged 20-29 increased in all three cities; for example in Melbourne it rose from 27% to 33%.

---

2   'Inner city' is defined as the central Local Government Area for Sydney and Melbourne (approximately 30 sq km). Brisbane's Local Government Area is unusually large (1,367 sq km) so data for Brisbane is drawn from four inner Statistical Local Areas (City – Inner, City – Remainder, South Brisbane, Spring Hill and Kangaroo Point).

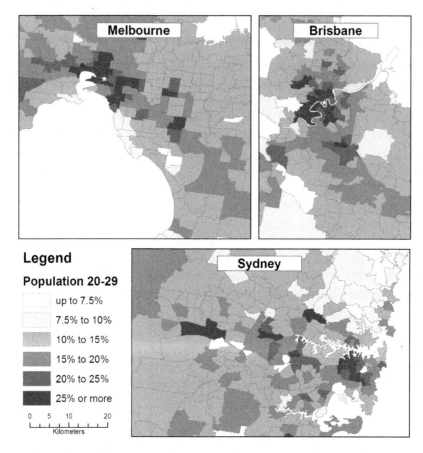

Figure 3.4: Percent of population aged 20-29, largest Australian capitals, 2011. Note: Star indicates city's central business district. Source: Australian Bureau of Statistics (2011b).

Table 3.1: Change in population of inner Sydney, Melbourne and Brisbane, 2001-2011. Source: Australian Bureau of Statistics (2011a).

		2001	2006	2011
Population age 20-29	Sydney	36,170	49,202	53,217
	Melbourne	19,853	31,962	39,440
	Brisbane	5,020	9,176	10,529
Total population	Sydney	153,200	180,475	196,781
	Melbourne	72,691	98,478	120,359
	Brisbane	23,828	35,713	39,941
Percent aged 20-29	Sydney	24%	27%	27%
	Melbourne	27%	32%	33%
	Brisbane	21%	26%	26%

Finally, there is strong evidence that these changes in mobility are a direct reflection of a delay in millennials' life transition from young adulthood into 'traditional adulthood'. This trend has important implications for the mobility of the millennial generation as they reach their 30s. Because this trend appears to be occurring in all developed countries, the discussion will now be expanded beyond Australia.

Breaking new ground or delaying the inevitable?

Compared to previous generations, millennials in the developed world are delaying full-time employment, cohabitation, marriage and child-rearing; they are more likely to be enrolled in post-secondary education and working part-time (Gray *et al.*, 2008; Office for National Statistics, 2011; Taylor *et al.*, 2012). Rates of educational participation have increased as the job market shifts toward skilled, technical jobs that require one or more degrees. For example the proportion of Australians age 20-24 in formal education has skyrocketed from 25% in 1991 to 44% in 2015 (Figure 3.5). Increasing rates of educational participation tends to delay full-time work. Not surprisingly, in Australia rates of full-time work among young adults have been plummeting. Indeed, for the first time in recent history young Australians are more likely to be in part-time work than full-time work (Figure 3.6). Similar trends are being expressed in the United States (Taylor *et al.*, 2012), New Zealand (Rive *et al.*, 2015) and the UK (Office for National Statistics, 2011).

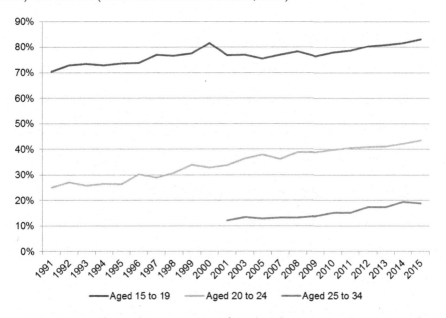

Figure 3.5: Percent of Australians age 15-34 in formal study, 1991-2015. Source: Australian Bureau of Statistics (2015b).

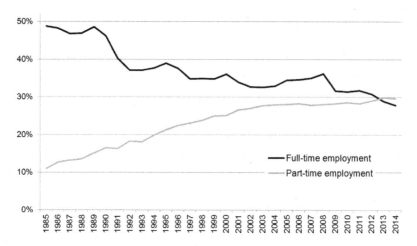

Figure 3.6: Percent of Australians age 15-24 in employment, 1985-2014. Note: Population and employment taken at 30 June. Employment seasonally adjusted. Source: Australian Bureau of Statistics (2015a; 2015c).

Millennials are also delaying the transition into long-term partnerships and child-rearing. For example, in Australia the proportion of 20-24 year-old women living with a partner dropped from 39% in 1986 to 24% in 2001 (Gray *et al.*, 2008). The median age of first marriage has also increased by over three years since the 1990s (Australian Bureau of Statistics, 2012) and the median age of first-time mothers is slowly approaching 30.

Taken together, all of these changes mean millennials have less need for a car and less means to pay for one. Traditionally 'adult' life stage markers of full-time work, home ownership, cohabitation and child-rearing are all strongly associated with driver licensing among millennials (Delbosc & Currie, 2014a). If the shift toward more sustainable mobility is driven almost entirely by delayed life stage, it follows that as millennials eventually reach these milestones, they will find themselves behind the wheel just like generation X and the baby boomers before them.

The way forward: Implications for a low carbon mobility transition

It may be tempting to take a defeatist attitude toward these findings and risk losing a real chance to improve the sustainability of our transport systems. Every year that a millennial delays car-dominated mobility is another year with fewer cars on the roads, fewer road deaths and reduced pollution. And every year that a millennial lives without a car provides an opportunity for them to familiarise themselves with new ways to travel, from public transport to car-sharing and ride-sharing. Yet as millennials transition into adulthood, there is a pressing need to support this transition through strong transport and land-use policy. It has been argued that transport planners and policymakers should focus more attention on parts of society who are 'not yet captives' to car-oriented mobility, rather than focus solely on changing car habits after they have formed (see Case Study 1, and Tal & Handy, 2010).

Two broad policy areas can potentially support this transition sustainably: by providing family housing in accessible areas, and by supporting sustainable transport. As previously discussed, most millennials in their 20s prefer to live in accessible, inner-city areas. From a transport perspective, the simplest way to help millennials continue to travel through sustainable methods is to provide family housing in accessible areas. European cities have long provided a variety of housing stock within cities and families living in apartments and townhouses are common. Yet in many newer cities, notably in North America and Australia, the inner-city housing 'boom' has been driven by small one and two-bedroom apartments that are not suitable for growing families. Furthermore, inner-city schools, hospitals and childcare centres have not kept pace with the young families that do choose to stay in place.

Yet changing the housing market is no easy task and the realities of housing prices will likely push many millennials away from the inner city. Instead, policy could focus on improving sustainable transport options that support full-time work and family life. Transit-oriented development should provide family housing near transit hubs. Local transport networks should encourage active travel to schools, childcare, parks and shops. Travel demand management and transit investments should provide as much opportunity as possible for millennials to make sustainable travel choices. Combined with developments such as car-sharing schemes, some families may be able to live comfortably with only one family car instead of two – and more as the children of the millennials reach their teenage years.

Millennials, like every generation, are diverse and most are happy to follow in the car-oriented footsteps of previous generations. Yet perhaps more than any previous generation, millennials are approaching cars from a utilitarian, rather than aspirational, perspective. If cities can provide them with that utility through alternatives to the car, many will take up those alternatives. Now is the time to provide them with that opportunity.

References

Australian Bureau of Statistics (2011a). Census Community Profiles. Available from: http://www.abs.gov.au/websitedbs/censushome.nsf/home/communityprofiles

Australian Bureau of Statistics (2011b). Census table builder. Available from: http://www.abs.gov.au/websitedbs/censushome.nsf/home/tablebuilder

Australian Bureau of Statistics (2012). *Australian social trends 2012: Commonwealth of Australia*. Report 4102.0. *Available from: http://www.abs.gov.au/AUSSTATS/abs@.nsf/Lookup/4102.0Main+Features30March+Quarter+2012*

Australian Bureau of Statistics (2015a). *Australian Demographic Statistics*. Report 3101.0.

Australian Bureau of Statistics (2015b). *Education and Work, Australia*. Report 6227.0.

Australian Bureau of Statistics (2015c). *Labour Force, Australia*. Report 6202.0.

Baslington, H. (2008). Travel socialization: A social theory of travel mode behaviour. *International Journal of Sustainable Transportation*, **2**(2): 91-114.

Belden Russonello & Stewart (2011). *The 2011 Community Preference Survey: What Americans are looking for when deciding where to live*. Washington DC, National Association of Realtors.

Bell, D. & Currie, G. (2007). *Travel & Lifestyle Impacts of New Bus Services in Outer Suburban Melbourne*, 30th Australasian Transport Research Forum.

Bergstad, C. J., Gamble, A., Hagman, O., Polk, M., Garling, T., Ettema, D., Friman, M. and Olsson, L. E. (2012). Influences of affect associated with routine out-of-home activities on subjective well-being. *Applied Research in Quality of Life*, **7**(1), 49-62.

Blumenberg, E., Wander, M., Taylor, B. D. & Smart, M. (2013). *The times, are they a-changin'? Youth, travel mode and the journey to work*. Transportation Research Board 92nd Annual Meeting. Washington, DC.

Cervero, R., Sandoval, O. & Landis, J. (2002). Transportation as a stimulus of welfare-to-work private versus public mobility. *Journal of Planning Education and Research*, **22**(1), 50-63.

Currie, G. (2007). Young Australians: No way to go. In *No Way to Go: Transport and social disadvantage in Australian communities*. G. Currie, J. Stanley and J. Stanley. Clayton, Victoria, Australia: Monash University ePress.

Dargay, J. M. & Vythoulkas, P. C. (1999). Estimation of a dynamic car ownership model: A pseudo-panel approach. *Journal of Transport Economics and Policy*, **33**(3), 287-302.

Davis, B., Dutzik, T. & Baxandall, P. (2012). *Transportation and the new generation: why young people are driving less and what it means for transportation policy*, Frontier Group: USA.

Delbosc, A. (2012). The role of well-being in transport policy. *Transport Policy*, **23**(0),25-33.

Delbosc, A. (2016). Delay or forgo? A closer look at youth driver licensing trends in the United States and Australia. *Transportation*, 1-8. DOI:10.1007/s11116-016-9685-7.

Delbosc, A. & Currie, G. (2011a). Exploring the relative influences of transport disadvantage and social exclusion on well-being. *Transport Policy*, **18**(4), 555-562.

Delbosc, A. & Currie, G. (2011b). Transport problems that matter – Social and psychological links to transport disadvantage. *Journal of Transport Geography*, **16**(1), 170-178.

Delbosc, A. & Currie, G. (2013). Causes of youth licensing decline: a synthesis of evidence. *Transport Reviews*, **33**(3), 271-290.

Delbosc, A. & Currie, G. (2014a). Changing demographics and young adult driver license decline in Melbourne, Australia (1994-2009). *Transportation*, **41**(3), 529-542.

Delbosc, A. & Currie, G. (2014b). Impact of attitudes and life stage on decline in rates of driver's license acquisition by young people in Melbourne, Australia. *Transportation Research Record*, **2452**, 62-70.

Delbosc, A. & Currie, G. (2014c). Using discussion forums to explore attitudes toward cars and licensing among young Australians. *Transport Policy*, **31C**, 27-34.

Department for Transport (2007). *Transport Trends 2007*. London.

Department of Infrastructure and Regional Development (2015). *State of Australian cities 2014-2015: progress in Australian regions.*

Department of Transport (2009). *Victorian integrated survey of travel and activity, 2007.*

Driller, B. K. & Handy, S. L. (2013). *Exploring the Influence of Parents on Children's Bicycling in Davis, California.* Transportation Research Board 92nd Annual Meeting.

Ettema, D., Gärling, T., Olsson, L. E. & Friman, M. (2010). Out-of-home activities, daily travel, and subjective well-being. *Transportation Research Part A: Policy and Practice,* **44**(9), 723-732.

Fonda, S. J., Wallace, R. B. & Herzog, A. R. (2001). Changes in driving patterns and worsening depressive symptoms among older adults, *Journals of Gerontology - Series B Psychological Sciences and Social Sciences.* **56**(6), S343-S351.

Fotel, T. & Thomsen, T. U. (2002). The surveillance of children's mobility. *Surveillance & Society,* **1**(4), 535-554.

Frank, L. D., Sallis, J. F., Conway, T. L., Chapman, J. E., Saelens, B. E. & Bachman, W. (2006). Many pathways from land use to health: associations between neighborhood walkability and active transportation, body mass index, and air quality. *Journal of the American Planning Association,* **72**(1), 75-87.

Gärling, T. & Axhausen, K. W. (2003). Introduction: Habitual travel choice. *Transportation,* **30**(1), 1-11.

Gray, M., Qu, L. & Weston, R. (2008). *Fertility and family policy in Australia,* Australian Institue of Family Studies.

Hofferth, S. L. & Sandberg, J. F. (2001). Changes in American children's time, 1981–1997. *Advances in Life Course Research,* **6**, 193-229.

Jones, A. P., Haynes, R., Sauerzapf, V., Crawford, S. M., Zhao, H. & Forman, D. (2008). Travel times to health care and survival from cancers in Northern England. *European Journal of Cancer,* **44**(2), 269-274.

Kenworthy, J. R., Laube, F. B., Newman, P., Barter, P., Raad, T., Poboon, C. & Guia Jr, B. (1999). *An International Sourcebook of Automobile Dependence in Cities 1960-1990,* University Press of Colourado: Boulder, USA.

Klein, N. J. & Smart, M. J. (2016). *Millennials and Car Ownership: Fewer Cars, Less Money.* Transportation Research Board Annual Meeting. Washington DC.

Kuhnimhof, T., Buehler, R., Wirtz, M. & Kalinowska, D. (2012). Travel trends among young adults in Germany: Increasing multimodality and declining car use for men. *Journal of Transport Geography,* **24**, 443-450.

Lachman, M. L. & Brett, D. L. (2011). *Generation Y: America's new housing wave.* Washington, DC, Urban Land Institute.

Lucas, K. & Jones, P. (2009). *The Car in British society,* RAC Foundation: UK.

McDonald, N. C. (2007). Active Transportation to school: Trends among U.S. Schoolchildren, 1969–2001. *American Journal of Preventive Medicine,* **32**(6), 509-516.

McDonald, N. C. (2015). Are millennials really the 'go-nowhere' generation? *Journal of the American Planning Association,* **81**(2), 90-103.

Metz, D. H. (2000). Mobility of older people and their quality of life. *Transport Policy,* **7**(2), 149-152.

Ministry of Infrastructure and the Environment (2014). *Not car-less, but car-later,* Netherlands Institute for Transport Policy Analysis.

Nakanishi, H. & Black, J. A. (2015). Travel habit creation of the elderly and the transition to sustainable transport: An exploratory research based on a retrospective survey. *International Journal of Sustainable Transportation,* **10**(7), 604-616.

NZ Transport Agency (2015). *Supporting senior drivers: how family and friends can help.* NZTA: Wellington, NZ. Available from: http://www.nzta.govt.nz/assets/resources/supporting-older-drivers/docs/supporting-senior-drivers.pdf.

Office for National Statistics (2011). *Young people in the labour market - 2011.* ONS: London.

Rayle, L., Dai, D., Chan, N., Cervero, R. & Shaheen, S. (2016). Just a better taxi? A survey-based comparison of taxis, transit, and ridesourcing services in San Francisco. *Transport Policy,* **45**, 168-178.

Reardon, L. & Abdallah, S. (2013). Well-being and transport: Taking stock and looking forward. *Transport Reviews,* **33**(6), 634-657.

Rive, G., Thomas, J., Jones, C., Frith, B. & Chang, J. (2015). *Public Transport and the Next Generation.* Wellington, NZ Transport Agency. Report 569.

Schoenduwe, R., Mueller, M. G., Peters, A. & Lanzendorf, M. (2015). Analysing mobility biographies with the life course calendar: a retrospective survey methodology for longitudinal data collection. *Journal of Transport Geography* **42**(0), 98-109.

Social Exclusion Unit (2003). *Making the Connections: Final Report on Transport and Social Exclusion,* Office of the Deputy Prime Minister (UK): London, UK.

Stanley, J. K., Hensher, D. A., Stanley, J. R. & Vella-Brodrick, D. (2011). Mobility, social exclusion and well-being: Exploring the links. *Transportation Research Part A: Policy and Practice,* **45**(8), 789-801.

Steg, L. (2005). Car use: lust and must. Instrumental, symbolic and affective motives for car use. *Transportation Research Part A,* **39**, 147-162.

Tal, G. & Handy, S. (2010). Travel behaviour of immigrants: An analysis of the 2001 National Household Transportation Survey. *Transport Policy,* **17**(2), 85-93.

Taylor, P., Parker, K., Kochhar, R., Fry, R., Funk, C., Patten, E. & Motel, S. (2012). *Young, underemployed and optimistic: Coming of age, slowly, in a tough economy,* Pew Research Center.

Thigpen, C. & Handy, S. (2016). *Driver's Licensing Delay: A retrospective study of the impact of attitudes, parental and social influences, and intergenerational differences.* Transportation Research Board Annual Meeting: Washington, DC.

Transport Research Centre (2001). *Victorian Activity and Travel Survey user manual.* Melbourne: Transport Research Centre.

Verplanken, B. & Orbell, S. (2003). Reflections on past behaviour: A self-report index of habit strength. *Journal of Applied Social Psychology,* **33**(6), 1313-1330.

VicRoads (2015). VicRoads license breakdown by age, 2001-2015.

WHO (2012). *Global status report on road safety: time for action.* Geneva, Switzerland, World Health Organisation Department of Violence and Injury Prevention.

4 Optimising Low Carbon Mobility for Health and Equity

Alex Macmillan

Department of Preventive and Social Medicine, University of Otago, New Zealand.

Hamish Mackie

Mackie Research and Consulting, New Zealand.

Introduction

Climate change has urgent and profound implications for humans and our quality of life (Watts *et al.*, 2015). Transport systems have complex links with health and well-being, not only through the contribution of transport to climate change (Reardon & Abdallah, 2013). In modern human habitats, the places people reside and the goods, services and people that contribute to their wellbeing are often separated geographically, and transport options confer a health benefit by enabling access. These benefits must be weighed against the negative impacts of different transport options on health, wellbeing and equity across a range of domains: physical, mental, cultural and spiritual, environmental and economic (Reardon & Abdallah, 2013). Direct effects include air pollution, road traffic injuries and levels of daily exercise. There are also important indirect impacts: the ease with which people can fairly access health-promoting goods and services (including work); contact with neighbours, friends and family; access to sites of cultural significance; and connection with nature. The notion that access for equitable human wellbeing is the purpose of a transport system challenges the current neoliberal transport policy discourse, dominated by a perceived need to move goods, capital and labour for economic growth.

Cities are increasingly the context for these transport and health relationships. Urban transport transitions therefore matter very much to public health and will be increasingly important as global rural to urban migration continues (United Nations, 2014). The complex links between the social and the technical aspects of transport require new approaches to urban transport policy-making to optimise co-benefits for health and fairness. In this chapter, we focus on low carbon transitions for land transport in cities, especially cities that are currently dominated by the use of private motor vehicles for most trips. We critically review the links between land transport and health using a broad public health framework. We demonstrate that transport policy-making needs to enable transport planners to understand future implications of policy choices, include a wider range of outcomes in analysis of costs and benefits, and involve the communities whose transport patterns are expected to change. We then provide two real world examples of these principles in action. The setting for both examples is Auckland, New Zealand, a city with 60 years of urban planning predicated on universal car ownership and use (Mees & Dodson, 2006, also see Chapter 7).

Transport, health, equity and climate change

In describing the links between land transport systems and human health and well-being, we combine a public health lens with current psychological knowledge about human behaviour change. A public health lens assumes that individual health is not just the absence of disease but a state of complete physical, mental, and social well-being (World Health Organisation, 1948) and takes an evidence-based view that the most important influences on health lie outside the health sector, as well as outside the control of individuals (Marmot & Bell, 2012). This means that changing policy and infrastructure systems at global, national, regional and local levels are often more effective than attempting to change the behaviour of individuals, or even directly attempting to shift social norms (Marmot & Bell, 2012).

Figure 4.1: Map of the social and environmental determinants of human wellbeing and equity. Reproduced with permission Barton & Grant (2006).

Figure 4.1 illustrates a combined public health and psychological understanding of how individual health and wellbeing is nested in social and environmental influences.

Much research about the links between transport and health has focused on the impacts on physical wellbeing through air pollution, injury and physical activity. However, there are broader implications of transport patterns on mental, social, environmental and economic aspects of wellbeing, as well as the unequal distribution of wellbeing by gender, socioeconomic status, and ethnicity. The evidence for these complex links between transport and health is summarised briefly below.

Physical health

Injury is the most comprehensively studied health impact of transport, and features prominently in prevention programmes and policy. Traffic injuries are among the leading causes of mortality and morbidity worldwide, responsible for a stable 3% of the global years of life lost (Institute for Health Metrics and Evaluation, 2016). The risk of road traffic injury is greatest for motorcyclists, cyclists and pedestrians, while public transport is the safest way to travel (World Health Organisation, 2010, 2015). Perceived risk of injury is also an important barrier for people to use active transport, especially cycling (Parkin *et al.*, 2007). Inequities in road traffic injury exist by income, education and ethnicity (see for example Camilloni *et al.*, 2013; Hosking *et al.*, 2013). Effective policies for reducing road traffic injury include lowering vehicle speeds and reducing the number of motor vehicles on the road, which also have the potential to reduce transport related carbon emissions. Both are especially important for reducing injury to people walking and cycling (Bhalla *et al.*, 2007; Elvik & Bjørnskau, 2016).

Vehicle-related air pollution is responsible for a growing burden of lung and heart disease and cancer, driven by increases in South and East Asia (Global Road Safety Facility & Evaluation, 2014). Exposure to vehicle exhaust pollutants varies by mode of transport. Although levels of pollutants may be higher within vehicles than outside, higher breathing rates and longer trips for walking and cycling can mean exposures are greater (de Hartog *et al.*, 2010). Socio-economic and ethnic gradients also exist for exposure to vehicular air pollution (Briggs *et al.*, 2008; Jacobson, Hengartner, & Louis, 2005).

To date, many policies to address transport air pollution have responded to the introduction of standards for specific pollutants with technological improvements, sometimes decreasing one pollutant while increasing the emission of others (HEI Panel, 2010), also a potential consequence of a single-focused technical standard for carbon emissions. Electric vehicles hold promise for reducing carbon and other air pollutants, but rely on clean, renewable sources of electricity and a rapid fleet turnover to achieve health and climate targets.

Transport and land use policies that reduce the number of vehicle kilometres travelled can also reduce air pollution impacts. For example, the London Congestion

Charge, has reduced air pollution deaths and illness, with air quality improvements greatest in areas of high deprivation (Tonne *et al.*, 2008).

Replacing motor vehicle trips with more active modes has the potential to benefit health through physical activity (Martin *et al.*, 2015), even in the most polluted cities (Tainio *et al.*, 2016). Urban planning over the past half century has built physical activity out of our daily lives, so that extra time and expense is often needed to achieve the levels of activity that can prevent heart disease, stroke, diabetes, cancer, depression and loss of bone density (Warburton, Nicol & Bredin, 2006). Even 2.5 hours of brisk walking per week can reduce mortality by about 10% (Woodcock *et al.*, 2011). Individual encouragement to be more physically active has achieved little sustained success (Ogilvie *et al.*, 2007), while building some walking and cycling into habitual trips like commuting can more successfully reduce mortality (Hamer & Chida, 2008), even as part of a public transport trip (Rissel *et al.*, 2012). Policies that improve safe, convenient accessibility of destinations are needed to achieve the benefits of more walking and cycling for transport. When such policies lead to successful substitution of motor vehicle trips by walking and cycling they also reduce transport carbon emissions (Macmillan *et al.*, 2014).

Mental wellbeing

Regular physical activity also benefits mental wellbeing, reducing the risk of depression. When daily transport trips are congested, unpredictable and perceived as having a high opportunity cost, then perceived stress is higher, with implications for mental and physical health (Gottholmseder *et al.*, 2009). This stress can manifest itself in more harmful behaviours when it leads to expressions of anger to other road users (Asbridge *et al.*, 2006). The opportunity cost of the time spent travelling and people's ability to manage other responsibilities is a further cause of stress, particularly for women, who are still mainly responsible for multiple care obligations (Schwanen, 2011).

Road traffic noise has further negative impacts on mental wellbeing. It is estimated that about 100,000 years of life are lost annually in Europe due to environmental noise, much of which is attributable to road traffic noise (Jantunen *et al.*, 2011), through cumulative impacts on stress and sleep disturbance. Railway noise has also been implicated in annoyance and sleep disturbance, especially in Japan (Lim *et al.*, 2006).

Social participation and economic wellbeing

Much research has assumed transport time is lost to other activities or opportunities (for example Mokhtarian & Chen, 2004). However, active transport can provide a 'double dividend' in the form of time saved on physical activity undertaken for fitness during leisure time. People may also use time on public transport for relaxation and social connection (Letherby & Reynolds, 2003), while walking provides opportunistic social and nature connection within neighbourhoods (Lund, 2003). In contrast, busy roads are detrimental to social wellbeing, by severing communities physically and psychologically, hampering connection with neighbours and access to local shops and services (Mindell *et al.*, 2011).

Urban transport design determines fair participation in the labour market, families and wider society (Lucas, 2011). Urban sprawl and car dependence creates a gradient of social exclusion by gender, income, ethnicity and disability (Clifton & Lucas, 2004; Stanley & Vella-Brodrick, 2009), thereby harming social wellbeing. Addressing transport social exclusion requires provision of improved, affordable public transport services, and high quality access by walking and cycling, which also contribute to a low carbon mobility transition (Battellino, 2009; Lucas *et al.*, 2009).

Environmental wellbeing

In addition to motorised transport's significant contribution to climate change (see Chapters 1 and 15), there are other impacts on human wellbeing mediated by negative impacts on local physical environments. Urban ecosystems including trees, parks, and water bodies all bring benefits for human wellbeing through microclimate regulation (of increasing importance as cities heat up due to climate change); air filtration; stormwater management; food production; and the cultural, spiritual and recreational benefits of nature contact (Tzoulas *et al.*, 2007). Road building and car parking result in a trade off with these urban ecosystems (Pickett *et al.*, 2001). Roads are ecological vacuums and fragment green spaces, limiting their ability to support biodiversity (Fahrig, 2003) and mitigate urban heat island effects (Pickett *et al.*, 2001). Water-impervious roads increase the risk of urban flooding, when high volumes of polluted storm water run off into vulnerable fresh and marine waters (Spellerberg, 1998). This run-off has negative effects on aquatic ecosystems and human health through recreational exposure (Trombulak & Frissell, 2000).

Achieving policies that optimise co-benefits for climate health

Many transport policies identified as effective in reducing land transport's contribution to climate change align well with policies to reduce other health effects of current transport patterns (Woodcock *et al.*, 2007). However, a significant re-balancing of transport investment is needed, prioritising:

1 Investment in safe, convenient walking and cycling for short trips and linking with public transport.

2 Slower urban speeds, improving traffic flow while encouraging safe active transport.

3 High quality public transport powered by renewable electricity.

4 When private vehicle use is necessary, ensuring they are the most energy efficient, low-emissions vehicles available.

Longer term urban land use planning is also crucial, to improve fair access to employment, education and health-promoting goods and services by walking, cycling and public transport. This planning needs to incorporate zoning rules, housing density and affordability and destination and service planning.

Perverse incentives for continued private motor vehicle use (for instance tax incentives for business fleets) also need to be addressed and replaced with disincentives that have a focus on fairness. Road pricing and fuel taxes have the potential to benefit the climate and health, but these taxes can be regressive – their economic burden falling unfairly on the poorest households, reducing the ability of these households to meet their health and wellbeing needs (Dhar *et al.*, 2009). Some policies that have been used to achieve a low carbon mobility transition have the potential to worsen health or increase inequalities. In one example, evidence suggests that crop-based biofuels compete with food crops for land, increasing the price of basic foods (Hill *et al.*, 2006).

The complex socio-technical relationships between urban transport and health and the potential for unintended negative consequences demand new approaches to policy-making that allow decision-makers to optimise co-benefits for health and fairness while planning for a low carbon transition (Banister & Hickman, 2013). Currently, climate impacts, health and wellbeing, and equity outcomes are poorly considered in transport policy-making. This is partly a result of difficulties with understanding the multiple long-term impacts of policy choices. There also remains a narrow range of interests dominating the transport policy discourse, which mean that transport's contribution to economic growth through freight and labour movements continue to dominate in many cities around the world. To integrate health, equity and environmental sustainability, decision-making must incorporate systems thinking; bring together the qualitative and quantitative knowledge of policy-makers, society and research in a collaborative learning process; and understand the impacts of policies across a wide range of agreed outcomes.

In the next section, we describe two examples of these principles in action to address the challenges of healthy, equitable, low carbon mobility. The first is a systems model of commuting and wellbeing developed using a participatory process. The second, *Future Streets*, is a participatory intervention study with dual aims: to generate high quality evidence for the effectiveness of suburban infrastructure for walking and cycling; and to understand and alter the architecture of transport decision-making. Both are examples from Auckland, New Zealand, a rapidly growing small city of 1.4 million people, where urban planning has for the last 60 years heavily favoured car dependence and sprawl. New Zealanders currently have among the highest per capita greenhouse gas emissions in the world (WRI, 2014), with 40% of carbon emissions coming from transport, mostly private motor vehicles (Ministry for the Environment, 2016). At the same time, New Zealand has the third highest rate of obesity in the world (Ministry of Health, 2015) partly due to physical inactivity. Significant transport inequities also exist in Auckland, by income and ethnicity (Fergusson *et al.*, 2016).

The trip to work and community wellbeing: a system dynamics model

Commuting is a special kind of trip because it allows access to employment, an important determinant of wellbeing. Because trips to work occur at congested times, commuting contributes more heavily to the negative impacts of transport than its share of trip numbers or distance suggests (André & Rapone, 2009). Furthermore, the habitual, mass nature of urban commute trips makes them an amenable target for shifting from car dependence to other modes.

We used participatory system dynamics modelling (SDM) to develop a trans-disciplinary understanding of the links between commuting and wellbeing as a complex system, starting with a broad health framework. By using SDM we were incorporating characteristics of complex systems, including many interacting variables whose relationships change over time and determine the trends in outcomes of interest. Interaction between variables in complex systems is characterised by feedback: positive, or reinforcing loops and balancing, or negative loops. The accumulation of 'stocks' (variables with measurable levels) is important, including people, information, capital, outcomes like pollution or injury, or material resources (Richardson, 2011).

We built on the cross-disciplinary literature summarised above by collecting primary qualitative data to develop a set of qualitative feedback loops, known as a causal loop diagram (CLD) that explained the system linking commuting and wellbeing in Auckland. The development of the CLDs was inductive and constructivist (Charmaz, 2005). Individual accounts of commuting and wellbeing were considered to be manifestations of the underlying socio-technical structures we aimed to understand (Braun & Clarke, 2006). We undertook 16 semi-structured interviews, using cognitive mapping (Eden & Ackermann, 2004), with Auckland community, policy and health stakeholders, using an *a priori* sampling frame with a focus on social exclusion. A dynamic definition of problem trends, a set of shared wellbeing outcomes and a preliminary set of feedback loops were developed from these interviews, triangulating with the literature about transport and public health. The preliminary feedback loops were refined in two workshops, as well as in meetings with individuals and organisations involving the interviewees and 21 representatives from across the sampling frame.

The dynamic problem was defined as an exponential growth in people commuting by private motor vehicle (cars, vans and motorcycles), with gradual declines in the use of walking, cycling and public transport. Together, the participants identified a range of problematic outcomes of these trends, including congestion, climate change, limited transport choice, poor quality public transport, escalating costs and air pollution. The wellbeing outcomes identified by participants covered environmental, social, cultural, economic, physical and mental wellbeing. There was a consensus desire for a reversal of these trends, which would not occur with a 'business-as-usual' approach.

Cognitive maps from the interviews represented the participants' internalised understandings of the complex relationships between the trip to work and self-defined wellbeing. During the first workshop, participants identified a set of wellbeing outcomes and clustered interview variables into themes. These were used to develop draft causal loop diagrams (CLDs) which were reviewed, debated and refined in a second workshop.

Some of these wellbeing outcomes are part of feedback loops in the resulting CLDs, while others are external to the feedbacks loops (exogenous outcomes). The interconnected set of CLDs is summarised in an overview model (Figure 4.2), comprising eight sectors. These sectors match the themes identified in the first workshop, and are described briefly below.

Walking and cycling

Concern for safety was considered a major barrier to walking and cycling, particularly cycling. A central balancing loop that is especially important for cycling means that increasing numbers of vulnerable road users translate into more reported injuries which dampens further growth. In addition, if more active transport leads to a reduction in road congestion, then this may make driving more attractive, undermining further growth in walking or cycling. There was also concern that if congestion was relieved, the remaining vehicles would travel faster, increasing the risk of injury and putting people off active modes. On the other hand, potentially helpful positive feedback loops were identified: safety in numbers (more walking and cycling leads to a reduced risk of injury per person); increased political will to invest in walking and cycling infrastructure; social normalisation of these commute modes.

Neighbourhood sense of safety from crime

A simple reinforcing loop was proposed, linking increased driving to work with a decline in neighbourhood social connection and declining sense of safety from crime in neighbourhoods. This was then thought to further increase people's car use as as a more secure mode of transport in the face of low sense of security.

Time pressure and employment accessibility

Participants perceived that car dependent urban planning was increasing the distance between home and work, increasing time pressure directly, while also increasing the cost of living. Increasing costs of daily living (especially through the vehicle-related costs) mean fewer people can afford to live conveniently to work places, worsening this vicious cycle. This theme is particularly important for low-income households. Participants considered that the decline of public transport exacerbates these issues.

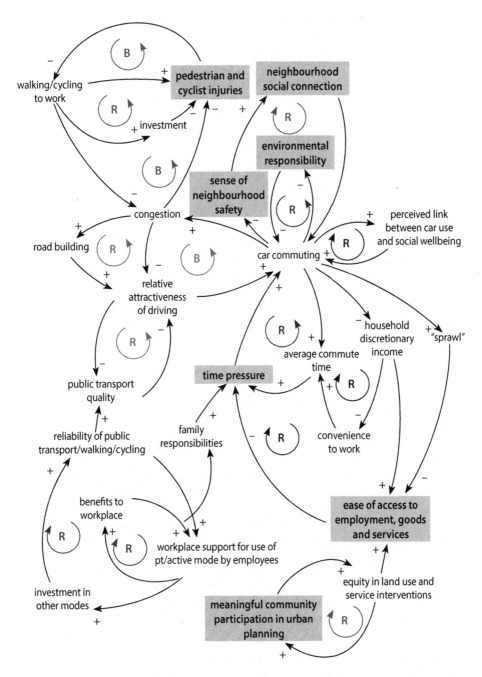

Figure 4.2: Causal loop diagram of the trip to work and wellbeing. Arrows with a positive sign (+) indicate a change in the variable at the arrow-tail leads to a change in the variable at the arrowhead in the same direction. Arrows with a negative (−) sign indicate a change in the arrow-tail variable leads to an inverse change in the arrowhead variable (opposite direction). R – Reinforcing loop, the result of which is an amplification of the initial pattern of behaviour. B – Balancing loop, the result of which may be to dampen the initial pattern of behaviour or create oscillation.

Relative attractiveness of public transport and car commuting

Participants considered that the viability of public transport is closely tied with the attractiveness of driving. As car commuting increases, so does congestion, which would serve as a natural limit to growth in car commuting (a balancing loop), in turn making public transport more attractive again. However, when congestion stimulates a policy response of further provision of road space, a reinforcing loop of driving attractiveness and congestion ensues (induced traffic). This in turn undermines public transport viability via reduced patronage, increasing fare costs and decreasing quality.

Workplace support

Declining workplace support for walking, cycling and public transport was also seen as problematic. It was considered possible to turn this around though, leading to two beneficial reinforcing loops. The first proposes that increased support for more active modes of transport would lead to a healthier, more productive workforce. This experienced benefit would then lead to further support. Workplace support could also take the form of advocacy for greater investment in high quality, reliable services and infrastructure. Increases in safety and reliability would then lead to further employer support.

Environmental and cultural wellbeing

Several factors were considered to be at play in the relationship between commuting and connection with nature. On the one hand, urban planning that places greenspace on the edges of the city meant that some people would be willing to live further from work, locking them into patterns of long car commutes, so that they could live closer to nature. On the other hand, car commuting in the city was considered to reduce daily contact with nature, reducing people's sense of stewardship for the environment. Car dependence was also considered to degrade the quality of urban cultural landscapes for people on foot or bike.

'Car culture' and social wellbeing

The dominance of car commuting is thought to be reinforced by a sense that this was the 'normal' way to get to work. The experience that car use brings an increased sense of control, independence and security, especially for women and young people, means that car commuting has become central to a sense of social wellbeing and status, reinforced by powerful messages from the media and advertising.

Participation and leadership in transport planning

Reinforcing feedback loops could potentially lead to helpful cycles of inclusive participation in urban transport planning, especially if equitable outcomes result.

However, it was thought that this helpful reinforcing cycle would need to be stimulated by political leadership.

The CLDs are a starting point for communities, researchers and policy-makers to explore effective policies for a transition in commuting that could have co-benefits for the climate, wellbeing and fairness. For example, the walking and cycling feedback loops have been developed into a simulation model of some specific policies to increase cycling in Auckland, contributing to a shift in national and regional cycling policy (Macmillan *et al.*, 2014).

Retrofitting streets for healthy low carbon suburbs – *Future Streets*

The *Future Streets* project combines the public health framework previously described, with road safety lessons from applied psychology and the policy-making principles outlined above: participatory action research; systems thinking for health, equity and sustainability; and combining policy, community and research knowledge. Building on the causal theories just described, *Future Streets* is an intervention study to enhance suburban streets for walking and cycling, with an equity focus.

Self-explaining roads

Building on well-established psychological concepts, the logic of 'Self Explaining Roads' (SER) (Theeuwes & Godthelp, 1995) is that well-designed roads evoke improved behaviours from road users (Weller *et al.*, 2008) leading to road safety improvements. The SER approach focuses on three principles: hierarchical road function (through roads, collector and local roads); consistency of mass and speed on each road type; and predictable behaviour through consistent design (van Vliet & Schermers, 2000).

In keeping with the structural influences on wellbeing (Figure 4.1), these principles make clear that road user behaviour is strongly influenced by road design. While educating and encouraging road users to change their behaviour may have some effect on behaviour, the design of roads, the behaviour they afford and the expectations that are reinforced are more powerful.

The safety implications of SER applied to suburban streets have been tested in Auckland, focusing on a small area with high levels of road traffic injury, concerns about safety and a heterogeneous road layout (Charlton *et al.*, 2010; Mackie *et al.*, 2012). Nine kilometres of local and collector roads were retrofitted to lower design speeds (Figure 4.3). On local streets, road marking removal, landscaping, 'community islands' and mountable crossroad islands were used to break sightlines, create uncertainty and encourage walking, aiming for a design speed of 30km/hr. Collector roads were differentiated with centre and edge lines and specific walking and cycling safety infrastructure, to create a 40km/hr design speed.

Figure 4.3: Self explaining roads retrofit.

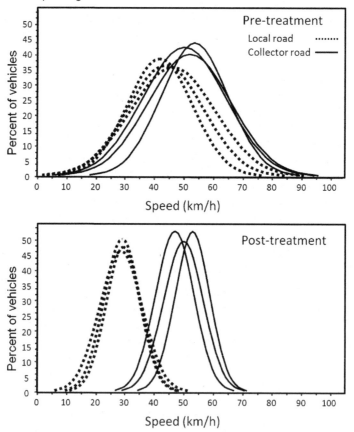

Figure 4.4: Speed distribution changes for local and collector roads following SER. Source: Charlton *et al.* (2010).

Pre- and post-intervention traffic speed and count data, a perceptions survey and video monitoring showed much lower traffic speeds on local roads (close to design speed) and less variation in speeds on both local and collector roads (Figure 4.4). The highest speeds (>70km/hr) were eliminated. The perceptions survey showed a closer match between actual and perceived safe speeds post SER construction. Five years later the annual social cost of crashes in the intervention area had halved, with more pedestrians and cyclists using local streets (Mackie *et al.*, 2012).

Te Ara Mua - Future Streets design

Combining these findings with the commuting SD model led to a participatory intervention study to assess the wider wellbeing benefits of retrofitting suburban streets for walking and cycling, with a focus on addressing transport and health inequities and enhancing cultural wellbeing for indigenous Māori.

We aimed to demonstrate community participatory street design, measure and model a wide range of health, environmental and social outcomes from SER and influence transport policy through collaborative learning.

We developed a funding partnership between research funders, the road controlling authority and the local community board. We chose two areas matched by urban form, neighbourhood deprivation, ethnic mix and size (600-900 households). They were then randomised to receiving an SER intervention and acting as a control. We used a participatory process to develop the street changes. This included developing a vision and objectives with the community to create a suburb that is safe and easy to travel around, prioritises walking and cycling, and reflects local identity. Safety from injury and crime were both important.

Māori principles of urban design (Hoskins, 2008) were incorporated in the design process, in partnership with local *hapū* (subtribes). This included naming of elements; use of indigenous narratives in patterns, colours and markers; connections with places of cultural significance; native plantings with historical connections; connecting *marae* (meeting houses) with *maunga* (significant local hill sites) through a walkway; and wayfinding that incorporates historical connections with the land. The intervention contextualises international best practice to increase walking and cycling within the local suburban social environment.

Incorporating environmental design for crime prevention was central to the design. Existing walking routes were identified by the community and through video analysis, including a number of 'green routes' through linear connecting parks that were considered unsafe, especially at night. Attention was paid to redesigning these spaces as safe walking and cycling routes. Examples of specific design elements are shown in Figure 4.5. The intervention is currently under construction.

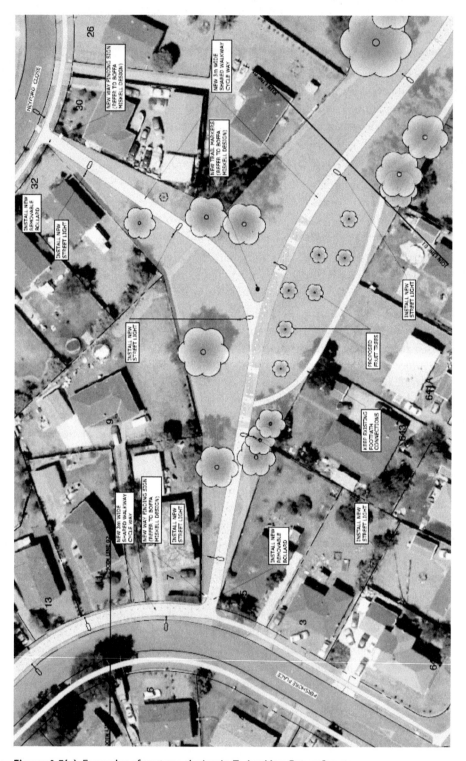

Figure 4.5(a): Examples of route re-design in *Te Ara Mua-Future Streets*

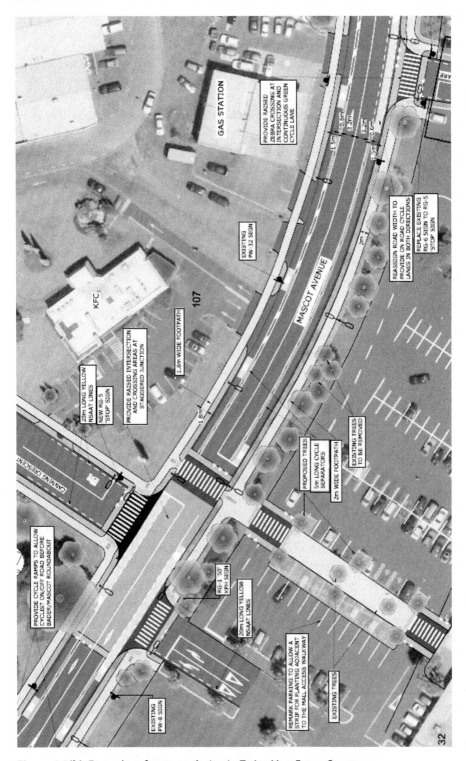

Figure 4.5(b): Examples of route re-design in *Te Ara Mua-Future Streets*

Te Ara Mua-Future Streets evaluation

Having a cross-disciplinary group of researchers from transport, human factors, social science and public health has meant that systems thinking, epidemiology, qualitative research and video analysis have all been incorporated into the integrated assessment of outcomes. The research design was based on an underlying complex theory about the relationships between street design and a range of health, social, economic and environmental outcomes. Measures in both areas include traffic behaviour (vehicles, pedestrians, cycling); random resident surveys measuring mode use, physical activity, neighbourhood perceptions and injury; injury data linkage; air quality measurements and modelling of greenhouse gas emissions. The results of the intervention study will then be used to create a simulation SD model to explore the costs and benefits for wellbeing, equity and carbon emissions of wider implementation at city or national level. It is hoped that the findings will generate supportive evidence for healthy, fair, low carbon suburban transport redesign.

Low carbon mobility transition processes

These two studies demonstrate how participatory decision-making and systems thinking can be used to identify and test transport policies that address climate change while also having immediate benefits for health and fairness. They also demonstrate that bringing trans-disciplinary stakeholders together can more rapidly translate research findings into change.

Both projects highlight challenges for rapidly achieving low carbon urban transport. We have highlighted the complex relationships between transport, climate and other aspects of human wellbeing and equity that need to be considered in a low carbon transport transition. The evolution of our research has seen the merging of multiple disciplines to test street designs that contribute to a healthy, fair, low carbon mobility transition in cities. This cross-disciplinary research has then been coupled with more challenging relationships between research, community and transport governance. Such partnerships are crucial to ensure the rapid uptake of the research findings into design standards and funding priorities.

Despite concerted engagement of individuals within transport governance, there are institutional challenges to undertaking these innovative projects within a system geared towards 'business-as-usual' roading infrastructure. There is enormous inertia in the current transport system, with barriers at all levels that require institutional change for a successful transition. In particular, economic evaluation of transport needs to be redesigned to recognise the wide range of climate and wellbeing benefits possible from investing in walking and cycling. Consistent transformation is needed in a changing political environment. A range of outcomes across wellbeing domains can be extremely useful for telling a story of benefit that speaks across political ideologies. Finally, meaningful participatory design and decision-making needs to be better incorporated into transport planning.

References

André, M. & Rapone, M. (2009). Analysis and modelling of the pollutant emissions from European cars regarding the driving characteristics and test cycles. *Atmospheric Environment,* **43**(5), 986-995.

Asbridge, M., Smart, R. G. & Mann, R. E. (2006). Can we prevent road rage? *Trauma, Violence & Abuse,* **7**(2), 109-121.

Banister, D. & Hickman, R. (2013). Transport futures: Thinking the unthinkable. *Transport Policy,* **29**(0), 283-293.

Barton, H. & Grant, M. (2006). A health map for the local human habitat. *The Journal of the Royal Society for the Promotion of Health,* **126**(6), 252-253.

Battellino, H. (2009). Transport for the transport disadvantaged: A review of service delivery models in New South Wales. *Transport Policy,* **16**(3), 123-129.

Bhalla, K., Ezzati, M., Mahal, A., Salomon, J. & Reich, M. (2007). A risk-based method for modeling traffic fatalities. *Risk Analysis,* **27**(1), 125-136.

Braun, V. & Clarke, V. (2006). Using thematic analysis in psychology. *Qualitative Research in Psychology,* **3**(2), 77-101. doi: 10.1191/1478088706qp063oa

Briggs, D., Abellan, J. J. & Fecht, D. (2008). Environmental inequity in England: Small area associations between socio-economic status and environmental pollution. *Social Science & Medicine,* **67**, 1612-1629.

Camilloni, L., Farchi, S., Chini, F., Giorgi Rossi, P., Borgia, P. & Guasticchi, G. (2013). How socioeconomic status influences road traffic injuries and home injuries in Rome. *International Journal of Injury Control and Safety Promotion,* **20**(2), 134-143.

Charlton, S., Mackie, H., Baas, P., Hay, K., Menezes, M. & Dixon, C. (2010). Using endemic road features to create self-explaining roads and reduce vehicle speeds. *Accident Analysis and Prevention,* **42**(6), 1989-1998.

Charmaz, K. (2005). Grounded Theory in the 21st Century. Applications for Advancing Social Justice Studies. In N. K. Denzin & Y. S. Lincoln (Eds.), *Sage Handbook of Qualitative Research* (3rd ed., 507-535). Thousand Oaks, California: Sage.

Clifton, K. & Lucas, K. (2004). Examining the empirical evidence of transport inequality in the US and UK. In K. Lucas (Ed.), *Running on Empty. Transport, social exclusion and environmental justice* (15-36). Bristol: The Policy Press.

de Hartog, J. J., Boogaard, H., Nijland, H. & Hoek, G. (2010). Do the health benefits of cycling outweigh the risks? *Environmental Health Perspectives,* **118**(8), 1109-1116.

Dhar, D., Macmillan, A., Lindsay, G. & Woodward, A. (2009). Carbon pricing in New Zealand: implications for public health. *New Zealand Medical Journal,* **122**(1290), 105-115.

Dora, C. & Phillips, M. (Eds.). (2000). *Transport, environment and health*: World Health Organisation Regional Office for Europe.

Eden, C. & Ackermann, F. (2004). Cognitive mapping expert views for policy analysis in the public sector. *European Journal of Operational Research,* **152**(3), 615-630.

Elvik, R. & Bjørnskau, T. (2016). Safety-in-numbers: A systematic review and meta-analysis of evidence. *Safety Science*. doi: http://dx.doi.org/10.1016/j.ssci.2015.07.017

Fahrig, L. (2003). Effects of habitat fragmentation on biodiversity. *The Annual Review of Ecology, Evolution, and Systematics*, **34**, 487-515.

Fergusson, E., Terruhn, J., Gilbertson, A., Ovenden, K. & Wildish, B. (2016). Youth mobilities in the Southern Initiative, Auckland: transport practices and experiences of 15-24 year olds. Auckland.

Gibson, J. (1977). The theory of affordances. In R. Shaw & J. Bransford (Eds.), *Perceiving, Acting and Knowing* (67-82): Lawrence Erlbaum.

Global Road Safety Facility and Evaluation. (2014). Transport for health: the global burden of disease from motorized road transport, Seattle, Washington (IHME) (The World Bank).

Gottholmseder, G., Nowotny, K., Pruckner, G. J. & Theurl, E. (2009). Stress perception and commuting. *Health Economics*, **18**, 559-576.

Hamer, M. & Chida, Y. (2008). Active commuting and cardiovascular risk: A meta-analytic review. *Preventive Medicine*, **46**(1), 9-13.

HEI Panel on the Health Effects of Traffic-Related Air Pollution [HEI Panel]. (2010). Traffic-related air pollution: A critical review of the literature on emissions, exposure, and health effects. Boston: Health Effects Institute.

Hill, J., Nelson, E., Tilman, D., Polasky, S. & Tiffany, D. (2006). Environmental, economic, and energetic costs and benefits of biodiesel and ethanol biofuels. *Proceedings of the National Academy of Sciences*, **103**(30), 11206-11210.

Hosking, J., Ameratunga, S., Exeter, D., Stewart, J. & Bell, A. (2013). Ethnic, socioeconomic and geographical inequalities in road traffic injury rates in the Auckland region. *Australian and New Zealand Journal of Public Health*, **37**(2), 162-167.

Hoskins, R. (2008). 'Our Faces in our Places': Cultural Landscapes – Māori and the Urban Environment. In G. Fougere (Ed.), *Re-thinking Urban Environments and Health*. Wellington: Public Health Advisory Committee.

Institute for Health Metrics and Evaluation. (2016). GBD Data Visualizations. Retrieved 11 June 2016, from University of Washington, http://www.healthdata.org/gbd/data-visualizations.

Jacobson, J. O., Hengartner, N. W. & Louis, T. A. (2005). Inequity measures for evaluations of environmental justice: a case study of close proximity to highways in New York City. *Environment and Planning A*, **37**(1), 21-43.

Jantunen, M., Kollanus, V., Leino, O., Happonen, E., Lim, T.-A. & Conrad, A. (2011). European perspectives on Environmental Burden of Disease: Estimates for nine stressors in six countries. In O. Hänninen & A. Knol (Eds.), *EBoDE Project*. Helsinki, Finland: World Health Organisation Europe.

Letherby, G. & Reynolds, G. (2003). Making connections: The relationship between train travel and the processes of work and leisure. *Sociological Research Online*, **8**(3), 1.1-6.10.

Lim, C., Kim, J., Hong, J. & Lee, S. (2006). The relationship between railway noise and community annoyance in Korea. *The Journal of the Acoustical Society of America*, **120**(4), 2037-2042.

Lucas, K. (2011). Driving to the breadline. In K. Lucas, E. Blumenberg & R. Weinberger (Eds.), *Auto Motives: Understanding Car Use Behaviours* (209-224). Bingley, UK: Emerald Group.

Lucas, K., Tyler, S. & Christodoulou, G. (2009). Assessing the 'value' of new transport initiatives in deprived neighbourhoods in the UK. *Transport Policy, 16*(3), 115-122.

Lund, H. (2003). Testing the claims of new urbanism: Local access, pedestrian travel, and neighboring behaviours. *Journal of the American Planning Association, 69*(4), 414-429.

Mackie, H. W., Charlton, S. G., Baas, P. H. & Villasenor, P. C. (2012). Road user behaviour changes following a self-explaining roads intervention. *Accident Analysis and Prevention, 50*, 742-750.

Macmillan, A., Connor, J., Witten, K., Kearns, A., Rees, D. & Woodward, A. (2014). The societal costs and benefits of commuter bicycling: simulating the effects of specific policies using system dynamics modeling *Environmental Health Perspectives, 122*(4).

Marmot, M. & Bell, R. (2012). Fair society, healthy lives. *Public Health, 126, Supplement 1*, S4-S10.

Martin, A., Panter, J., Suhrcke, M. & Ogilvie, D. (2015). Impact of changes in mode of travel to work on changes in body mass index: evidence from the British Household Panel Survey. *Journal of Epidemiology and Community Health, 69*(8), 753-761.

Mees, P. & Dodson, J. (2006). Backtracking Auckland: bureaucratic rationality and public preferences in transport planning. In J. Dodson (Ed.), *Urban Research Program Issues Papers*. Brisbane: Griffith University.

Mindell, J., Rutter, H. & Watkins, S. (2011). Urban Transportation and Human Health. In J. O. Nriagu (Ed.), *Encyclopedia of Environmental Health* (578-589). Burlington: Elsevier.

Ministry for the Environment. (2016). *New Zealand's Greenhouse Gas Inventory 1990–2014*. Wellington: New Zealand Government Retrieved from http://www.mfe.govt.nz/publications/climate-change/new-zealand-greenhouse-gas-inventory-1990-2014.

Ministry of Health. (2015). Understanding excess body weight: New Zealand Health Survey. Wellington: Ministry of Health.

Mokhtarian, P. L. & Chen, C. (2004). TTB or not TTB, that is the question: a review and analysis of the empirical literature on travel time (and money) budgets. *Transportation Research Part A: Policy and Practice, 38*(9-10), 643-675.

Ogilvie, D., Foster, C. E., Rothnie, H., Cavill, N., Hamilton, V., Fitzsimons, C. F. & Mutrie, N. (2007). Interventions to promote walking: systematic review. *British Medical Journal, 334*, 1204-1214.

Parkin, J., Ryley, T. J. & Jones, T. (2007). Barriers to cycling: an exploration of quantitative analysis *Civil Engineering: Book Chapters*.

Pickett, S. T. A., Cadenasso, M. L., Grove, J. M., Nilon, C. H., Pouyat, R. V., Zipperer, W. C. & Costanza, R. (2001). Urban ecological systems: Linking terrestrial ecological, physical, and socioeconomic components of metropolitan areas. *Annual Review of Ecology and Systematics, 32*, 127-157.

Reardon, L. & Abdallah, S. (2013). Well-being and transport: Taking stock and looking forward. *Transport Reviews, 33*(6), 634-657.

Richardson, G. P. (2011). Reflections on the foundations of system dynamics. *System Dynamics Review*, **27**(3), 219-243.

Rissel, C., Curac, N., Greenaway, M.,& Bauman, A. (2012). Physical activity associated with public transport use—a review and modelling of potential benefits. *International Journal of Environmental Research and Public Health*, **9**(7), 2454-2478.

Schwanen, T. (2011). Car use and gender: The case of dual-earner families in Utrecht, The Netherlands. In K. Lucas, E. Blumenberg & R. Weinberger (Eds.), *Auto Motives. Understanding Car Use Behaviours* (pp. 151-171). Bingley, UK: Emerald Group.

Spellerberg, I. F. (1998). Ecological effects of roads and traffic: A literature review. *Global Ecology and Biogeography Letters*, **7**(5), 317-333.

Stanley, J. & Vella-Brodrick, D. (2009). The usefulness of social exclusion to inform social policy in transport. *Transport Policy*, **16**(3), 90-96.

Tainio, M., de Nazelle, A. J., Götschi, T., Kahlmeier, S., Rojas-Rueda, D., Nieuwenhuijsen, M. J. & Woodcock, J. (2016). Can air pollution negate the health benefits of cycling and walking? *Preventive Medicine*, **87**, 233-236.

Theeuwes, J. & Godthelp, H. (1995). Self-explaining roads. *Safety Science*, **19**(2-3), 217-225.

Tonne, C., Beevers, S., Armstrong, B., Kelly, F. & Wilkinson, P. (2008). Air pollution and mortality benefits of the London Congestion Charge: spatial and socioeconomic inequalities. *Occupational and Environmental Medicine*, **65**(9), 620-627.

Trombulak, S. C. & Frissell, C. A. (2000). Review of Ecological Effects of Roads on Terrestrial and Aquatic Communities. *Conservation Biology*, **14**(1), 18-30.

Tzoulas, K., Korpela, K., Venn, S., Yli-Pelkonen, V., Kaźmierczak, A., Niemela, J. & James, P. (2007). Promoting ecosystem and human health in urban areas using Green Infrastructure: A literature review. *Landscape and Urban Planning*, **81**(3), 167-178.

United Nations, (2014). *World Urbanization Prospects: The 2014 Revision. Highlights*, (ST/ESA/SER.A/352). Department of Economic and Social Affairs, Population Division, United Nations: New York. Available from: https://esa.un.org/unpd/wup/Publications/Files/WUP2014-Highlights.pdf.

van Vliet, P. & Schermers, G. (2000). Sustainable safety: A new approach for road safety in the Netherlands. Rotterdam, The Netherlands: Traffic Research Centre.

Warburton, D. E., Nicol, C. W. & Bredin, S. S. (2006). Health benefits of physical activity: the evidence. *Canadian Medical Association Journal*, **174**(6), 801-809.

Watts, N., Adger, W. N., Agnolucci, P., Blackstock, J., Byass, P., Cai, W., Chaytor, S., Colbourn, T., Collins, M., Cooper, A., Cox, P.M., Depledge, J., Drummond, P., Ekins, P., Galaz, V., Grace, D., Graham, H., Grubb, M., Haines, A., Hamilton, I., Hunter, A., Jiang, X., Li, M., Kelman, I., Liang, L., Lott, M., Lowe, R., Luo, Y., Mace, G., Maslin, M., Nilsson, M., Oreszczyn, T., Pye, S., Quinn, T., Svensdotter, M., Venevsky, S., Warner, K., Xu, B., Yang, J., Yin, Y., Yu, C., Zhang, Q., Gong, P., Montgomery, H. & Costello, A. (2015). Health and climate change: policy responses to protect public health. *The Lancet*, **370**(9592), 1078-1088.

Weller, G., Schlag, B., Friedel, T. & Rammin, C. (2008). Behaviourally relevant road categorisation: A step towards self-explaining rural roads. *Accident Analysis and Prevention*, **40**(4), 1581-1588.

Woodcock, J., Banister, D., Edwards, P., Prentice, A. M. & Roberts, I. (2007). Energy and transport. *The Lancet*, **370**(9592), 1078-1088.

Woodcock, J., Franco, O. H., Orsini, N. & Roberts, I. (2011). Non-vigorous physical activity and all-cause mortality: systematic review and meta-analysis of cohort studies. *International Journal of Epidemiology*, **40**(1), 121-138.

World Health Organisation. (1948). Preamble to the Constitution of the World Health Organisation as adopted by the International Health Conference, New York, 19-22 June, 1946; signed on 22 July 1946 by the representatives of 61 States (Official Records of the World Health Organisation, no. 2, p. 100) and entered into force on 7 April 1948.

World health Organisation. (2010). *Health in the green economy. Co-benefits to health of climate change mitigation: Transport Sector. Preliminary findings - initial review*. Geneva: WHO Public Health & Environment Cluster (HSE).

World Health Organisation. (2015). *Global Status Report on Road Safety 2015*. Geneva.

World Resources Institute. (2014). Climate Analysis Indicators Tool: WRI's Climate Data Explorer. Historical Emissions 2012. Retrieved 26 June 2016, from World Resources Institute http://cait2.wri.org/.

5 Hypermobile Business and Leisure Lifestyles: Will wellbeing concerns stimulate environmental co-benefits?

Scott A. Cohen

School of Hospitality and Tourism Management, University of Surrey, UK.

Introduction

Travelling far, fast and frequently is increasingly common in contemporary lifestyles. Hypermobile lifestyles are normally associated with affluence, which affords the power to move, and materialises in corporeal movements such as frequent business travel and leisure trips, lifestyle migration or visits to spatially dispersed friends and relatives. These mobilities often fold into each other as complex hybrids. A unifying feature of such mobilities however is that they are often carbon intensive, requiring spatial mobility that in many cases relies on transport via air travel.

A wide body of scientific literature has in recent years examined if and how mobilities can be made more environmentally sustainable, with concern heavily centred on the climate impacts of varying forms of mobility (Banister, 2008; Higham, Cohen, Peeters & Gössling, 2013). Research has shown that a disproportionate amount of mobility emissions are generated from a small proportion of individuals, that is, the hypermobile elite (Frändberg & Vilhelmson, 2003; Gössling *et al.*, 2009). An array of studies have also demonstrated that those who travel frequently are largely unwilling to change their travel patterns because of environmental concern (e.g. McKercher *et al.*, 2010).

Against this background, this chapter focuses on two types of corporeal mobility, leisure-motivated lifestyle mobility and frequent business travel, with the aim of appraising if and how these forms of movement might undergo low carbon mobility transitions as a result of evidence indicating they have negative impacts on wellbeing. Lifestyle mobility refers to sustained mobility practices where travel, leisure, migration and work blur together, such as in the cases of many seasonal ski resort workers, long-term backpackers or ocean cruisers (Duncan, Cohen & Thulemark, 2013). Corporeal mobility is central to the performance of these lifestyles (Cohen, Duncan & Thulemark, 2015). But rather than focus on the environmental impacts of lifestyle mobility and frequent business travel, which to varying degrees are carbon intensive mobility practices, this chapter takes a new direction in probing whether attention to the negative personal and social consequences for individuals who undertake these hypermobile lifestyles, that is, concern over wellbeing aspects, could provide a basis for leveraging behavioural change.

The dark side of hypermobile lifestyles

The impetus for this chapter stems from a recent study examining the 'darker sides' of hypermobility (Cohen & Gössling, 2015). This work drew upon a range of interdisciplinary secondary literature to argue that frequent travel entails a number of physiological, psychological and social consequences that tend to be overshadowed in society by the popular representation of travel as glamorous. Travel is glamorised by a range of social mechanisms, such as visualisations on social media that encourage mobility competition, frequent flyer programme status levels and the mass media and travel industry which depict tourism and business travel as desirable (ibid).

This glamorisation comes at the expense of attention to frequent travel's negative impacts on personal wellbeing. The darker sides of travel are to a degree contingent on the type of travel. As the focus in this chapter is on two broad types, leisure-motivated lifestyle mobility and business travel, it is helpful to compare and contrast some of the negative personal and social consequences that adherents to these hypermobile lifestyles may experience. It is important however to note that the level of choice between these two types of travel may differ greatly: while lifestyle mobilities would typically be perceived as voluntary, business travel is often viewed as an obligation, although a nuanced reading of these two types of travel would suggest a dichotomous view of choice versus obligation would be an oversimplification. It is also important to recognise that darker elements of hypermobility may be perceived brightly by some individuals, vice versa and all shades in between (Cohen & Gössling, 2015).

Darker sides of lifestyle mobilities

Given that lifestyle mobilities are closely related to forms of lifestyle migration, with the latter associated with the search for a 'better' way of life (Benson & O'Reilly, 2009), it is unsurprising that few studies of either lifestyle mobilities or lifestyle migration have given significant voice to their negative sides. There is abundant evidence however on the ills of migration more generally (e.g. Nowok *et al.*, 2013), and emerging evidence that lifestyle mobilities may also be experienced as 'discordant' (Botterill, 2016). The negative personal consequences of lifestyle mobilities can be viewed as largely social-psychological, centring on the disruption of social relationships and personal identities. While there are myriad forms of lifestyle mobility (see Duncan *et al.*, 2013), 'lifestyle travellers' are drawn upon here as an insightful case. Lifestyle travellers are backpackers who, by travelling for years, often mixed with working in order to fund travel, sustain backpacking as an ongoing way of life (Cohen, 2011).

Lifestyle travel has been associated with a building sense of isolation as a lack of co-presence with friends and family who remain home can lead to divergent interests and worldviews. This sense of isolation has been shown to engender depression among returnees, often driving them to travel or 'escape' again (Pocock & McIntosh, 2011). It pushes young, western travellers back into searching for social cohesion through mobile lifestyles (Cohen, 2011), and ironically cages them within the very same corporeal mobilities through which they sought ideals of freedom. Despite the opportunities taking a trip can open for making fresh social connections (Bergström, 2010), both Adler and Adler's (1999) study of transient resort workers and Cohen's (2011) work on lifestyle travellers illustrate how new friendships and romantic relationships forged through mobility have a tendency to be situational and short-lived. Mobile lifestyles left many of the participants in these studies looking for more enduring relationships.

Lifestyle mobilities not only provoke psychological and emotional strains in social cohesion, but also in how one perceives personal identity and how one relates to place (Cohen *et al.*, 2015). Although lifestyle travellers are well connected to global networks, this is often at the expense of local place-bounded identities (Frändberg & Vilhelmson, 2003), that is, a weakening of ties at local and community scales. The counter side of this physical absence at those scales is more presence 'away', often in varied socio-spatial environments. Sustained and repeated exposure to different cultural practices, whilst associated with the development of cosmopolitan sensibilities and global citizenry (Hannerz, 2002), may also lead to a sense of identity confusion: indeed, studies of lifestyle travellers show evidence of participants who had developed a sense of being metaphorically 'lost' (Cohen, 2010). In more extreme cases, sustained mobility can even engender psychological disorders and mental illness. Studies from consular psychiatry have examined how 'pathological tourism' fosters 'mad travellers' who have severely disrupted conceptions of personal identity (Hacking, 1998). Maoz's (2007) study of Israeli backpackers in India observes that an institute in Israel has emerged to provide residential care for 'mentally damaged' backpackers upon their return from long-term travel, although this is closely tied to the use of drugs while travelling. Whilst such a clinical perspective has not been taken towards the study of lifestyle travellers, significant social psychological costs are evident, with these darker sides also manifesting in the case of frequent business travel, but in different ways.

Darker sides of frequent business travel

The negative personal and social consequences of frequent business travel share many of the social psychological costs that can be found in lifestyle mobilities, but also expose travellers to a range of further physiological consequences due to the short and episodic, but repeated, nature of recurrent business travel, as shall be discussed further below. Similar to lifestyle mobility, frequent business travellers can incur costs at kinship, friendship and community levels. Isolation is also experienced amongst business travellers, both for the traveller and those left behind at home (Gustafson, 2014): spouses left behind report resentment and anger while travelling staff report guilt at leaving behind family members (Espino *et al.*, 2002). Here again connections to global networks often come at the expense of ties at local and community scales. Frequent business travellers have been found to sacrifice local collective activities and instead prioritise immediate family in between trips (Gustafson, 2014). In communities where hypermobility is prevalent it thus has the potential to undermine social cohesion (Putnam, 2000).

Despite advances in communication technologies, frequent business travel is associated with decreasing time for co-present social life at home and locally (Bergström, 2010). This may include a negative impact on children's behaviour stemming from emotional upset of a parent being away frequently or for extended periods (Johnson *et al.*, 2013). The business traveller's family role may be reduced through repeated absence from key family events and milestones, such as birthdays, and even when at home, the limited time there may be spent recovering from fatigue in between trips (Black & Jamieson, 2007).

There is a strong gender dimension to business travel. It is a traditionally male sphere (Bergström Casinowsky, 2013); for instance, 77% of US citizens on business trips in 2002 were male (Aguilera, 2008). In households with a male frequent business traveller, there is also often a 'stay at home' partner who is prevented from engaging in some dimensions of the labour market because of domestic commitments (Black & Jamieson, 2007). In such cases women tend to shoulder the bulk of household and childcare duties. When it is women who are both frequent business travellers and mothers, research shows that they perceive pressure from others, and pressure themselves, to fulfil the role of mother while away (Black & Jamieson, 2007; Bergström Casinowsky, 2013).

In addition to these social and psychological consequences, there are a range of physiological consequences from frequent business travel that are rarely discussed (Cohen & Gössling, 2015). Whereas lifestyle mobility is typically associated with longer trips, and/or periods of migration, business travel is characterised by short trips, by car or train, but often by airplane. When trips become frequent, especially by air, business travellers are exposed to an array of threats to their wellbeing. The most commonly discussed physiological impact of frequent business travel is jet lag, but it is little known that jet lag can persist up to six days after flying (Waterhouse, Reilly & Edwards, 2004), and that its interference with the body's circadian rhythm can disrupt biological processes such as gene expression that influences aging, and switch off genes linked to the immune system, which raises the risk of heart attack or stroke (Archer *et al.*, 2014). The accumulation of fatigue from repeated jet lag, combined with travel stress, has the potential to turn chronic (Black & Jamieson, 2007; Striker *et al.*, 2000), and has been termed 'frequent traveller exhaustion' (Ivancevich *et al.*, 2003).

While the risk of developing deep-vein thrombosis during air travel received considerable media coverage, little attention was given to the radiation exposure frequent flyers receive. Exposure to radiation at high altitude is hundreds of times higher than at ground level. Some have argued that frequent business travellers, along with airline crew, should be classified as 'radiation workers', as for instance flying New York to Tokyo seven times return annually (about 85,000 miles) exceeds the regulatory limit for exposure to radiation (Barish & Dilchert, 2010). Radiation exposure from flying heightens the risk of initiating cancer, with pregnant women at the greatest risk, for whom the possibility of leukaemia forming in unborn babies is significantly increased (ibid).

These potential physiological impacts for frequent business travellers are accompanied by the further stress of work continuing to accumulate while away (Beaverstock *et al.*, 2009), acutely felt differences upon arrival at distant or socio-spatially different destinations (in terms of temperature, humidity, altitude or pollution) (Anderson, 2015), and/or the stress of getting there: weather delays, technical failures and additional security checks (Ivancevich *et al.*, 2013). The demands of business travel can be unrelenting, with sensitive data in the hands of tired travellers who may put their businesses at risk, and who may be asked to operate in unfamiliar environments and navigate cultural differences while meeting rigid schedules (Welch *et al.*, 2007). This is in the context of early mornings, late evenings and intense working days, with fewer opportunities for exercise, typically worse eating habits than at home and sometimes the overconsumption of alcohol (Beaverstock *et al.*, 2009; Gustafson, 2014). The majority of this travel is facilitated, at a global level, by flying (Beaverstock *et al.*, 2009).

Differential impacts on climate change

Even though both leisure-motivated lifestyle mobility and frequent business travel are characterised by a number of risks to travellers' personal and social wellbeing, their dynamics in terms of their impacts on climate change will in most cases be quite different. Whereas business trips tend to be short episodes, these can often come in succession for frequent business travellers, and in most cases the recurrent travel will require many air, car or train trips and miles. When these trips lean towards long distances and/or frequent flights, which is often the case (Beaverstock *et al.*, 2009), business travel becomes more carbon intensive, and even more so when within a mode of travel, such as flying, which is already a heavy emitter, frequent flyers may upgrade to business or first class, or even use private or company planes (Cohen & Gössling, 2015), only adding to the emission intensity of the flyer's trip.

The recent introduction of unlimited flying passes aimed at business travellers, by the startup company OneGo, who received media coverage with the headline 'Get ready to binge-fly with unlimited flight subscriptions', drew comparisons with a 'Netflix-style approach to air travel' (Bachman, 2016: n.p.), and is emblematic of the potential for frequent business travel by air to be taken to an environmentally destructive extreme (Cohen, Higham & Cavaliere, 2011).

In contrast, leisure-motivated lifestyle mobility tends to involve fewer short and episodic trips, and certainly fewer upgrades to business or first class, or the use of private jets. With its emphasis on leisure aspects, rather than a logic of work or production, adherents of lifestyle mobility, for whom corporeal mobility is also a central facet of their lives, tend to engage in *rhythms* of mobility that will often be less carbon intensive than business travel. Lifestyle mobility, whether in the form of travelling rock climbers (Rickly, 2016) or the residential mobility and multiple dwelling of retirees (Åkerlund, 2016), will often be on constrained budgets, involve fewer trips, or adopt a slower mode of transport, such as hitchhiking, recreational vehicle or sailboat. While lifestyle mobility will certainly still in many cases involve air travel, including long-haul segments, whether that be to chase endless winters (e.g. skiing or snowboarding) or summers (e.g. wind surfing or surf boarding), the cumulative carbon intensity of these movements on an annual basis, while not yet empirically investigated in comparison to that of frequent business travel, can speculatively be estimated to be less. When lifestyle-led activities become professionalised, however, such as in the case of surfing, it is likely that the carbon intensity of the mobilities associated with the practices will change significantly, as the rhythm and speed of the associated movements will be subject to the same pressures of time-space compression as much of business travel. That is, they will travel faster, farther and more frequently.

In light of these differential impacts on climate change between leisure-motivated lifestyle mobility and frequent business travel, and the earlier discussion of the darker sides of hypermobility, two key points emerge: 1) the wellbeing consequences of business travel seemingly outweigh those of lifestyle mobility, mainly due to the physiological costs of frequent, episodic travel; 2) the carbon intensity of business travel seemingly outweighs that of lifestyle mobility, mainly due to the increased emissions from frequent, episodic travel. In relation to both of these forms of hypermobility, previous studies have clearly demonstrated that leisure (Cohen, Higham & Reis, 2013; McKercher *et al.*, 2010) and business travellers (Lassen, 2010) are largely unwilling to change their travel patterns because of environmental concern (Gössling & Cohen, 2014). This raises crucial questions with regards to what types of hypermobility are most urgent in terms of addressing their climate impacts, alongside which ones the most convincing evidence base can be presented that mobility practices should be changed due to their negative impacts on personal and social wellbeing. Less travel in such cases will often feature the *co-benefit* of less damage to one's wellbeing and the wider natural environment. In the two cases of hypermobility discussed here, frequent business travel is the most promising arena in terms of both its carbon intensity and the potential for wellbeing concerns to be leveraged to stimulate behavioural change.

These observations however do not address at least two further points, and only one of these will be taken up in detail in the final section of this chapter. The first is that not all forms of leisure-motivated mobility are lifestyle mobility. Certainly frequent breakneck speed weekend getaways abroad, romantic rendezvous between spatially distanced lovers, annual family holidays and a whole gamut of leisure-related mobilities, which can be integrated with those for work (see Høyer & Naess, 2001 on conference tourism), have varying carbon intensities depending on the mobility practices involved, and they are largely outside the scope of the present discussion. The crucial question that is taken up here, based on the argument this chapter has built, is whether wellbeing concerns hold potential to stimulate behavioural change among business travellers, which would also be reflective of a low carbon mobility transition.

Will wellbeing consequences stimulate behaviour change?

The evidence base for the wellbeing consequences of lifestyle mobilities is presently centred on social psychological dimensions, and it is unlikely that these personal and social costs will provide sufficient leverage to stimulate behaviour change among those engaging in lifestyle mobilities. Studies of lifestyle mobility have shown that those engaging in these ways of life are heavily invested in their activities in terms of their personal and social identities (Duncan et al., 2013) and other research demonstrates that identities play a significant role in travel decisions, and may override environmental issues (Hibbert, Dickinson & Gössling, 2013).

In contrast, it is within frequent business travel, which tends to require frequent air travel (with its concomitant higher emissions), and where the consequences of this hypermobility can entail severe physiological costs, that the most leverage for behavioural change based on concerns over personal wellbeing exists. This was also evidenced in the media coverage that ensued from the publication of the Cohen & Gössling (2015) article 'A darker side of hypermobility', which like this chapter, considered dimensions of some forms of leisure- and work-related hypermobility. The media honed in on the business travel aspect from this study, resulting in a range of coverage in outlets such as The Telegraph (Anderson, 2015) and The Economist (A.W., 2015), culminating in a 10 minute TV segment on the research on the show CNN Business Traveller (2015). The article in The Economist, titled 'The sad, sick life of the business traveller' was shared more than 100,000 times alone on social media, including more than 15,000 comments on Facebook. This is evidence of the impact of the research on the general public, influencing at a minimum public awareness, and most likely also the public's attitude to the wellbeing consequences of frequent business travel, although the Facebook comments are not publicly available to be studied empirically.

What this reaction by the public to the media coverage does not tell us is if and how knowledge of the consequences of frequent business travel may actually impact travel behaviour. To a degree this puts the academic conversation on this issue circularly back to the widespread recognition that there is an awareness-attitude and/or attitude/behaviour gap amongst travellers, with regards to both the climate impacts of air travel (Hibbert *et al.*, 2013; Cohen *et al.*, 2016), and potentially frequent travel's effects on wellbeing. This was anecdotally illustrated in the *CNN Business Traveller* (2015) TV segment on this issue, wherein a frequent business traveller who was interviewed by the show's host voiced concern about the consequences for his health and family life, but said he would keep travelling anyways, eliciting the accusation from the host that the interviewee was 'his own worst enemy'.

This conundrum is further exasperated by the conventional view that business travel is not a matter of personal choice, although Lassen (2010: 734) problematises this assumption by showing in a case study of Danish business travellers that *'employees have much more space for individual decisions in relation to travel frequency and destinations than the conventional understanding of work-related travel assumes'*. Nonetheless, much of the decision making surrounding business travel will be driven by the needs of the employer, and embedded in the socio-technical systems of human resource management and corporate travel agents, including the broader resistance of companies to forgo face-to-face business meetings in favour of virtual communication, wherein it is recognised that 'being there in person' plays a vital role in conveying respect and value in workplace meetings (Strengers, 2015).

These insights suggest that the socio-technical systems that pattern business travel must be changed in order to facilitate less frequent business travel. This is not unlike the conclusions of Cohen *et al.* (2016) and Hall (2013) with regards to reducing the climate impact of the tourism and transport sectors. These studies also point to the necessity of altering the structures of provision in which practices are embedded. The difference is that the environmental case for altering socio-technical systems in this context, such as human resource management policies that guide how much business travel employees may undertake in a space of time, are unlikely to be changed by employers, based on climate concern. Economic imperatives will win out over environmental justice in these cases. However, if the necessity to change becomes based on the health and safety of employees, and this discourse is able to be convincingly linked to protecting the economic interests of businesses, and the capacity of their employees to carry out their work safely and effectively, only then will organisations take notice of the dangers of continued hypermobility by workers. Once these systems begin to change, and the cultural icon of the 'road warrior' is no longer institutionally condoned in workplaces, a co-benefit for the environment will begin to take hold, and a low carbon mobility transition will be underway.

References

Adler, P. A. & Adler, P. (1999). Transience and the postmodern self: The geographic mobility of resort workers, *The Sociological Quarterly*, **40**(1), 31–58.

Åkerlund, U. (2016). Strategic lifestyle management in later life: Swedish lifestyle movers in Malta seeking the 'best of both worlds', *Population, Space and Place*, doi: 10.1002/psp.1964.

Aguilera, A. (2008). Business travel and mobile workers, *Transportation Research Part A*, **42** 1109–1116.

Anderson, J. (2015). Exploring the consequences of mobility: Reclaiming jet lag as the state of travel disorientation, *Mobilities*, **10**(1) 1–16.

Anderson, E. (2015). How business travel can make you seriously sick, *The Telegraph*, 19/8/15, Accessed 5/2/2015 http://www.telegraph.co.uk/finance/newsbysector/transport/11811449/How-business-travel-can-make-you-seriously-sick.html.

Archer, S., Laing, E.E., Möller-Levet, C.S., van der Veen, D.R., Bucca, G., Lazar, A.S., Santhi, N., Slak, A., Kabiljo, R., von Schantz, M., Smith, C.P. & Dijk, D-J. (2014). Mistimed sleep disrupts circadian regulation of the human transcriptome, *Proceedings of the National Academy of Sciences*, **111**(6), E682-E691.

A.W. (2015). The sad, sick life of the business traveller, *The Economist*, 17/8/15, Accessed 5/12/15 http://www.economist.com/blogs/gulliver/2015/08/frequent-flyers.

Bachman, J. (2016). Get ready to binge-fly with unlimited flight subscriptions, *BloombergBusiness*, 1/2/16, Accessed 4/2/16 http://www.bloomberg.com/news/articles/2016-02-01/get-ready-to-binge-fly-with-unlimited-flight-subscriptions.

Banister, D. (2008). The sustainable mobility paradigm, *Transport Policy*, **15**(2), 73-80.

Barish R.J. & Dilchert, S. (2010). Human resource responsibilities: Frequent flyer radiation exposure, *Employee Responsibilities and Rights Journal*, **22**, 361–369.

Beaverstock, J.V., Derudder, B., Faulconbridge, J.R. & Witlox, F. (2009). International business travel: Some explorations, *Geografiska Annaler: Series B, Human Geography*, **91**(3), 193–202.

Benson, M. & O'Reilly, K. (2009). *Lifestyle Migration – Expectations, Aspirations and Experiences*. Farnham: Ashgate.

Bergström, G. (2010) Consequences of overnight work travel for personal social relations: Problems, promises, and further repercussions, *Mobilities*, **5**(3), 369–386.

Bergström Casinowsky, G. (2013). Working life on the move, domestic life at standstill? Work-related travel and responsibility for home and family, *Gender, Work and Organisation*, **20**(3), 311–326.

Black, I. & Jamieson, S. (2007). Up, up and fading away: The work and family life of executive international travellers, *Policy and Practice in Health and Safety*, **5**(2) 63–78.

Botterill, K. (2016). Discordant lifestyle mobilities in East Asia: Privilege and precarity of British retirement in Thailand, *Population, Space and Place*, doi: 10.1002/psp.2011.

Cohen, S. A. (2010). Personal identity (de)formation among lifestyle travellers: A double edged sword, *Leisure Studies*, **29**(3), 289–301.

Cohen, S.A. (2011). Lifestyle travellers: Backpacking as a way of life, *Annals of Tourism Research*, **38**(4), 1535-1555.

Cohen, S.A., Duncan, T. & Thulemark, M. (2015). Lifestyle mobilities: The crossroads of travel leisure and migration, *Mobilities*, **10**(1), 155-172.

Cohen, S.A. & Gössling, S. (2015). A darker side of hypermobility, *Environment and Planning A*, **47**, 1661-1679.

Cohen, S.A., Higham, J.E.S. & Cavaliere, C.T. (2011). Binge flying: Behavioural addiction and climate change, *Annals of Tourism Research*, **38**(3), 1070-1089.

Cohen, S.A., Higham, J.E.S., Gössling, S., Peeters, P. & Eijgelaar, E. (2016). Finding effective pathways to sustainable mobility: Bridging the science-policy gap, *Journal of Sustainable Tourism*, **24**(3), 317-334.

Cohen, S.A., Higham, J.E.S. & Reis, A.C. (2013). Sociological barriers to developing sustainable discretionary air travel behaviour, *Journal of Sustainable Tourism*, **21**(7), 982-998.

CNN *Business Traveller* (2015). The dark side of travel, 15/10/15, Accessed 5/2/15 http://edition.cnn.com/videos/world/2015/10/15/spc-business-traveller-dark-side-of-travel-a.cnn.

Duncan, T. Cohen, S.A. & Thulemark, M. (2013). *Lifestyle mobilities: Intersections of travel, leisure and migration*, Farnham: Ashgate.

Espino, C.M., Sundstrom, S.M., Frick, H.L., Jacobs, M. & Peters, M. (2002). International business travel: Impact on families and travellers, *Occupational and Environmental Medicine*, **59**, 309–322.

Frändberg, L. & Vilhelmson, B. (2003). Personal mobility: A corporeal dimension of transnationalisation. The case of long-distance travel from Sweden, *Environment and Planning A*, **35**, 1751–1768.

Gössling, S. & Cohen, S. A. (2014). Why sustainable transport policies will fail: European Union climate policy in the light of transport taboos, *Journal of Transport Geography*, **39**, 197-207.

Gössling, S., Ceron, J-P., Dubois, G., Hall & C. M. (2009). Hypermobile travellers, in *Climate Change and Aviation*, Eds. S. Gössling, P. Upham, Earthscan: London, 131–149.

Gustafson, P. (2014) Business travel from the traveller's perspective: Stress, stimulation and normalization, *Mobilities* **9**(1), 63–83.

Hacking, I. (1998). *Mad Travellers: Reflections on the Reality of Transient Mental Illnesses*, Free Association Books: London.

Hall, C.M. (2013). Framing behavioural approaches to understanding and governing sustainable tourism consumption: beyond neoliberalism, 'nudging' and 'green growth'?, *Journal of Sustainable Tourism*, **21**(7), 1091-1109.

Hannerz, U. (2002). Where we are and who we want to be, in *The Postnational Self: Belonging and Identity*, Eds. U. Hedetoft and M. Hjort, University of Minnesota Press: Minneapolis, 217–232.

Hibbert, J.F., Dickinson, J.E. & Gössling, S. (2013). Identity and tourism mobility: An exploration of the attitude-behaviour gap, *Journal of Sustainable Tourism*, **21**(7), 999-1016.

Higham, J.E.S., Cohen, S.A., Peeters, P. & Gössling, S. (2013). Psychological and behavioural approaches to understanding and governing sustainable mobility, *Journal of Sustainable Tourism*, **21**(7), 949-967.

Høyer, K. & Naess, P. (2001). Conference tourism: A problem for the environment, as well as for research?, *Journal of Sustainable Tourism*, **9**(6), 451–470.

Ivancevich, J.M., Konopaske, R. & DeFrank, R.S. (2003). Business travel stress: A model, propositions and managerial implications, *Work & Stress: An International Journal of Work, Health & Organisations*, **17**(2) 138–157.

Johnson, S., Li, J., Kendall, G., Strazdins, L. & Jacoby, P. (2013). Mothers' and fathers' work hours, child gender, and behaviour in middle childhood, *Journal of Marriage and Family* **75**, 56-74.

Lassen, C. (2010). Environmentalist in business class: An analysis of air travel and environmental attitude, *Transport Reviews*, **30**(6), 733–751.

Maoz, D. (2007). Backpackers' motivations: The role of culture and nationality, *Annals of Tourism Research'* **34**(1), 122-140.

McKercher, B., Prideaux, B., Cheung, C. & Law, R. (2010). Achieving voluntary reductions in the carbon footprint of tourism and climate change, *Journal of Sustainable Tourism*, **18**(3), 297-317.

Nowok, B., Ham, M. V., Findlay, A. M. & Gayle, V. (2013). Does migration make you happy? A longitudinal study on internal migration and subjective well-being, *Environment and Planning A*, **45**(4), 986–1002.

Pocock, N.J. & McIntosh, A.J. (2011). The return from travel: A new beginning?, *Current Issues in Tourism*, **14**(7) 631–649.

Putnam, R. (2000). *Bowling Alone: The Collapse and Revival of American Community*, Simon & Schuster: New York.

Rickly, J.M. (2016). Lifestyle mobilities: A politics of lifestyle rock climbing, *Mobilities*, **11**(2) 243-263.

Strengers, Y. (2015). Meeting in the global workplace: Air travel, telepresence and the body, *Mobilities*, **10**(4), 592-608.

Striker, J., Dimberg, L. & Liese, B.H. (2000). Stress and business travel: Individual, managerial and corporate concerns, *Journal of Organisational Excellence*, Winter, 3–9.

Waterhouse, J., Reilly, T. & Edwards, B. (2004). The stress of travel, *Journal of Sport Sciences*, **22**, 946–966.

Welch, D.E., Welch, L.S. & Worm, V. (2007). The international business traveller: A neglected but strategic human resource, *International Journal of Human Resource Management*, **18**(2), 173–183.

Case Study 1: The low carbon mobilities of Chinese migrant communities in Sydney, Australia

Sophie-May Kerr, Natascha Klocker and Gordon Waitt

School of Geography and Sustainable Communities, University of Wollongong, Australia.

Introduction

In Australia, as in many other industrialised societies, there is an urgent need to transition to low carbon mobilities. Australians have amongst the highest rates of car ownership in the world. In 2014, there were 756 motor vehicles per 1000 residents (Australian Bureau of Statistics, 2014). In Australia's most populous city – Sydney – 68.1 per cent of trips are made by private motor vehicle (Bureau of Transport Statistics, 2013). Transitioning to low carbon mobility futures in a highly car dependent society will not hinge solely on technology but requires changes to places, policies, ideas, and behaviours, as well as technologies. And there is evidence to suggest that low carbon mobilities are *already* being practised by some social groups – even in otherwise heavily car dependent places. This case study foregrounds one such group: Chinese migrants living in Sydney.

Our point of departure is evidence gathered in quantitative transport studies. Large-scale USA travel surveys show that migrants and ethnic minorities have significantly lower rates of car ownership and use than ethnic majority and native-born populations (Douma, 2004; Valenzuela *et al.*, 2005; Bohon *et al.*, 2008; Lovejoy & Handy, 2008; Grengs, 2010; Golub *et al.*, 2013; Modarres, 2013). This trend is replicated in Australia. For instance Klocker *et al.* (2015) reported that individuals of north-east Asian ancestry (primarily Chinese) owned and used cars at significantly reduced rates when compared with Anglo-European Australians. This trend was particularly pronounced amongst first-generation migrants of north-east Asian ancestry. These differences remained statistically significant *after* controlling for income differences – suggesting that cultural factors are likely at play (see Tal & Handy, 2010 for similar findings in the USA).

The qualitative findings reported on in this case study draw from interviews with first-generation Chinese migrants living in Sydney. These interviews help to shed light on the quantitative trends outlined above. The narratives presented here unsettle dominant understandings of car dependence in Australia. They demonstrate that diverse cultures of transport already exist within the Australian population. Our central argument is that the *already existing* low carbon mobilities of migrants demand greater research attention and support.

Methods

This case study reflects on project findings from an investigation of Chinese migrant households' everyday mobility cultures in Sydney. The term 'Chinese' refers to participants' self-defined ethnicity. While transport practices are undoubtedly also influenced by age, gender, professional status and family structure; participants' narratives underscored the power of ethnicity and country of birth. Recruitment occurred through Chinese community organisations, personal networks and snowballing. The participants were born (and/or grew up) in mainland China or affiliated territories (Hong Kong, Macau and Taiwan) and subsequently migrated to Australia.

In total, 14 Chinese migrants were interviewed (5 male and 9 female), with interviews ranging from 1-2 hours in duration. The interviews sought to gain insights into the lay knowledge which informed Chinese migrants' mobility choices. Questions explored migration histories, how migration disrupted or confirmed particular transport choices, and participants' understandings of how mobility choices helped maintain particular individual and collective identities, including their Chinese ethnicity. Open-ended style questions encouraged participants to share lived experiences of daily travel. Interviews were recorded and transcribed verbatim. Analysis occurred by combining both narrative and discourse analysis.

A preference for public transport

Most of the Chinese migrants interviewed in this study owned and used cars. Yet, they did not position the car as essential for all trips, or as their main transport mode (discussed further below). In contrast to wider patterns of extensive car use in Australia, our participants reported intentionally orienting their lives around Sydney's public transport nodes. They did so based on pre-migration transport norms, established in contexts where public transport use remains ubiquitous. These migrants arrived in Australia with a lay embodied knowledge that made them receptive to using public transport. 'Habit' was a common term that participants used to explain their continued public transport use, *post-migration*. Thus Lei (male, mid 30s, born in China, migrated 5+ years ago) commented: *'I used to take a lot of public transportation [in China] and I think it's like a habit'*. Similarly, Linda (female, early 30s, grew up in Taiwan, migrated 10+ years ago) noted: *'I just take public transportation because that's how I used to live back in Taiwan'*.

When making Sydney-based transport choices, the participants' pre-migration embodied routines and experiences fostered tolerance for the felt discomforts and inconveniences of public transport. Lei spoke of his higher tolerance thresholds for crowded trains than Australian-born people, '*I probably prefer public transport slightly more than the local [Australian] people… Because I'm more tolerant than others to the crowded people… that's one reason*'. Similarly, Anthony (male, 35, born in China, migrated 5+ years ago) said:

> *I don't think here it's a big problem for me to stand in a very crowded car[riage] or for many Chinese people, [be]cause we used to this crowded…it's still okay if I have to stand up with a lot of people, it's okay for me.*

Personal space tolerances are culturally embedded (Hall *et al.*, 1968). While our interviewees conceded that public transport is not always 'comfortable', it remained acceptable within their tolerance thresholds. This stands in stark contrast to affluent Anglo-European Australians living in suburban Sydney that expressed a preference for driving because the smells and sights of trains (and train passengers) evoked strong feelings of disgust and discomfort (Waitt and Harada, 2012).

Having grown up in contexts where private car ownership was atypical, our research participants arrived in Australia with little or no driving experience. This too shaped their subsequent transport choices. Contrary to common proclamations of Australians' 'love affair' with the car (Motavalli, 2001), our interviewees' feelings towards cars ranged from pragmatism and ambivalence, to discomfort and in some instances – outright fear and hostility (Kerr, 2014; Waitt *et al.*, 2016):

> *If I had the choice I mostly would go for public transport because I don't have to think about where I am going, am I going to crash? So for me it's [a] more… relaxing trip. And even though sometimes it might take a bit longer on the train it doesn't bother me (Chen: female, 23, born in China, migrated 10+ years ago).*

> *I think the speed [of driving] here is much faster compared to Taiwan where I come from…I [am] kind of scared to drive in Sydney because the speed [is] so fast (Linda)*

> *I'm not that good at driving so maybe that's more safe to others if I am not driving…I don't want to make dangerous situations, so [I] just catch the train (Fred: male, 26, born in China, migrated 4 years ago)*

Our participants' emotions contradict standard assertions that Australians love cars and enjoy driving, and view public transport with disdain (Motavalli, 2001; Waitt & Harada, 2012). Multiple cultures of transport co-exist in Australia. Yet, car-dependent norms remain dominant – putting intense pressure on migrants to adopt higher carbon mobilities over time.

Whither low carbon mobilities?

Despite their stated preference for public transport, many participants found it difficult to maintain low carbon mobilities post-migration (see Waitt *et al.*, 2016). Public transport remained their entrenched choice for many trips – especially regular commuting to work. Only one participant owned a car in China, however, 13 of 14 eventually felt compelled to do so in Sydney. Participants' low carbon mobilities succumbed – to a certain extent – to the spatially and temporally fragmented character of their post-migration lives. Sydney's public transport networks proved inadequate to manage grocery shopping, childcare and social lives (see Waitt *et al.*, 2016). For example, Xia explained how the car became imperative for her as a mother:

> *Time is so precious for [a] mum. So if we go and get somewhere [by car] it is much easier than public transport… If I have to bring him to school that's [the car is] very important because the school [is] not close to the station, but close to the bus stop but the bus take a very long time to his pre-school. So if I drive it take 5-10 minutes, if I take the bus it takes about 45minutes!*

Xia further commented, '*I didn't want to learn to drive… I had to. I have no choice*'.

Given the clear need for low carbon mobility transitions (see Chapman, 2007), these findings are discouraging. The mobility practices of these Chinese migrants moved in the opposite direction – they became more carbon intensive over time. Most did not readily acculturate to car dependence in Australia, and delayed ownership until they felt they had no other choice (Kerr, 2014). Even after owning a car, these migrants continued to use public transport whenever possible. However, the car dependent society these Chinese migrants found in Sydney was not sufficiently conducive to support the full continuation of their low carbon, pre-migration transport norms. These findings indicate the deep failings of the Sydney's public transport system, when even the most committed public transport users (and reluctant car drivers) feel compelled to purchase and use cars. They are also indicative of a lost opportunity.

Concluding remarks

The findings of this research unsettle dominant narratives of car dependence, demonstrating that multiple relationships to automobility already co-exist in Australia; and indeed in other immigrant societies. We conclude that attentiveness to ethnic diversity provides an opportunity to think through different ways of being mobile, even within societies in which the majority of people remain heavy car users. The Chinese migrant participants in this study demonstrated a cultural preference and disposition towards low carbon mobilities. While not motivated by a desire to be 'green', these cultural preferences are environmentally beneficial. Our research thus speaks to a broader body of literature that has drawn attention to the significance of inadvertent or unintentional sustainabilities (Evans, 2011; Klocker *et al.*, 2012; Hitchings *et al.*, 2015).

Given the profound environmental implications of car use, research and policy attention should arguably focus on better understanding, heralding and supporting the
practices of groups who are already making low carbon transport choices - to avoid
turning avid public transport users into reluctant car drivers. Transport behaviours
are just one element of everyday life, shaped by cultural norms, with implications
for environmental sustainability. In western countries of high immigration – like
Australia – the environmental skills and capacities of migrants remain poorly understood (Klocker & Head, 2013). In Australia, and elsewhere, attentiveness to ethnically
diverse sustainabilities may provide fertile ground for re-thinking and re-shaping
the ingrained habits of ethnic majority and native-born populations – where these
are environmentally problematic.

References

Australian Bureau of Statistics. (2014). Motor Vehicle Census, Australia, 31 Jan 2014,
cat.no. 9309.0, accessed 5 August 2014, http://www.abs.gov.au/ausstats/abs@.nsf/
mf/9309.0.

Bureau of Transport Statistics (2013). 201/12 *Household Travel Survey, Summary Report
2013 Release*, NSW Government, Sydney.

Bohon, S., Stamps, K. & Atiles, J. (2008). Transport and migrant adjustment in Georgia.
Population Research and Policy Review **27**, 273–291.

Chapman, L. (2007). Transport and climate change: a review, *Journal of Transport
Geography*, **15**, 354-367.

Douma, F. (2004). Using ITS to better serve diverse populations. Report prepared for
Minnesota Department of Transportation Research Services Section, Minnesota.

Evans, D. (2011). Thrifty, green or frugal: Reflections on sustainable consumption in a
changing economic climate, *Geoforum*, **42** (5), 550-557.

Golub, A., Marcantonio, R. & Sanchez, T. (2013). Race, space and struggles for mobility:
Transportation impacts on African Americans in Oakland and the East Bay. *Urban
Geography* **34**, 699–728.

Grengs, J. (2010). Job accessibility and the modal mismatch in Detroit, *Journal of
Transport Geography* **18**, 42–54.

Hall, E., Birdwhistell, R., Bock, B., Bohannan, P., Diebold, A.R., Durbin, M., Edmonson,
M., Fischer, J., Hymes, D., Kimball, S., Barre, W., Lynch, F., McClenllan, J., Marshall,
D., Milner, G., Sarles, H., Trager, G. & Vayda, A. (1968). Proxemics, *Current
Anthropology*, **9** (2/3), 83-108.

Hitchings, R., Collins, R. & Day R. (2015). Inadvertent environmentalism and the
action-value opportunity: Reflections from studies at both ends of the generational
spectrum, *Local Environment*, **20** (3), 369-385.

Kerr, S., (2014). Exploring everyday cultures of transport in Chinese migrant
households in Sydney, Honours thesis, University of Wollongong, Wollongong.

Klocker, N., Gibson, C. & Borger, E. (2012). Living together, but apart: Material geographies of everyday sustainability in extended family households, *Environment and Planning A*, **44** (9), 2240–2259.

Klocker, N. & Head, L. (2013). Diversifying ethnicity in Australia's population and environment debates, *Australian Geographer*, **44** (1), 41-62.

Lovejoy, K. & Handy, S. (2008). A case for measuring individuals' access to private-vehicle travel as a matter of degrees: Lessons from focus groups with Mexican immigrants in California. *Transportation* **35**, 601–612.

Modarres, A. (2013). Commuting and energy consumption: Toward an equitable transportation policy. *Journal of Transport Geography* **33**, 240–249.

Motavalli, J. (2001). *Forward Drive: The Race to Build 'Clean' Cars for the Future*, CA: Sierra Club Books, San Francisco.

Tal, G. & Handy, S. (2010). Travel behaviour of immigrants: An analysis of the 2001 National Household Transportation Survey. *Transport Policy* **17**, 85–93.

Valenzuea, A., Schweitzer, L. & Robles, A. (2005). Camionetas: Informal travel among immigrants, *Transportation Research Part A*, **39** (10), 895-911.

Waitt, G. & Harada, T. (2012). Driving, cities and changing climates, *Urban Studies*, **49** (15), 3307-3325.

Waitt, G., Kerr, S. & Klocker, N. (2016). Gender, ethnicity and sustainable mobility: A governmentality analysis of migrant Chinese women's daily trips in Sydney, *Applied Mobilities*, **1** (1), 68-84.

Case Study 2: Opening Cape Town streets for a low carbon future

Leanne Seeliger

Unit for Environmental Ethics, University of Stellenbosch, South Africa.

Lisa Kane

Centre for Transport Studies, University of Cape Town, South Africa.

Introduction

Cape Town's apartheid spatial form combined with its weak and under resourced public transport system has resulted in a resource inefficient city where many people rely on carbon-intensive private vehicles, or taxis for mobility (Wilkinson, 2000; Statistics South Africa, 2014a) More than half of the energy used in the Cape Town metro area is consumed by the transport sector (City of Cape Town, 2015). At a macro level, the city authorities and partners have drawn up strategies including the Comprehensive Integrated Transport Plan (Transport for Cape Town, 2014) and the Low Carbon Central City Strategy (Cape Town Partnership, 2014) to encourage 'own-steam' transport (e.g. walking, cycling), public transport and smarter private vehicle use (e.g. car-pooling). However, despite these policy interventions the carbon footprint of transport continues to grow (City of Cape Town, 2015).

While it is true that the current transport system, with its prioritisation of private vehicles and lack of adequate public transport, has traditionally favoured the affluent, it is not clear whether increasing the financial resources allocated to public transport will be sufficient to encourage a shift to low carbon alternatives. This case study addresses a civil society movement called Open Streets through the lens of transition theory. It suggests that this movement is a niche development in which a transformation of the way people and places are valued could occur. This niche has the potential to significantly alter the regime of the urban transport system in Cape Town and assist in shifting the city towards a low carbon urban mobility future.

The co-evolution of urban transport systems

Transportation systems are intricate socio-technical systems (Rees *et al.*, 2016) that are difficult to change because they often involve heavy infrastructure costs and profound changes to people's behaviour patterns (Geels, 2012). Major shifts need to happen within civil society, among firms, politicians and policy makers. This process is co-evolutionary and can take decades to happen. This case study highlights two overlooked factors in co-evolution: 'conscientisation' about these often taken-for-granted systems; and experiences of streets outside of the mundane every day.

In Cape Town, like many South African cities, the issue of place-making is complicated. The city's apartheid patterns of settlement disadvantaged Black South Africans by placing them on the outskirts of cities and forcing them to spend high proportions of their low wages on public transport to get to work in the city centre (Cape Town Partnership, 2014). Now, despite the democratic political situation, the outskirts of Cape Town remain places where affordable housing is available and the central city is home to a large proportion of the jobs. This means the underprivileged remain reliant on the city's substandard public transport system.

The racial segregation of the past created a fearful society (Lemanski, 2004). Many White South Africans lived behind high walls and their use of public street space was very limited. By contrast Black and Coloured South Africans used streets for access and as playgrounds (Coetzer, 2004), in part because of limited access to amenities. Now, more than 20 years after the arrival of democracy, as South Africa seeks to transition to a lower carbon future with fewer cars and more community interaction, the privileged are still hesitant to switch to lower carbon modes of transit that require a great utilisation of what they have traditionally considered unsafe public open spaces and and are less convenient in terms of flexibility (Statistics South Africa, 2014b). Moreover, the previously disadvantaged, often forced to use public transport, still see the private car as the preferred mode of transportation.

South Africa's National Department of Transport, in an attempt to address the inefficiency of travel in the country's cities and motivated in part by the hosting of the 2010 Football World Cup (ITDP, 2008; Boulle & Van Ryneveld, 2015), began a bus rapid transport (BRT) system in the country's five metropolitan areas and 10 smaller cities. This programme, which is called the MyCiti bus in Cape Town, is ambitious. The city plans to expand it so that most residents are within 500 metres of a trunk (BRT/rail) or bus feeder route, allowing for even those on the periphery of the city to be able to reach their destinations within an hour (Boulle & Van Ryneveld, 2015; City of Cape Town, 2014). However, despite these good intentions, the system has struggled to be financially viable (Lewis, 2015) and widespread public transport uptake by the higher income segment of the Cape Town population has been limited (Donaldson, 2015).

To address access, and other related 'street' concerns, the Open Streets movement was initiated in Cape Town 2012. It was formed by a diverse group of actors, ranging from those interested in climate change and low carbon forms of travel to others focused on civil rights and the allocation of urban space, social cohesion, creative arts, job creation, security, sports and recreation. All believed in the power of street design and street use to contribute to these diverse policy agendas[1]. A decision was taken early on to embrace the wide ranging, and often eclectic possibilities for street development and to find ways to work across the various interests in a productive way. In this way, Open Streets aimed from the beginning to break down the silos commonplace in government thinking about urban development.

We argue that Open Streets provides an example of a *niche* development that could assist in addressing the social transformation needed to assist South African travellers to move to lower carbon forms of mobility in Cape Town, and possibly elsewhere in South Africa.

Transition theory is an attempt to explain how sustainability innovations occur in large systems (Hodson & Marvin, 2010; Horisch, 2015). It does this with the help of multi-level perspective that consists *niches*, *regimes* and *landscapes* (Geels, 2002). A regime is the prevailing socio-technical system that is characterised by a specific logic because technologies are inevitably linked to a variety of interests including political, business, cultural and consumer interests. Occasionally, cracks occur in a regime as a result of external long-term macro-level tensions at the landscape level (i.e. societal values, political ideologies or macro-economic patterns) and then new practices emerge.

Niche developments are the protected spaces within regimes that support emerging innovations and alternative practices. These niches allow learning processes that enable communities to overcome both technical and social problems in one regime, to transition to another regime (Geels, 2012). They create space for the articulation of the visions and expectations of people as well as facilitate social networking opportunities. If these innovations grow in support and attract funding and they coincide with the emergence of gaps in the regime (influenced by the macro landscape level) then they break through the existing practices of the current regime and create new and alternative practices. It is with this transition theory lens that we examine the impact of the Open Streets movement in Cape Town.

During the first six months of Open Streets, attention was focused on its manifesto, which set out to promote shared places in Cape Town that *'embody respect for all and help bridge the social and spatial divides of our city'*. The manifesto promoted a vision for streets that should *'enable safer and more cohesive communities; provide platforms for creative expression of local cultures and values; be places for recreation and social*

---

1   One of the paper's authors was a co-founder and has been able to observe the development of the movement at close hand.

interaction; contribute to job creation and local economic activity and provide choice how people move around the city' (Open Streets website, 2015a, np).

Over the lifespan of the project, the interests represented have changed. Early on, it was necessary first to engage the public and to place 'streets' on the agenda as a conversation piece. before Open Streets could be used as a platform for change. Media interest and the development of a cohort who were interested to engage further was seen as essential. As funding was not secured, the group made intense use of social media, especially Twitter and Facebook to gain attention and interest. One member wrote a regular newspaper column and the group were proactive in writing and publishing opinion pieces.

To date, the flagship programme used to raise awareness about the Open Streets manifesto and movement has been a series of Open Streets Days. The first of these took place in Observatory, an eclectic suburban area about 5km from central Cape Town which has a strong creative community. The Open Streets organisation generated local buy-in through a series of public meetings and on-the-ground, conventional and social media networking over two months (April-May 2013). Open Streets then facilitated the day by closing the road to traffic and ensuring the soft and hard infrastructure necessary was in place for about five hours initially on a Sunday and subsequently on a Saturday. The Observatory Improvement District, a strong and enthusiastic local area partner, ensured local support and engagement. The setting brought an estimated 5000 participants, performers, activists and enthusiasts to the first Open Streets days and generated positive media interest from the outset.

Subsequent surveys of more than 100 participants at the Open Streets Days conducted by Open Streets volunteers revealed that citizens enjoyed the diversity of the crowds who came to Open Streets days and although this has varied over the eight Open Streets Days (in Observatory, Langa, central Cape Town and Bellville) it seems that this somewhat taken-for-granted quality of Open Streets Days is seen as a powerful positive, in a political context currently of high awareness of unresolved racial division and inequity. Survey participants also remarked on a sense of freedom (especially for children) which Open Streets Days provide, and a safe, relaxed 'vibe'.

By late 2015, the Open Streets movement had attracted sufficient public interest that it began being seen as a possible platform for change agendas. The Western Cape Provincial Government tested a concept ('Streetiquette') for using street theatre to raise awareness about pedestrian street safety (one of the manifesto aims) with the help of Open Streets (Western Cape Government website, 2015). The organisation has also recently received funding from World Wide Fund for Nature (WWF) Nedbank Green Trust for the development of more Open Streets Days with an associated low carbon transport focus. This will mean developing a programme for rail, bus, mini-bus taxi and bike access to Open Streets days, and a series of campaigns and research in low carbon transport.

There are many factors that influence whether niche innovations such as the Open Streets programme in Cape Town are able to become mainstream, and challenge the hegemony of the dominant regime. One such factor is timing. If tensions within existing transport regimes are too small and the current regime is able to handle the pressure within the system for decades, then insufficient windows of opportunity open up for niche innovations to grow (Geels, 2012). However, it is perhaps the systemic pressures on South Africa's transport systems which will compel the uptake of innovative solutions: gridlocks in the city centre and on major arterials; reaction against the on-going high loss of life on roads and associated costs and the increasing and stubborn contribution of the transport sector to carbon emissions. One could also argue that the worldwide shift at a 'landscape level' towards a new sustainability paradigm also stands in the Open Streets programme's favour for gaining acceptance.

The following quotes on the Open Streets website (2015b) posted on 11 May 2015, are an indication of the diversity of interest groups that it appeals to:

- *'Open Streets is an opportunity to see what the city might be like if priority was placed on people - skaters, cyclists, pedestrians and families - instead of cars'* (Marco Morgan, National Skate Collective)

- *'The City is really excited to be part of [Open Streets], to be supporting this. By removing cars I think we really do make a statement about sustainability and liveability and that's what this City and this government is about.'* (Brett Herron, Mayco Member for Transport, Roads and Stormwater)

- *'Streets matter, they do not only connect us with each other they also connect us to ourselves… The phrase 'I grew up in that street', says so much. Open Streets have connected Lower Main Road in Obs, Bree Street in the City and Bunga Avenue in Langa by simply allowing ordinary people to lay claim to these streets albeit for a short while. May this brave little initiative grow from strength to strength and may we open our hearts and minds to rediscover the importance of the streets we walk every day!'* (Nico McLachlan, MyCiti and N2 Express Facilitator)

As the above quotes indicate, the problems Open Streets face going forward are not ones of popularity. Instead the growth of Open Streets faces a series of organisational, logistical, regulatory and funding barriers. It is not clear, for example, where Open Streets, and similar initiatives fit within current governance structures, even those that are focused on transforming the city to a low carbon future. This begs questions therefore about how such cross-disciplinary initiatives can be funded and supported into the future. The apparently simple act of closing a road to traffic has proven to be expensive due to event regulations in place to offset perceived risks. These regulations require traffic and security officers, advanced and same-day signage, toilets and cleaning, the transport of barriers and cones, and public liability insurance. These posts mean that the roll out of Open Streets at scale is not currently financially viable.

Despite the currently prohibitive costs of Open Streets Days, the organisation has a mandate from the City to explore ways of growing the Open Streets Day network in a financially sustainable manner. Now that Open Streets has a higher profile, and with funding from WWF Nedbank Green Trust, Open Streets will be focusing on three key areas over the next three years:

1   Highlighting concerns of street design and use, transport and roads within the public realm and media through targeted campaigns. The management team consider this essential to addressing and reversing existing private vehicle ownership and use aspirations.

2   Giving all people, but in the case of low carbon work especially the affluent car driving South Africans, a different outside-the-car experience of the street and the city and so to raise awareness and facilitate engagement in alternative visions of the city.

3   Allowing children, whose parents are often justifiably fearful of the street, to experience a different city. Inspiring them is one key to Cape Town's immediate low carbon prospects, and to South Africa's long term future.

References

Boulle, M. & Van Ryneveld, P. (2015). Unpacking implementation: The case of the MyCiti Bus Rapid Transit in Cape Town. http://www.mapsprogramme.org/wp-content/uploads/MYCITI_IMPLEMENTATION-1.pdf. Accessed 3 March 2016.

Cape Town Partnership. (2014). The low carbon central city strategy. http://www.capetownpartnership.co.za/wp-content/uploads/2014/02/low_carbon_central_city_strategy.pdf. Accessed 3 March 2016.

City of Cape Town. (2015). Cape Town Energy2040 Vision. https://www.capetown.gov.za/en/EnvironmentalResourceManagement/publications/Documents/Cape_Town_Energy2040_Vision_pres_2015-09.pdf. Accessed 3 March 2016.

Coetzer, N. R. (2004). The production of the city as white space: Representing and restructuring identity and architecture, Cape Town 1892-1936. PhD, University of London, unpublished).

City of Cape Town. (2014). City-wide public transport plan to ensure mobility into the year 2032. June, 17. Media Release 429. www.capetown.gov.za/en/MediaReleases/Pages/Citywidepublictransportplantoensure mobilityintotheyear2032.aspx. Accessed 3 March 2016.

Donaldson, A. (2015). Cape Town's cunning plan to deal with traffic congestion. http://www.politicsweb.co.za/opinion/cape-towns-cunning-plan-to-deal-with-traffic-conge. Accessed 17 March 2016.

Geels, F. W. (2002). Technological transitions as evolutionary reconfiguration processes: A multi-level perspective and a case-study, *Research Policy*, **31** (8-9), 1257-1274.

Geels, F. W. (2012). A socio-technical analysis of low carbon transitions: Introducing the multi-level perspective into transport studies. *Journal of Transport Geography*, **24**, 471-482.

Hodson, M. & Marvin, S. (2010). Can cities shape socio-technical transitions and how would we know if they were? *Research policy*, **39**(4), 477-485.

Hörisch, J. (2015). The role of sustainable entrepreneurship in sustainability transitions: A conceptual synthesis against the background of the multi-level perspective. *Administrative Sciences*, **5**(4), 286-300.

ITD (2008). Cape Town considers BRT. https://www.itdp.org/cape-town-considers-brt/. Accessed 17 March 2016.

Lemanski, C. (2004). A new apartheid? The spatial implications of fear of crime in Cape Town, South Africa. *Environment and Urbanization*, **16**(2), 101-112.

Lewis, A. (2015). MyCiTi faces R52m deficit. http://www.iol.co.za/business/news/myciti-faces-r52m-deficit-1834748. Accessed 17 March 2016.

Open Streets website. (2015a). Open Streets Manifesto. http://openstreets.org.za/about-us/manifesto-for-open-streets-cape-town. Accessed 3 March 2016.

Open Streets website. (2015b). What Capetonians are saying about open streets. May, 11. http://openstreets.org.za/news/what-capetonians-are-saying-about-open-streets. Accessed 3 March 2016.

Rees, D., Stephenson, J., Hopkins, D. & Doering, A. (2016). Exploring stability and change in transport systems: combining Delphi and system dynamics approaches. *Transportation*, 1-17.

Statistics South Africa. (2014a). *National household travel survey Western Cape profile* No. Report No. 03-20-02 (2014)). Pretoria: Statistics South Africa.

Statistics South Africa. (2014b). *National household travel survey. Attitudes and perceptions about transport*. Pretoria: Statistics South Africa. https://www.arrivealive.co.za/documents/P03202013. Accessed 17 March 2016.

Transport for Cape Town. (2014). *Comprehensive integrated transport plan 2013-2018. May 2014*. Cape Town: City of Cape Town.

Western Cape Provincial Government website. 2015. Streetiquette performers take over Cape Town CBD to promote pedestrian safety. November, 22. https://www.westerncape.gov.za/news/streetiquette-performers-take-over-cape-town-cbd-promote-pedestrian-safety. Accessed 3 March 2016.

Wilkinson, P. (2000). City profile: Cape Town. *Cities*, **17**(3), 195-205.

Part 2: Structures in Transition

6 The Challenges of Changing the Paradigms, Regimes and Structures of Low Carbon Mobility

C. Michael Hall

Department of Management, Marketing and Entrepreneurship, University of Canterbury, New Zealand.

Introduction

Transitions are broadly defined as processes in which society changes fundamentally within comparatively short periods of time, usually of the order of just over a generation or 25 years (Rotmans et al., 2001). Transitions refer to the change in dynamic equilibrium from one state of equilibrium to another. They are also referred to as regime change (Smith et al., 2005), and are often seen as equivalent to, or occurring in concert with, paradigm change (Vanloqueren & Baret, 2009). Geels and Kemp (2007) distinguish between a 'transformation', referring to a change in the direction of trajectories, related to an alteration in the rules that guide innovation, and 'transition', referring to a discontinuous shift to a new trajectory and system. However, the terms are often used interchangeably. The topic of sustainable or low carbon mobility transitions has attracted reasonable levels of academic interest (Nykvist & Whitmarsh, 2008; Köhler et al., 2009; Cohen, 2010; Farla et al., 2010; Geerlings et al., 2012; Upham et al., 2015), with concerns over sustainable or low carbon mobility also often embedded in or overlapping with other policy fields, such as urban design and planning (Mäkinen et al., 2015; Strandell & Hall, 2015), or tourism (Hall, 2009; Gössling et al., 2012).

This chapter aims to provide a brief introduction to some of the issues associated with enabling low carbon mobility transitions. It first discusses issues of regime change and transition and highlights the desire for specific types of transition. However, the nature of desired regime change appears to inherently require the involvement of the state and therefore this also raises significant issues of policy change and learning. The chapter then goes on to discuss the complexity of multi-scale transitions and the extent to which this raises issues of agency and structure, with emphasis on the capability to enable transition and positive change itself being related to different framing of policy interventions and learning. The chapter then concludes by noting the limitations of capacities to enable low carbon mobility transitions without there being third degree policy learning and major paradigm change.

Regime change and transition

Regimes can be understood as the rules, institutions and structures, which are recursively reproduced, used and changed by policy actors (Giddens, 1984). Policy in this sense needs to be understood not just as what is written but more so what is done and not-done with respect to decision-making and the flows and trajectories of decisions and their implementation over time. Such decisions and flows are also dominated by particular policy paradigms. For Hall (1993: 279) a 'policy paradigm' is the *'framework of ideas and standards that specifies not only the goals of policy and the kind of instruments used to attain them, but also the very nature of the problems they are meant to be addressing'*. Although concerns have been expressed about the capacity for paradigm change (Weaver, 2009) and policy learning with respect to sustainable tourism and mobility (Hall, 2011), this *'agency-structure dynamic, which is also crucial in [transition pathways], leaves space for different kinds of action'* (Geels & Schot, 2007: 415).

Regime change, which has been incorporated into multi-level perspectives on technological transitions (Geels, 2011), is primarily a function of two partially coupled processes: (1) shifting selection pressures on the regime, and (2) the co-ordination of resources (capabilities, factor endowments, knowledge) available inside and outside the regime to adapt to these pressures. Selection pressures include not only economic pressures operating at the level of the firm and the region (such as pricing, competition, contracts, taxes and charges, regulations, standards, liability, profitability, skills and knowledge), but also broad political, social and economic pressures emanating from institutional structures and conventions (e.g. demographic shifts, consumer culture, societal environmental attitudes, urbanisation, neoliberal model of globalisation), as well as pressures that 'bubble up from below, from innovative niches that are not yet so established as to constitute a regime' (Smith *et al.*, 2005: 1495). An example of the latter would be the demands that arise in some jurisdictions from the pressures of the so-called 'piecemeal' or 'sharing economy' (Hall & Veer, 2016).

Table 6.1 illustrates some of the different types of changes in the regime environments. Importantly the types of change may shift over time. For example, coral bleaching appears to be shifting from being an occasional specific shock to a situation of hyper-turbulence over time as a result of increased frequency of bleaching events in response to the growing intensity of climate change (Slezak, 2016). The activity of interests with respect to regime change is significant because such debates affect the manner in which policy learning occurs and therefore consequently frames the function reproduction and potential for change of policy paradigms (Hall, 2011) and socio-technical regimes (Smith *et al.*, 2005). Indeed, without at least some form of internal or external pressure '*it is unlikely that substantive change to the developmental trajectory of the regime will result*' (Smith *et al.*, 2005: 1495).

In utilising the two dimensions of regime change and assuming that different selection pressures are always present it is possible to present a typology of four transitions (Figure 6.1) (Berkhout *et al.*, 2004; Smith *et al.*, 2005; Gössling *et al.*, 2012). The reorientation of trajectories and emergent transformations are evolutionary transitions in which the outcome is not planned in a significant way, endogenous renewal and purposive transition are goal-oriented (teleological) transitions in which a diffuse goal or vision of the end state is guiding policy-makers and orienting their strategic decisions (Kemp & Rotmans, 2004: 138). This latter type of regime transformation or regime shift is also referred to as transition management.

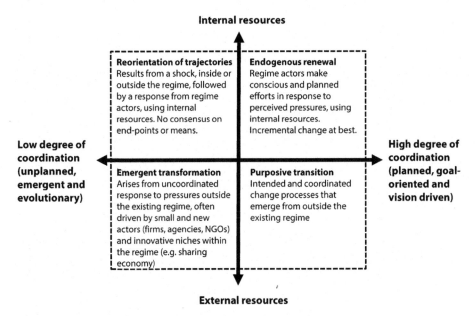

Figure 6.1: A typology of transitions. Source: After Berkhout *et al.* (2004); Kemp & Rotman (2004); Smith *et al.* (2005); Gössling *et al.* (2012).

Transition management is usually regarded as requiring integrative and multi-level governance to encourage and shape development processes, and choice of policy instruments and actions by individuals and private and public organisations,

Table 6.1: Types of changes in environment. Source: After Wholey & Brittain (1989); Suarez & Oliva (2005); Geels & Schot (2007); Hall (2010).

Type of change in environment	Examples	Frequency (number of environmental disturbances per unit time)	Amplitude (magnitude of deviation from initial conditions caused by a disturbance)	Speed (rate of change of disturbance)	Scope (number of environmental dimensions affected by simultaneous disturbances)	Predictability
Regular (low intensity, gradual change)	Business cycle; election cycle; regulatory change	Low	Low	Low	Low	High
Hyper-turbulence (high frequency of change in one dimension)	Hypercompetition in rapidly changing markets; social fashion; increase in droughts, floods, coral bleaching, and high magnitude storm events under climate change	High	Low	High	Low	Low-medium
Specific shock (rare, rapid and high intensity environmental changes)	Industry deregulation; oil/energy crises; political revolution; technological substitution	Low	High	High	Low	Low
Disruptive (Infrequent gradual change in one dimension but with a high-intensity effect)	Disruptive technologies, e.g. mobile technologies, mass automobiles; peak oil; sea level rise; ocean acidification	Low	High	Low	Low	medium
Avalanche / institutional upheaval (Infrequent but high intensity and fast change in multiple dimensions)	Neoliberal economic reforms; biodiversity loss; deforestation	Low	High	High	High	Low

based on common visions (Gössling *et al.*, 2012). Its main objective is to empower stakeholders to develop their knowledge base and to implement new practices and technology change (Kemp *et al.*, 2007). Some authors (e.g. Kemp & Rotmans, 2004), argue that it should be understood not as being a policy instrument in its own right, even though it perhaps serves this role at a meta-policy level by serving to shape policy processes, but is instead a prescription on how policy *should* function. Rotmans *et al.* (2001: 22) summarise the main characteristics of transition management as follows:

- Long-term thinking (at least 25 years) as a framework for shaping short-term policy
- Thinking in terms of more than one domain (multi-domain) and different actors (multi-actor) at different scale levels (multi-level)
- A focus on learning and a special learning philosophy (learning-by-doing and doing-by-learning)
- To bring about system innovation alongside system improvement (encourage new ways of doing)
- Keeping a large number of options (maintaining a wide playing field)

Transition management has been investigated in various contexts, including energy (Loorbach, 2010), mobility (Kemp & Rotmans, 2004), waste management (Kemp *et al.*, 2007), water (van der Brugge *et al.*, 2005; van der Brugge & Rotmans, 2007) and, as noted in the introduction, is also increasingly being applied to low carbon and sustainable mobility, though its application is very limited in tourism (Gössling *et al.*, 2012). Yet, many of the processes that have been initiated to achieve sustainable mobility would fall within the broad frame of transition management as well as associated fields such as resilience. The concept has mainly been applied at the regional level (Geels & Schot, 2007), which clearly raises significant issues with respect to how the concept can be used to frame and influences the field of sustainable mobility at various scales of governance from the supranational to the national and through to the local (Gössling *et al.*, 2012).

As a result of the systems basis of transition management, Loorbach (2007) suggests that the approach to policy design within a transition management framework has five main elements:

1 Establishing a transition arena (i.e. a broad constituency of representatives from industry, politics, and society that accompany the ongoing planning and implementation process),

2 Developing a vision of a future sustainable sector structure,

3 Identifying pathways towards these future states by means of back-casting methods,

4 Setting up experiments for particularly interesting development options,

5 Monitoring, evaluating and revising.

Interestingly, van den Bergh *et al.* (2011) argue that one could see the search for transition policy as a kind of 'third best' policy approach, which aims to add greater realism to understanding the complex political and socio-economic system in which policies, such as those required for low carbon mobility, need to be implemented and function. They further suggest that the systems basis of transition thinking allows more attention to be given to the policy evaluation criterion of 'social–political feasibility', as well as the usual criteria of effectiveness and efficiency, as part of broader policy learning processes (Hall, 2011).

However, as well as providing a way of framing policy processes, the nature of change may also be an important factor in influencing mobility transitions. For example, in their study of transition management in Norwegian tourism, Gössling *et al.* (2012) suggested that the change environment appeared significant for the nature of the process. They noted that Norway had appeared to have benefited from a regular change environment, rather than one of the other types of change, as a result of its relative socio-economic and environmental stability. Yet, the Norwegian transition management process seemed geared in anticipation of one of the more rapid and higher magnitude forms of change that threaten the sustainability of tourism, such as rapid climate change or economic crisis. Ironically, even though non-regular forms of change also create their own transition pathways (see Table 6.1), the capacity to actively manage such regime transitions is much more difficult given the degree of turbulence they create in socio-technical regimes (Geels & Schot, 2007). This meant that policy actors appeared to be waiting for much more government intervention in the transition process than would be 'normal' given the actual rate of change. Such discontinuities clearly raises significant questions with respect to stakeholder capacity to both envision the future and take action in the absence of perceived high levels of risk or turbulence.

Although some caution has been expressed about the value of transition management (Shove & Walker, 2007), the combination of the advantages of incrementalism (small, achievable steps which are not immediately disruptive) with those of planning (articulation of desirable futures and use of goals and objectives) in transition management (Rotmans & Kemp, 2008), would appear to be of direct relevance to the goal of more sustainable forms of mobility. As Rotmans & Kemp (2008: 1010) comment, '*It is a model by which to work towards a sustainability transition, even when the very idea of achieving this is revealed as illusionary... We make our histories but not our future. Yet we can do things that help to achieve better futures, even in the face of perplexing complexity and overwhelming uncertainty.*' Similarly, Rip (2006: 94) argues '*illusions are productive because they motivate action and repair work, and thus something (whatever) is achieved.*' Indeed, given that in the majority of cases the long-term outcomes of policy actions, even though well intended and focussed, are by definition unknowable, the system hard to steer and the effects of deliberate intervention inherently unpredictable, it is perhaps ironic that it is this that actually sustains concepts of agency and management in seeking sustainable change (Shove & Walker, 2007), and it is to these issues that this chapter will now turn.

From process to policy

Within the transition management approach to regime transformation, decision-makers support what they hold to be desirable socio-technological configurations. This is achieved by promoting institutional and market niches '*in which favoured configurations are supported and allowed to prosper, enabling them either to replace or transform dominant, unstable regimes*' (Berkhout et al., 2004: 50). Transition management therefore deliberately attempts to change regimes according to a consensus guiding vision in order to clearly articulate selection pressures and favoured niches. However, the emergence of post-sovereign governance and the new public management which provides a more market- and network-based approach to policy development and implementation, have meant that the range of social and political actors, both in articulating pressure for change, and in providing the resources, capabilities and networks that condition responses (Smith et al., 2005), has expanded enormously (Kemp et al., 2007). However, rather than being less important, in such a complex policy environment, and given its responsibility for much of the past 150 years for public supported mobility, the state's role has actually become more rather than less important, given the importance of steering the system in an appropriate low carbon direction. Furthermore, there is clearly a significant issue if the regime is actually progressing along a non-sustainable or low carbon trajectory. How, then can it be changed? As van den Bergh et al. (2011: 8) commented, '*Transition policy also needs to account for bounded rationality of agents, system failures like lock-in, unpredictability and surprise in innovation systems, and network interactions between agents. Especially, lock-in and network interactions have not yet seen systematic translation into policy thinking.*'

The social and technical dimensions of mobility are central to understanding the capability of individuals to engage in low carbon mobility. Social in the sense of what is perceived as appropriate for travel (an immaterial dimension of mobility) and technical in the sense of what is available for use for travel (a material dimension). Here policy regimes need to be understood as being bound up in 'infrastructures of provision' (Southerton et al., 2004), institutions, and 'systems of provision'. These are the vertical commodity chains comprising production, finance, marketing, advertising, distribution, retail and consumption that '*entail a more comprehensive chain of activities between the two extremes of production and consumption, each link of which plays a potentially significant role in the social construction of the commodity both in its material and cultural aspects*' (Fine & Leopold, 1993: 33). However, the significance of the systems of provision approach is that it highlights that particular socio-technical systems constrain choice to that available within the system of provision. This means that consumers, and to an extent policy makers and other actors can be 'locked-in' to particular social practices of behaving, consuming and producing/ supplying (Unruh, 2000; Lorenzoni et al., 2007; Maréchal, 2010; Seyfang, 2011), including with respect to low carbon forms of mobility.

'Lock-in' to a particular socio-technical system of provision, such as the carbon economy, has been recognised as a major constraint to emissions reduction and avoidance of dangerous climate change (Maréchal, 2010). However, many policy actors continue to support the carbon economy, arguably because they continue to believe in the technocentric, market-oriented and ecological modernisation values that underpin the economy (Bailey & Wilson, 2009). Policy paradigms and technological paradigms, the latter defining an idea of 'progress' by embodying prescriptions on the directions of technological change to pursue and those to neglect (Dossi, 1982), therefore potentially become mutually reinforcing. In such a situation, policy learning by actors within the decision-making system becomes extremely difficult (Hall, 2011), with changes occurring only at the margin or in limited terms, but without challenging the basic policy paradigm. Such a situation reflects Geels' (2011) arguments that to enable sustainability transitions the roles of agency, (bounded) rationality and power need greater elaboration along with regime and socio-technical system processes.

Within discussions of sustainable and low carbon mobility there are arguably two major paradigms at play: eco-efficiency and sustainable consumption (Table 6.2). These are based on different objectives and economic policy orientations.

Table 6.2: Different technological/policy paradigms for sustainable mobility

Paradigms	Eco-efficiency	Sustainable Consumption
Basic definition	More productive use of materials and energy as a result of technological innovation leading to lower use of energy on a per passenger kilometre basis	Reducing the absolute use of energy by changing consumption patterns, and reducing throughput of products and services
Implicit objective	Maintaining business as usual but on a 'greener' basis. Implies the same or even increased personal travel demand. No fundamental changes in consumption choice or destination choice.	Reduction in personal demand and distance travelled; resuse and recycle. Fundamental change in nature of demand and consumption choice.
Economic policy orientation	'Green growth'/'Green economy'	'Reorientation'/'Degrowth'
Examples of sub-trajectories	Market mechanisms, competitiveness, biofuels, improved traffic management, green finance, behavioural economics and nudging	Cradle to cradle design, slow consumption/slow travel, compact cities, public and active transport, social practices

Although not included in the table, the two technological/policy paradigms are also potentially based on different scientific paradigms: reductionism in the case of eco-efficiency and holism with respect to sustainable consumption. The paradigms pursue different trajectories, with eco-efficiency constituting only incremental shifts in policy and constituting a supposedly more low carbon version of *business as usual*. The focus on mobility infrastructure and practices is also narrow. In contrast, a sustainable consumption approach takes a broader system-wide perspective of the requirements for sustainable mobility and seeks to make all parts of the consumption structure work in an integrated fashion towards reducing carbon reliance; for example, emphasising that urban design needs to be integrated with public and active transport initiatives in order to encourage greater sustainability by developing new social practices (Hall *et al.*, 2017). While both paradigms present themselves as 'green', the interpretation of low carbon mobility is very different, with eco-efficiency focussing on per capita relative consumption, and sustainable consumption looking to enable absolute reductions in carbon emissions (Hall, 2015). However, the efficiency approach is currently the dominant paradigm in the discourses of policy actors on low carbon mobility in most parts of the world and especially in terms of long-distance mobility.

Drawing on the policy learning literature (Hall, 2011, 2013), it can be suggested that the eco-efficiency regime represents a continuation of previous paradigms regarding growth and innovation and the approach to low carbon mobility is an example of first and second order change at best (Hall, 2015). First order change is characterised by incremental, routinised, satisficing behaviour that is based around policy actors that leads to a change in the '*levels (or settings) of the basic instruments of... policy*' (Hall, 1993: 279). Second order change is characterised by the selection of new policy instruments and techniques and policy settings due to previous policy experience, but the overarching policy goals remain the same (Hall, 2013). In contrast, third order change, or a policy paradigm shift, takes place when a new goal hierarchy is adopted by policy actors because the coherence of existing policy paradigm(s) has been undermined, '*where experiment and perceived policy failure has resulted in discrepancies or inconsistencies appearing which cannot be explained within the existing paradigm*' (Greener, 2001: 135).

A sustainable consumption approach, which recognises that systems of provision of low carbon mobility and the capability of individuals to utilise them are constrained by socio-technical regimes, does represent an alternative to the dominant paradigm, but a key question remains as to why it is not being readily adopted. Arguably one reason is the lock-in that exists in the dominant socio-technical paradigm in which recognition of relevant alternatives is typically restricted to those that are theoretically consistent with it (Shove, 2010). Policy makers fund and legitimise lines of enquiry that generate results which they can accept and manage, even if they do not necessarily provide the 'solution' to the policy problem. The result is a self-fulfilling cycle of credibility (Latour & Woolgar, 1986), in which evidence of relevance and value to policy makers helps in securing additional resources for that approach. As Shove (2010: 1283) noted, policy actors '*are highly selective in the models of change on which they draw, and that their tastes in social theory are anything but random. ... to ask how options are structured, or to inquire into the ways in which governments maintain infrastructures and economic institutions, is perhaps too challenging to be useful.*'

Conclusions

The mutual interdependence between policy paradigms and socio-technical regimes frame the policy options for, and therefore the trajectories of, low carbon mobility. One cannot be understood without the other. Policy learning is constrained by the dominant policy paradigm which is, in turn, reinforced by the nature of the socio-technical regime. The reinforcement between modes of governance and policy actions also creates a path dependency in which solutions to low carbon mobility are only identified within 'green growth' arguments for greater efficiency and market-based solutions, and an ideology that frames the problem of sustainable consumption in terms of individual consumption and responsibility (Whitmarsh *et al.*, 2011; Hall, 2013).

When there is a paradigm that pervades the entire policy making process, policy learning is extremely difficult (Hall, 2011), with changes occurring only at the margin or in limited terms, such as the development of biofuels and incremental improvements in technological efficiencies, but without challenging the dominant growth paradigm. Alternative paradigms that lie outside of the dominant policy discourses *'are doomed to be forever marginal no matter how interactive or how policy-engaged their advocates might be. To break through this log jam it would be necessary to reopen a set of basic questions about the role of the state, the allocation of responsibility, and in very practical terms the meaning of manageability'* (Shove, 2010: 1283). At the national and supranational level, opportunities to challenge the dominant approach to low carbon mobility that focusses on efficiency are extremely limited. Greater optimism may exist at the local state level where alternative articulations of public and active transport exist (Hall *et al.*, 2016) and where polycentric innovation systems can be encouraged. However, long term prospects for sustainable transition towards low carbon mobility will depend on the capacity for innovations to diffuse within existing structures of governance that currently favour efficiency-based solutions. Although regions are the ideal basis for sustainable transitions, being *'islands of sustainability'* that *'can be seen as "trouble makers" which infiltrate the whole unsustainable system and act as cells of development'* (Wallner *et al.*, 1996: 1763), they remain framed by national and supranational institutions. Nevertheless, it is the growing awareness of the contradictions in, and policy failure of, green growth strategies towards low carbon mobility that may also provide the best opportunity for third order change.

References

Bailey, I. & Wilson, G.A. (2009). Theorising transitional pathways in response to climate change: Technocentrism, ecocentrism, and the carbon economy. *Environment and Planning A*, **41**, 2324–2341.

Berkhout, F., Smith, A. & Stirling, A. (2004). Socio-technological regimes and transition contexts. In Elzen, B., Geels, F.W., Green, K. (Eds.), *System Innovation and the Transition to Sustainability: Theory, evidence and policy* (pp. 48-75). Cheltenham: Edward Elgar.

Cohen, M. J. (2010). Destination unknown: Pursuing sustainable mobility in the face of rival societal aspirations. *Research Policy*, **39**, 459-470.

Dosi, G. (1982). Technological paradigms and technological trajectories: A suggested interpretation of the determinants and directions of technical change. *Research Policy*, **11**, 147–162.

Farla, J., Alkemade, F. & Suurs, R.A. (2010). Analysis of barriers in the transition toward sustainable mobility in the Netherlands. *Technological Forecasting and Social Change*, **77**, 1260-1269.

Fine, B. & Leopold, E. (1993). *The World of Consumption*. London: Routledge.

Geels, F.W. (2011). The multi-level perspective on sustainability transitions: responses to seven criticisms. *Environmental Innovation and Societal Transitions*, **1**, 24–40.

Geels, F.W. & Kemp, R. (2007). Dynamics in socio-technical systems: typology of change processes and contrasting case studies. *Technology in Society*, **29**(4), 441-455.

Geels, F.W. & Schot, J. (2007). Typology of sociotechnical transition pathways. *Research Policy*, **36**, 399-417.

Geerlings, H., Shiftan, Y. & Stead, D. (Eds.). (2012). *Transition towards Sustainable Mobility: The role of instruments, individuals and institutions*. Farnham: Ashgate Publishing.

Giddens, A. (1984). *The Constitution of Society: Outline of the theory of structuration*. Berkeley: University of California Press.

Gössling, S., Hall, C.M., Ekström, F., Brudvik Engeset, A. & Aall, C. (2012). Transition management: a tool for implementing sustainable tourism scenarios? *Journal of Sustainable Tourism*, **20**, 899-916.

Hall, C.M. (2009). Degrowing tourism: Décroissance, sustainable consumption and steady-state tourism. *Anatolia*, **20**, 46-61.

Hall, C.M. (2010). Crisis events in tourism: Subjects of crisis in tourism. *Current Issues in Tourism*, **13**, 401–417.

Hall, C.M. (2011). Policy learning and policy failure in sustainable tourism governance: From first and second to third order change? *Journal of Sustainable Tourism*, **19**, 649-671.

Hall, C.M. (2013). Framing behavioural approaches to understanding and governing sustainable tourism consumption: Beyond neoliberalism, 'nudging' and 'green growth'? *Journal of Sustainable Tourism*, **21**, 1091-1109.

Hall, C.M. (2015). Economic greenwash: On the absurdity of tourism and green growth. In V. Reddy and K. Wilkes (Eds.), *Tourism in the Green Economy* (pp. 339-358). London: Earthscan by Routledge.

Hall, C.M., Le-Klähn , D-T. & Ram, Y. (2016). *Tourism, Public Transport and Sustainable Mobility*. Bristol: Channelview.

Hall, C.M. & Veer, E. (2016). The DMO is dead. Long live the DMO (or, why DMO managers don't care about post-structuralism). *Tourism Recreation Research,* http://dx.doi.org/10.1080/02508281.2016.1195960.

Hall, P.A. (1993). Policy paradigms, social learning, and the state: The case of economic policymaking in Britain. *Comparative Politics,* **25**, 275-296.

Kemp, R., Loorbach, D. & Rotmans, J. (2007). Transition management as a model for managing processes of co-evolution towards sustainable development. *International Journal of Sustainable Development and World Ecology,* **14**(1), 78-91.

Kemp, R. & Rotmans, J. (2004). Managing the transition to sustainable mobility. In B. Elzen, F.W. Geels, K. Green (Eds) *System Innovation and the Transition to Sustainability: Theory, evidence and policy* (pp. 137-167). Cheltenham: Edward Elgar.

Köhler, J., Whitmarsh, L., Nykvist, B., Schilperoord, M., Bergman, N. & Haxeltine, A. (2009). A transitions model for sustainable mobility. *Ecological Economics,* **68**, 2985-2995.

Latour, B. & Woolgar, S. (1986). *Laboratory Life: The construction of scientific facts.* Princeton: Princeton University Press.

Loorbach, D. (2007). *Transition Management. New mode of governance for sustainable development.* Utrecht: International Books.

Loorbach, D. (2010). Transition management for sustainable development: A prescriptive, complexity-based governance framework. *Governance,* **23**, 161-183.

Lorenzoni, I., Nicholson-Cole, S. & Whitmarsh, L. (2007). Barriers perceived to engaging with climate change among the UK public and their policy implications. *Global Environmental Change,* **17**, 445–459.

Maréchal, K. (2010). Not irrational but habitual: The importance of 'behavioural lock-in' in energy consumption. *Ecological Economics,* **69**, 1104–1114.

Mäkinen, K., Kivimaa, P. & Helminen, V. (2015). Path creation for urban mobility transitions: Linking aspects of urban form to transport policy analysis. *Management of Environmental Quality: An International Journal,* **26**, 485-504.

Nykvist, B. & Whitmarsh, L. (2008). A multi-level analysis of sustainable mobility transitions: Niche development in the UK and Sweden. *Technological Forecasting and Social Change,* **75**, 1373-1387.

Rip, A. (2006). A co-evolutionary approach to reflexive governance – and its ironies, in, Voss, J-P., Bauknecht, D. and Kemp, R. (Eds), *Reflexive Governance for Sustainable Development* (pp. 82-100), Cheltenham: Edward Elgar.

Rotmans, J. & Kemp, R. (2008) Detour ahead: a response to Shove and Walker about the perilous road of transition management. *Environment and Planning A,* **40**, 1006-1012.

Seyfang, G. (2011). *The New Economics of Sustainable Consumption: Seeds of change.* Basingstoke: Palgrave Macmillan.

Shove, E. (2010). Beyond the ABC: Climate change policy and theories of social change. *Environment and Planning A*, **42**, 1273-1285.

Shove, E. & Walker, G. (2007) CAUTION! Transitions ahead: politics, practice, and sustainable transition management. *Environment and Planning A*, **39**, 763-770.

Slezak, M. (2016). The Great Barrier Reef: a catastrophe laid bare. *The Guardian*, 7 June, http://www.theguardian.com/environment/2016/jun/07/the-great-barrier-reef-a-catastrophe-laid-bare

Smith, A., Stirling, A. & Berkhout, F. (2005) The governance of sustainable socio-technical transitions. *Research Policy*, **34**, 1491–1510.

Southerton, D., Chappells, H. & Van Vliet, B. (Eds) (2004). *Sustainable Consumption: The implications of changing infrastructures of provision*. Cheltenham: Edward Elgar.

Strandell, A. & Hall, C.M. (2015). Impact of the residential environment on second home use in Finland - testing the compensation hypothesis. *Landscape and Urban Planning*, **133**, 12-33.

Suarez, F.F. & Oliva, R. (2005). Environmental change and organisational transformation. *Industrial and Corporate Change*, **14**, 1017–1041.

Unruh, G.C. (2000). Understanding carbon lock-in. *Energy Policy*, **28**, 817–830.

Upham, P., Virkamäki, V., Kivimaa, P., Hildén, M. & Wadud, Z. (2015). Socio-technical transition governance and public opinion: The case of passenger transport in Finland. *Journal of Transport Geography*, **46**, 210-219.

van den Bergh, J., Truffer, B. & Kallis, G. (2011). Environmental innovation and societal transitions: Introduction and overview. *Environmental Innovation and Societal Transitions*, **1**, 1–23.

van der Brugge, R. & Rotmans, J. (2007). Towards transition management of European water resources. *Water Resources Management*, **21**, 249-267.

van der Brugge, R., Rotmans, J. & Loorbach, D. (2005). The transition in Dutch water management. *Regional Environmental Change*, **5**(4), 164-176.

Vanloqueren, G. & Baret, P.V. (2009). How agricultural research systems shape a technological regime that develops genetic engineering but locks out agroecological innovations. *Research Policy*, **38**, 971–983.

Wallner, H.P., Narodoslawsky, M. & Moser, F. (1996). Islands of sustainability: A bottom-up approach towards sustainable development. *Environment and Planning A*, **28**, 1763-1778.

Weaver, D. (2009). Reflections on sustainable tourism and paradigm change. In Gössling, S., Hall, C.M. and Weaver, D.B. (Eds), *Sustainable Tourism Futures* (pp. 33-40). New York: Routledge.

Whitmarsh, L., Seyfang, G. & O'Neill, S. (2011). Public engagement with carbon and climate change: To what extent is the public 'carbon capable'? *Global Environmental Change*, **21**, 56–65.

Wholey, D. & Brittain, J. (1989). Characterizing environmental variation. *Academy of Management Journal*, **32**, 867-882.

7 Institutions, Path Dependency and Public Transport

Muhammad Imran

School of People, Environment and Planning, Massey University, New Zealand.

Jane Pearce

Department of Geography, University of Canterbury, New Zealand.

Introduction

The aim of this chapter is to provide a historical overview of urban transport policies in Auckland, New Zealand, and to investigate the nature of institutional barriers and opportunities for change that have emerged since the early 2000s. The chapter reviews literature on political-institutional factors by considering how political and institutional power and finance have influenced transport policy making in Auckland.

The central-local relationships in urban transport planning

For cities, urban planning decides 'who gets what, when, where, why and how?' and includes political-institutional dimensions (Forester, 1982; Sandercock, 2004). These dimensions are characterised by unequal power relations between different actors (such as tiers of government, the private sector and community groups), and procedures that favour some actors over others. Central governments formulate transport legislation and policies and therefore set priorities and funding mechanisms (Banister, 2005; Curtis & Low, 2012), thereby setting *the parameters within which local authorities operate* (Laffin, 2009: 25). Hierarchies generate necessarily collaborative relationships between central and local governments (McGarvey, 2012) with local government following central government policy direction to receive funding for mega-development projects (Lee & Rivasplata, 2001). Planning practice works through national frameworks implemented by regional or local government (Friedmann, 1993; Laffin, 2009); planners facilitate government policy and make these policies acceptable to the public via community engagement (Sandercock, 2005; Gunder, 2010). As a result, urban planning cannot act outside the scope of politics and institutional contexts; planners should embrace the polit-ical context of planning as *'there is no way to avoid being political'*, and openly invite examination and debate concerning political and institutional values (Sandercock, 2004:136).

It follows that transport planning is also very political cum institutional (Curtis, 2005; Loh & Sami, 2013), with both central and local government exerting power over agenda-setting and funding. The political-institutional direction of transport planning and policies controls whether the focus of a city transport system will be automobile dependent or transit oriented (Vuchic, 1999). Historically, a posi-tive central-local relationship has been observed in road building (Merrill, 2012). For example, in Australia and the US, road building is mostly federally funded, whereas public transport is rarely funded in this way (Curtis, 2005). The 1956 USA Federal Aid Highway Act and Highway Revenue Act provided the policies and funding to build the Interstate Highway network (Headicar, 2009; Vigar, 2001). Federal government provided 90 per cent of funds, the remaining funds coming from state governments. Positive relationships ensued between central and state governments, generating cost–effective interstate networks. In the UK, the 1949 Special Roads Act allowed motorway building, which peaked in 1972 at 400 miles (643 kilometres) per year (Headicar, 2009). The Commonwealth government in Australia funded interstate highways in collaboration with State governments (Curtis, 2005).

After World War II (1939–45), transport policies in the UK, US and Australia favoured cars and motorway development, justifying investment on the basis of economic growth and societal freedom (Banister, 2005). These policies have resulted in a bias toward mobility, rather than accessibility for all members of society (Banister, 2005). Car manufacturing industries and oil and road construc-tion companies have lobbied central government to influence agenda-setting and decision-making processes to favour on-going road building and to give the car priority over other modes of transport (Gunder, 2002). Vasconcellos (1997) argues that economic prosperity, automobile subsidies, urban resource policies and public transport policies have all acted together to make transit impractical, whilst making the automobile 'highly demanded'. Indeed, Urry (2004: 27) describes the system of automobility as a world-wide *'self-organising autopoietic, non-linear system … which generates the preconditions for its own self-expansion'*. Central and local government transport policies and funding mechanisms are elements within that autopoietic system.

Policy and funding mechanisms have caused tensions between central and local governments in relation to transport policies. International research demonstrates that transport challenges can be overcome through fresh conceptualisation and empirical investigation of institutional challenges (Curtis & Low, 2012; Vigar, 2001) as '*institutions both limit intentional action, and make action possible by providing definitions of problems, solutions to those problems, the knowledge to implement those solutions and a corps of personnel bearing that knowledge*' (Curtis & Low, 2012: 49).

Path dependence & development – a theoretical framework

'Path dependence' explains how a particular solution to a policy issue becomes selected over time by probing the history, small events, coincidences and circumstances in an institutional context (Arthur, 1988; David, 1985; Greener, 2005; Kay, 2005; North, 1990; Pierson, 2004). In the literature, David (1985) uses path dependence to explain technological selection and growth. He explains how 'historical causes' favour the QWERTY keyboard even in the presence of better alternatives. Other examples include the selection of the narrow gauge of British railways, the petrol engine, colour television system and the 1950s programming language FORTRAN, which benefited from certain circumstances in history. Arthur (1988) applies the concept to the selection of physical locations of firms and patterns of urbanisation. He argues that city structure did not develop by economic determination alone but that there were events, coincidences and socio-political circumstances that shaped the current patterns of our cities. North (1990) employs the concept of path dependence in the sphere of governance and argued that the competition is not between technologies and economies but amongst institutions that make decisions. These authors make a strong case for the importance of history in identifying path dependence in technological evolution, economic rationality and policy processes.

However, some scholars criticise historical approaches. For example, Mahoney (2000: 507) argues that path dependence is defined within the vague terms 'history matters' or 'the past influences the future'. He stresses that identification of path dependence should involve tracing a given outcome to a particular set of historical events, and showing how these events are themselves contingent occurrences that cannot be explained on the basis of prior historical conditions. Goldstone (1998: 832) suggests that history leads to purely narrative explanations of particular sequences. Pierson (2004) argues that to assert that 'history matters' is insufficient, unless we are able to explore why, where and how. He stresses that systematically situating particular moments, including the present, in a temporal sequence of events and processes can greatly enrich our understanding of complex social dynamics. In summary, path dependence does not simply analyse what is being planned and implemented but also examines all the factors that influence the way in which policymakers conceive of and address problems. Thus the path dependence process is understood as intrinsically historical, with initial steps in a policy direction encouraging further movement along that path, with path stabilisation being conditioned by earlier choices, and changed bounded by institutional continuity (Imran & Matthews, 2011).

Low and Astle's (2009) and Curtis and Low's (2012) research on urban transport in Australian cities shows that structural changes, land use planning, access to funding, accountability frameworks and forums of other stakeholders in the roads and public transport sectors exhibit institutional path dependence. Imran's (2010) research in Pakistan found institutional, technical and discursive forms of path dependence in the development of sustainable urban transport. The studies cited show that urban transport policies become stable over time as a result of past decisions on infrastructure investment, funding systems, transport techniques and the mind-set of key decision makers concerning both the nature of the problem and its solution. Moreover they show that policy and funding mechanisms have caused tensions between central and local governments in many parts of the world. Local governments carry out land-use planning and set transport policies, but funding remains controlled by central government. Local governments have to raise their own funds for projects not supported by central government (McGarvey, 2012). Transport is important for local government because it provides local mobility solutions, which may not align with central government solutions and policies. For example, Curtis (2005) argues that the Australian federal government adopted a 'windscreen approach' to providing transport infrastructure, giving priority to cars, with other modes being afterthoughts. In contrast, Perth favours investment in walking, cycling and public transport. As a result, solutions delivered by one tier do not satisfy the expectations of the other (Curtis & Low, 2012). Similarly, Banister (2005) notes that Edinburgh, Scotland, is unable to achieve suitable transport solutions due in part to constraints in funding from central government. Positive central-local relations are found to have been generally absent in public transport investment.

In spite of this, a new and sustainable path is under development. For example, in recent years central governments in the UK, US and Australia have become aware of the unsustainable nature of transportation networks and have formulated responses: in the UK, the Traffic Management Act 2004 and the Planning Policy Guidelines 7 (PPG); in Australia, the Australian National Charter of Integrated Land Use and Transport Planning 2003 (Curtis, 2005); and in the US, the Safe, Accountable, Flexible, Efficient Transportation Equity Act 2005, showing a significant move towards transit investment and land use and transport integration. This change toward a multi-modal approach has also come about due to the recognition by central governments that cities are economically, socially and environmentally important at a national level, and politically influential (Hull, 2008). This is an exciting time in history when the path-dependent nature of transport policies is being challenged and a new policy path is emerging.

Transport planning and policies in Auckland

According to the 2013 census, approximately 85 per cent of the New Zealand population reside in urban areas. Auckland, with a population of 1.5 million, is New Zealand's largest city; it is located in the north of the North Island (see Figure 7.1).

The population of Auckland is growing rapidly, with estimates suggesting that by 2033 two million people will live in Auckland. Auckland is vital to New Zealand's economy, and is the hub of the service sector. Currently, Auckland contributes 35 per cent of the nation's GDP (MBIE, 2015). In the period from 2009 to 2014, Auckland's economy grew by 25 per cent, well above the national average of 22 per cent. Since 2010, a single metropolitan council, the Auckland Council (AC) and its subsidiary council-controlled organisation, Auckland Transport (AT), are responsible for transport planning in Auckland. The Auckland Plan (2012-2042), New Zealand's first ever spatial plan, states an aspiration for the city to become the world's most liveable city by promoting sustainable transport as a central component of liveability. Often, it has been argued that Auckland's geography and population growth push the city into a pattern of creating linear motorways and public transport corridors (MoT, 2016), and that development spreads at relatively low densities in suburbs (19 people per hectare) across a visually spectacular landscape. The following sections investigate these assertions through critical historical lenses.

Figure 7.1: Location of Auckland. Source: MBIE (2015: 20).

Before WWII: Public transport based transport policies

Auckland transport and its institutional structures have evolved in the 175 plus years since the signing of New Zealand's founding document, the Treaty of Waitangi in 1840. The initial development of suburban Auckland was constrained to areas reached by the early rail and tram systems, which became symbols of municipal pride, superiority, economic growth and progress (Bloomfield, 1975; Watson 1996). From 1884, Auckland City Council (ACC) regulated the tram network and placed strict terms and conditions on frequency, hours of operation, and fares. The trams became popular due to the fast, smooth and relatively cheap service they offered, contributing to the first 'peak hour' in the city (Stewart, 1973). Tram overcrowding was addressed by introducing bus services, ultimately creating tram versus bus competition. Public transport thus supported outward but compact suburban expansion (Stewart, 1973).

Auckland's tram network was electrified in 1902, improving the service and further encouraging outward urban expansion, and ultimately increasing adjacent land values. Auckland's tram network was developed further chiefly as a means to increase land values, the benefit of which was captured by the developers, the tramway company and to a lesser extent the government (Bloomfield, 1975; Dahms, 1980; Hickman, 2003; Sinclair, 1999). Auckland's publicly-owned trams made a profit until the early 1950s (except in the economic recession of the 1930s). Huge profits were made during World War II because petrol for private vehicles was rationed and rubber tyres were in short supply (Bush, 1971). Moreover, the Motor Omnibus Traffic Act 1926 and the 1928 Auckland Transport Board Act allowed freer movement of the publicly-owned trams by compelling buses to move to different streets. These Acts aimed to reduce wasteful competition, maintain minimum safety levels and provide timetabling and fare guidelines, but also introduced subsidies for private bus operators (McDonald, 1974; McLeod, 1966).

After WWII – Road-based transport policies

By the middle of the 20th century, Auckland's public transport network (rail, tram and buses) was run predominately by the public sector (except some private bus and ferry services). In addition to the total monopoly of tram and rail services, in 1954 bus services were 60 per cent publicly owned (McDonald, 1974). During the 1950s, public transport patronage averaged over 100 million passenger trips per annum, comparable to figures for many successful Australian and Canadian cities (data extracted from information available at the Auckland Transport website). Furthermore, during the 1950s New Zealand Rail provided its own bus fleet to act as feeder services to and from the rail network. Initially, rail and bus integration worked well, but over time rail patronage dropped due to increasing car ownership (McDonald, 1974). Similar losses of patronage and profit were experienced by the local authority bus networks, due to fare increases on the one hand and the large number of concession fares offered on the other hand (McLeod, 1966; Stewart, 1973).

Declining patronage was also due to the failure to progress the *Ministry of Works 1946 Rail Plan* to expand and electrify the rail network. This plan was abandoned in 1954, coinciding with the introduction of the Auckland Regional Planning Authority's (ARPA) *1955 First Master Transportation Plan for Auckland*, which changed the city's transport focus from public transport to private vehicle travel. This plan recommended the construction of an inner ring road around the CBD, fed by express urban motorways, and the building of extensive parking facilities within the inner city. Through the further recommendation to abandon rail upgrades until justified by future population growth, this plan almost exclusively favoured private over public transport and active travel alternatives (Harris, 2005; Mees & Dodson,

2007). Consequently, the Auckland rail system was not electrified or expanded during the 1950s. These decisions coincided with withdrawal of the popular and well-patronised electric tram network. Following this change in transport planning direction, patronage levels per capita started to drop despite continuous population growth (Mees & Dodson, 2007).

Auckland's second attempt to electrify and expand the rail network was made in the Auckland Regional Authority's (ARA) *1965 Regional Transit Plan* and *1967 Regional Master Plan*. A rapid-rail scheme was proposed in these plans in conjunction with coordinated bus services. However, the motorway network proposed in the 1965 *Comprehensive Transportation Plan* superseded the rapid-rail scheme. The Mayor of Auckland City Council, Sir Dove-Myer Robinson, believed rapid rail was the only way to reverse the extreme decline of over 105 million public transport trips per annum in 1956 to 45 million trips per annum in 1969 (Edgar, 2012). He worked with the National (1960-1972) and Labour (1972-1975) governments to get them to commit to rapid rail. Increasing petrol prices due to the effect of the 1973 worldwide oil crisis on New Zealand made private vehicle travel expensive and strengthened Robinson's arguments (Dravitzki & Lester, 2007). However, the National government (1975-1984) dropped this project in light of the *1976 Comprehensive Transportation Plan*, which marginalised public transport development in favour of motorways (ACC, 1998).

In 1983, the *ARA Rail Report* seriously considered replacing rail services with buses. However, this proposal was postponed due to strong public opposition. The 1986 *Operational Plan for Auckland Urban Transport* focused mainly on extending motorways, boosted by the establishment of Transit New Zealand and Transfund to direct and fund major state highway developments, including urban motorways in Auckland. The 1989 *Transport Licensing Act* privatised Auckland's bus and rail network in the name of economic rationalisation and free market ideology. Throughout the 1990s private companies reduced and removed inefficient and uneconomic routes, resulting in a further decline in public transport patronage.

The 21st century transition to sustainable transport

The decline in public transport patronage and an increase in road congestion compelled planners in Auckland, and New Zealand more generally, to reconsider their policy options in the 21st century. First, the *ARC Regional Policy Statement, Regional Land Transport Strategy and Regional Growth Strategy* produced in 1999 and 2000 sought to refocus Auckland around a rapid transit system (using bus, light, or heavy rail as appropriate) and aimed at reducing car travel in the longer term.

The *New Zealand Transport Strategy* (NZTS) 2002, released by the Labour government (1999-2008), was the first comprehensive document, post 2000, to recognise all modes and users of transport. Sustainability was promised through improving public transport, reducing congestion, providing alternatives to the private car and providing infrastructure for walking and cycling. A new patronage funding system for public passenger transport was suggested to improve access and mobility; and the government purchased the Auckland regional rail network in 2002, with the 'longer term goal of reducing car travel' (p. 28).

NZTS 2002 was updated in 2008 and the development of public transport targets to 2040 was supported by an accompanying *Government Policy Statement* (GPS). *NZTS 2008* determined that a public transport focus would help alleviate congestion in Auckland, justifying central and local government investment in the metropolitan rail network and the country's first Bus Rapid Transit (BRT) system, locally called the Northern Busway. It is estimated that approximately 5.7 million passengers travelled on the city's rail network in 2007, an increase from 2.3 million in 2000. The *GPS 2008* allocation of funding placed particular emphasis on reducing travel by single occupancy vehicles (SOVs).

In concert with national-level transport strategising, the Auckland *Regional Land Strategy 2005* focuses on the integration of public transport services by introducing integrated ticketing and fares for different transport modes. The *Rail Development Plan 2006* refocused on rail-based public transport in Auckland. This Plan represented the first time in more than 40 years that rail had been seen as '*extremely efficient at moving people*' and as the '*essential backbone of the Rapid Transit Network*' (ARTA, 2006: 6). ARTA aimed to have 30 million trips per annum by rail by 2030, concluding that electrifying the rail network and purchasing electrical multiple unit trains was the right long-term strategy for Auckland. To overcome funding gaps for public transport projects, the *Auckland Transport Plan 2007* proposed a regional fuel tax for Auckland.

A centre-right National-led government assumed office after the 2008 election. The 2009 GPS reflects the government's priorities for land transport, namely economic productivity and growth, with '*investment in the SH [state highway] network especially the Roads of National Significance (RoNS) as a key to the efficient movement of freight and people*' (MOT, 2009: 11). Regardless of the focus on RoNS, government did not cut funding to public transport in Auckland because it saw public transport as critical in reducing congestion and contributing to economic growth, at least in the metropolitan cities. Auckland received a large proportion of the 30 per cent increase in nationwide funding for public transport services revealed in the 2009 GPS. Most of that investment was to be in rail rolling stock and services.

In 2009, Auckland underwent New Zealand's most extensive local government reform in two decades to become a 'super city' under one unitary authority – Auckland Council – with seven Council Controlled Organisations (CCOs), including Auckland Transport (AT). The largest CCO, AT, is responsible for providing the region's transport infrastructure and services, using about half of the Council's rate-take to manage NZ$ 14.5 billion of assets, representing significant budget-spending power. The first 'metropolitan' Mayoral election was held in October, 2010. It was won by Len Brown, a left-leaning politician who campaigned for better public transport, including mega rail projects. New Zealand's first spatial plan – the Auckland Plan – was prepared under the new super-city Mayor's leadership. The Auckland Plan sets out a hierarchy of development strategies for Auckland from 2012 to 2042. The overarching goal is presented as the *vision* of making Auckland the world's most liveable city by 2042. The plan acknowledges the regional transport system is 'overburdened and inefficient' (p. 313), due to years of under-investment in public transport, and to settlement patterns; both compounded by decision-making in the previous half century. It is argued that to lessen congestion, accommodate future business and population growth, and complete the existing road and rail network, require a move to a single transport system, a shift to public transport, and the maximising of the environmental and health benefits of walking and cycling. To solve Auckland's transport problems the Plan proposes projects that include the City Rail Link (CRL) (a 3.5km underground rail link in central Auckland), the Auckland-Manukau Eastern Transport Initiative (AMETI) and East-West Link, and an additional Waitematā Harbour crossing (including a rail link).

Discussion – path dependence to path development

Critical juncture leading to path dependent policies

The previous section provides a historical overview of transport planning and policy in Auckland. Historically, public transport was the backbone of transport policies in Auckland. Despite the competition that has existed between buses, trams, and rail services, Auckland public transport patronage has in the past been comparable to that of world-leading cities. However, trends changed following the implementation of the 1955 *Transportation Plan for Auckland* and the 1965 *Comprehensive Transportation Plan*; this era was thus a critical juncture (Imran & Matthews, 2011) which has shaped present-day transport policy in Auckland. In the period from 1955 to 1965 Auckland could have improved its train and tram system or taken a new path of motorway network development. The city chose the latter, largely due to expert and government bias for 'modernising transport system' (Gunder, 2002). The implementation of modernising the transport system narrowed paths of alternative transport, and favoured motorway development. This road development path stabilised due to the formulation of an alternative set of policies and economic, mobility, safety, consumer, funding and environmental discourses (Imran & Pearce, 2015a) which persisted into the 21st century, when a new critical juncture started to emerge.

Critical juncture in motion leading to path development policies

Disruption of path dependent policies in order to facilitate the generation of a new critical juncture requires the resetting of policy goal hierarchies in political 'path development' (Torfing, 2001; Stele, 2011). The Labour-led government (1999-2008) received support on matters of confidence and supply from the Green Party. The *New Zealand Transport Strategy* 2002 was the first comprehensive document post

2000 to reset policy goals by focusing on sustainable transport to promote resilience and flexibility. Sustainability was promised by improving public transport, reducing congestion, providing alternatives to the private car, and providing infrastructure for walking and cycling. The focus on sustainability was strengthened by the Land Transport Management Act (LTMA) 2003, and later the Public Transport Management Act (PTMA) 2008 and the formulation of specific targets in the NZTS 2008. Central government policy changes appeared to have a positive impact on Auckland's transport, particularly following the buy-back of Auckland's regional rail (which had been privatised in 1993 when the National Party was in government), refurbishment of Britomart CBD transport interchange, and the preparation of the Rail Development Plan.

Although Mees and Dodson (2007) call these policies Labour–Green sustainability rhetoric, we argue that these initiatives were launched against the backdrop of pre-existing path dependent transport policies. It is clear that transformative change requires the dismantling of road-based transport policies, but invoking sustainability in transport policies was a first step towards undermining the path dependence of road-based transport policies. This positioning had an effect on the subsequent right-leaning National-led government (2008-current), which did not halt public transport projects (including Auckland Rail electrification, the integrated fare system, and the reorganisation of bus services) in Auckland.

Despite central government's commitment to RoNS, local government governance reform has strengthened the political voice of Auckland. The Auckland Plan, at least on paper, strengthens the alternative sustainability-focused path of transport planning by proposing three mega public transport projects. Gunder (2014) is critical of the Auckland Plan, declaring these projects 'impossible fantasy'. Similarly, Imran and Pearce (2015b) argue that attention should be given to small fixes rather than mega public transport projects. However, there is no doubt that these projects (especially prioritising the CRL), in association with strong local political leadership, have compelled central government to change the policy direction followed since the mid-1960s of not funding Auckland's rail network extension.

In June 2013, the Prime Minister, John Key, for the first time showed support for the $NZ2.5 billion CRL, a project necessary to increase the capacity of Auckland's rail-based public transport system. This support marks the first real shift in central government's vision for Auckland's transport since 1955, when central government started investing in the Auckland motorway system, and comes 45 years after the then Prime Minister, Keith Holyoake, first announced support for a rail project in October 1969. The central government wants to delay the CRL until 2020, suggesting that only by then will there be enough patronage (20 million trips per year) to justify it. However, Auckland rail patronage increased by 23 per cent in 2015 and reached a total of over 15 million trips per year. It therefore appears that the patronage target of 20 million will be achieved earlier than 2020 (data extracted from AC website).

Torfing (2001: 277) argues that *'political attempts to reform existing policies often fail to bring about substantial change … [and when] they succeed, the new policy is heavily influenced by the pre-existing policy path'*. In Auckland's case, this research does not deny Torfing's (2001) findings and Mees and Dodson's (2007) claim concerning green rhetoric, but it does argue that cracks in the old policy path have become evident and that a new critical juncture is emerging. Like the first critical juncture, the new critical juncture, which supports a sustainable transport path, will take one to two decades to mature. A new critical juncture also depends on small events, coincidences and circumstances in an institutional context (North, 1990; Pierson, 2004), which in the case of Auckland have occurred continuously. As referred to earlier, the sustainability focus of the Labour-led government's NZTS, the adoption of a rail-based transport vision for Auckland, strong regional leadership emerging from the local government governance reforms and 'conditional' funding commitments by a right-leaning central government have all occurred in the first decade of the 21st century, – and are all either events, coincidences or circumstances which could lead to future institutional change. Moreover, Auckland's transport path development is not happening in a vacuum. Increasing global commitments to climate change mitigation after the IPCC's Fifth Assessment Report, new Sustainable Development Goals to expanding public transport, the introduction of new technologies (smart phones etc., see Chapter 13) that reduce the need to travel (Lyons 2014), and the effects of globalisation bring new creative working ideas to the city and impact Auckland's new path development.

This new policy path is emerging within complex interactions between central and local government and the long-standing traditions of road-based transport planning. This new path is weak and does not guarantee a sustainable transport future, especially in the absence of institutional mechanisms and a deep-seated will to fund public transport projects. To make institutional change more stable, public transport should develop 'instrument constituencies', as happened in the case of road development policies (Burke, 2016). In the past, road regimes initiated fuel taxes, vehicle registration and other fees to secure a stable funding mechanism to build and extend motorways. Later, road advocates built coalitions with developers, logistics operators, oil producing and road construction companies and motoring associations to continue building mega road projects. One-off CRL funding will not guarantee that the current critical juncture will bring permanent change to Auckland; for change to be permanent, innovative ways of funding public transport (such as value capture) will have to be developed.

The predecessor of AC suggested a regional fuel tax, but that was later rejected by the central government. A fuel tax for funding public transport projects is not a smart idea in the light of the fact that vehicle kilometre travel (VKT) is declining in New Zealand. Further, that government has set a target of converting 90% of the vehicle fleet into electric vehicles by 2025 will ultimately reduce fuel revenue in the future. The central government and the Auckland Council launched a transport alignment project for a long-term strategic approach to transport development in

Auckland and it appears to be the right time to reach consensus on new funding mechanisms for the development of public transport. Moreover, a broader and proactive constituency should be established including new public-transport users (such as immigrants, youth and the elderly), community groups (such as TransportBlog, Generation Zero, the Campaign for Better Transport, and the Public Transport Users Association), and business groups (the Chamber of Commerce and the Property Council NZ). These are all ways in which public transport polices are becoming permanent methods of meeting the demands of a future Auckland.

Conclusion

This chapter uses path dependence and development as a theoretical framework providing a structured approach with which to explain the nature of transport planning and policies in Auckland. The Auckland case study is significant for New Zealand as, due to its size, transport planning challenges, and unique governance structure, it has developed an entirely new relationship with central government since 2010. The research finds that events such as replacement of trams with buses and policy directions such as selection of motorway projects over rapid rail in the mid-1950s to mid-1960s locked Auckland's transport policies into a road-based paradigm. However, this road-based transport policy paradigm has been challenged since the early 2000s, with subsequent events, policies and institutional restructuring all shaping a new critical juncture in favour of sustainable transport. In spite of this emerging critical juncture, transport policies to deliver greater sustainable transport outcomes have largely been placed on hold due to resistance from path-dependent transport policies that promote RoNS.

It is unlikely that institutional change will occur quickly, and without further resistance, unless two key opportunities of transition to a low carbon transport system in Auckland are explored. First, local political leadership is important to generate constructive debate in resisting carbon-intensive policies and in setting a new policy direction toward a low carbon mobility future. Local leadership should be strengthened by public transport funding autonomy at regional or metropolitan level to deliver a low carbon transport system and to develop public transport policy instruments and constituencies. Second, an integrated relationship between transport and land use is fundamental in promoting sustainable transport in the 21st century. National level policy guidelines, clear mechanisms, evaluation criteria and procedures are required to achieve land use and transport integration for low carbon transition in New Zealand and beyond.

Acknowledgements

We would like to acknowledge the financial support of the Royal Society of New Zealand, Marsden Fast-Start Project No MAU1208 for this research project. Some parts of this chapter have been presented previously in conference papers co-authored with Teryll Lepper and Lee Matthews.

References

Arthur, B. (1988). Urban Systems and Historical Path Dependence, in, Ausubel, J. & Herman, R. (Eds.), *Cities and their Vital Systems: Infrastructure, Past, Present and Future*, Washington, National Academy Press, 85-97.

Auckland Regional Transport Authority (ARTA). (2006). *Rail Development Plan 2006*. Auckland.

Banister, D. (2005). *Unsustainable Transport: City transport in the new century*. London: Spon Press.

Bloomfield, G. (1975). Urban tramways in New Zealand 1862-1964, *New Zealand Geographer*, **31**(2), 99-123.

Burke, M. (2016). Problems and prospects for public transport planning in Australian cities. *Built Environment*, **42**(1), 37-54.

Bush, G. (1971). *Decently and in Order: The centennial history of the Auckland City Council*. Auckland, London: Collins Bros and Co Ltd.

Curtis, C. (2005). The windscreen world of land use transport integration: Experiences from Perth. *Town Planning Review*, **76**(4), 423-453.

Curtis, C. & Low, N. (2012). *Institutional Barriers to Sustainable Transport*. Farnham: Ashgate.

Dahms, F. (1980). Urban passenger transport and population distribution in Auckland: 1860-1961, *New Zealand Geographer*, **36**(1), 2-10.

David, P. (1985). Clio and the economics of QWERTY, *The American Economic Review*, **75**(2): 332-337.

Dravitzki, V. & Lester, T. (2007). *Can we Live by Public Transport Alone? Transport: The Next 50 Years*, Christchurch, New Zealand.

Edgar, J. (2012). *Urban Legend*, Auckland, Hachette.

Forester, J. (1982). Planning in the face of power. *Journal, American Planning Association*, **48**(1), 67-80.

Friedmann, J. (1993). Toward a non-euclidian mode of planning. *Journal of the American Planning Association*, **59**(4), 482.

Goldstone, J. (1998). Initial conditions, general laws, path dependence and explanation in historical sociology, *American Journal of Sociology* **104**(3), 829-845.

Greener, I. (2005). The potential of path dependence in political studies, *Politics* **25**(1), 62-72.

Gunder, M. (2002). Auckland's motorway system: A New Zealand genealogy of imposed automotive progress 1946-66. *Urban Policy and Research*, **20**(2), 129-142.

Gunder, M. (2010). Planning as the ideology of (neoliberal) space, *Planning Theory*, **9**(4), 298-314.

Gunder, M. (2014). Fantasy in planning organisations and their agency: The promise of being at home in the world, *Urban Policy & Research*, **32**(1), 1-15.

Harris, C. (2005). Slow train coming: The New Zealand State changes its mind about Auckland Transit, 1949-56, *Urban Policy and Research*, **23**(1), 37-55.

Headicar, P. (2009). *Transport Policy and Planning in Great Britain.* London: Routledge.

Hickman, H. (2003). Riding the Rails *New Zealand Memories, 3*, 40-45.

Hull, A. (2008). Policy integration: What will it take to achieve more sustainable transport soluations in cities?, *Transport Policy,* **15**(2), 94-103.

Imran, M. (2010) .*Institutional Barriers to Sustainable Urban Transport in Pakistan.* Oxford, Oxford University Press.

Imran, M. & Matthews L. (2011). Discursive path dependence: Keeping the supremacy of road-based urban transport planning in Auckland, *Road & Transport Research,* **20**(1), 52-68.

Imran, M. & Pearce, J. (2015a). Discursive barriers to sustainable transport in New Zealand cities, *Urban Policy & Research,* **33**(4), 1-24.

Imran, M. & Pearce, J. (2015b). Auckland's first spatial plan: Ambitious aspirations or furthering the status quo?, *Cities,* **45**, 18-28.

Kay, A. (2005). A critique of the use of path dependency in policy studies, *Public Administration,* **83**(3), 553-571.

Laffin, M. (2009). Central-Local relations in an era of governance: Towards a new research agenda, *Local Government Studies, 35*(1), 21-37.

Lee, W. & Rivasplata, R. (2001). Metropolitan transportation planning in the 1990s: comparisons and contrasts in New Zealand, Chile and California. *Transport Policy,* **8**(1), 47-61.

Loh, G. & Sami, N. (2013). Death of a planning department: Challenges for regionalism in a weak mandate state. *Land Use Policy, 32*(0), 39-49.

Low, N. & Astle, R. (2009). Path dependence in urban transport: An institutional analysis of urban passenger transport in Melbourne, Australia 1956-2006, *Transport Policy,* **16** (2): 47-58.

Lyons, G. (2014). *Future Demand.* Wellington: NZ Ministry of Transport.

Mahoney, J. (2000). Path dependence in Historical Sociology, *Theory and Society* **29**, 507-548.

McDonald, T. (1974). *Urban Transportation and Land Use: A Study for the Urban Public Passenger Transport Council* Wellington, New Zealand Institute of Economic Research Incorporated.

McGarvey, N. (2012). Expectations, assumptions and realities: Scottish local government post-devolution. *British Journal of Politics & International Relations,* **14**(1), 153-174.

McLeod, N. (1966). *The Policies of Transport in New Zealand: A History of the Policies of Several Governments Towards the Transport Industry from 1918 to Present Day,* Unpublished Master of Arts in History Thesis, Victoria University, Wellington.

Mees, P. & Dodson, J. (2007). Backtracking Auckland?: Technical and communicative reason in metropolitan transport planning. *International Planning Studies,* **12**(1), 35-53.

Merrill, S. (2012). Looking forward to the past: London Underground's 150th anniversary. *Journal of Transport History,* **33**(2), 243-252.

Ministry of Business, Innovation and Employment (MBIE) (2015). *Regional Economic Activity Report*. Wellington: MBIE.

Ministry of Transport (MOT). (2009). *Government Policy Statement on Land Transport Funding 2009/10-2018/19*. Wellington.

Ministry of Transport (MOT) (2016). *Auckland Transport Alignment Project: Foundation Report*. Wellington: MoT.

North, D. (1990). *Institutions, Institutional Change and Economic Performance*, Cambridge: Cambridge University Press.

Pierson, P. (2004). *Politics in Time: History, Institutions and Social Analysis*, Princeton, Princeton University Press.

Sandercock, L. (2004). Towards a planning imagination for the 21st century. *Journal of the American Planning Association,* **70**(2), 133-141.

Sandercock, L. (2005). The democratization of planning: Elusive or illusory? *Planning Theory & Practice,* **6**(4), 437-441.

Sinclair, K. (1999). *A History of New Zealand*, Auckland, Penguin Books.

Stele, W. (2011). Strategy-making for sustainability: An institutional learning approach to transformative planning practice, *Planning Theory & Practice*, **12**(2), 205-211.

Stewart, G. (1973). *The End of the Penny Section: A History of Urban Transport in New Zealand*, Wellington, A.H & A.W Reed.

Torfing, J. (2001). Path dependent Danish welfare reforms: The contribution of the new institutionalisms to understanding evolutionary change, *Scandinavian Political Studies,* **24**(4), 277-309.

Urry, J. (2004). The 'system' of automobility. *Theory, Culture and Society,* **21**(4-5), 25-39.

Vasconcellos, A. (1997). The demand for cars in developing countries. *Transportation Research Part A,* **31**(3), 245-258.

Vigar, G. (2001). *The Politics of Mobility: Transport, the environment and public policy*. New York: Spoon Press.

Vuchic, V. (1999). *Transportation for Livable Cities*. New Brunswick: Center for Urban Policy Research.

Watson, J. (1996). *Links: A History of Transport and New Zealand Society*, Wellington, Ministry of Transport.

8 The Structures of Mobility and Challenges of Low Carbon Transitions in India

Rutul Joshi

Faculty of Planning and Centre for Urban Equity, CEPT University, Ahmedabad, India.

Yogi Joseph and Vivek Chandran

Centre for Urban Equity, CEPT University, Ahmedabad, India.

Introduction

Sustainable mobility describes all forms of transport which minimise fuel consumption and carbon emissions by minimising the need to travel (Knoflacher, 2007; Banister, 2008), and includes modes such as shared or public transport, walking and cycling (Agarwal & Zimmerman, 2008). Knoflacher (2007) argues that the hypothesis of traditional urban transport planning 'growth of mobility' and 'travel time saving by increasing speed' end up creating more transport, environmental and socio-economic problems all over the world. The traditional Indian city was oriented towards the use of low carbon and low-energy transport modes like walking and cycling. High rates of economic growth and rising household incomes in the last decade and a half contributed to the emergence of a new, carbon-intensive mobility pattern centred on the automobile. The growth in transport-related emissions presents a large challenge for India, particularly in achieving a low carbon society (Schipper *et al.*, 2009; Woodcock *et al.*, 2009). In this chapter, the growth and domination of high-carbon, motorised transport in Indian cities is presented as a major challenge, and opportunities and challenges by way of efforts to respond to growing car-dependence in India are examined.

Non-motorised transport (NMT) modes, including cycles, pedal rickshaws, and animal-driven carts, were once the dominant way of moving around in Indian and other Asian cities (Pucher *et al.*, 2007). Replogle (1991) estimated in the 1990s that

NMT accounted for 25-80% of trips in Asian cities, significantly higher than other parts of the world. A Government of India-sponsored study (WSA & MoUD, 2008), based on a sample of 87 Indian cities estimated that the share of cycling declined from an average of 30 percent in 1994 to 11 percent by 2008. The same study also reported a 12 percent rise in the share of personal modes of transport and declining public transport trips in the same time period. These are not encouraging signs from the point of view of reducing emissions or encouraging sustainable transportation, as noted by National Transport Policy Development Committee (NTPDC) working group on Urban Transport (NTDPC, 2012). Consequently, rising numbers of fatalities, overall congestion, and poor air quality have affected the quality of life in Indian cities (Badami, 2009; Mohan, 2013). Lack of integration between land use and transportation, the absence of an enabling environment for NMT modes and poor transportation demand management (TDM) have raised questions over Indian cities' preparedness to transition to a low carbon future.

The Government has made attempts to address the many negative externalities of rising motorisation in the last decade. An example of this is the framing of the National Urban Transport Policy that puts people, rather than vehicles at the centre stage of cities (MoUD, 2006). This landmark change in policy was followed by other interventions including the adoption of bus-based and rail-based mass rapid transit systems in several Indian cities like Delhi, Mumbai, Chennai, Bengaluru, Hyderabad and Kochi, among others. However, these interventions have been criticised for their fragmented response to the problem (Mahadevia *et al.*, 2013). This chapter argues that the translation of progressive policies into action has been marred by confusion and ad-hocism which has harmed the cause of low carbon transitions even further. It traces how an early post-independence obsession with modernity drove cities away from a low carbon sustainable model to a more energy-intensive model. A narrow re-imagining of roads as mere thoroughfares combined with borrowed motifs of modernity led to a culture of automobility that prioritises personal mobility over other low carbon alternatives. The chapter argues that despite the many challenges facing the prospect of low carbon transitions, recent government interventions in the form of policies and programmes present some hope.

Urban planning in India prioritises motorised traffic

Ancient Indian cities were only large enough to be easily traversed on foot or other modes like animal carts. Together with the lack of modern modes of intra-city travel seen today, this led to a limitation of the size of ancient Indian cities (Schlingloff, 2014). Colonial settlements such as those of Fort St. George (Madras) and Fort William (Calcutta) were compact on account of the limitations of transport modes in the seventeenth and eighteenth century, respectively (Ghose, 1960).

The planning of New Delhi by Edwin Lutyens in the 1920s was considered by some to be a landmark event in the history of modern urban planning in India (Gordon, 2006). However, notwithstanding the symbolism in the adoption of local building materials, the plan had little in common with the traditional Indian city (Volwahsen, 2002). Unlike the typical chaotic intersection of roads, New Delhi was designed with wide roads accompanied by ceremonial pathways and monuments. This was accompanied by strict zoning and adoption of a low-density approach to residential settlements. This new urban form not only contradicted traditional Indian use of road space but also disadvantaged NMT whilst prioritising motorised transport.

The problem with the idea of wide motorised streets as an integral part of the modern Indian city is that it delegitimises other traditional low carbon uses of the street as not being modern enough (Joshi & Joseph, 2015; Anjaria, 2014). For example, pedal rickshaws and cyclists are often victimised in Indian cities and barred from using many streets on account of their low speed 'causing congestion' (Roychowdhury et al., 2013; Bandyopadhyay & Chakraborty, 2013). Meanwhile, automobiles are encouraged to consume road space. This duplicity in allowing 'higher' modes like cars to ply while discouraging the use of low carbon modes (e.g. cycles and pedal rickshaws) is symptomatic of a system that prioritises motorisation.

Existing conditions of urban transport

Indian cities have seen massive growth and spatial expansion over the last few decades (MGI, 2010). With expanding city boundaries, trip lengths and trip times increased, creating the desire for 'faster' options of mobility. As a result, private modes of transport became more desirable over modes that were low carbon and low energy.

Mode share

Figure 8.1 presents the mode share among cities with varying population sizes. This data is a compilation of various studies, using different methodologies, and hence, a large variation is observed between cities of similar category and across categories (WSA & MoUD, 2008). Broad patterns reveal that in cities with larger populations, the share of NMT decreases, PT increases, and personal motorised modes decreases. The share of NMT modes reduces by as much as half. While the share of personal motorised modes decreases in cities with large populations, that of cars alone increases to levels greater than that of two-wheelers.

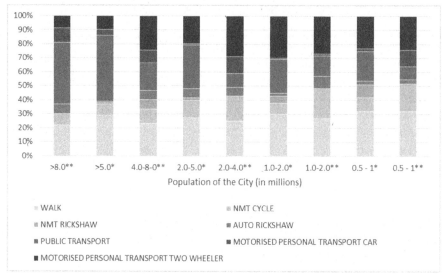

Figure 8.1: Mode share in Indian cities by city population. Source: *Tiwari (2011) and ** WSA (2008).

Increase in urban transport demand

The two pan-India studies (WSA & MoUD, 2008; RITES, 1994), indicate that except for the largest cities, mean trip length has not risen within the same population categories. However, the challenge in the provision of sustainable transport alternatives has been the sheer growth in the number of cities with large populations and added population growth in large cities. During the last decade, India's urban population grew by 91 million to reach 377 million. While half this growth was in cities with less than 0.5 million population (adding 174 new cities with populations between 0.1 and 0.5 million), the other half of the growth was in 97 cities with populations above 0.5 million (Census of India, 2011b). Increased transport demand in Indian cities is not just a result of rising incomes, but also due to expanding city sizes. This translates into longer trip lengths for a greater proportion of the population.

City Category	Population (million)	Cities in 2001	Cities in 2011	Urban Population 2001	Urban Population 2011	Trip Length (in km) WSA, 2007	Trip Length (in km) RITES, 1994
1	< 0.5	220*	372*	49%	49%	2.1- 3.0	3.70 - 4.38
2	0.5 - 1.0	39	44	9%	8%	2.6 - 4.5	4.38 - 4.86
3	1.0 - 2.0	22	34	9%	12%	4.1 - 5.5	4.86 - 5.51
4	2.0 - 4.0	6	11	5%	8%	5.0- 6.0	5.51- 6.40
5	4.0 - 8.0	4	3	7%	5%	6.1- 8.6	6.40 - 7.62
6	> 8.0	3	5	21%	18%	9.6- 11.9	7.62 - 8.32
Totals		294	468	286 million	377 million		

Table 8.1: Trip Length of cities with varying populations. Source: Census of India (2011); WSA (2007); RITES (1994). Note: * Cities with population between 0.1 million and 5 million.

Non-motorised transit modes

NMT is the predominant mode of transport used in India, with 47% share of all work trips. Walking is used for 30% of all work trips while the remaining 17% of trips are made using bicycles (Census of India, 2011a). Although NMT is the predominant mode of transport, cities rarely provide adequate infrastructure to support it. Unobstructed, continuous sidewalks of adequate widths are rare in Indian cities. Consequently, it is common to see pedestrians walking on the vehicular carriageway, and with cyclists, struggling to negotiate the space between curb-side parking and moving vehicles. It is also common in Indian cities to find students travelling to school on cycles (Tiwari, 2011; Badami, 2009; Mohan, 2013). However, rates of cycling to school have declined with rising safety concerns. NMT modes, especially cycling, have also become less desirable as they suffer from a loss of image owing to its association with being a 'poor man's' mode (Joshi & Joseph, 2015).

There is, however, a growing realisation of the benefits of NMT, and the role of sidewalks and cycling infrastructure in facilitating it. NMT is gradually being seen as part of the solution to achieve a low carbon, low-energy mobility with associated health benefits. This change in infrastructure allocation can be seen in cities such as Delhi, Chennai, and Bangalore, where several streets and neighbourhoods are being redesigned to prioritise pedestrians (Narayanan, 2014). Cities such as Ahmedabad and Pune have created several kilometres of cycling lanes, however, their efficacy is questionable (Datey et al., 2012). Citizen initiatives such as Raahgiri and car-free days have also helped raise awareness among citizens, to aspire towards a NMT-friendly public realm (ANI, 2014).

Public transport modes

PT services are responsible for 21% of all work trips in India (Census of India, 2011a). They are predominantly bus-based, with few rail-based options, and fewer cities with water-based transport options (Singh, 2005). City bus services, provided by public and private operators, are common in most Indian cities, carrying 15% of all work trips in India (Census of India, 2011a). Smaller cities often rely on small private bus operators in the absence of publicly owned bus service. These private buses are allowed to function through loose government regulations.

While populations in metropolitan cities in India increased over the last two decades, bus fleets experienced depletion in the very time period they should have expanded in order to deal with growing demand (WSA & MoUD, 2008). State governments (who control the financial autonomy of cities) and city governments under-invested in PT making them inefficient over the years. As a result, poor reliability of service, poor maintenance and overcrowding became common (Badami & Haider, 2007). A small number of metropolitan cities (e.g. Bengaluru) have been able to raise the standard of bus services, but through higher fares. As a result, PT becomes unattainable for lower socio-economic groups, who are most dependent on them for access to livelihood opportunities. The unmet demand for cheap, frequent and reliable PT services in Indian cities gives rise to Intermediate Public Transit (IPT) services that try to address the deficit.

The commuter rail service run by the Indian Railways is another transport option in cities with rail connectivity, especially in Mumbai, where it is the largest PT mode. However, mass adoption of commuter rail in India has been rare except where the city's geography and existing spread of rail networks were inherently advantageous (Acharya, 2000). Metro rail and the Bus Rapid Transit System (BRTS) have been the most common Mass Rapid Transit (MRT) services introduced in India. Driven by national policies and schemes, the last decade witnessed a healthy growth in rapid transit services. Nine cities have a partly functional or under construction metro rail, with a total service coverage of 300 kilometres of which a majority (208 kilometres) is in the Delhi NCR region, serving 2.3 million trips daily. Another 200 kilometres of metro is under construction in these cities and an additional 500 kilometres is planned. The metro has become a popular rapid transit mode, with 27 other cities in the process of planning their metro rail service which could amount to approximately 1000 kilometres of new service (NTDPC, 2014). The BRTS, on the other hand, has not had the same scale of adoption in Indian cities as the metro rail. Despite being a low-cost alternative to metro rail, it has faced several difficulties in adoption owing to its need for dedicated lanes. The Delhi BRTS, built in 2008, was dismantled on January 16th, 2016. The system was plagued by criticism from private transport users for the 'disproportionate' amount of road space allocated to it, which was perceived to cause congestion and delays in the remaining mixed vehicular lanes (Tiwari, 2016).

Intermediate public transport modes

IPT, also known as 'paratransit', is situated between PT and private motorised modes. Several types of services can be classified as IPT, based on variation in routing, fare and personalised or shared use of the service. However, for ease they can be classified into two predominant types; (1) those that provide door-to-door services such as autorickshaws and taxis and (2) those that are informal public transport services such as shared autorickshaws and mini buses. In India, the auto rickshaw is the predominant IPT mode, along with other modes such as pedal rickshaws and tempo services that also provide IPT services to a lesser extent. They cater collectively to 4% of work trips in India (Census of India, 2011a).

The autorickshaw is the most widely used IPT mode, with registrations growing at 8% per annum since 2001 (MoSPI, 2016). Autorickshaw services are similar to the traditional taxi service. They are hired to provide door-to-door service for which they charge a distance-based fare. They work predominantly as a formal service, regulated by the city government, requiring registration and fares fixed in conjunction with autorickshaw unions. Due to their slow speeds, some cities have restricted their movement. Mumbai banned the entry of autorickshaws into South Mumbai, while Bangalore has restricted their movement into dedicated lanes on certain streets (Rao, 2011; TNN, 2014). Furthermore, it is common for autorickshaw users to experience denial of service or to be asked to pay a fare much higher than that prescribed by the government. In the absence of other cheap door-to-door services, users are captive to this mode. Attempts have begun to reform the autorickshaw sector. In several cities autorickshaws have been ordered to adopt cleaner fuels such as CNG (Mani *et al.*, 2012). Autorickshaws have also become part of aggregator services recently, offering bookings over the internet or telephone (Mishra, 2016).

In smaller cities and peripheries of metropolitan cities with low PT penetration, it is common to find another variant of the autorickshaw namely, 'shared autorickshaw'. This service operates on a fixed to semi-fixed route with no designated stops, passengers share their ride with others, and fares are based on the distance travelled. The service runs outside of formal government regulations, without registrations, and fares based on consensus among drivers and unions. They are often overcrowded since operators try to make the most profit out of each trip.

Until recently, taxicab services were only common in large metropolitan cities like Delhi, Mumbai, and Kolkata. With the rapid uptake of mobile and online taxi aggregator services, many cities in India have gained access to taxi services. Registration of taxis has grown in the last decade at 11 per cent per annum (MoSPI, 2016). However, the legal status of cab aggregator services like Uber has become an area of concern, with several states banning them for lack of licences. This reflects the government's inability to respond to developments in cab services (Chakraborty & Poovanna, 2015). In their bid to adapt to new markets, cab aggregator services such as Ola have also started rideshare services (Kashyap, 2015).

The most low carbon, low-energy mode of transport among IPT modes in India would have to be the pedal rickshaw. However, this low carbon mode is fast disappearing, with city governments keen to marginalise this slow, space consuming, congestion causing, IPT mode (Ravi, 2016). Pedal rickshaws are popular on the streets of Old Delhi, ferrying people to the metro station and back, however, they were barred from entering congested areas such as Chandni Chowk (Sudworth, 2006). Ravi (2016) argues that pedal rickshaws could be modernised, used to provide sustainable last-mile connectivity between metro stations and nearby residential areas.

Private motorised modes

Since India did not experience rapid industrialisation, and average incomes in the late 1980s were low, cars and motorised two-wheelers were available only to the privileged. Post economic liberalisation in the early 1990s, aspirational commodities like cars became available to middle-income groups. Indian roads now see an addition of a hundred thousand passenger vehicles every year (WSA & MoUD, 2008). 8.5 million cars were added between 2001 and 2011 as compared to 7 million cars from 1951 to 2000 (MoSPI, 2016). Car ownership levels are expected to rise to around 35 cars per thousand population (Ghate & Sundar, 2013), marked by the addition of another 30 million new cars. Another estimate expects the number of motor vehicles in India to grow to about 200 per thousand persons by the year 2050. These figures point towards a rapid motorisation of India (Chamon *et al.*, 2008).

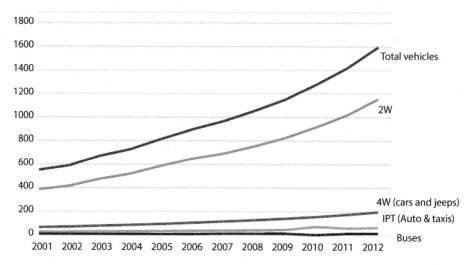

Figure 8.2: Growth of vehicle registration in India (in lacs). Source: MOSPI (2016).

Private motorised modes used in India include two-wheelers (2W) such as scooter and motorbikes and four-wheelers (4W) such as cars, jeeps and vans. 2Ws are the largest private transport mode with 22% of work trips being made on them while 5% of work trips are made on 4Ws (Census of India, 2011a). Two wheelers accounted for 74% of all vehicles registered in the last decade, growing at 10% per annum, while only 12% of all vehicles registered in the same period were cars, but growing at a rate higher than two-wheelers at 12% per annum (MoSPI, 2016). This recent growth of personalised motor vehicles can be attributed to rising personal incomes, easier financing options, and a growing second-hand vehicle market. Large metropolitan cities have begun experiencing the many side-effects of increased vehicular mobility. Trip times have increased while associated issues such as vehicular pollution and reduced road safety have become concerns. Two-wheelers may, however, be a solution to a low carbon future. Schipper *et al.* (2008) looked into various scenarios involving vehicle ownership patterns and fuel efficiency increases with respect to a transition to a low carbon future. One of four models created was a Two Wheeler World (TWW) scenario which assumes that with rising congestion two wheelers become a preferred mode choice over cars. The TWW scenario was the second best scenario to a full-fledged Sustainable Urban Transport option.

The prevailing conditions of transport in India indicate a rapid growth in personal motorised modes. PT options would have an important role to play in a low carbon transition, along with NMT and IPT options. However, there is a tendency within governments to provide lip service in support of transit and NMT, while not following up on them later (Tiwari, 2016). There is a need for a system of negative feedback against excessive consumption, and positive feedback for low carbon, low energy modes (Mohan, 2013). This means that walking and cycling environments need to be enhanced, and last mile connectivity options improved while introducing the negative feedback to personal vehicle use in the form of parking and congestion charges.

A culture of automobility

As data presented in the previous section indicates, Indian cities have experienced a decline in the share of NMT over the last two decades. Before 1983, buying a car meant having to choose between Hindustan Motors and Premier Motors, coupled with a long wait time for delivery (Yoganandan & Pugazh, 2015). However, with the arrival of Maruti Suzuki in 1983, automobiles became easily accessible to those with aspirations (India Today, 2009). Today, advertisements in print and visual media portray the automobile as the ultimate aspirational good; fueling the demand for their production. Over the last decade, automobile manufacturers have been encouraged to set up shop in various parts of the country to address the demand for automobiles while generating employment (TNN, 2008). Automobile loans were made available at rates lower than for education loans. These factors contributed to a large-scale proliferation of cars as discussed earlier. Clearly, this is not in line with a low carbon transition agenda.

Badami (2009), Tiwari (2011) and Mohan (2013) describe the struggles of NMT users in Indian cities where they must constantly fight the stigma attached to their use. Given the all-pervasive presence of the automobile around them, NMT modes are made to look out-of-place in the city. Demand for wider roads and easing of traffic congestion fuels popular media and political rhetoric in cities. The effect of motorisation triggers wider social and political constituencies, which go beyond the demand for wider roads, flyovers (grade separators) and uninterrupted traffic flows. Combined with lenient taxation on automobiles, freely available parking spaces and absence of effective road pricing mechanisms, automobiles are seen as 'king of the roads.' The space occupied by automobiles – while moving or when parked – are viewed as inevitable and more legitimate over other urban activities such as play areas, sitting areas or street trading. The contest for spaces in cities tilts in the favour of automobile users who protect their territories. These factors lead to a culture of automobility, where the NMT modes are deemed lowly.

There is also pressure from the automobile lobbies on city administrators when they prepare progressive plans to prioritise public modes. The planning (and later dismantling) of the Delhi BRT project is an interesting example. Debates in Delhi centred on whether it was a good idea to dedicate median lanes of multi-lane roads for the exclusive use of BRT project (Tiwari, 2016). The lobbies representing private car owners petitioned the Delhi High Court DHC claiming that as 'job creators' in the economy they were more legitimate users of road space compared to the 'wastage' of space for the BRT corridor. The court rejected the petition and supported the retaining of the BRT corridor (IANS, 2012). In spite of the positive verdict, the BRT corridor has since been dismantled with the promise of a comprehensive re-planning of the BRT (Mathur, 2016). The dismantling of the Delhi BRT corridor is a symbolic setback for sustainable mobility initiatives in the country. Chaplin (2011) points out, through examples of other basic urban services, that the nature of the postcolonial state has been dominated by coalitions of private interests conspiring to usurp public funds for their benefits. This appears to be true in the case of the transport sector. Overall, this culture of automobility is not in line with the agenda of low carbon transitions.

Attempts at addressing motorisation

In view of the arguments made in the previous section, it is important to understand how the state and civil society have responded to rising levels of motorisation. This section looks at the government's interventions, which have largely been in the form of policies, missions and isolated one-off programmes/events, and civil society movements that have strived to attract attention to the cause of equitable access to streets and public realm.

National Urban Transport Policy, 2006

The conventional transportation planning paradigm of facilitating traffic movement in the city was a product of social aspirations and political outlook of mobility in cities. The idea of sustainable transport had a belated entrance into Indian policymaking. It was only in 2006 that the 'National Urban Transport Policy' was formulated. This policy proposed a dramatically pronounced shift from 'roads for vehicles' to 'streets for people'. However, the twelfth national five-year plan (2012-2017) identified that about 44% of 871 billion USD of funds are to be spent on 'urban roads' with only 11% on 'urban (mass) transport' over the next 20 years.

Jawaharlal Nehru National Urban Renewal Mission

The Jawaharlal Nehru National Urban Renewal Mission (JnNURM) was launched in 2005 as a major initiative to improve urban quality of life. The mission envisaged an expenditure of 20 billion USD over a period of seven years. One of the two sub-missions focused on urban infrastructure and governance which had components of street network, urban transport, and redevelopment of old city areas. Taking a cue from the National Urban Transport Policy, cities were encouraged to invest in PT including BRTS and metro rail. These had to be accompanied by investments in NMT enabling infrastructure. However, the rhetoric of 'sustainable mobility' did not find much resonance in the transport investment priorities of cities. After seven years of disbursements, the assigned funds were mostly concentrated in road infrastructure, favouring general traffic and not necessarily sustainable transport investments. IIHS (2011) reports that 57% of transport-related funding was allocated to roads and flyovers and 33% to mass rapid transit and PT. Cities eventually had more JnNURM-funded road and flyover projects than any other type of projects (CSE, 2011).

Civil society movements

Several cities, most notably Delhi, jave organised car-free days in the last two years. These were a response to rising levels of pollution, as reported by the media, that forced the government to intervene (ENS, 2015; WHO, 2014; PTI, 2015). In Delhi, four car-free days were organised last year. This was followed by the odd-even policy under which alternate days saw the use of vehicles with odd or even registration numbers only. The positive response was centred more on the visible drop in congestion than environmental concerns (Khanna & Mehta, 2016; Goel & Pant, 2016). The increased patronage of PT systems during these days makes a case for strengthening them while restricting the use of private modes of transport. The state government proposed a second phase of the odd-even initiative in April 2016 which did not enjoy the success of its previous edition (Hindustan Times, 2016).

Many civil society movements have begun questioning the usurping of street space by automobiles while advocating for a return of these spaces to people. Raahgiri Day is a popular, multi-city event inspired by the idea of Open Streets and Ciclovía. During such events, stretches of streets are closed to vehicles for a few hours in the day, usually a Sunday, and opened to street activities like skating and dance. Participants mostly belong to the middle class. Critics have called these events 'elitist icons of urban renewal movement', that do not reflect any actual concern for the environment or equitable transport (Srivastava, 2015). However, counter arguments also claim that any improvements in NMT environment could support an equitable low carbon transition (Anjaria, 2015).

Areas of concern for low carbon mobility

Road Safety

In 2014, traffic accidents were responsible for 47% of all unnatural deaths in India. They also accounted for 39% of all unnatural deaths in urban India (MoSPI, 2016). Traffic accidents in India have grown at a CAGR of 4%, with 13.69 deaths/100,000 being reported in urban India and a slightly lower 13.21 deaths/100,000 as the national average. The WHO (2015) estimates the rate to be higher at 16.6 deaths/100,000 owing to underreporting.

The highest fatalities reported were of two-wheeler users at 33.9% followed by 17.2% four-wheeler users, 9.1% pedestrians and 3.5% cyclists. A large segment of deaths (36.2%) did not have specific details about the nature of the accident and causalities. With a global average of pedestrian fatalities at 25% (15.9% more than in India) and cyclists at 4% (0.5% more than India), it is highly likely that pedestrian and cyclist deaths would be a large proportion of the unspecified fatalities. The road infrastructure design in Indian cities does not ensure the safety of NMT users.

Road traffic injury needs to be seen as a public health issue (Badami *et al.*, 2004) and it should be acted upon accordingly.

Lagging street infrastructure

There are no mandatory norms regulating the design of urban streets and corresponding infrastructure. The India Road Congress (IRC) codes developed in the 1980s that attempted to regulate the design of urban streets prioritise the smooth flow of automobiles over facilitating NMT modes. Other organisations developed their own guidelines, however they were not legally binding. In addition, no checks ensure that quality standards for infrastructure provided on streets are upheld. The Tender SURE guidelines used by Bengaluru are definitely a move in the right direction (JUSF 2011). They were developed for use by Bangalore city administrators to tender street improvement works, and ensure the maintenance of standards, while prioritising NMT over motor vehicles.

Absence of land use transport integration

The National Urban Transport Policy (MoUD, 2006) calls for greater integration of land use planning with transport, stressing the need to minimise travel distances and maximise access to opportunities, especially for the marginalised sections. The working group on urban transport of the National Transport Policy Development Committee (NTPDC), constituted by the erstwhile Planning Commission of India, submitted a report that reinforced the ideas of the NUTP (NTDPC, 2012). Planning in India has relied on the 'predict and provide' approach and despite recent attempts by academics to use quantitative analysis based models, such as Adhvaryu and Echenique (2012) and Munshi *et al.* (2014), land use allocation continues to be based on decisions that may not always justify sustainability goals. As a result, average trip lengths have increased and people are forced to travel more to be able to access opportunities. Low levels of accessibility are a function of strict zoning and greater sprawl leading to the need for ownership of private motorised vehicles.

Parking policies

Parking management can play a significant role in the transition to a low carbon future. However, most cities in India have yet to identify its potential as an effective TDM measure. The few cities that have attempted parking reforms have found them difficult to implement due to resistance from citizens, and fear of political backlash. Parking provisions in Indian cities are commonly provided through on-street parking, within buildings and to a lesser extent in parking plots and multi-storied structures. On-street parking is the most common form of parking available in cities, generally in the form of uncharged curbside spaces (Barter, 2011). Several large cities in India, have begun regulating on-street parking spaces, due to greater demand for street space. Regulating on-street parking is a challenge in Indian cities, where the norm is to park in no-parking zones and over footpaths.

Conclusion

The main challenge for transport policy-makers is understanding the nature of Indian modernity with its multiple nuances and for them to place the transport needs of a city in that context. It is assumed incorrectly that modernisation means inevitable motorisation (domination of motorised modes over cityscapes) while viewing NMT modes as pre-modern and thus not futuristic. Modernity could also mean seeking new ideas to bring greater social justice and fairness into the city without burdens of the past. Comprehensive planning for NMT in a city can go a long way in achieving pathways to sustainability while addressing the issues of transport inequities. A paradigm shift is required in the mainstream urban transport planning, which should be more inclusive of the needs of the poor in Indian cities.

A transport paradigm that looks at mobility and speed would invest in infrastructure for automobiles, thereby discouraging investments in infrastructure for non-motorised modes. There is a need for a more context-sensitive transport paradigm which is well-integrated with land use. Changes in urban land use patterns can have important effects on the viability and attractiveness of NMT and PT. These modes are vital to allowing low-cost mobility and accessibility to a range of urban opportunities with wider housing and livelihood choices.

The emerging automobile culture in Indian cities and how it impacts urban transport governance and decision-making is an important area that policymakers must address to ensure a successful transition to a low carbon future. This would invariably mean that PT projects are placed in priority along with city level plans for NMT and actively pursuing TDM tools like parking policies.

References

Acharya, R. (2000). Indian Railways: Where the commuter is king. *Japan Railways and Transport Review*, **25**, 34–45.

Adhvaryu, B. & Echenique M. (2012). SIMPLAN: A SIMplified PLANning model. *Environment and Planning B: Planning and Design*, **39**(1), 96–119.

Agarwal, O. & Zimmerman, S. (2008). Toward sustainable mobility in urban India. Transportation Research Record: *Journal of the Transportation Research Board*, **2048**, 1-7.

ANI (2014). Bhopal celebrates Raahgiri Day to spread awareness about road safety. *ANI News*, Available at: http://aninews.in/newsdetail2/story184358/bhopal-celebrates-raahgiri-day-to-spread-awareness-about-road-safety.html. Accessed 11 Feb. 2016.

Anjaria, J.S. (2014). How we define the street. *The Indian Express*, Available at: http://indianexpress.com/article/opinion/columns/how-we-define-the-street. Accessed 11 Feb. 2016.

Anjaria, J.S. (2012). Is there a culture of Indian streets? *The Seminar*, Available at: http://www.india-seminar.com/(2012)/636/636_jonathan_s_anjaria.htm#top. Accessed 11 Feb. 2016.

Anjaria, J.S. (2015). The cyclist and the Marxist: Why everything should not be reduced to class conflict. *Scroll*, Available at: http://scroll.in/article/766391/the-cyclist-and-the-marxist-why-everything-should-not-be-reduced-to-class-conflict. Accessed 11 Feb. 2016.

Badami, M., Tiwari, G. & Mohan, D. (2004). Access and mobility for the urban poor in India: bridging the gap between policy and needs. In Forum on *Urban Infrastructure and Public Service Delivery for the Urban Poor*, National Institute of Urban Affairs, Delhi, India.

Badami, M.G. (2009). Urban transport policy as if people and the environment mattered: pedestrian accessibility the first step. *Economic and Political Weekly*, **XLIV**(33), 43-51.

Badami, M.G. & Haider, M. (2007). An analysis of public bus transit performance in Indian cities. *Transportation Research Part A: Policy and Practice*, **41**(10), 961–981.

Bandyopadhyay, K. & Chakraborty, A. (2013). Cops slam brakes on bicycles. *The Times of India*, Available at: http://timesofindia.indiatimes.com/city/kolkata/Cops-slam-brakes-on-bicycles/articleshow/21968076.cms. Accessed 11 Feb. 2016.

Banister, D. (2008). The sustainable mobility paradigm. *Transport Policy*, **15**(2), 73–80.

Barter, P.A. (2011). *Parking Policy in Asian Cities*. Mandaluyong: Asian Development Bank. Available at: http://www.adb.org/sites/default/files/publication/28935/parking-policy-asia.pdf. Accessed 8 Apr. 2015.

Census of India (2011a). *B-28 'Other Workers' by distance from residence to place of work and mode of travel to the place of work*, Available at: http://www.censusindia.gov.in/(2011) census/B-series/B_28.html. Accessed 13 Jan. 2016.

Census of India (2011b). *Cities having population 1 lakh and above*. Available at: http://censusindia.gov.in/(2011)-prov-results/paper2/data_files/India2/Table_2_PR_Cities_1Lakh_and_Above.pdf. Accessed 13 Jan. 2016.

Chakraborty, S. & Poovanna, S. (2015). Govt. frames rule for cab aggregators like Ola, Uber. *Livemint*, Available at: http://www.livemint.com/Politics/hh9iHhNFi7aDMdVipC0dyK/Govt-drafts-rules-to-regulate-Uber-other-ridehailing-firms.html. Accessed 11 Jan. 2016.

Chamon, M., Mauro, P. & Okawa, Y. (2008). Mass car ownership in emerging market giants. *Economic Policy*, **23**(54), 243–296.

Chaplin, S.E. (2011). Indian cities, sanitation and the state: the politics of the failure to provide. *Environment and Urbanization*, **23**(1), 57–70.

CSE, (2011). Clean and sustainable mobility for all. New Delhi: CSE. Available at: http://www.cseindia.org/userfiles/anumita_1stday.pdf. Accessed 13 Jan. 2016.

Datey, A., Darji, V., Patel, T. & Mahadevia, D. (2012). *Walking and cycling in Indian cities: A struggle for reclaiming road edges*, Working Paper no. 18, Centre for Urban Equity, CEPT University.

ENS (2015). Most polluted city in the world, Delhi suffers from a toxic blend, says UK study. *Indian Express,* Available at: http://indianexpress.com/article/cities/delhi/the-most-polluted-city-in-the-world-delhi-suffers-from-a-toxic-blend-study/. Accessed 20 Jan. 2016.

Ghate, A.T. & Sundar, S. (2013). Can we reduce the rate of growth of car ownership? *Economic and Political Weekly,* **48**(23), 32-40.

Ghose, B. (1960). The colonial beginnings of Calcutta urbanisation without industrialisation. *The Economic Weekly,* (August 13), 1255–1260.

Goel, R. & Pant, P. (2016). Vehicular pollution mitigation policies in Delhi. *Economic & Political Weekly,* **51**(9), 41.

Gordon, D. (2006). *Planning Twentieth Century Capital Cities,* Abingdon: Routledge.

HT Correspondent, (2016). Delhi to conduct a second round of odd-even from April 15. *Hindustan Times,* online Available at: http://www.hindustantimes.com/delhi/delhi-to-conduct-second-round-of-odd-even-kejriwal/story-DcownpCt7Q96FEAkSfMulO.html. Accessed 6 Apr. (2016).

IIHS (2011). *Urban India (2011): Evidence.* Bengaluru: IIHS. Available at: http://iihs.co.in/wp-content/uploads/2013/12/IUC-Book.pdf. Accessed 7 Apr. 2015.

India Today (2009). 1983-Maruti 800 is launched: Driving the India story. *India Today,* Available at: http://indiatoday.intoday.in/story/1983-Maruti+800+is+launched:+Driving+the+India+story/1/76373.html. Accessed 7 Mar. 2016.

IANS (2012). Delhi high court dismisses BRT corridor review plea. *NDTV,* Available at: http://www.ndtv.com/delhi-news/delhi-high-court-dismisses-brt-corridor-review-plea-505363. Accessed 7 Mar. 2016.

JUSF (2011). *TENDER SURE (Specifications for Urban Roads Execution),* Bengaluru: JUSF.

Joshi, R. (2014). Mobility practices of the urban poor in Ahmedabad (India). PhD thesis, Faculty of Environment and Technology, The University of the West of England, available at: http://eprints.uwe.ac.uk/25016. Accessed 10 Oct. 2015.

Joshi, R. & Joseph, Y. (2015). Invisible cyclists and disappearing cycles: The challenges of cycling policies in Indian cities. *Transfers,* **5**(3), 23–40.

Kashyap, S. (2015). With 'Ola Share' and 'uberPOOL' has ride-sharing come of age in India. *Your Story,* Available at: http://yourstory.com/2015/10/ola-share-and-uberpool. Accessed 8 Mar. 2016.

Khanna, P. & Mehta, N. (2016). Odd-even rule ends in Delhi; Effect on air quality unclear. *Livemint,* Available at: http://www.livemint.com/Politics/lhm0PbZRp4BMTRaOkG3L9N/Oddeven-rule-ends-in-Delhi-verdict-on-air-qualityunclear.html. Accessed 8 Mar. 2016.

Knoflacher, H. (2007). Success and failures in urban transport planning in Europe-understanding the transport system. *Sadhana,* **32**(4), 293–307.

Mahadevia, D., Joshi, R. & Datey, A. (2013). Ahmedabad's BRT system - A sustainable urban transport Panacea? *Economic and Political Weekly,* **XLVIII**(48), 56–64.

Mani, A., Pai, M. & Aggarwal, R. (2012). Sustainable urban transport in India: role of the auto-rickshaw sector. Mumbai: Embarq India. Available at: http://www.wri.org/publication/sustainable-urban-transport-india. Accessed 7 Mar. 2016.

Mathur, A. (2016). The dismantling of Delhi's BRT corridor to begin today, to cost around INR 12 Crore. *India Today*, Available at: http://indiatoday.intoday.in/story/dismantling-of-brt-corridor-to-begin-today/1/573942.html. Accessed 7 Mar. 2016.

MGI (2010). India's urban awakening: Building inclusive cities, sustaining economic growth. New Delhi: MGI. Available at: http://www.mckinsey.com/global-themes/urbanization/urban-awakening-in-india. Accessed 17 Mar. 2015.

Mishra, B.R. (2016). Ola to expand auto service to eight more cities. *Business Standard*, Available at: http://www.business-standard.com/article/companies/ola-to-expand-auto-service-to-eight-more-cities-116031101004_1.html. Accessed 12 Apr. 2016.

Mohan, D. (2013). Moving around in Indian Cities. *Economic and Political Weekly*, **XLVIII**(48), 40–48.

MoSPI (2016). *Statistical year book 2016*. New Delhi: MoSPI. Available at: http://mospi.nic.in/Mospi_New/upload/SYB(2016)/index1.html. Accessed 17 Apr. 2016.

MoUD (2006). *National Urban Transport Policy*. New Delhi: MoUD. Available at: http://mospi.nic.in/Mospi_New/upload/SYB2016/index1.html. Accessed 17 Jan. 2016.

MoUD (2016). *Handbook of Urban Statistics*. New Delhi: MoUD. Available at: http://www.indiaenvironmentportal.org.in/files/file/handbook%20of%20urban%20statistics%202016.pdf. Accessed 23 Apr. 2016.

Munshi, T., Zuidgeest, M., Brussel, M. & van Maarseveen, M. (2014). Logistic regression and cellular automata-based modelling of retail, commercial, and residential development in the city of Ahmedabad, India. *Cities*, **39**(0), 68–86.

Narayanan, N. (2014). Showing the path to other Indian cities, Chennai starts pedestrianising its roads. *Scroll*, Available at: http://scroll.in/article/687775/showing-the-path-to-other-indian-cities-chennai-starts-pedestrianising-its-roads. Accessed 7 Sep. 2015.

NTDPC (2014). *India transport report: Moving india to 2032*. New Delhi: Routledge. Available at: http://planningcommission.nic.in/reports/genrep/NTDPC_Vol_01.pdf. Accessed 8 Apr. 2016.

NTDPC (2012). *National Transport Policy Development Committee on Urban Transport: Final report*. New Delhi: MoUD. Available at: http://planningcommission.nic.in/sectors/index.php?sectors=National%20Transport%20Development%20Policy%20Committee%20(NTDPC). Accessed 18 Mar. 2014

PTI (2015). Delhi to observe third 'car-free' day on December 22; DTC to deploy special shuttles. *The Indian Express*. Available at: http://indianexpress.com/article/cities/delhi/delhi-to-observe-third-car-free-day-on-december-22-dtc-to-deploy-special-shuttles/. Accessed 15 Dec. 2015.

Pucher, J., Peng, Z., Mittal, Z., Zhu, Y. I. & Korattyswaroopam, N. (2007). Urban transport trends and policies in China and India: Impacts of rapid economic growth. *Transport Reviews*, **27**(4), 379–410

Rao, S. (2011). South Mumbai doesn't want to ride in autos. *Hindustan Times*. Available at: http://www.hindustantimes.com/mumbai/south-mumbai-doesn-t-want-to-ride-in-autos/story-qWgJTJfRdeAL3rplf991gN.html. Accessed 10 Jul. 2014.

Ravi, R. (2016). No space for cycle rickshaws. *Economic and Political Weekly*, **LI**(9), 49–51.

Replogle, M., (1991). *Non-motorized Vehicles in Asia: Lessons for sustainable transport planning and policy*. World Bank Technical Report No. 162. Washington DC: The World Bank. Available at: http://www.gtkp.com/assets/uploads/20091125-110428-2262-2293_NonmotorizedVehiclesAsia.pdf. Accessed 17 Dec. 2011.

RITES (1994). *Comprehensive Study of 21 Cities in India*. New Delhi: RITES.

Roychowdhury, A., Bansal, R., Bhattacharjee, A. & Gandhi, S. (2013). On foot and pedal. *Down To Earth*. Available at: http://www.downtoearth.org.in/coverage/on-foot-and-pedal-38071. Accessed 11 Jun. 2015.

Schipper, L., Banerjee, I. & Ng, W. S. (2008). CO_2 Emissions from land transport in India: Scenarios of the uncertain. In: *Annual Meeting Proceedings*. Washington DC: TRB. Available at: http://www.irfnet.ch/files-upload/knowledges/CO2%20Emissions%20from%20land%20transport%20in%20India_TRB.pdf. Accessed 13 Jan. 2016.

Schipper, L., Fabian, H. & Leather, J. (2009). Transport and carbon dioxide emissions: Forecasts, options analysis and evaluation, *ADB Sustainable Development Working Paper*, no. 9, Asian Development Bank.

Schlingloff, D. (2014). *Fortified Cities of Ancient India: A comparative study*, New Delhi: Anthem Press.

Singh, S.K. (2005). Review of urban transportation in India. *Journal of Public Transportation*, **8**(1) 79–97.

Srivastava, S. (2015). Why the sports bicycle should not be a symbol of urban renewal. *Scroll*. Available at: http://scroll.in/article/765917/why-the-sports-bicycle-should-not-be-a-symbol-of-urban-renewal. Accessed 11 Feb. 2016.

Sudworth, J. (2006). Delhi court bans pedal rickshaws. *BBC News*. Available at: http://news.bbc.co.uk/2/hi/south_asia/5388374.stm. Accessed 11 Feb. 2016.

Tiwari, G. (2016). Are we ready for public transport? *Economic and Political Weekly*, **LI**(9), 51–54.

Tiwari, G. (2011). *Key Mobility Challenges in Indian cities*, Leipzig: International Transport Forum, OECD.

TNN (2014). Autos get a dedicated lane in the heart of Bangalore. *Times of India*. Available at: http://timesofindia.indiatimes.com/city/bengaluru/Autos-get-a-dedicated-lane-in-the-heart-of-Bangalore/articleshow/44137211.cms. Accessed 11 Feb. 2016.

TNN (2008). Nissan, Renault ink MoU for plant in Tamil Nadu. *The Economic Times*. Available at: http://articles.economictimes.indiatimes.com/2008-02-23/news/28458614_1_carlos-tavares-patrick-pelata-nissan-motor-and-renault. Accessed 11 Feb. 2016.

Volwahsen, A. (2002). *Imperial Delhi: The British Capital of the Indian Empire*, New York: Prestel.

WHO (2015). *Global Status Report on Road Safety 2015*. Geneva: WHO. Available at: http://www.who.int/violence_injury_prevention/road_safety_status/(2015)/GSRRS(2015)_Summary_EN_final.pdf. Accessed 22 Feb. 2016.

WHO (2014). *WHO's Ambient Air Pollution Database-Update 2014*. Geneva: WHO. Available at: http://www.who.int/phe/health_topics/outdoorair/databases/AAP_database_results_2014.pdf. Accessed 22 Dec. 2014.

Woodcock, J., Edwards, P., Tonne, C., Armstrong, B.G., Ashiru, O., Banister, D., Beevers, S., Chalabi, Z., Chowdhury, Z., Cohen, A. & Franco, O.H. (2009). Public health benefits of strategies to reduce greenhouse-gas emissions: urban land transport. *The Lancet*, **374**(9705), 1930-1943.

WSA & MoUD (2008). Study on traffic and transportation policies and strategies in urban areas in India. New Delhi: MoUD. Available at: http://moud.gov.in/traffic_transport. Accessed 27 Dec. 2013.

Yoganandan, G. & Pugazh, E. (2015). *Male Car Owners' Perception and Buying Behaviour*, New Delhi: EduPedia Publications Pvt. Ltd.

9 Low Carbon Transition in Finnish Mobility: The clash of experimental transport governance and established practices?

Paula Kivimaa

Science Policy Research Unit, University of Sussex, UK and Finnish Environment Institute, Helsinki, Finland.

Armi Temmes

School of Business, Aalto University, Helsinki, Finland.

Introduction

With a population of 5.4 million people and a northern location between Sweden and Russia, Finland is a country of few people and relatively long distances. This places pressure on maintaining an efficient private transport infrastructure, while at the same time visions of low carbon mobility systems exist and are increasingly created, particularly in more densely populated areas. Even in the southern urban areas, such as the Helsinki metropolitan region (1.1 million inhabitants) and Tampere city region (close to 0.7 million inhabitants), where more opportunities for mobility innovations to replace private car use and ownership exist, urban sprawl tends to complicate the process. However, there are also signs of action on the political, institutional and societal levels supporting a low carbon mobility transition in Finland.

The Finnish context from the multi-level perspective

The multi-level perspective (MLP) of the sustainability transitions literature views long-term transformative change to occur as an interaction between three different levels: landscape, regime and niches (Geels, 2002, 2012). Innovation and experimental activities take place at the niche level with potential to initiate regime-level transition. This is the locus of more radical technological, social, organisational and behavioural innovations that can disrupt how existing systems of consumption and production function. Niche building at this level depends on processes of voiced expectations deviating from the mainstream, forming supportive networks, and learning on multiple dimensions (e.g. Hoogma *et al.*, 2002; Smith & Raven, 2012).

The key constraining and enabling factor for such disruptive innovation is the socio-technical regime that is characterised as a rather persistent deep structure composed of technology and infrastructure, institutions and policy often influenced by existing networks of actors, and prevailing practices, beliefs and habits (Geels, 2002, 2012). Destabilising an existing regime can be a very long process (Turnheim and Geels, 2012), as multiple path dependencies need to be overcome (e.g. Unruh, 2002, also see Chapter 7).

Landscape is the exogenous environment comprising macro-economic, macro-political and cultural forces and development trends that may impose pressure to change existing socio-technical regimes (e.g. Geels, 2002, 2012). We use the concept of *landscape* to show the context in which mobility systems change, of *regime* to describe the various dominant elements in the Finnish transport system, and of *niche* to focus on selected new developments with potential to overturn the high-energy and fossil-fuel dependent mobility system.

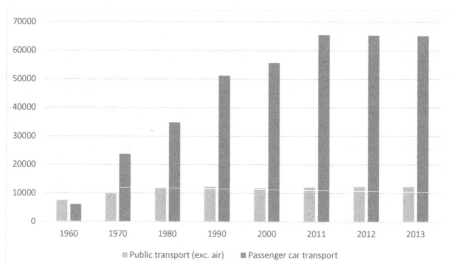

Figure 9.1: Passenger kilometres travelled in public transport and passenger cars. Source: Transport and Communications Statistical Yearbook for Finland, 2014.

Greenhouse gas emissions (GHG) from domestic transport were circa 11 million tons in 2014, reducing 14 percent from peak emissions in 2005 (Statistics Finland, 2015). This corresponds to about 19% of Finland's GHG emissions excluding land use change and forestry (Statistics Finland, 2015a). The reduction is largely explained by the increased use of biofuels in transport, whereas there is little change in passenger kilometres travelled in private cars (Figure 9.1). In Finland, looking at both the expansion of the use of biofuels and significant changes in how transport policy is planned (described later in this chapter), the transport regime has clearly begun the process of change towards low carbon mobility. However, at the same time, it continues to be much restricted by the historically dominant private vehicle and fossil fuel based-regime.

Several landscape factors set the context for the Finnish transport regime and its change in recent years. Many of these are global, including international climate change commitments, fluctuating oil prices and the availability of oil, and digitalisation. For example, new information communication technologies (ICT) (see Chapter 13) have enabled the early small-scale emergence of business concepts for more efficient use of private cars; including ride sharing and car lending (Temmes et al., 2014). In addition, there are landscape factors particular to Finland, namely the cold climate, long distances in a relatively sparsely populated country, and the urban sprawl phenomenon that jointly contribute to making low carbon mobility transition difficult. At the same time, however, more than two thirds of the people in Finland live in an area that covers only 5% of the country, i.e. cities and their surroundings, creating opportunities for intelligent use of public and intermodal transport (Temmes et al., 2014). Megatrends including the aging population and online shopping will gradually change the transport regime in terms of what kind of transport and delivery services are needed in the future. At the end of 2014, 20% of the population was over 65 years old, and this is estimated to reach 25% by 2030 (Statistics Finland, 2015b).

As in many Western countries, the transport regime is dominated by privately-owned internal combustion engine vehicles. As Figure 9.1 shows, passenger kilometres by private cars increased steeply until 2011 and have stagnated since then, while journeys made by public transport have stayed at the same level since the 1980s. Despite the long distances in the country, interestingly '64% of the journeys travelled by car in Finland are less than 10 kilometres in distance. Moreover, the use of private passenger vehicles is most common in journeys that are only 1-3 kilometres long' (Temmes et al., 2014: 13). While private cars dominate the transport system, '[o]ther modes of passenger transport (cycling and walking, public transport, and transport services) co-exist as important elements. In addition, practices such as teleworking or internet shopping provide opportunities to reverse' the historically high levels of private car-based transport (Temmes et al., 2014: 7).

There are also regional differences in the use of different transport modes; public transport and walking being the most common in the Helsinki metropolitan region, while private car and cycling are more common in smaller and more northern cities, such as Oulu (Upham *et al.*, 2015). Also in terms of public perception, the transport regime is not homogenous throughout the country. For example, support for biofuels is much stronger in the Northern city of Oulu than in the more Southern cities of Helsinki and Tampere (Upham *et al.*, 2015).

On the institutional side, path-dependent and transformative elements co-exist. The need to combine processes of land-use planning and transport has been recognised for decades to create a more efficient and sustainable transport system (See Chapter 7). More recently, both public and private actors have advocated a range of experiments and programmes to develop new technologies and services enabling systemic change in transport. Examples of this include a portfolio of experiments initiated in 2014 by the Ministry of Transport and Communications and the Transport Safety Agency, the Mobility as Service (MaaS) concept launched also by the Ministry of Transport and Communications (see below), the TransEco and TransSmart Programmes (TransEco, 2016; TransSmart, 2016) pooling together around 20 projects and a range of actors, and the capital city Helsinki adopting a radical turning point in the principles of transport planning starting in 2013 – putting pedestrians and cyclists before motorised transport (Helsingin Sanomat, 2016). Simultaneously, however, removing tax credits to commuting largely based on private motorised transport, on a national level, and introducing parking fees to a larger area around cities, on a local level, have been very difficult (cf. Mäkinen *et al.*, 2015).

The niche level includes a range of technologies and service concepts with already realised or potential influence over different parts of the current transport regime, the largest being the biofuels niche that has, according to Nylund *et al.* (2015), reached large commercial scale. Electric vehicles and related infrastructure are growing but the numbers are still small (ElectricTraffic, 2016). Public transport, which cannot be considered a novel niche as such, has started to renew itself through low carbon vehicles, improved services and infrastructure, connected to investments in new rail and metro networks. In terms of more demand-related niches, while interest in a range of services reducing transport demand and travelled passenger kilometres exist, still many '*car sharing and ride sharing concepts tend to be restricted by the rules of the existing regime, e.g. taxation, business licensing and insurance policies*' (Temmes *et al.*, 2014: 34). These have not received the same level of innovation policy support as the solutions maintaining with the ideology of private motorised transport (Kivimaa & Virkamäki, 2014).

Changing institutional and policy for sustainable mobility

In 2011, the Government Programme, drafted by each new government and laying out a four-year plan for the government term, stated as the main goal of Finnish transport policy to be '*to secure smooth and safe mobility in accordance with the needs of the economy and the inhabitants of Finland, along with measures to reduce transport-*

related emissions and promote sustainable development' (Council of State, 2011: 83). The latest government programme from 2015 continued many of the plans presented in 2011, including changing the balance of taxation income from car tax (of newly purchased cars) to the annual vehicle tax, and relying on transport biofuels to achieve reductions in GHG emissions from transport. More specifically, the government proposed to increase the share of renewable transport fuels to 40% by 2030, to build a digital business growth platform aiding mobility as a service, and to reduce unnecessary regulation across sectors (Council of State, 2015). These measures are likely to impact a transition towards low carbon transport systems positively. However, much focus is placed by the government on biofuels, whereas simultaneously it reduced its subsidies to public transport – an important measure reducing per capita GHG emissions by approximately 15%.

Two agencies operate under the Ministry of Transport and Communications. In 2010, previously separated agencies for aviation, rail, road and marine transport were merged into a new transport infrastructure agency called the Finnish Transport Agency and the Finnish Transport Safety Agency (Trafi). This enables more coordinated planning of different transport modes with potential benefits to low carbon transition. Also Tekes, the Finnish Funding Agency for Technology and Innovation, falling under the Ministry of Employment and the Economy, influences the transport sector by funding R&D projects. Local authorities also have a strong role in Finland because municipalities have many discretionary rights concerning land-use, housing and regional transport planning, influencing transport demand and modality. Key development needs lie in better coordination between national and local policies (Mäkinen *et al.*, 2015) and coordination between land-use, housing and transport in the regional level (Loikkanen, 2013).

Since 2010, changes in the institutional and policy content in support of a low carbon transport regime have been seen. Significantly, the Ministry of Transport and Communications and its agencies have engaged in a systemic change agenda and have, therefore, been able to support experimenting and policy development in that field. Also, the largest city region, the Helsinki Metropolitan region has been active in developing a more sustainable transport system, starting with new policies on parking, infrastructure for cycling, and experiments in public transport (Mäkinen *et al.*, 2015), and continuing with changes regarding the transport planning principles and mobility as a service (Guardian, 2014; Helsingin Sanomat, 2016). These changes are very welcome from the perspective of advancing low carbon transport, particularly as the existing mix of policies has gaps that need to be addressed to more effectively support such a transition.

On a national level, a range of policies exist in the four categories of development with potential to reduce GHG emissions: transport demand (passenger kilometres), transport mode (vehicle kilometres per passenger kilometres), fuel efficiency of vehicles, and carbon content of fuels. As an example, biofuels reduce the carbon content of fuels and electric vehicles improve fuel efficiency but neither directly affect transport demand. In contrast, an extensive public transport network can reduce vehicle kilometres per passenger, and novel services replacing transport demand can reduce passenger kilometres all together. On a national level, there has been '*a clear difference in policies supporting low carbon development in vehicles and fuels as opposed to transport demand and modal selection*' (Kivimaa & Virkamäki, 2014: 37). This is in line with previous research on the technology dominance of transport policy and research (see, e.g., Goodwin, 1999; Schwanen *et al.*, 2011).

Policy instruments encouraging transport demand reduction and modal change through entrepreneurial experimentation and market formation have been largely missing (Kivimaa & Virkamäki, 2014), while the latest government programme from 2015 partly addresses these points.The role of local authorities and agencies can be crucial in creating a test market for innovative transport solutions, such as the Kutsuplus On-demand automated transport service, developed by a group of researchers, that provided an on-call minibus service with non-fixed routes by the Helsinki Region Transport during 2012-2015 (Kivimaa, *et al.*, unpublished; Mäkinen *et al.*, 2014). Yet, most innovation funding is still targeting vehicle and fuel technology development; innovation policies have particularly focused on creating a market for electric vehicles, and experiments and demonstration for the production of transport biofuels (Kivimaa & Virkamäki, 2014).

Akin to recent institutional changes, some recent policy changes show promise. However, an analysis of recently introduced transport policy instruments both in the local level of the Helsinki metropolitan region and nationally show that the 'transformative' impact of such promising policies depends on other policies they are implemented with and the existing mix of policies they are embedded in: '*single policy measures create multiple and sometimes conflicting signals for urban mobility transitions. Their potential effects can indicate elements of path dependence, path desta-bilisation and path creation simultaneously as shown by our analysis of, for instance, the Helsinki region's metro extension*' (Mäkinen *et al.*, 2015: 499). The extension of the metro network may actually increase private car transport, as (a) impact assessments suggest that park-and-ride facilities encourage people move further away from the city centres and (b) previously designated bus lanes become available for private vehicles when metro replaces bus connections (path dependence). However, through the metro investment contributing to multi-modal transport, this policy measure may also encourage some car users at least partly to switch to other modes (path destabilisation) and the aim to create walking city fabrics around new metro stations can promote path creation. At the regional level, how transport policies cohere with employment policies (influencing, e.g. commuting patterns and distances) and economic policies (affecting, e.g. the competitiveness of city regions) is crucial in terms of the effects they generate (Mäkinen *et al.*, 2015).

Low carbon transition niches in Finland

Three exemplary cases in the development of low carbon niches in Finnish transport will now be presented.

Low carbon niches supporting the continuation of private passenger cars: Biofuels and electric vehicles

Technological development of both fuels and vehicles are the most progressed niches in the transition towards low carbon mobility (Nyqvist & Whitmarsh, 2008; Geels, 2012). This is related to the ease of the transition, as fuel and vehicle developments do not impose many changes to mobility practices of individuals but rather changes in supportive infrastructure and delivery networks, being the least disruptive form of abating greenhouse gas emissions from the perspective of the dominant car-based transport regime (cf. Upham *et al.*, 2014). In Finland, the active niches are those of liquid biofuels and electric vehicles (Temmes *et al.*, 2014). Interestingly they have developed in very different ways and paces.

Biofuels can be divided into two distinct technology groups: first-generation (1G) and second-generation (2G) biofuels, the former based on conventional technologies and agricultural crops and the latter involving the conversion of e.g. woody biomass and various waste streams, often into products having better user properties than 1G fuels (e.g. hydrated vegetable oil, HVO) (Lovio & Kivimaa, 2012). The niche discussed in the Finnish context relates to the latter. The development of the 2G biofuels niche in Finland has been relatively rapid. When the EU Directive 2003/30/EC setting a 5.75% biofuels target for 2010 and later increasing to 10% by 2020 was proposed, support for biofuels in Finland was very low causing Finland to oppose the directive and postpone its enforcement (Lovio & Kivimaa, 2012).

Finnish fuel companies never entered the 1G biofuel market, like many others that were motivated largely by agricultural policies enhancing the use of food crops for fuel production (Lovio & Kivimaa, 2012; Peixoto *et al.*, 2013). Instead, Neste Oil started the development of HVO-diesel in 2001, in anticipation of the EU biofuels directive. This development was based on earlier technology exercises, and was supported by public funding and the deliberate delay of the Finnish government to implement the biofuels directive (Peixoto *et al.*, 2013). Another fuel company St1 started the production of fuel ethanol from food industry waste based on a novel production technology.

Despite long standing R&D, politically the situation remained fairly stagnant until 2009-2010, when a national biofuels target exceeding EU demands was set, creating a market for rapid expansion. This prompted, for example, large investments by Neste Oil in HVO production and an increase in the ethanol content of regular petrol from 5% to 10% (Temmes *et al.*, 2014). Subsequent to actions by Neste Oil and St1, incumbent forest companies became interested in developing technologies to produce biodiesel from wood-based feedstock (Lovio & Kivimaa, 2012), but only tall-oil-based HVO production started by UPM has been commercially viable. Biofuels development has led to large scale business of second generation biofuels in Finland. The success is based on several factors: demand creation through both EU and national policy, long-standing tradition in bioenergy research in Finland due to abundant forest resources, and innovative actors aiming at 2G biofuels.

Contrarily to biofuels, the electric vehicles niche has developed slowly to approximately 1600 cars at the end of 2015 (0.5 % of all passenger cars), and some Finnish businesses actively marketing charging infrastructure and services for EVs. The development of this niche has been a result of systematic 'expectations work' of private actors towards politicians and policy-makers (Temmes et al., 2013), which has resulted in tax reductions and subsidies by the government for purchasing a limited number of electric vehicles. An initial barrier to policy action in the field of electric vehicles was a general belief that any support would leak to foreign automotive manufacturers, because very little automotive manufacturing exists in Finland. After extensive lobbying emphasising the broader scope of the field (Apajalahti et al., 2015) and private experimentation activities, a national vision-setting working group was appointed. The ambitious recommendations, published in 2009 by the group, generated a new wave of business activities in Finland both around EVs themselves and charging infrastructure during 2009-2010. They received much public attention resulting in remarkable media hype (Temmes et al., 2013).

Businesses on vehicles and their components were not successful and a major disappointment which reduced government support and media attention followed. Therefore actors especially in the infrastructure area gathered to reframe the field from EVs to the broader concept of electromobility including infrastructure and services (Temmes et al., 2013). As a result a major innovation programme was run from 2011 to 2015. The programme lead to the development of a community of actors around electric vehicles and a number of interesting start-ups. The increase in the numbers of electric vehicles continues, however, to be slow.

Biofuels and electric vehicles represent two competing niches for low carbon transition, even if neither of them is able to fully solve the climate issues of transport. The main characteristics of the transitions are summarised in Table 9.1. These characteristics show that biofuels are clearly a fit-and-conform transition, which means that the new technology rather easily fits in the existing regime and conforms to it (Smith & Raven, 2012; Upham et al., 2014), whereas electric vehicles require some change in the regime (i.e. the transition can be characterised as stretch-and-transform by which the new niche transforms the existing regime rather than conforming to it) even if the private vehicles still remain. The Finnish policy-makers widely refer to the principle of technology neutrality in regulation (cf. Azar & Sandén, 2011). This tends to enhance incremental niches, in Finland, especially biofuels (Temmes et al., 2014).

Table 9.1: Comparison of the transition elements of the biofuels and electric vehicles niches in Finland. Source: based on Peixoto *et al.* (2013), Temmes *et al.* (2013), Temmes *et al.* (2014).

	Biofuels	Electric vehicles
Regime change	Very little ʹ existing cars and driving practices existing fuel distribution network	Moderate new cars, new driving practices new cost structure new infrastructure with new business logic
Niche protection mechanisms	long tradition of innovation support in bioenergy market formation through EU regulation	no tradition of innovation support, because of lack of automotive companies few actions for market formation
Actors	innovative incumbent companies prepared to significantly change their supply chains	very versatile group of actors from incumbent utilities to start-ups and educational organisations

Protection of low carbon niches in public transport: Innovative public procurement

Demonstrations and public procurement are considered as important measures to enhance market formation for innovations in general (Breznitz *et al.*, 2009; TEM, 2010) and specifically in transport (Harborne *et al.*, 2007; Yarime, 2009). The Helsinki Region Transport Authority (HSL) has actively engaged in both full-scale experimentation of new technologies and innovative public procurement in bus transport. The principal tasks of HSL are to plan and organise public transport in the Helsinki metropolitan region and improve its operating conditions and to procure bus, tram, metro, ferry and commuter train services. Some 345 million journeys are made on HSL's transport services annually. HSL has ambitious strategic targets, including an objective to reduce its CO_2 emissions by 90% by 2025 (HSL, 2016).

HSL has actively developed its procurement system for bus transport in order to support the achievement of its strategic targets. The contracts with the bus operators are seven years in length, allowing time and motivation for the contractors to invest in a modern fleet. HSL has an extensive set of criteria either required or affecting the price of the tender. These include specifications for the traveling comfort and for the emissions (both CO_2 and local emissions) and noise levels of the buses. In order to give a proper incentive for the contractors to reduce the emissions during the seven-year tender period, HSL has introduced a system that they call an environmental bonus. This is a refunding mechanism for those bus operators who can prove that they have reduced their emissions.

To further enhance low carbon bus transport HSL is active in participating in vehicle technology development by being a partner in research programmes, such as TransSmart/ eBUS (TransSmart, 2016) and EVE (EVE, 2016). In recent years one important area of development has been electrical buses that are regarded as potential solutions especially for shorter routes that connect the railway stations with suburbs. The cold climate is problematic for charging but short routes and regular charging at the end stations have been found to reduce the requirement for battery capacity. HSL's partnerships with research institutions and publicly funded research programmes has resulted in successful public-private funding structures for research. The first experiment was carried out in the city of Espoo, part of the Helsinki Metropolitan area, where the buses have been tested in the field by actually running a bus line in harsh climatic conditions (Erkkilä *et al.*, 2013).

As part of eBUS programme, a special full-size electric vehicle was built to serve as a platform for component and vehicle testing. This platform combined electric bus technology with a lightweight construction (Laurikko *et al.*, 2015). As a result a company called Linkker was founded to commercialise the bus. Linkker and its partners are also working on charging infrastructure and smart mobility solutions to be integrated in the buses. These include, for example, vehicle control systems and ice detectors – solutions that help improve traffic safety and driving techniques. While in its normal operations HSL only procures bus transport from private operators, it has in 2015 ordered 12 electric buses from Linkker to carry out systematic experimentation with the buses and the infrastructure requirement. It is a four-year multi-partner pilot project funded by both private actors and Tekes. The aim of the project is to familiarise bus operators with electric buses and to build a   charging infrastructure (Laurikko *et al.*, 2015). The buses will also serve as a platform for testing innovations, studying their impacts and developing them further. Similarly, HSL has been active in other areas testing novel public transport solutions, such as demand-based route transport, by partnering with research and SMEs (Mäkinen *et al.*, 2015; Kivimaa *et al.*, unpublished).

A future radical niche transforming the idea of transport: MaaS – Mobility as a Service

The transport sector is so complex that a major transition affects numerous actors and requires very consistent and visionary policy-making. The idea of Mobility as a Service (MaaS) depicts such a major transition, which is forecasted to completely change the paradigm of transport. A commonly accepted clear definition for MaaS, however, is still missing. In the Finnish discourse it includes '*a transport service package to users that allows easy and reliable travel from door to door, which eventually allows the users to give up their own cars without a reduction in the level of service*' (LiVi, 2015). MaaS started off as an idea by a few private actors in the transport and ICT sectors, but is now a concept promoted actively by the public administration and e.g. the Minister of Transport and Communications. It is in a very early stage of development and, therefore, one of the major activities has been to create expectations (cf. Borup *et al.*, 2006) and general willingness among policy-makers to act with the purpose of a completely transformed way of how we think about transport, disrupting the institutional and regulatory regime (cf. Kivimaa & Kern, 2016). The concept of Mobility as a Service (MaaS) is experiencing somewhat of a hype in

Finland at the moment (Sampo Hietanen, CEO of ITS Finland, personal communication) and generally seen to offer business opportunities (LiVi, 2015).

MaaS is considered a major transition by the Finnish Transport Authorities (New Transport Policy Club, 2016), who see their role as enablers of this transition. The vision is that MaaS-services will be offered to users by 'mobility operators' with the help of modern digital solutions. The consumer would choose a suitable monthly package of various forms of transportation and communications, such as leased car, public transport, video-conferencing and on-demand transport from the operator. The first such operator has been founded at the beginning of 2016 – MaaS Finland Ltd. Its owners comprise transport service operators and technology providers and a significant loan from Tekes. The challenges in the business of an operator include the contracting, pricing and cost-sharing between the actors in these service packages. The prerequisite is open access to the timetables, real-time location information, and payment systems of existing transport service providers (e.g., railway operators, taxis, local transport operators, car sharing). It is also necessary that the operator is independent of transport service providers to avoid favouring of any single transport mode or operator. Even if the MaaS-concept is presently most actively used in Finland there are many similar activities emerging in Europe as seen in the programme of the recent Intelligent Transport conference (ITS World Conference, 2016), where some actors founded Mobility as a Service Alliance (Maas Alliance, 2016). The founding partners include both universities, authorities, innovation funding agencies and associations from various countries.

Summary of drivers and barriers of low carbon mobility transition in Finland

In this chapter we have analysed drivers and barriers for low carbon mobility in Finland. The various findings described earlier in the chapter are summarised in Table 9.2. The recent years have witnessed a phase where several structures have become more supportive of change than ever before both through long-term focus and experimental governance. Transition towards low carbon transport regimes shows promise particularly in the Helsinki Metropolitan region of Finland.

Even when the transition towards sustainable mobility is advancing, barriers and drivers co-exist both at the level of the global and national landscapes and of national and metropolitan regimes (Table 9.2). Yet, transition can be evidenced by an increasing number of regime drivers and a reducing number of barriers. In the metropolitan region, significant policy and institutional barriers were no longer detectable in our analysis. Interestingly, however, when looking at landscape developments, barriers tend to be national, while all drivers are more global trends.

Table 9.2: Summary of drivers and barriers of low carbon transition in Finland. Impacts of the landscape and regime.

	Global and national landscape		National transport regime in Finland		Transport regime in Helsinki Metropolitan area	
	Drivers	Barriers	Drivers	Barriers	Drivers	Barriers
Infrastructure	Price and availability of oil	Long distances; Urban sprawl	Attempts to coordinate land use and transport planning; Gradual development of infra and services for EV	Slowly changing infrastructure	Investments in new public transport; Free parking is decreasing in central Helsinki; Improved cycling infrastructure	Free parking is still common; Centralisation of services (e.g. health centres, libraries)
Innovation	Rapid development of ICT	Domination of technological solutions in innovation debates	Several transport R&D programmes and extensive networking; Biofuels development; High-level recognition and networks for MaaS	Domination of technological solutions in innovation debates	Public-academia-private partnerships in innovative developments; High level recognition for MaaS	
Policy	International climate commitments	Heavy demand of licensing of transport services	Supportive policy mixes for biofuels and EVs; Revisions of vehicle taxation; High target for biofuels	Commuting tax credits; Reducing support for public transport; Few demand-oriented policies	New parking and cycling policies; Renewed transport planning	Incoherence with employment and economic policies (?)
Institutions			Mergers of previously separate transport agencies; MinTC engaged in systemic change and experimenting	Main government action oriented towards biofuels	City of Helsinki transformed principles of transport planning; HSL engaged in piloting and partnerships	
People & practices	On-line shopping	Cold climate; Ageing population	Interest in owning private cars decreasing among young people	Private cars still dominate, especially in less populated areas; Varying support for biofuels and EV's	Public transport and cycling are generally accepted transport modes	Dependence on cars outside central areas

Conclusions

This chapter has demonstrated that Finland is on the path towards low carbon mobility while the transition is still in a relatively early phase and encounters clashes through the co-existence of drivers and barriers on multiple domains and levels. Key advances have not only been made in terms of niche building around technological solutions, including biofuels in transport and electric vehicles, but importantly in changing institutions and governance. On both national and metropolitan levels the responsible administrations have taken on the challenge of systemic change, endorsed this idea and engaged in both experimentation and policy change towards this effect. This shown in the reduced number of institutional and policy barriers, while there are still issues to be tackled in particular in licencing and taxation related to transport. Mostly the activities have also gained high level support from the standing government, the Ministry of Transport and Communications and Innovation Funding organisations.

The move towards experimental transport governance combined with other policy and institutional changes have been of crucial importance. Yet much remains to be done to achieve change in people's values, attitudes and practices connected to mobility. It is clear that until now the concrete steps taken in terms of reducing greenhouse gas emissions are due to 'technical fixes' to the private car-based personal transport regime rather than replacing private car use. Biofuels have certainly already contributed, whereas electric vehicles are up and coming. Many structures and people's preferences prevent more transformative change in personal transport, including how cities have been planned and built to create urban sprawl and dependence on private cars and limited public funds to support public transport. Nevertheless the level of attention given lately to experimenting with new transport services and the idea of transforming to transport as a service and a gradual change in the planning culture, create much hope for a future low carbon mobility system in Finland.

Acknowledgements

Empirical work presented in this chapter is largely based on the FIP-Trans project funded by the Finnish Funding Agency on Technology and Innovation Tekes during 2012-2014. The work has been updated in the context of the SET project funded by the Strategic Research Council of Finland (Grant Number 293405), in 2015-2016, and the Centre on Innovation and Energy Demand funded by RCUK (Grant Number EP/KO11790/1).

References

Apajalahti, E-L., Temmes, A. & Lempiälä, T. (2015). Incumbent organisations engaging to field-changinginnovations: cases of PV and EV charging. Submission 18764 Accepted to Academy of Management Annual Meeting 2015.

Azar, C. & Sandén, B. (2011). The elusive quest for technology-neutral policies. *Environmental Innovation and Societal Transitions* **1**, 135-139.

Borup, M., Brown, N., Konrad, K. & van Lente, H. (2006). The sociology of expectations in science and technology. *Technology Analysis & Strategic Management* **18**, 285-298.

Breznitz, D., Ketokivi, M. & Rouvinen, P. (2009). Demand- and user-driven innovation. In *Evaluation of the Finnish National Innovation System*, Taloustieto Oy: Helsinki, 71-102

ElectricTraffic (2016). http://www.sahkoinenliikenne.fi/sites/sahkoinenliikenne_fi/files/attachments/sahkoautokanta_suomessa_2015-q3_asl_1.pdf. Accessed 26 Feb 2016.

Erkkilä, K., Nylund, N-O., Pellikka, A-P., Kallio, M., Kallonen, S., Kallio, M., Ojamo, S., Ruotsalainen, S., Pietikäinen, O. & Lajunen, A. (2013). eBUS - Electric bus test platform in Finland. EVS27 International Battery, Hybrid and Fuel Cell Electric Vehicle Symposium, Barcelona. http://www.transsmart.fi/files/35/eBUS_Electric_Bus_Test_Platform_in_Finland.pdf.

EVE programme (2016). http://www.tekes.fi/globalassets/julkaisut/eve_final_report.pdf. Accessed 21 Jan. 2016.

Geels, F. W. (2002). Technological transitions as evolutionary reconfiguration processes: a multi-level perspective and a case-study. *Research Policy*, **31**, 1257–1274.

Geels, F. W. (2012). A socio-technical analysis of low carbon transitions: introducing the multi-level perspective into transport studies. *Journal of Transport Geography*, B, 471-482.

Goodwin, P. (1999). Transformation of transport policy in Great Britain. *Transportation Research Part A: Policy and Practice* **33**, 655–669.

Guardian (2014). 10 July, http://www.theguardian.com/cities/2014/jul/10/helsinki-shared-public-transport-plan-car-ownership-pointless. Accessed 26 Feb. 2016.

Harborne, P., Hendry, C. & Brown, J. (2007). The development and diffusion of radical technical innovation: The role of bus demonstration projects in commercializing fuel cell technology. *Technology Analysis and Strategic Management* **19**, 167-187.

Helsingin Sanomat (2016). http://www.hs.fi/kaupunki/a1453445641199?jako=8525e7c86a 615c7fc7317a619ea8d940&ref=tw-share. Accessed 26 Feb. 2016.

Hoogma, R, Kemp, R, Schot, J. & Truffer, B. (2002). *Experimenting for Sustainable Transport: The approach of Strategic Niche Management*. Spon Press, London.

HSL (2016). https://www.hsl.fi/en/helsinki-regional-transport-authority. Accessed 21 Jan. 2016.

ITS World Conference (2016). http://itsworldcongress.com/schedule/. Accessed 26 Feb. 2016.

Kivimaa, P., Boon, W. & Antikainen, R. (unpublished). Commercialising university inventions for sustainability – a case study of (non-)intermediating 'cleantech' at Aalto University. Submitted for review in *Science and Public Policy*.

Kivimaa, P. & Kern, F. (2016). Creative destruction or mere niche support? Innovation policy mixes for sustainability transitions. *Research Policy*, **45**(1), 205-217.

Kivimaa, P. & Virkamäki, V. (2014). Policy mixes, policy interplay and low carbon transitions: The case of passenger transport in Finland. *Environmental Policy and Governance*, **24** (1), 28-41.

Laurikko, J., Pihlatie, M., Nylund, N-O., Halmeaho, T., Kukkonen, S., Lehtinen, A., Karvonen, V., Mäkinen, R. & Ahtiainen, S. (2015). Electric city bus and infrastructure demonstration environment in Espoo, Finland. EVS28 International Electric Vehicle Symposium and Exhibition, Kintex, Korea.

LiVi (The Finnish Transport Agency) (2015) MaaS services and business opportunities. Reports of the Finnish Transport Agency 56/ 2015. http://www2.liikennevirasto.fi/julkaisut/pdf8/lts_2015-56_maas_services_web.pdf.

Lovio, R. & Kivimaa, P. (2012). Comparing alternative path creation frameworks in the context of emerging biofuel fields in the Netherlands, Sweden and Finland. *European Planning Studies*, **20**(5), 773-790.

Maas Alliance (2016). http://maas-alliance.eu/. Accessed 26 Feb. 2016.

MaaS programme (2016). https://www.tekes.fi/en/programmes-and-services/tekes-programmes/mobility-as-a-service/. Accessed 25 January 2016.

Mäkinen, K., Kivimaa, P. & Helminen, V. (2015). Path creation for urban mobility transitions - Linking aspects of urban form to transport policy analysis. *Management of Environmental Quality* **26**(4), 485 – 504.

New Transport Policy Club (2016). http://www.lvm.fi/documents/20181/859937/P%C3%A4%C3%A4+pilviss%C3%A4%2C+jalat+maas.+Uuden+liikennepolitiikan+klubin+fu turiikki/e0ccbf7e-9937-4abc-bbf9-3dd412890c1b?version=1.0. Accessed 7 March 2016.

Nylund, N-O., Tamminen, S., Sipilä, K., Laurikko, J., Sipilä, E., Mäkelä, K., Hannula, I. & Honkatukia, J. (2015). Tieliikenteen 40 %:n hiilidioksidipäästöjen vähentäminen vuoteen 2030: Käyttövoimavaihtoehdot ja niiden kansantaloudelliset vaikutukset. VTT Research Report VTT-R-00752-15 (Report on economic impacts of decreasing carbon dioxide emissions of transport. In Finnish)

Nyqvist, B. & Whitmarsh, L. (2008). A multi-level analysis of sustainable mobility transitions: Niche development in the UK and Sweden. *Technological Forecasting & Social Change* **75**, 1373-1387.

Peixoto, I., Temmes, A. & Lovio, R. (2013). How the emergence of multiple paths shapes a new field: examining variety and deviation in fuel production. *Fifth International Symposium on Process Organisation Studies*. Theme: The Emergence of Novelty in Organisations. 20-22 June. Greece.

Schwanen, T., Banister, D. & Anable, J. (2011). Scientific research about climate change mitigation in transport: a critical review. *Transportation Research Part A: Policy and Practice* **45**, 993–1006.

Smith, A. & Raven, R. (2012). What is protective space? Reconsidering niches in transitions to sustainability. *Research Policy* **41**, 1025–1036

Statistics Finland (2015a). http://www.tilastokeskus.fi/til/khki/2014/khki_2014_2015-12-14_tie_001_en.html. Accessed 26 Feb 2016.

Statistics Finland (2015b). http://www.stat.fi/til/vaenn/2015/vaenn_2015_2015-10-30_tie_001_en.html. Accessed 7 March 2016.

TEM (Ministry of Employment and the Economy) (2010). Demand and user-driven innovation policy. Publications of the Ministry of Employment and the Economy 48/2010. https://www.tem.fi/files/27547/Framework_and_Action_Plan.pdf.

Temmes, A., Räsänen, R-S., Rinkinen, J. & Lovio, R. (2013). The Emergence of Niche Protection through Policies: The Case of Electric Vehicles Field in Finland. *Science & Technology Studies* **26**, 37-62.

Temmes, A., Virkamäki, V., Kivimaa, P., Upham, P., Hildén, M. & Lovio, R. (2014). Innovation policy options for sustainability transitions in Finnish transport. *Tekes Reviews* 306/2014.

TransEco & TransSmart (2016). http://www.transeco.fi/en, http://www.transsmart.fi/transsmart/in_english. Accessed 25 January 2016.

Turnheim, B. & Geels, F.W. (2012). Regime destabilisation as the flipside of energy transitions: lessons from the history of the British coal industry (1913–1997). *Energy Policy* **50**, 35–49.

Unruh, G.C. (2000). Understanding carbon lock-in. *Energy Policy*, **28**, 817–830.

Upham, P., Kivimaa, P., Mickwitz, P. & Åstrand, K. (2014). Climate policy innovation: a socio-technical transitions perspective. *Environmental Politics*, **23** (5), 774-794.

Upham, P., Kivimaa, P. & Virkamäki, V. (2013). Path dependence and expectations in transport innovation policy: the case of Finland and the UK, *Journal of Transport Geography*, **32**, 12-22.

Upham, P., Virkamaki, V., Kivimaa, P., Hilden, M. & Wadud, C. (2015). Socio-technical transition governance and public opinion: The case of passenger transport in Finland. *Journal of Transport Geography* **46**, 210-219.

Yarime, M. (2009). Public coordination for escaping from technological lock-in: its possibilities and limits in replacing diesel vehicles with compressed natural gas vehicles in Tokyo. *Journal of Cleaner Production* **17**, 1281-1288.

10 The Underlying Structures of Low Carbon Mobility

Peter Newman

Curtin University Sustainability Policy Institute (CUSP), Curtin University, Australia.

Introduction

Carbon structural adjustment is as difficult and controversial as are financial structural adjustment programs in developing countries (Bird, 2001). The process of financial change is painful because it by necessity challenges the very structures and foundations on which economies have been built. Carbon structural adjustment is also much needed but is not yet a program of the International Monetary Fund (IMF) or World Bank. The same kind of fundamental change that came from the UN-inspired Breton Woods conference in 1944 on ending poverty is now on the agenda from the Paris Conference of the Parties (COP 21) in 2015 on ending dependence on fossil fuels.

The main focus of most carbon structural adjustment policy has been the need to replace coal-fired power stations with combinations of technological change (renewable energy, energy efficiency and new energy storage systems) and structural change such as finance, regulation and incentive programs (IPCC, 2014; Hargroves, 2015). These are now well underway and coal is clearly decoupling from wealth due to the structural success of these alternative technologies and institutional systems (IEA, 2016). Although oil and mobility has also been on the same agenda, it has received far less attention on structures, with most attention on technology, new vehicles and new fuels (e.g. WBCSD, 2004). Mobility structures are now being addressed much more since the Intergovernmental Panel on Climate Change (IPCC) and the International Energy Agency (IEA) began to focus more on such matters (IPCC, 2014; IEA, 2014).

This chapter will seek to understand how the structures of mobility, both existing and new, are helping or hindering a low carbon transition. It will assess why three underlying transport structural changes: peak car use, the second rail revolution and the decoupling of wealth and car use, are happening. And these will be explained in terms of three underlying urban structural changes: the re-urbanisation of cities, the economic trends towards the knowledge economy and the cultural trend towards smart phones and tablets. The shift of modes and the re-urbanisation processes together are replacing the previous era of urban car dependence with a polycentric low carbon city. The chapter will end by suggesting how this momentum can continue and enable a low carbon mobility transition.

Low carbon mobility: Transport structural adjustment

The most recent data on urban passenger mobility shows the start of some rather extraordinary and unexpected trends. Each of these are providing some hope for low carbon mobility structural change that will be explained further below.

Peak car

The Global Cities Database, developed by Jeff Kenworthy and many research students, presents data on cities, transport, energy and land use for nearly 40 years (Kenworthy & Laube, 2001; Kenworthy *et al.*, 1999). This research illustrates an interesting trend downwards in car use growth from 1950 to 2005 (Figure 10.1).

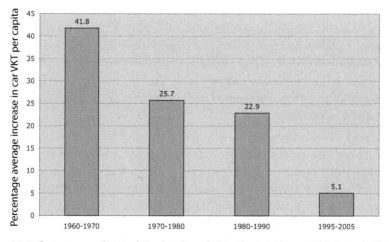

Figure 10.1: Car use growth trends in developed cities from 1960 to 2005. Source: Global Cities Database (Kenworthy & Laube, 2001; Newman & Kenworthy, 2015).

It became particularly interesting from 2004, when the US, most of Europe and Australia saw a *reduction* in car use per person for the first time in a hundred years. Figure 10.2 shows the US data and Figure 10.3 shows the Australian data with every city, including the congestion-free cities of Canberra, Darwin and Hobart, all going into reverse on car use. The same patterns have been seen in Europe (Jones, 2016). Newman and Kenworthy (2015) present evidence to suggest that the first signs of this trend can also be seen in emerging cities across Eastern Europe, Latin America, China and India.

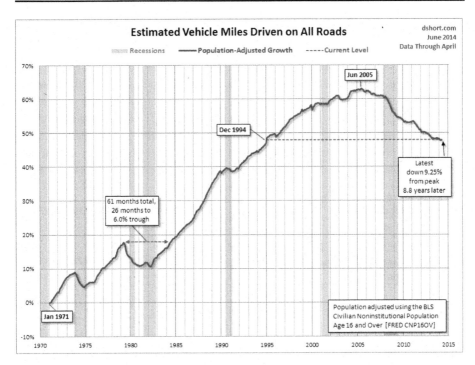

Figure 10.2: Car use per person peaks and declines in the US. Source: compiled from US Department of Transportation data.

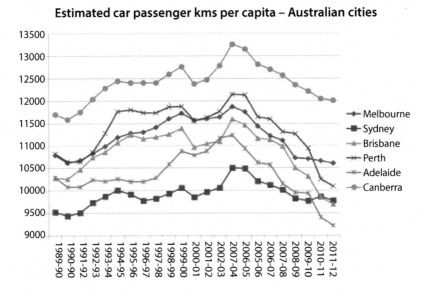

Figure 10.3: Car use per person declines in Australian cities. Source: BITRE, 2012.

The second rail revolution

Urban rail went into a hiatus during the expansion of the car-based city and the freeway era (1940s to 1990s). However, starting in the 1990s and accelerating this century, there has been a dramatic increase in urban rail across all the world's developed and developing cities (Newman *et al.*, 2013). Urban rail is expanding across Europe, North America and Europe and there are 81 Chinese cities building metro rail as well as 50 Indian cities (Newman & Kenworthy, 2015). The data from our Global Cities Database are summarised in Table 10.1 to show how automobile speeds have slowed in relation to transit, and especially where there is a rail option.

Ratio of overall public transport system to road speed	1960	1970	1980	1990	1995	2005
American cities	0.46	0.48	0.55	0.50	0.55	0.54
Canadian cities	0.54	0.54	0.52	0.58	0.56	0.55
Australian cities	0.56	0.56	0.63	0.64	0.75	0.75
European cities	0.72	0.70	0.82	0.91	0.81	0.90
Asian cities	-	0.77	0.84	0.79	0.86	0.86
Global average for all cities	0.55	0.58	0.66	0.66	0.71	0.70
Ratio of metro/suburban rail speed to road speed	1960	1970	1980	1990	1995	2005
American cities	-	0.93	0.99	0.89	0.96	0.95
Canadian cities	-	-	0.73	0.92	0.85	0.89
Australian cities	0.72	0.68	0.89	0.81	1.06	1.08
European cities	1.07	0.80	1.22	1.25	1.15	1.28
Asian cities	-	1.40	1.53	1.60	1.54	1.52
Global average for all cities	0.88	1.05	1.07	1.11	1.12	1.13

Table 10.1: Ratio of overall average transit system and rail speed to general road traffic speed in cities, 1960 to 2005. Source: Newman & Kenworthy, 2015.

The ratio of overall public transport system speed compared to general road traffic has increased from 0.55 to 0.70 between 1960 and 2005, the ratio of rail system speed to general road traffic has gone from rail being slower than cars in 1960 (0.88) to a situation in 2005 where rail was on average faster (1.13). And this trend has been steadily increasing (as shown in Table 10.1).

This trend is evident in a range of countries, for instance, in American and Canadian cities, overall public transport is barely half as fast as general traffic speed, whereas their rail systems are about 90% to 95% as fast, meaning that in many cases, trains are competitive with the car, especially in dense urban centres where the saturated road infrastructures are consistently being outperformed by fast urban rail systems. Australian cities do a little better with public transport overall now only about 25% slower than cars, while the rail systems are now on average about 8% faster and have generally been improving their competitive position since the 1960s and 1970s. When major corridors into city centres are considered, the rail systems are at a clear competitive advantage in terms of speed of transit.

European cities have generally had quite competitive rail systems in terms of speed which now sits on average 28% faster than cars. Their overall public transport systems, as a result of their fast rail systems, are on average 90% as fast as the car. It is interesting to note, however, that their rail speed relative to traffic dropped from 1.07 to 0.80 during the 1960s when they opened up to the car and built a lot of roads. A similar trend can be seen in Australian cities, but after that, rail speeds relative to the car rose quite consistently.

Asian cities in the sample have very fast rail systems compared to their crowded road systems; in 2005, rail speeds were 52% higher. This has fluctuated somewhat over the decades, but rail speeds on average were never less than 40% better than cars, even in the 1970s. Such data give hope to the many emerging cities struggling with the car, that rail systems can help them to develop a very different kind of overall urban transport system that is not determined by the private automobile. In emerging cities, traffic speeds were very slow (around the low 20s km/h) and bus speeds are always slower than this. Bangkok, for instance, had a traffic speed of 14 km/h and a bus speed of 9 km/h in 1990 (Newman & Kenworthy, 1999). Thus as these emerging cities build rail (often above or below the traffic) the data are likely to reflect transit speed improvements as shown in Table 10.1.

Decoupling of wealth and car use

The first sign of a peak in global GHG has been observed by the IEA (2016) and this is clearly decoupling from the growth in wealth. Most policy writing in this area remains rather pessimistic about change but these are encouraging signs. Although changes in the growth of coal and the dramatic growth in renewables have been noticed for some time, the decline in oil and its decoupling from wealth have not been as obvious in the popular commentary. This may be because, for many commentators, the structural changes in oil consumption are so obviously related to the highly fixed structures in cities that have been based around cars for so long (Newman & Kenworthy, 1989, 1999, 2015). There are going to be many factors causing the decline in greenhouse gases but the trends do seem to have begun around the same time as the above structural changes in coal use and car use that have set in since the early part of this century. Thus the next section examines how the structural decoupling of wealth and car use is linked to the structural changes within cities.

Low carbon mobility: Urban structural adjustment
Re-urbanisation of cities

Cities are structured by transport. Marchetti (1994) and Zahavi & Talvitie (1980) were among the first to show that there is a universal travel-time budget of a little over one hour on average per person per day, i.e. around 30 minutes on average for the journey to work. This Marchetti constant has been found to apply in every city studied; we found it holds true in all 100 or so cities in our Global Cities Database

(Kenworthy & Laube, 2001), as well as in data on UK cities for 600 years (Standing Advisory Committee on Transport, 1994). There are differences of opinion about the measurement of travel time and thus the size of its budget (Ahmed & Stopher, 2014) but given the universality of its application and the value of time in all urban transport studies, it is of some significance. Our work has shown how such travel time is the basis of urban structuring.

The Marchetti constant aids understandings of how cities are structured, because if people need to keep within a travel time budget then it is transport modal priorities and policies that will shape the form of cities (Newman & Kenworthy 1999, 2006, 2015). This suggests that cities grow to being about 'one-hour wide' based on the speed by which people can move in them. If cities go beyond this, they start to become dysfunctional and thus begin to change infrastructure and land use to adapt again to this fundamental principle (Van Wee *et al.*, 2006). This structuring suggests how cities can be transformed for agendas such as low carbon mobility.

There are three main city types or urban fabrics based on the 'one hour wide city' concept:

1 **Walking cities** (pre-historic cities until 1850s that grew outwards about 3 to 4 kms due to walking speeds, and hence very dense with narrow streets).

2 **Transit cities** (from the early trains in the 1850s and trams from the 1880s up until the 1950s, cities could grow outwards for 10 to 20 kms due to the speed of transit (trams 10 kph and trains around 20 kph) enabling long corridors of urban development with dense walkable centres at stations. This enabled medium density transit cities to be built.

3 **Automobile cities** (post 1950s cities that grew outwards with the popularity of the automobile to 50 kms or so). This era ushered in the phenomenon of low density automobile dependence.

Most cities today have a mixture of all three urban fabrics (Figure 10.4).

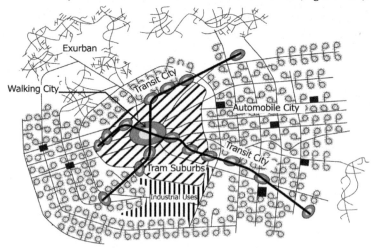

Figure 10.4: Growth of three city types based on transport modes. Source: Author.

Those cities built mostly in the automobile era are heavily oil-dependent (Figure 10.5), which shows there is an exponential link between car use/fuel use and urban density. However there is a new world emerging in terms of this fundamental structuring of cities: re-urbanisation. Cities have been reducing in density for the last 100 years as the benefits arising from faster movement have rebuilt urban development opportunities around mechanised transport, first rail-based then road-based. Figure 10.6 suggests that cities have stopped declining in density, plateaued, and are now increasing in density.

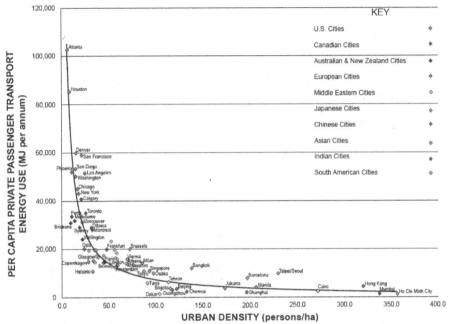

Figure 10.5: Transport fuel use and urban density in global cities. Source: Newman & Kenworthy (2015).

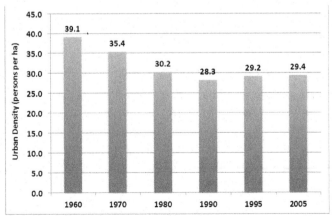

Figure 10.6: Urban density trend in 23 cities in the USA, Australia, Canada and Europe, 1960-2005. Source: Newman & Kenworthy (2015).

If cities increase in density then in structural terms it is more likely that a reduction in both car use and fuel use will follow. Re-urbanisation is a structural move supporting low carbon mobility and can explain the peak car and transit growth phenomenon, but it is important to critically consider why this may be happening. The growth in travel time budget in Australian cities due to urban sprawl and traffic congestion is now very evident (Figure 10.7). All these cities are now structurally dysfunctional as they have moved beyond the 30 minute average travel time for the journey to work.

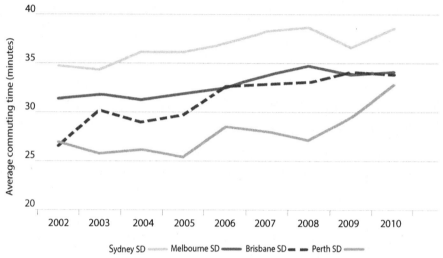

Figure 10.7: Trends in journey to work times in Australian cities. Source: BITRE (2016).

It is not hard to see why cities would respond to such increases in travel time by:

- Enabling rail projects that can go around, over or under the traffic and generate some real travel time savings, and/or

- Enabling re-urbanisation so that people can live nearer their work and so save time. This suggests that work is centralising so residential opportunities and transport opportunities are recognising this new market. Economic trends can help explain why this market has emerged.

Knowledge economy and city form

The biggest change in the economy during the period leading up to and including the period of car use decline and rail growth has been the digital transformation and the consequent knowledge/service economy. Despite this being global and enabling long distance communication, it has in fact been a concentrating force in terms of city structure and fabric. The knowledge economy and digital jobs are focused in city centres, as these are where the creative synergies between people occur (Kane, 2010; Glaeser, 2011). Old city centres have been transformed back into functional Walking cities and, those which have done this best, have attracted the most capital and young talent to work there (Gehl, 2012; Matan & Newman, 2012).

Other centres have also done similar transformations and the linkages between them have become the basis for the revival of the Transit city. Universities, health campuses and IT job clusters have created their own centres for jobs and have attracted housing and transit to link them together.

Other parts of the economy such as manufacturing, small and large industry, freight transport and storage, have remained car-based and are outside this new knowledge economy. They will remain so but they are also not where the growth in jobs or the growth in wealth is happening. Thus the Automobile city economy and culture has become somewhat distinct from the new regenerated urban economy of knowledge/services with their basis in Walking and Transit city locations.

Culture and technology

As with many economic changes, there is also a cultural dimension to this change that perhaps explains the rapidity of the changes observed above as well as the demographic complexion of the change (Florida, 2010). Young people (especially those involved in knowledge economy jobs) are moving to reduce their car use and switch to alternative transport faster than any other group (Davis *et al.*, 2012; and see Chapter 3, of this book). This has been recognised by a few commentators and related to the use of social media devices (Florida, 2010). On transit or walking (and even to an extent while biking) young people are already connected by their smart technology phones and tablets. They are hardly usable while driving a car. Davis *et al.* (2012) suggest that the mobile phone is a far more important device than a car for younger people. This is a cultural revolution that partly underlies the rail revolution.

While Baby-boomers gained freedom and connection with a car, generation Y (born 1980 onwards) may not have the same need for private vehicle ownership (Delbosc & Currie, 2013). They like to save time on a fast train but they also like to use the time constructively, relating to their friends and work through smart technology devices. The other structural expression of this change is that younger people are moving to live in the Walking city or Transit city as these locations more readily enable them to express the kind of urban experience and culture that they aspire to (Florida, 2010; Glaeser, 2011) as well as save to precious time. Thus they feed the market that enables peak car, the rail revival and city centre renewal to continue.

Low carbon mobility futures

There are not many guidelines to the future of our cities and regions that enable us to imagine out into the far future when we know there are so many techno-logical changes that will be happening that are beyond our imagination and present knowledge. However, if we do not go through this process of imagina-tion we can get submerged under an avalanche of despair as people can see only disaster once the days of climate change begin to hit more obviously. It is also very good economics to be better prepared for a low carbon future by creating a high performance city (IEA, 2016; UN Habitat, 2016). The alternatives futures around low carbon mobility all require substantial commitment to change in both how we live and the technologies we use in our cities and regions. By imagining some of the changes as suggested above, it is possible to see how we can continue on the track to cities without automobile dependence and its associated fossil fuel dependence.

The first signs of change towards these emerging technologies and urban systems can now be seen: the dramatic growth in electric transit; the rapid move towards electric vehicles and smart grids with a 40% per annum growth in global renewables; the large growth in the use of Pedelecs and E-bikes in many places; the emerging use of natural gas and biofuels; new technologies such as Skype and tele-presence (see Chapter 13); and the emergence of revitalised dense urbanism in a polycentric city framework (Newman & Kenworthy, 2015). Their application into large-scale urban demonstrations is now underway in places such as Kronsberg and Vauban in Germany, Masdar in UAE, the Low Carbon Cities of China, UC Davis's West Village, as well as the dramatic example of Singapore that is not just managing automobile dependence but is demonstrating the greening of density (Newman, 2014; Newman & Matan, 2013).

The potential for creating cities free of automobile dependence enables us to create oil-free cities that are strongly economically competitive and highly liveable. The technologies and practices outlined above suggest that we can be oil-free by 2050 and renewably based oil-free by 2100 as outlined by the IPCC (2014).The structural changes outlined above suggest that the changes in transportation, urban design and city planning, are well underway. This is the structural change to low carbon mobility that has begun but must continue if we are to meet global carbon goals. Continuing   reduction in automobile dependence and the growth in new technologies can enable us to create cities that are oil-free, based on options that are viable and attractive.

References

Ahmed, A. & Stopher, P. (2014). Seventy minutes plus or minus 10 – a review of travel time budget studies, *Transport Reviews* **34** (5), 607-625.

Bird, G. (2001). IMF Programs: Do they work? Can they be made to work better?, *World Development* **29** (11).

BITRE (2012). *Traffic Growth in Australia*, Report 127, Bureau of Infrastructure, Transport and Regional, Economics, Canberra, Australia. http://www.bitre.gov.au/publications/2012/report_127.aspx.

Delbosc, A. & Currie, G. (2013). Causes of youth licensing decline: A synthesis of evidence, *Transport Reviews*, **33** (3), 271-290.

Glaeser, E. (2011) *The Triumph of the City*, London: Penguin Press.

Hargroves, C. (2015). Carbon Structural Adjustment: Designing, Motivating, and Delivering an Economy-Wide Transition to Low Greenhouse Gas Emissions, PhD Thesis, CUSP, Curtin University.

Intergovernmental Panel on Climate Change (2014). *Climate Change 2014: Mitigation of Climate Change.* Contribution of Working Group III to the Fifth Assessment Report of the Intergovernmental Panel on Climate Change. UK: Cambridge University Press.

International Energy Agency (2015). *World Energy Outlook*, IEA, Paris.

International Energy Agency (2016). *Energy Technology Perspectives*, IEA, Paris.

Kenworthy, J., Laube, F., Newman, P., Barter, P., Raad, T., Poboon, C. & Guia B. (1999). *An International Sourcebook of Automobile Dependence in Cities, 1960~1990*, University Press of Colorado, Boulder, Colorado.

McIntosh, J., Trubka, R. & Newman P. (2015). Tax increment financing framework for integrated transit and urban renewal projects in car dependent cities. *Urban Policy and Research* **33**(1), 37-60.

Newman, P. (2015). Transport infrastructure and sustainability: a new planning and assessment framework, *Smart and Sustainable Built Environment*, **4** (2), 1-15.

Newman, P. (2014). Density, the sustainability multiplier: Some myths and truths with application to Perth, Australia, *Sustainability* **6**, 6467-6487.

Newman, P. (2014). Biophilic Urbanism: A Case Study of Singapore, *Australian Planner*, **51**, 47-65.

Newman, P. & Kenworthy, J. (2011). Peak car use: Understanding the demise of automobile dependence, *World Transport Policy and Practice*, **17**(2), 32-42.

Newman, P. & Kenworthy, J. (2015). *The End of Automobile Dependence: How Cities are Moving Beyond Car-based Planning*, Island Press, Washington DC.

Newman, P., Kenworthy, J. & Glazebrook, G. (2008). How to create exponential decline in car use in Australian cities, *Australian Planner* **45**(3), 17-19.

Newman, P., Glazebrook, G., & Kenworthy, J (2013). Peak car and the rise of global rail, *Journal of Transportation Technologies*, **3** (4), 272-287.

Newman, P. & Matan, A. (2013). *Green Urbanism in Asia*, World Scientific Publications, Singapore.

Newton, P., Newman, P., Glackin, S. & Trubka, R. (2012) Greening the greyfields: Unlocking the development potential of middle suburbs in Australian cities, *World Academy of Science, Engineering and Technology*, **71**, 138-157.

McIntosh, J., Newman, P. & Glazebrook, G. (2013). Why fast trains work: An assessment of a fast regional rail system in Perth, Australia, *Journal of Transportation Technologies*, **3**, 37-47.

Rauland, V. & Newman, P. (2015). *Decarbonising Cities: Mainstreaming Low Carbon Urban Development*, Springer, London.

Trubka, R., Newman, P. & Bilsborough, D. (2010). Costs of Urban Sprawl (1) – Infrastructure and Transport, *Environment Design Guide*, **83**, 1-6.

Trubka, R., Newman, P. & Bilsborough, D. (2010). Costs of Urban Sprawl (2) – Greenhouse Gases, *Environment Design Guide*, **84**, 1-16.

Trubka, R., Newman, P. & Bilsborough, D. (2010). Costs of Urban Sprawl (3) – Physical Activity Links to Healthcare Costs and Productivity, *Environment Design Guide*, **85**, 1-13.

UN Habitat (2016). *World Cities Report 2016,* UN Habitat, Nairobi, Kenya.

World Business Council on Sustainable Development (2004). *Sustainable Mobility,* WBCSD, Switzerland.

Case Study 3: Why the car is key to low carbon mobility in Brazil

Tobias Kuhnimhof

Institute of Transport Research, German Aerospace Center, Berlin, Germany.

Christine Weiss

Institute for Transport Studies, Karlsruhe Institute of Technology, Karlsruhe, Germany.

Introduction

The challenge of transitioning to low carbon mobility differs between industrialised countries and emerging economies. Industrialised countries – where mobility is high but its growth has slowed down – must reduce absolute levels of transport emissions, i.e. they have to transition from high carbon to low carbon mobility. Emerging economies – where continued growth of both transport and associated emissions appear inevitable – have to find mobility pathways that allow for growth of transport while curbing the growth of transport emissions. Different strategies are required to achieve this objective in an emerging economy, depending on respective framework conditions. Brazil is a particularly interesting case. As this chapter will illustrate, Brazil is headed toward an auto-dominated mobility system. We argue that Brazil must achieve low carbon automobility in order to achieve low carbon mobility.

With a population of 204 million and a GDP of $3.276 trillion in 2014, Brazil is the 6th largest country and the 8th largest economy worldwide (CIA, 2016), and is one of the most important developing economies. Thus Brazil is not only a major market itself – its economic and political leadership position causes Brazil to be influential beyond its own borders on a regional and global scale. Against this background it is evident, that Brazil, with transport accounting for 42% of total carbon dioxide (CO_2) emissions (CAIT, 2016), presents an important case for climate change mitigation and the decarbonising of transport.

The current model of transport in Brazil

During the last decades, car ownership and usage has increasingly shaped transport in Brazil as both new car registrations and the total car fleet grew substantially. With 2.9 million new car registrations in 2014 (doubling from 2005 figures), Brazil was the fourth largest new cars and light commercial vehicle market in the world (Fenabrave, 2006, Fenabrave, 2015). The used car market is even bigger; in 2014 8.7 million used cars changed hands, 3.1 times the number of new car registrations (Fenabrave, 2015). At 162 cars per 1000 inhabitants, the car ownership rate in Brazil exceeds that of India and China; however, it is still far below those of Germany and the USA, yet the average annual mileage is similar to that of China and India but low compared to Germany and the USA (see Table 1). The car, however, is not the only important private motor vehicle: a surge in motorcycle ownership in the recent years has led to 20 million motorbikes on register in 2015 (Fenabrave, 2015).

Table 1: Car fleet and car usage figures in Brazil and in four other countries. Sources: OICA (2016), progtrans (2010), KBA (2016), BTS (2013), National Bureau of Statistics of China (2012), Ministry of Statistics and Programme Implementation (2013).

	New car registrations [millions] (data from 2014)	Car fleet [millions] (data from 2012)	Car ownership rate [cars/1,000 inhabitants] (data from 2011)	Average annual mileage of the car fleet [km] (data from 2010)
GER	3.0	44	547	12,400
USA	7.7	234	722	19,800
BRA	2.9	33	162	7,000
CHN	19.7	61	45	9,300
IND	2.6	19	15	6,200

As exemplified by its 1.5 million km interurban roads compared to 28,500 km railway infrastructure, Brazil has a predominantly road-based transport system (CIA, 2016). This has also contributed to a bus dominated public transport system with long distance bus lines connecting metropolitan areas across Brazil. In various Brazilian cities, bus rapid transit (BRT) systems enable fast connections within the cities; for example in Rio de Janeiro, where about 9 million passengers use the BRT every month (Colin, 2015).

In Brazilian cities with more than 60,000 inhabitants, walking still forms an important part of everyday mobility accounting for 37% of all trips (across all trip purposes) in 2013. The car (as driver or passenger) is used for 27% of all trips, followed by public road transport (25%). Rail, motorbike and bicycle all have a modal share of about 4% (ANTP, 2014).

To obtain a better understanding of how the transport system in Brazilian cities compares to other cities worldwide, we draw on a cluster analysis of over 40 metropolitan transport systems from around the world (Kuhnimhof & Wulfhorst, 2013, Priester *et al.*, 2013). Figure 1 visualises the result of this cluster analysis including two Brazilian cities (Sao Paulo and Campinas). It also includes a brief characterisation of the clusters. The original cluster analysis included 41 cities – among them Sao Paulo – which were categorised on the basis of data from the millennium cities data base (Kenworthy & Laube, 2001), including 59 transport system indicators for the year 1995. Despite the fact that some of these 1995 indicators are likely to be outdated, the clusters still provide a good indication about the general pathway that cities are on (Kuhnimhof & Wulfhorst, 2013). Campinas was fitted into the clusters later on the basis of more current transportation system data dating from around 2010 (WBCSD, 2016).

Figure 1 shows that high income cities typically fall into one of three clusters: 'Transit' cities (mostly high density Asian cities), 'Hybrid' cities (European and most North American and Australian cities) and 'Auto' cities (low density US cities and Riyadh, Saudi Arabia). Cities from emerging economies typically fall into the 'Non-motorised' cluster (some Asian cities), 'Traffic-saturated' cluster (some Asian cities, cities in the Middle East and North Africa) and the 'Paratransit' cluster (cities in Africa and South America). Interestingly, both Sao Paulo (1995) and Campinas (2010) did not fall in line with other cities from emerging economies and clustered as 'Hybrid' cities. Relevant differences between these Brazilian cities and typical 'Hybrid' cities in Europe and North America were relatively low GDP, a low car mode share and a high level of motorcycle ownership.

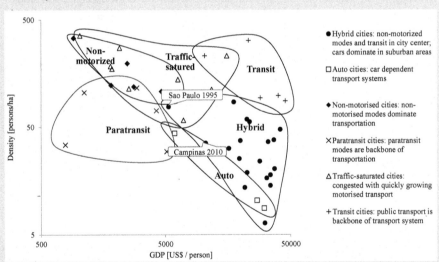

Figure 1: The position of Brazilian cities among global cities clustered based on mobility system characteristics. Source: Figure adapted from Kuhnimhof and Wulfhorst (2013).

Of course, there are important factors that make Brazilian cities unique. However, it is interesting to note that on a global scale Brazilian cities are not so different from European and many North American cities, for instance with regard to density. Moreover, the clusters in Figure 1 can also be interpreted as stages of development of urban mobility systems: as the economy grows, cities move from left to right in the graph. Often population densities decrease with rising incomes (Angel et al., 2010). Hence, cities tend to move towards the lower right corner of the graph (with the notable exception of some Asian cities that manage to maintain high densities as incomes grow). If Sao Paulo and Campinas follow this path, they seem to be heading towards a relatively low density, auto-oriented section of the 'Hybrid' cluster. This is a first indication of the direction that Brazil is taking in terms of its future development which we will discuss in more detail in the remainder of the paper.

Factors shaping Brazilian automobility in the next decades

Economic development

Figure 2 shows the historic evolution of car ownership over change in GDP in four selected industrialised countries as well as in the BRIC countries (Brazil, Russia, India and China). For GDP per capita, we used data from Bolt and van Zanden (Bolt & van Zanden, 2013) which are based on conversion using purchasing power parity (PPP) applying a particular conversion developed for international comparisons called Geary-Khamis dollars (GK$). Other than ordinary exchange rates, these purchasing power parities do not only consider income differences across countries but also cost-of-living differences. In other words: a given amount of Geary-Khamis dollars (GK$) buys the consumer an equivalent set of consumer products in different study countries.

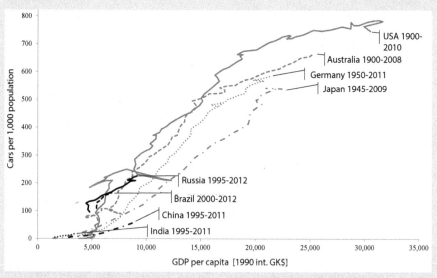

Figure 2: Car ownership over GDP per capita for USA, Australia, Germany, Japan, Russia, Brazil, China, and India. Authors' own representation using data from the Maddison Project (2013), US Census Bureau (2010), BITRE (2012b), BMVBS (2013), KBA (2016), Statistics Japan (2014b), BTS (2012), progtrans (2010), National Bureau of Statistics of China, (2012), Ministry of Statistics and Programme Implementation (2013), and Knott (2000).

Car ownership evolution tends to follow an s-shaped curve, as has been observed in countries with growing car ownership all around the globe (Dargay *et al.*, 2007). It grows non-linearly with income, growing more slowly at the lowest income levels, then growing more rapidly as incomes increase, and finally slowing down as saturation is approached. When using 1990 Geary-Khamis dollars, the period of economic development between a GDP of $5,000 and $20,000 has historically been characterised by strong growth of car ownership in many industrialised and newly industrialised countries. There is no indication that car ownership trends over GDP in emerging economies such as Brazil will not follow a similar s-shaped curve. Hence, Brazil appears to have entered a period of strong car ownership growth in the last decade. It is likely to remain in that stage of car ownership growth for another two to three decades before growth will level off and there might be signs of saturation. This means that Brazilian automobility – and with it emissions – will continue to grow at rapid pace for years to come.

Figure 2 also shows that at comparable levels of GDP per capita, car ownership varies substantially across countries. This indicates that GDP development falls short of fully explaining automobility development; other factors also influence automobility levels. In the following sections we present other relevant factors and analyse how they play out in the case of Brazil.

However, before discussing additional factors, we want to point out two specific characteristics of the Brazilian economy and private household income situation, which might help to interpret average household car ownership. First, with a Gini coefficient of 0.52 Brazil is one of most unequal countries in terms of income distribution. The wealthiest 10% of Brazilian households dispose of 43% of the country's cumulated household income (CIA, 2016). Hence, speaking in the terms of Figure 2, a small proportion of the Brazilian population has moved far ahead on the x-axis and towards associated high levels of car ownership. The vast majority, however, lags behind and has car ownership levels far below the average. Second, the private debts of Brazilian households have substantially risen within recent years. While in 2005 private households had debts of about 20% of their annual disposable income, these increased to about 45% in 2013 (Banco Central do Brasil, 2013). The high propensity of private households to take out loans might cause the current level of car ownership to be higher than what one would expect given Brazil's average income.

Demography and workforce participation

Different age/life cycle groups exhibit different travel behaviour (Dios Ortúzar & Willumsen, 2011). As a consequence it is evident that a country's demographic structure influences its aggregate travel demand structure. Commuters are a key factor in this context because they tend to generate more travel demand and more car use than other segments of the population. In the next decades the proportion of the total Brazilian population in working age is higher than the respective proportion in the selected industrialised countries during the past decades (OECD, 2012). This means that this relatively active and mobile group constitutes a substantial share of the population, likely leading to high aggregate mobility demand. Moreover, in Brazil workforce participation of women has risen rapidly in the past decades and is relatively high compared to the other countries (World Bank, 2010). Taken together, this means that workers, and thus commuters, represent a large share of the Brazilian population today and this is likely to continue in the next years. Given the fact that commuters tend to increase car ownership and car use, this demographic set-up is likely to give additional strength to the growth of automobility in Brazil.

Oil and energy

An affordable energy supply is a precondition for individual motor transport. Today, fossil fuels are the dominant source of energy for automobile travel on the global scale. Annually, Brazil produces roughly the same amount of oil as it consumes (EIA, 2014). This puts Brazil in a much better position than most industrialised countries during their historic period of strong growth of car ownership. In other countries, dependence on foreign energy was considered a barrier against developing an automobile dependent transport system (Ecola *et al.*, 2014). In Brazil this is less of an issue; even more so, because fossil fuels are supplemented by ethanol. The relevance of ethanol as an alternative to conventional gasoline is illustrated by the rapid market take up of flexible fuel cars. These cars are equipped with an ethanol-ready engine and a single fuel tank for both fuels. Car owners can refuel their flexible fuel vehicles with either gasoline or ethanol or with gasoline-ethanol-mixtures of any mixture-ratio (Busch, 2010). Introduced in 2003, the flexible fuel drive is the dominant technology at the car market today with 93% of new cars being equipped with a flexible fuel drive (Anfavea, 2015).

However, the projected global growth of energy demand in the next decades raises the question whether energy for individual motor transport will be affordable for the average Brazilian. To inform this discussion, Figure 3 shows long term trends of petrol prices relative to income (in purchasing power parities) for Brazil and other countries. The figure illustrates that to date, the affordability of fuel in Brazil compares quite well to the situation in industrialised countries at historic times when their GDPs were much lower. Fuel prices grew substantially in absolute terms in Brazil within the recent years. 2015 fuel prices in Brazil were at 0.92 USD per litre gasoline and 0.68 USD per litre ethanol (ANP, 2015). However, in the long term, fuel prices decreased in the industrialised countries relative to income as incomes grew more rapidly than fuel prices. Given that economic growth and income growth continues in Brazil, a similar development of fuel becoming less expensive relative to incomes is likely for Brazil.

Of course, global energy prices will influence fuel price in Brazil – however, this is unlikely to change the structural development towards more affordable fuel for the average Brazilian. Fuel taxation, which can explain why fuel in Germany is almost three times as expensive as in the USA, for instance, will be just as important for fuel affordability as the crude oil price. The Brazilian ethanol policy and the expected diversification and increased efficiency of vehicle powertrains in the next decades will also help to mitigate the expected impact of crude oil price increases.

Future fuel price development is unlikely to hamper the growth of automobility substantially in Brazil in the next years. However, an increasing price differential between fossil fuels and other energy sources for automobiles might foster the shift towards alternative power trains and low carbon automobility that Brazil has already started with the introduction of ethanol fuel and flexible fuel vehicles.

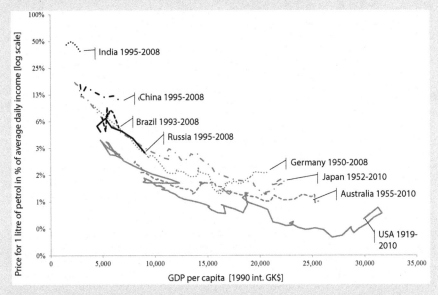

Figure 3: Fuel price relative to income for Brazil and seven other selected countries. Authors' representation based on data from the Maddison-Project (2013), World Bank (2010), BITRE (2012a), BMVBS (2013), Statistics Japan (2014a), Office of Energy Efficiency & Renewable Energy (2014) and GIZ (2011).

Car industry

In many developing economies, the automotive industry is regarded as a pillar of economic growth. Brazil is no exception. Car production is an increasingly important part of Brazil's industrial sector. Relative to its population Brazil produces more cars than China and Australia (Figure 4). In 2011, Brazil produced more cars per population than the USA. This, however, was in the aftermath of the economic crisis and the situation has reversed again. For a successful car industry, a domestic market is important. In such a situation the automotive industry lobby – representing a large number of jobs – usually forms an influential group in the political decision making process and measures that could curb automobility are more difficult to implement (Douglas *et al.*, 2011). Hence, a strong focus of the economy on the automotive industry is also likely to be a driver of automobility growth.

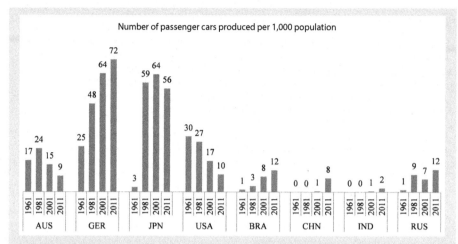

Figure 4: Car production relative to population for Brazil and seven other selected countries. Authors' representation based on data from BTS (2013).

Urbanisation, population densities and transport infrastructure

Other important factors that influence demand for automobility are urbanisation, population densities and infrastructural conditions (Priester *et al.*, 2013). A factor that potentially curbs automobility in Brazil is the large population share that lives in large and very large cities, where travel tends to be less auto-oriented than in other environments. About 50% of Brazilians, as opposed to about 30% of Germans or Americans, reside in cities of over 100,000 people. Of these, about 20% live in cities with a population of over 1 million, compared to about 10% of Germans or Americans (UNESA, 2016). However, lower population densities within urban areas tend to increase automobile orientation of urban dwellers. Brazil's urban population densities are on a similar level as those in Germany and likely to decrease further in the future (Lincoln Institute of Land Policy, 2016, Angel *et al.*, 2010). Moreover, even today per capita road supply in Brazil compares to that in Europe – also with a trend to increase further (CIA, 2016). These factors indicate that despite high urbanisation, spatial structure factors in Brazil are likely to be relatively conducive to automobility in the next decades.

Brazil's automobile future – consolidated outlook

In the previous section we presented a number of factors which are likely to play a key role in shaping the framework conditions for the development of transport in Brazil. With regard to low carbon mobility, understanding the impact of these factors is essential. Before drawing conclusions about how to achieve low carbon mobility in Brazil, we therefore ask the question: How car oriented will Brazil's future transportation be? Will it be car dominated as in the USA or more balanced as in Europe or even Japan?

Ecola *et al.* (2014) examined the future of automobility in Brazil, Russia, India and China (BRIC countries). The study combined quantitative analysis of historical data from the BRIC countries and from selected industrialised countries with data derived from an expert-based qualitative approach. The latter was used to transfer historic experiences about how automobility evolution was shaped in industrialised countries and how these experiences may affect the future of automobility in the BRIC countries. The study indicated that Brazil is likely to be the most car-oriented country among the BRICs with a potential long-term level of automobility higher than in Europe but lower than in the USA. China and India, on the other hand, were projected to be heading towards lower levels of automobility than Germany but higher than Japan.

An important feature of Brazil's path towards automobility is the increase of the proportion of car owners among its population. This proportion increases because of new consumer groups entering an income stratum that enables them to acquire a car, becoming first time car buyers of either new or used cars. Weiss *et al.* (2013) analysed the relevance of this group for the Brazilian car market for the period from 2000 to 2030 using a system dynamics model. The number of cars bought by first time car buyers peaked in 2010 with 830,000 cars. In 2010 the vast majority (about 90%) of cars in Brazil were sold to households as a second or third car or to replace an existing vehicle. After 2010, car sales to first time car buyers decrease constantly. The reason for this development is the decreasing number of households without a car and the shift of the car market from new car buyers to car buyers who are replacing an existing vehicle or buying a second or third vehicle in the household.

This system dynamics model projects the proportion of households with car in 2030 in Brazil to be about 50%. This is still low, compared to industrialised countries today (Germany: 80%; USA: 90%) (infas, 2010, FHWA, 2016). Likewise, 2030 car ownership rate projections for Brazil – ranging from 350 to 400 cars per 1,000 population – will remain low compared to car ownership in Europe (500 cars/1,000 inhabitants) and the USA (760 cars/1,000 inhabitants) today. However, even when assuming relatively optimistic GDP growth rates of 3% per annum until 2030, Brazil's GDP per capita will only reach about 12,000 USD (GK$) in that year. Hence, as can be seen in Figure 2, Brazil will likely still be in the middle of a period of strong growth of car ownership in 2030. So, when in 2030 car ownership in Brazil is still far lower than in industrialised countries today the reason is simply that saturation of automobility growth will still be far out of reach then.

Conclusion for low carbon mobility transitions in Brazil

This case study examined the future of automobility in Brazil in order to derive implications for a low carbon mobility transition. We presented several factors which may form framework conditions that are conducive to automobility in Brazil. Car ownership and car travel are likely to increase with economic development in the coming decades in Brazil, heading toward levels of automobility that could well be higher than in Europe today. Demographic and socio-economic factors, the availability of domestic fuel, a strong car industry as well as infrastructural conditions are key drivers of this development.

Against a background of projected high levels of car ownership and use we suggest a focus on 'Improve' strategies (e.g. increasing efficiencies) for Brazil. However, examples from other countries illustrate a strong path dependency, e.g. because it takes years or even decades to replace a country's vehicle fleet. Hence, measures and regulations to shape Brazil's future vehicle fleet appear to be paramount. With many first time car buyers entering the Brazilian market in the next decades, there is still the possibility to shape the automobile system – from car purchasing behaviour to everyday travel routines – around alternative fuels and powertrains including electric vehicles. This includes various measures such as emission limits for new vehicles and fuelling/charging infrastructure. With the successful introduction and market uptake of ethanol fuel and flexible fuel vehicles, Brazil has already made a first substantial step in this direction. Other bold measures to improve the efficiency of the future vehicle fleet should follow.

Aside from improving vehicle efficiency, strategies for decarbonisation include fostering the use of non-auto modes of transport (i.e. the Shift-approach) or reducing the need to travel long distances (i.e. the Avoid-approach). It is evident that measures such as public transport improvements, transit oriented development, emphasis on non-motorised modes, increasing local accessibility etc. all contribute to decarbonising transport (Priester et al., 2013). They should also be pursued because they bring about numerous additional benefits ranging from reducing congestion across improving the quality of public space to health benefits through active transportation. This is particularly true for Brazil's metropolitan megacity areas where large parts of the Brazilian population live. In these locales, increased personal travel will lead to increased congestion, severe health issues due to local emissions, substantial parking problems and other negative concomitants of urban personal transport. Under these conditions policy emphasis on other transport modes or other personal vehicles (motor cycles, mini cars) appears inevitable. Along with mitigating local transport problems, these measures will also contribute to low carbon mobility.

However, for Brazil as a whole one should not have high hopes that fostering alternative transport modes can be a major contributor to decarbonising transport. This would not fit the realities in large parts of the country that have set out on a relatively auto-oriented path. This makes improving vehicle efficiency and moving to alternative fuels and powertrain technology key factors for achieving decarbonisation of transport. In other words: If Brazil is to achieve low carbon mobility it must develop into a showcase of *low carbon automobility*.

References

Anfavea (2015). *Anuario da Industria Automobilisica Brasileira.* Sao Paolo: Brazilian Automotive Industry Association.

Angel, S., Parent, J., Civco, D. L. & Blei, A. M. (2010). The persistent decline in urban densities: global and historical evidence of 'sprawl'. In: Lincoln Institute Of Land Policy (ed.) *Lincoln Institute of Land Policy Working Paper.*

ANP. (2015). *Gás Natural e Biocombustíveis* Available at: http://www.anp.gov.br/preco/. Accessed 18 Jan 2016.

ANTP. (2014). *Sistema de Informações da Mobilidade Urbana da ANTP - Relatório Comparativo 2003/2012.* Available at: http://www.antp.org.br/_5dotSystem/userFiles/SIMOB/Relatorio%20Comparativo%202013.pdf. Accessed 12 Dec 2015.

Banco Central Do Brasil (2013). *Relatório de Inflacao.* Brasilia.

BITRE (2012a). Traffic growth in Australia. *Research Report 127.* Canberra ACT: Bureau of Infrastructure, Transport and Regional Economics (BITRE).

BITRE (2012b). Traffic growth: Modelling a global phenomenon. *Research Report 128.* Canberra ACT: Bureau of Infrastructure, Transport and Regional Economics (BITRE).

BMVBS (2013). *Verkehr in Zahlen 2012/2013* (German Transport in Figures). Berlin: Bundesministerium für Verkehr, Bau und Stadtentwicklung (BMVBS).

Bolt, J. & Van Zanden, J. L. (2013). The first update of the Maddison Project, Re-estimating growth before 1820. *Maddison Project Working Paper.*

BTS. (2012). *National Transportation Statistics.* Washington D.C.: Bureau of Transportation Statistics (BTS). Available at: http://www.bts.gov/publications/national_transportation_statistics/. Accessed 20 Feb 2012.

BTS. (2013). *National Transportation Statistics.* Bureau of Transportation Statistics (BTS). Available at: http://www.rita.dot.gov/bts/publications/nationaltransportationstatistics/. Accessed 29 July 2013.

Busch, A. (2010). *Wirtschaftsmacht Brasilien: Der grüne Riese erwacht,* Bonn, Bundeszentrale für Politische Bildung.

CAIT. (2016). *CAIT Climate Data Explorer, Historical Emissions.* Available at: http://cait.wri.org/historical/. Accessed 18 Jan 2016.

CIA. (2016). *The World Factbook: Brazil.* Available at: https://www.cia.gov/library/publications/the-world-factbook/geos/br.html. Accessed 18 Jan 2016.

Colin, B. (2015). *4 Inspirations for Sustainable Transport from Rio de Janeiro.* World Resources Institute. Available at: http://www.wri.org/blog/2015/03/4-inspirations-sustainable-transport-rio-de-janeiro. Accessed 18 Jan 2016.

Dargay, J., Gatley, D. & Sommer, M. (2007). Vehicle ownership and income growth, worldwide: 1960-2030. *Energy Journal,* **28**(4),143–170.

Dios Ortúzar, J. D. & Willumsen, L. G. (2011). *Modelling Transport,* Chichester, Wiley.

Douglas, M. J., Watkins, S. J., Gorman, D. R. & Higgins, M. (2011). Are cars the new tobacco? *Journal of Public Health, 33,* 160-169.

Ecola, L., Rohr, C., Zmud, J., Kuhnimhof, T. & Phleps, P. (2014). *The Future of Driving in Developing Countries*, Santa Monica, CA, RAND Corporation.

EIA. (2014). *EIA Beta*. U.S. Energy Information Administration (EIA). Available: http://www.eia.gov/beta/. Accessed 20 March 2014.

Fenabrave (2006). Semestral 2005 da Distribuicao de Veículos Automotores no Brasil.

Fenabrave (2015). Semestral 2014 da Distribuicao de Veículos Automotores no Brasil.

FHWA. (2016). *NHTS Online Analysis Tools*. US Department of Transportation, Federal Highway Administration (FHWA). Available: http://nhts.ornl.gov/tools.shtml. Accessed 27 Jan 2016.

GIZ (2011). *International Fuel Prices 2010/2011*. Gesellschaft für Internationale Zusammenarbeit (GIZ).

INFAS, D. (2010). *Mobilität in Deutschland 2008*.Tabellenband. Bonn; Berlin: Institut für Angewandte Sozialwissenschaft GmbH (INFAS), Deutsches Zentrum für Luft- und Raumfahrt (DLR).

KBA. (2016). *Zahlen zum 1. Januar 2015 im Überblick*. Kraftfahrtbundesamt (KBA). Available at: http://www.kba.de/DE/Statistik/Fahrzeuge/Bestand/bestand_node. html. Accessed 18 Jan 2016.

Kenworthy, J. & Laube, F. (2001). *UITP Millennium Cities Database for Sustainable Transport*. Brussels: International Union of Public Transport (UITP).

Knott, J. W. (2000). The 'conquering car': Technology, symbolism and the motorisation of Australia before World War II. *Australian Historical Studies*, **31**, 1–26.

Kuhnimhof, T. & Wulfhorst, G. (2013). The reader's guide to mobility culture. *In:* Institut Für Mobilitätsforschung (ed.) *Megacity Mobility Culture. How Cities Move on in a Diverse World*. Heidelberg, New York; Dordrecht; London: Springer.

Lincoln Institute Of Land Policy. (2016). *The Atlas of Urban Expansion*. Available at: http://www.lincolninst.edu/subcenters/atlas-urban-expansion/documents/table-urban-land-cover-data.xls. Accessed 29 Jan 2016.

Ministry of Statistics and Programme Implementation. (2013). *Statistical Year Book, India 2013*. Available at: http://mospi.nic.in/mospi_new/upload/SYB2013/index1.html. Accessed 25 March 2014.

National Bureau of Statistics of China. (2012). *Annual Data*. Available at: http://www.stats.gov.cn/english/. Accessed 31 Jan 2012.

OECD. (2012). *OECD Statistics*. Available at: http://stats.oecd.org/Index.aspx .Accessed 31 Jan 2012.

Office of Energy Efficiency & Renewable Energy. (2014). *Vehicle Technologies Office: Modeling, Testing, Data and Results*. Available at: http://energy.gov/eere/vehicles/vehicle-technologies-office-modeling-testing-data-and-results. Accessed 20 March 2014.

OICA. (2016). *New PC Registrations or Sales*. International Organisation of Motor Vehicle Manufacturers. Available at: http://www.oica.net/wp-content/uploads//pc-sales-20151.pdf. Accessed 19 April 2016.

Priester, R., Kenworthy, J. & Wulfhorst, G. (2013). The diversity of megacities world-wide: Challenges for the future of mobility. In: Institut Für Mobilitätsförschung (ed.) *Megacity Mobility Culture. How Cities Move on in a Diverse World.* Heidelberg, New York; Dordrecht; London: Springer.

Progtrans (2010). *World Transport Report: Analyses and Forecasts, Edition 2010/2011,* Basel, Progtrans.

Statistics Japan. (2014a). *Historical Statistics of Japan, Chapter 12 Transport.* Available at: http://www.stat.go.jp/english/data/chouki/12.htm. Accessed 26 March 2014.

Statistics Japan. (2014b). *Statistical System, Chapter 12 Transport.* Available at: http://www.stat.go.jp/english/data/chouki/12.htm. Accessed 20 March. 2014.

The Maddison-Project. (2013). *New Maddison Project Database.* Available at: http://www.ggdc.net/maddison/maddison-project/home.htm. Accessed 26 March 2014.

UNESA. (2016). *2014 Revision of World Urbanization Prospects.* Available at: http://esa.un.org/unpd/wup/. Accessed 29 Jan 2016.

US Census Bureau. (2010). *International Data Base (IDB).* Available at: http://www.census.gov/population/international/data/idb/informationGateway.php. Accessed 04 July 2011.

WBCSD. (2016). *Sustainable Mobility 2.0.* Available at: http://www.wbcsd.org/work-program/sector-projects/mobility.aspx. Accessed 27 Jan 2016.

Weiss, C., Kuehn, A. & Schade, W. (2013). Car purchasing potential of first time buyers in Brazil and Russia. In: *World Conference on Transport Research Society,* ed. 13th World Conference on Transport Research, Rio de Janeiro.

World Bank (2010). World Development Indicators (WDI). Washington D.C.

Case Study 4: Low carbon transition – potentials and limitations for tour operators

Melanie Stroebel

Institute for Environmental Sciences, University of Koblenz-Landau, Germany.

Introduction

The role of businesses in climate change is complex. From a political economy perspective, businesses are crucial actors in reducing emissions, simply by adapting products and operations. In this process, they are influenced by their wider societal, political, and economic environment, whilst simultaneously governing climate change mitigation by shaping rules and norms of how the issue is best addressed (Newell, 2008a, 2012; Bulkeley & Newell, 2010). The low carbon transition of travel and tourism is situated in this political economy context. Ideally, industry's projections for technological innovation and operational changes around aircraft, infrastructure, and fuel would come together to halve 2005 emissions by 2050, as mapped by the International Air Transport Association (IATA, 2013).

However, researchers modelling tourism's emissions development have questioned such optimism, let alone change at the scale necessary to avoid dangerous climate change (Scott *et al.*, 2010; Gössling *et al.*, 2010). They consider more substantial adaptations to tourism to be essential in order to avoid dangerous climate change; including modal shift away from flying to travel by train and road as well as travel to nearby destinations alongside efficiency improvements (Peeters & Dubois, 2010; UNWTO, 2008). Hall (2009: 59) makes the case for de-growth as a guiding concept on the path towards 'sufficient and efficient' sustainable tourism.

The political economy literature on global environmental governance can help to explore the connection between business and climate change. It recognises that global environmental politics is not exclusively conducted by nation states via formal regulatory processes, but is shaped by a complex set of stakeholders from the local to the global, and entails binding regulation as well as formal and informal rules and norms of how to deal with the environmental impacts of economic activities (Levy & Newell, 2006; Bulkeley & Newell, 2010; Newell, 2012). Self-regulation and market-based mechanisms are increasingly common forms of environmental governance; they are often characterised by the privatisation and commodification of natural resources, building on an understanding that the market is the ideal place to trigger innovation (Haufler, 2001; Bakker, 2005; Newell, 2008b). The influence of private actors in global environmental governance has not always been positively perceived. In particular the power of transnational corporations has sprung a debate around whether regulation is *'regulation* for *business rather than regulation* of *business'* that enables and protects investment (Newell, 2001: 910 – emphasis in original). Overall, Newell (2008b, 2012) argues, concerns around trade and a globalising economy have overshadowed and shaped how environmental issues are governed.

A political economy approach therefore explores environmental issues by engaging with questions of *'Who governs and who is governed? How do they govern? On whose behalf? With what implications?'* (Newell, 2008a: 507). To this, this case study adds the question of why tour operators address, and in the process govern, climate change in a particular way.

A political economy approach sees governance and business as interlinked. Businesses do not shape rules and norms in isolation; they are influenced by the dynamic regulatory, discursive, technological, and productive environment, in which they operate (Newell, 2008a). This duality draws attention to the potential political implications of a discrepancy between how tourism businesses address climate change and how the tourism industry at large needs to address the issue in order to keep global warming below 2 degrees Celsius. Models on emissions development clearly show conflicts between business as usual and necessary emissions reductions (Scott *et al.*, 2010). Against this background, a political economy approach draws attention to the potential contradictions between corporate interests and solving societies' wider environmental concerns; a conflict also captured by Naomi Klein (2014).

In particular, a Neo-Gramscian perspective on global environmental governance is useful to contextualise business measures around climate change and better understand business responses (Levy & Egan, 2003; Levy & Newell, 2005). It draws on Gramsci's (1971) work on hegemony, a dominance of the ruling class that is achieved not through coercive control, but by ensuring that society identifies with the political and material interests as well as with the ideologies of the dominant class. When applied to the economic and environmental realm, climate change may constitute a threat to the hegemonic corporate market position; consequently, business reactions to environmental risks can be understood as strategies to *'sustain corporate dominance and legitimacy in the face of environmental challenges'* (Levy & Newell, 2005: 58).

Respective corporate strategies to environmental problems can be material, discursive, and organisational, intended to shape perceptions and understandings of tourism and climate change in civil society and governments (Levy & Newell, 2005; Levy & Egan, 2003; Duffy & Stroebel, 2016). Material strategies to protect corporate market positions take the form of developing low-impact products and techno-logical strategies, such as carbon offsetting and investments into biofuel research. Discursively, businesses can attempt to protect their position by presenting them-selves as environmentally responsible and engaged actors as well as by shaping the public debate, for instance by challenging scientific knowledge and making the case for tourism's economic importance. At the organisational level, building coalitions between business actors and institutions supports the protection of hegemony fur-ther (Levy & Egan, 2003; Levy & Newell, 2005). By employing and coordinating these strategies, businesses and their representatives influence perceptions around envi-ronmental impacts and solutions and secure market positions and legitimacy (Levy & Egan, 2003; Levy & Newell, 2005).

The measures listed above are familiar in the corporate social responsibility (CSR) literature. However, the Neo-Gramscian perspective on environmental governance differs from much of this literature in that it recognises the political implications of these activities (for an exception see Levy & Kaplan, 2008; Scherer & Palazzo, 2011). In effect, this means addressing emissions is not only environmentally and/or eco-nomically motivated; the measures and discourses around CSR are highly political. They create and promote rules and norms around how an environmental issue is best addressed (Haufler, 2001; Levy & Newell, 2005).

While corporate responsibility has helped reduce environmental impacts in many industries, CSR generally requires a business case that is either financial or related to positive stakeholder perception (Carroll & Shabana, 2010; Kurucz *et al.*, 2008). Argu-ably, CSR only takes place when it is profitable (Doane, 2005). This limitation is crucial when CSR is viewed as a form of governance (Haufler, 2001; Levy & Kaplan, 2008). It means that limits for corporations may limit positive outcomes of governance more broadly. It is therefore important to understand the potential for a low carbon tran-sition at the level of individual businesses and reflect upon the implications for gov-erning a low carbon transition.

Business approaches to climate change

For businesses, environmental concerns are but one aspect shaping strategic and operational decision-making. Sustainable growth and profitability are the fun-damental paradigms that underpin tour operator activities (Thomas Cook Group, 2013; TUI Group, 2016). In recent decades, businesses have been able to draw from ever-growing international arrival numbers, which were expected, promoted, and celebrated (UNWTO, 2012; 2014). However, researchers forecast that under a busi-ness-as-usual scenario, growth in demand for travel will lead to an increase in abso-lute CO_2 emissions of tourism-related activities from 1,167 Mt in 2005 to 3,057 Mt by 2035 (UNWTO, 2008). Absolute emissions reductions in tourism cannot rely on technology alone – they require a combination of technological, behavioural, and operational changes – yet models reveal conflicts between forecast growth and technological progress at the global level (UNWTO, 2008; Scott *et al.*, 2010; Peeters & Dubois 2010; Mayor & Tol, 2010). This conflict also exists for individual tour operators, where potentials and limitations for a low carbon transformation become apparent.

Tour operators employ technological innovations and operational changes to improve efficiency along their entire supply chain: Energy audits in hotels and offices have resulted in the introduction of heating and energy saving measures; power from renewable sources has further decreased carbon footprints; coach fleet renewals and navigational systems have reduced emissions from ground operations; and aircraft fleet renewals, winglets, operational changes, better planning, and maintenance have all improved fuel-efficiency of flights (Thomas Cook Group, 2015; TUI Group, 2015). In corporate reports, efficiency has become a key indicator, permitting comparison of environmental performance against competitors (see for example Thomas Cook Group, 2015; TUI Group, 2015).

Crucial in all this is that tour operators are users – not producers – of technologies. Efficiency improvements beyond operational and behavioural changes depend on progress on airframes, engines, and fuels made by aircraft manufacturers, their suppliers, and researchers. There is one notable exception where a tour operator has become active. The TUI Group, alongside other airlines, is engaged in the development of biofuels. TUI Group's Thomson Airways was the first UK airline to fly on a blend of kerosene and biofuels in 2011, its Dutch airline sponsored an algae photobioreactor, and, recently, TUI joined Boeing's ecoDemonstrator program to tests green diesel (TUI Group, 2015; TUI Travel, 2013). Technological progress in aviation has been achieved in recent years, but more radical technological innovation towards low carbon emissions is a lengthy process; implementing change in aircraft technology can take decades (Enders, 2012; Lee *et al.*, 2009). In the meantime, tour operators need to make do with the available technologies to reduce GHG emissions.

While tour operators have lowered relative emissions of trips in recent years, reducing absolute emissions presents a challenge. Absolute emissions of some tour operators that address climate change (like Thomas Cook Group and TUI Group) are gradually declining (TUI Group, 2015; Thomas Cook Group, 2015). However, they remain subject to fluctuations as a result of changes in demand and corporate structures. For 2014, TUI Group (2015, 18) reports: *'we fell short of our 20,000 [tonnes reduction of carbon from ground operations] target as the hotel occupancy rates increased significantly.'* In 2009/2010 TUI airlines achieved an absolute reduction target early, in part, as a result of a strategic co-operation with Air Berlin, which took over operations with poorer efficiency performance (Carbon Disclosure Project, 2012). These cases demonstrate the interdependence of demand and absolute emissions reductions and draw attention to potential conflicts between emissions reductions and corporate strategies to grow. With limited technological potential for quick and significant efficiency improvements in aviation, tour operators are faced with two competing strategies: to supply products to a growing demand and risk increasing emissions or to reduce absolute emissions by shifting the product portfolio to more low carbon products or fewer flight-based holidays.

Demand limitations

A more immediate measure for tour operators to reduce emissions would be to adapt product portfolios by moving away from high impact products and processes. With aviation responsible for the majority of emissions from tourism operations – 88.4 percent of carbon emissions of TUI Group in 2014 (TUI Group, 2015) – reducing the number and distance of flights seems like the logical way forward. Peeters and Dubois' (2010) scenarios clearly demonstrate that avoiding dangerous climate change requires radical changes in transport modes and destination choices. Such substantial changes are, however, not reflected in current product portfolios of tour operators, not even those of responsible or environmental operators, many of which are specialised on destinations that require travel by aeroplane.

The scarcity of low carbon products may be associated with the current lack of demand. While consumers are aware of the environmental impacts of travel – more than 90 percent of TUI customers expect their tour operators to act responsibly – customers do not follow up their concerns with respective travel decisions (TUI Travel, 2010; personal communication). Behavioural addiction, inconsistent environmental concerns when away from home, and rationalising contradictions have all been identified to cause this lack in action (Cohen et al., ,2013; Cohen et al., 2011). Tour operators found that weather/climate and price take priority over environmental concerns in the decision-making process. Despite this current shortcoming, tour operators are taking the steps outlined above to pre-empt potential criticism and demand implications of perceived irresponsibility; for the next ten to fifteen years, they foresee increasing behavioural adaptation and a growing demand for carbon offsetting schemes.

Encouraging consumers to reflect on and reconsider travel decisions (whether it is transport modes or destination choices) to reduce emissions is uncommon, yet necessary, in marketing and booking processes. While much recent research focuses on consumers and their potential and limitations for change (Cohen et al., 2013; Gössling et al., 2012; Higham et al., 2013), attention to how environmental impacts are communicated to consumers is also essential.

Carbon offsets are rarely offered in the booking process and carbon footprints remain unknown to many consumers, unless they retrieve information from third party websites of offset providers. Such product descriptions on websites (and in brochures) indicate that in the communication with consumers other messages are prioritised. While the information provided may be targeted to the information needs of consumers, product descriptions can side-line environmental impact information at the point where travel decisions might be influenced.

Only few businesses include transparent details on emissions. The brochure of Forum Anders Reisen (n.d.), an association of responsible tour operators in Germany, is one exception. It recommends reconsidering transport means, clearly identifies emissions, and suggests carbon offsetting if flights cannot be avoided.

The concern with this kind of environmental leadership and with restricting destination choices on environmental grounds is that consumers may simply book elsewhere to satisfy their demand or to make use of a cheaper offer. For businesses that want to grow, meeting and exceeding demand is key and where environmental concern and willingness of consumers to pay extra costs or reconsider holiday travel is insufficient, it may not be in the businesses' best financial interests to adapt product portfolios – especially at the scale necessary to achieve a low carbon transition.

Governing climate change

In the absence of transformational changes in supply and demand, it seems that a low carbon transition requires a stringent regulatory framework to reduce emissions from travel. However, for now, global regulation does not require binding emissions reductions from tourism: international aviation was left out of the Kyoto Protocol (United Nations, 1998) and has again been overlooked in the agreement reached at the 21st Conference of the Parties in Paris in 2015 (United Nations, 2015). The integration of aviation into the European Union Emissions Trading Scheme was also severely amended, following pressure from airlines and governments outside of the European Union (BBC, 2012). It now only affects flights within the European Economic Area (EEA) rather than all flights arriving and departing the EEA. This modification was made to grant the International Civil Aviation Organisation time to develop market-based measures, which it is scheduled to do by 2016 (Court of Justice of the European Union, 2011; European Commission, 2016).

In this void of binding global regulation, private actors are establishing rules and norms around climate change mitigation that set the tourism industry up for future growth (Duffy & Stroebel, 2016) – an approach that differs notably from the shifts in transport modes, frequency, and distance of air travel that researchers deem to be essential (Gössling *et al.*, 2010; Peeters & Dubois, 2010; Mayor & Tol, 2010). Materially and organisationally, private actors, such as leading tour operators and industry associations like IATA (2013), promote efficiency improvements in aviation and other services as the go-to strategy to address climate change. Discursively, they present tourism as a low-impact industry that is actively engaged in reducing environmental problems, while highlighting tourism's crucial role in global development (Gössling & Peeters, 2007; Duffy & Stroebel, 2016). These measures and framings foster a climate change governance that permits exploiting growing demand for tourism products by making a low carbon transition appear possible alongside growth.

Conclusion

There is little doubt that emissions from tourism must be reduced, yet a low carbon transition needs to take place (and is debated) within the existing growth-centred and fossil fuel-driven political economy, which offers potentials but also sets limitations. This case study has provided evidence from two large tour operators groups, which are addressing emissions from their products and operations, but also demonstrated that the context in which they operate sets limitations to how much change can be implemented.

Technological innovation is slow and, on its own, will be insufficient to achieve necessary emissions reductions (Lee *et al.*, 2009; Peeters & Dubois, 2010, Scott *et al.*, 2010). A low carbon transition is also not reflected in demand. Consumers do not actively seek low carbon products, despite environmental concerns (TUI Travel, 2010). From a regulatory perspective, there is no binding global requirement that sets limits to absolute emissions from travel and tourism and directs future development. For tour operators, addressing emissions very much occurs at the voluntary level.

From a Neo-Gramscian perspective, the legitimacy of the tourism industry is not yet under threat, as demand for tourism products, despite their significant contribution to climate change, continues largely unabated. Nonetheless, tourism industry actions can be seen as pre-emptive strategies to secure the industry's legitimacy – a protection of the future of tourism (Duffy & Stroebel, 2016). However, the difficulty for tour operators to contribute to a low carbon transition in the current context of production and consumption is also evident. It is within this complexity of corporate, economic, environmental, political, and consumer interests and their links and interactions that a low carbon transition needs to be debated.

References

Bakker, K. (2005). Neoliberalizing nature? Market environmentalism in water supply in England and Wales, *Annals of the Association of American Geographers*, **95**(3), 542-565.

BBC (2012). EU suspends extension of plane emissions trading rules, 12 November, available at: http://www.bbc.co.uk/news/business-20299388. Accessed: 24 Jan. 2016.

Bulkeley, H. & Newell, P. (2010). *Governing Climate Change*, Abingdon: Routledge.

Carbon Disclosure Project (2012). CDP 2012 Investor CDP 2012 Information Request: TUI Travel.

Carroll, A.B. & Shabana, K.M. (2010). The business case for corporate social responsibility: a review of concepts, research and practice, *International Journal of Management Reviews*, **12**(1), 85–105.

Cohen, S.A., Higham, J.E.S. & Cavaliere, C.T. (2011). Binge flying, *Annals of Tourism Research*, **38**(3), 1070–1089.

Cohen, S.A., Higham, J.E.S. & Reis, A.C. (2013). Sociological barriers to developing sustainable discretionary air travel behaviour, *Journal of Sustainable Tourism*, **21**(7), 982–998.

Court of Justice of the European Union (2011). Press Release No 139/11: Judgement in Case C-366/10, Air Transport Association of America and Others v Secretary of State for Energy and Climate Change, 21 December, available at: http://curia.europa.eu/jcms/upload/docs/application/pdf/2011-12/cp110139en.pdf. Accessed 24 Jan. 2016.

Doane, D. (2005). Beyond corporate social responsibility: Minnows, mammoths and markets, *Futures*, **37**(2-3), 215–229.

Duffy, R. & Stroebel, M. (2016). Protecting holidays forever: Climate change and the tourism industry, *Brown Journal of World Affairs*, **22**(1), 7-23.

Enders, T. (2012). One born every minute, in G. Lipman; T. Delacy; S. Vorster; R. Hawkins and M. Jiang (eds.), *Green Growth and Travelism: Letters from Leaders*, Oxford: Goodfellow, 27-32.

European Commission (2016). Reducing emissions from aviation, available at: http://ec.europa.eu/clima/policies/transport/aviation/index_en.htm, accessed; 24 Jan. 2016.

Forum Anders Reisen (n.d.). Reiseperlen 2016, available at: http://konradinheckel.tpk6.de/smart3/pub/reiseperlen-2016/. Accessed 24 Jan. 2016.

Gössling, S. & Peeters, P. (2007). 'It does not harm the environment!' An analysis of industry discourses on tourism, air travel and the environment, *Journal of Sustainable Tourism*, **15**(4), 402–417.

Gössling, S., Hall, C.M., Peeters, P. & Scott, D. (2010). The future of tourism: Can tourism growth and climate policy be reconciled? A mitigation perspective, *Tourism Recreation Research*, **35**(2), 119-130.

Gössling, S., Scott, D., Hall, C.M., Ceron, J.-P. & Dubois, G. (2012). Consumer behaviour and demand response of tourists to climate change, *Annals of Tourism Research*, **39**(1), 36-58.

Gramsci, A. (1971). *Selections from the Prison Notebooks*, edited and translated by Quintin Hoare and Geoffrey Nowell Smith. New York: International Publishers.

Hall, C.M. (2009). Degrowing tourism: Décroissance, sustainable consumption and steady-state tourism, *Anatolia*, **20**(1), 46–61.

Haufler, V. (2001). *A Public Role for the Private Sector: Industry Self-Regulation in a Global Economy*, Washington: Carnegie Endowment for International Peace.

Higham, J., Cohen, S.A., Peeters, P. & Gössling, S. (2013). Psychological and behavioural approaches to understanding and governing sustainable mobility, *Journal of Sustainable Tourism* **21**(7), 949-967.

IATA (2013). IATA Technology Roadmap, available at: http://www.iata.org/whatwedo/environment/Documents/technology-roadmap-2013.pdf, viewed 8 Jan. 2016.

Klein, N. (2014). *This Changes Everything: Capitalism vs. the Climate*. London: Penguin Books.

Kurucz, E., Colbert, B. & Wheeler, D. (2008). The business case for corporate social responsibility, in A. Crane; D. Matten; A. McWilliams; J. Moon & D.S. Siegel (eds.)

The Oxford Handbook of Corporate Social Responsibility, Oxford: Oxford University Press, 83–112.

Lee, D.S., Fahey, D.W., Forster, P.M., Newton, P.J., Wit, R.C.N., Lim, L.L., Owen, B. & Sausen, R. (2009). Aviation and global climate change in the 21st century, *Atmospheric Environment*, **43**, 3520-3537.

Levy, D.L. & Egan, D. (2003). A Neo-Gramscian approach to corporate political strategy: Conflict and accommodation in the climate change negotiations, *Journal of Management Studies*, **40**(4), 803–829.

Levy, D.L. & Kaplan, R. (2008). Corporate social responsibility and theories of global governance: Strategic contestations in global issue arenas, in A. Crane; D. Matten; A. McWilliams; J. Moon and D.S. Siegel (eds.) *The Oxford Handbook of Corporate Social Responsibility*, Oxford: Oxford University Press, 432-451.

Levy, D.L. & Newell, P. (2005). A Neo-Gramscian approach to business in international environmental politics: an interdisciplinary, multilevel framework, in: D. Levy and P. Newell (eds.) *The Business of Global Environmental Governance*, Cambridge, MA: MIT Press, 47-69.

Levy, D. L. & Newell, P. (2006). Multinationals in global governance, in Vachani, S. (ed.) *Transformations in Global Governance: Implications for multinationals and other stakeholders*. Cheltenham: Edward Elgar Publishing, 146-167.

Mayor, K. & Tol, R.S.J. (2010). Scenarios of carbon dioxide emissions from aviation, *Global Environmental Change*, **20**(1), 65–73.

Newell, P. (2001). Managing multinationals: The governance of investment for the environment, *Journal of International Development*, **13**, 907-919.

Newell, P. (2008a). The political economy of global environmental governance, *Review of International Studies*, **34**, 507-529.

Newell, P. (2008b). The Marketization of global environmental governance: Manifestations and implications, in J. Park, K. Conca and M. Finger (eds.) *The Crisis of Global Environmental Governance: Towards a New Political Economy of Sustainability*, London: Routledge, pp.77–95.

Newell, P. (2012). *Globalization and the Environment: Capitalism, Ecology and Power*, Cambridge: Polity Press.

Peeters, P. & Dubois, G. (2010). Tourism travel under climate change mitigation constraints, *Journal of Transport Geography*, **18**(3), 447–457.

Scherer, A. & Palazzo, G. (2011). The new political role of business in a globalized world: a review of a new perspective on CSR and its implications for the firm, governance, and democracy, *Journal of Management Studies*, **48**(4), 899-931.

Scott, D., Peeters, P. & Gössling, S. (2010). Can tourism deliver its 'aspirational' greenhouse gas emission reduction targets?, *Journal of Sustainable Tourism*, **18**(3), 393–408.

Thomas Cook Group (2013). New Growth Strategy and Updated Profit Improvement Plans, 13 March 2013, available at: http://www.thomascookgroup.com/wp-content/uploads/2014/04/130313-CMM-RNS-FINA-LN-C-DOC.pdf. Accessed 8 Jan. 2016.

Thomas Cook Group (2015). Transforming for a Better Future – Year 2: Sustainability Report 2014, available at: https://www.thomascookgroup.com/wp-content/uploads/2015/01/ThomasCook_SR14.pdf. Accessed 5 Jan. 2016.

TUI Group (2015). Sustainable Holidays Report 2014, available at: http://www.tuigroup.com/damfiles/default/tuigroup-15/en/sustainability/tui_group_sustainable_holidays_report_2014-4fece29831504fe07cd5b5eeae5023fd.pdf. Accessed 5 Jan. 2016.

TUI Group (2016). Strategy & Equity Story, available at: http://www.tuigroup.com/en-en/investors/tui-group-at-a-glance/strategy-and-equity-story. Accessed 8 Jan. 2016.

TUI Travel (2010). Sustainable Development Report 2009: Taking on Responsible Leadership, available at: http://www.tuitravelplc.com/system/files/susrep/12009SustainableDevelopmentReport1.pdf. Accessed: 26 Jan. 2016.

TUI Travel (2013). Sustainable Holidays Report 2012: Spreading smiles, available at: http://www.tuitravelplc.com/system/files/susrep/TUI-Travel-PLC-Sustainable-Holidays-Report-2012.pdf. Accessed 26 Jan. 2016.

United Nations (1998). Kyoto Protocol to the United Nations Framework Convention on Climate Change, available at: http://unfccc.int/resource/docs/convkp/kpeng.pdf. Accessed 14 March, 2016.

United Nations (2015). Paris Agreement, available at: http://unfccc.int/files/meetings/paris_nov_2015/application/pdf/paris_agreement_english_.pdf. Accessed 14 March 2016.

UNWTO (2008). *Climate change and tourism: responding to global challenges,* available at: http://www.unep.fr/shared/publications/pdf/WEBx0142xPA-ClimateChangeandTourismGlobalChallenges.pdf. Accessed 3 March 2016.

UNWTO (2012). UNWTO Welcomes the World's One-Billionth Tourist 2012, available at: http://media.unwto.org/press-release/2012-12-13/unwto-welcomes-world-s-one-billionth-tourist. Accessed 26 Jan. 2016.

UNWTO (2014). UNWTO Tourism Highlights: 2014 Edition, available at: www.e-unwto.org/doi/pdf/10.18111/9789284416226. Accessed 26 Jan. 2016.

Part 3: Innovations for Low Carbon Mobility

11 The Constrained Governance of Socio-technical Transitions: Evidence from electric mobility in Scotland

Craig Morton

Institute for Transport Studies, University of Leeds, UK.

David Beeton

Urban Foresight, Newcastle, UK.

Introduction

The everyday use of cars to service the mobility requirements of citizens in most economically developed nations represents a firmly embedded social phenomenon. In 2013, 83.2% of all passenger kilometres were conducted in cars in the European Union, with little variation away from this statistic across the different member states (Eurostat, 2015). Whilst strategies to encourage multimodal behaviour by promoting the wider utilisation of public and active transport may assist in rebalancing the provision of transport (Graham-Rowe *et al.*, 2011; Santos *et al.*, 2010), the car is likely to remain the dominant form of mobility for the foreseeable future. Consequently, developing strategies through which to shift car based mobility onto a sustainable trajectory represents a prominent transport policy issue.

In an effort to address the considerable environmental externalities associated with the current mobility system, including the emission of greenhouse gases and local pollutants, focus has been on the development and deployment of technical innovations which may offer partial solutions to these problems (King, 2007, 2008; Schwanen *et al.*, 2011; The Committee on Climate Change, 2015). Most apparent in the technical innovations put forward involve alternative vehicle propulsion systems. Electric vehicles (EVs) are considered to be the most realistic alternative propulsion system and are currently entering the mainstream automotive market (Offer *et al.*, 2010). EVs have zero tailpipe emissions, allowing them to respond to the growing concerns around air quality, and they have the potential to offer low carbon mobility as a growing proportion of renewable energy generation comes online. With these benefits in mind, fostering an electric mobility (e-mobility) socio-technical transition has established itself as the primarily mechanism through which a sustainable future for the transport system in most economically developed nations will be achieved (Dijk *et al.*, 2013).

Due to the highly competitive nature of the mainstream automotive market combined with the current deficiencies of EVs regarding a number of key vehicle performance attributes (such as vehicle range and cost premiums), a natural introduction of EVs into the market will likely be ineffective (Steinhilber *et al.*, 2013). The continuity of the status quo in the automotive market is further supported by the high level of resilience displayed by the existing internal combustion engine regime (Wells & Nieuwenhuis, 2012). Governments are becoming increasingly aware of the need to assist and steer the purposive transition towards e-mobility. With this in mind, the government of Scotland has established a transition strategy aimed at promoting the adoption of EVs (Transport Scotland, 2013).

The specific circumstance of the Scottish Government, which represents a devolved administration of the United Kingdom (UK) with restricted authority, offers an interesting case through which to consider the governance of the e-mobility transition. It is the purpose of this chapter to consider this governance strategy by charting its development, implementation and evaluation. To assist in structuring the analysis, Loorbach's (2010) governance framework is employed which categorises aspects of transition policy into four different types of governance activity. Specific attention is paid in the analysis to ways in which governance activity is constrained as a result of the particular circumstances of the Scottish Government. These constraints cover issues related to restrictions in the Scottish Government's agency in certain areas due to powers reserved by the UK Government, the transference of regulatory authorities to the European Commission and the local conditions which exist within Scotland.

This chapter proceeds with an overview of socio-technical transition theory and the literature which discusses the governance of transition before outlining the strategy developed and so far implemented by the Scottish Government in an effort to support the transition to e-mobility.

The governance of socio-technical transition

The field of socio-technical transitions examines the processes of long-term structural change which involve transformations in technologies and shifts in the configurations of social activities within and between major sectors such as energy generation (Foxon *et al.*, 2010) and transportation (Cohen, 2012). Transition research pays specific attention to how these shifts and transformations lead to technological innovations progressing from niche applications to attaining a mainstream presence in the established socio-technical regime. These processes are often illustrated through the Multi-Level Perspective (MLP: Geels, 2002, 2005) which is displayed in Figure 11.1 and utilises three analytical levels to chart system evolution. These analytical levels cover technological niches, which encompass laboratories of variation and innovation, socio-technical regimes, which represent semi-coherent and established systems, and the socio-technical landscape, which represents deep structures that govern system operation.

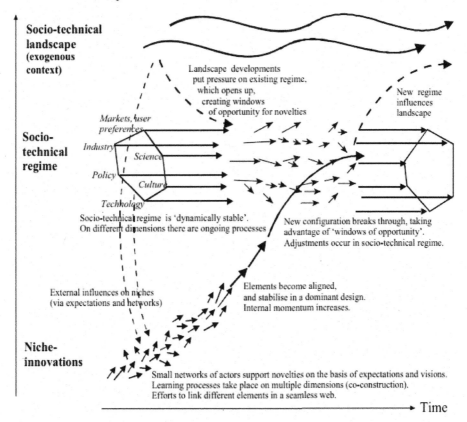

Figure 11.1: Multi-Level Perspective of the process of socio-technical transition. Source: Geels (2002).

Transitions can be generated by a mixture of emerging conditions and issues which produce selection pressures on the incumbent regime that induce change. Smith *et al.* (2005) suggest that the context which defines the nature of a transition can be mapped by considering the juncture of two dimensions. The first of these dimensions relates to the *level of coordination* displayed by regime actors and transition managers in their response to the changing selection pressures. The second dimension concerns the *locus of resources* required to respond to the changing selection pressures and whether these resources are internal to the regime or exist externally. Geels and Schot (2007) propose an alternative classification of transitions which makes use of the MLP to format a series of transition pathways which socio-technical transitions may follow. Their classification first acknowledges that selection pressures are highly varied, generating diverse responses from the regime actors and niche innovators. Moreover, both the *timing of the interactions* which occur in socio-technical transitions and the *nature of these interactions* will likely foster different types of transition.

Whilst the transition classification systems proposed by both Smith *et al.* (2005) and Geels and Schot (2007) use different approaches, they both recognise the role of *agency* in transition. Smith *et al.* (2005) argues that the ability of agency to make an appreciable difference in the transition process necessitates the exercise of political, economic and institutional power. The political expression of agency in the transition process is often referred to as transition management (Meadowcroft, 2009), which involves active governance that aims to guide transitions along desirable pathways. with increasing attention being paid to the facilitation of transitions towards sustainability (Markland, 2012).

The application of governance to facilitate desirable socio-technical transitions represents an intricate web of expressed visions, policy frameworks and intervening actions. In an effort to bound transition management into a series of issues, Loorbach (2010) put forward a governance framework which outlines the cycle which transition management tends to follow and classifies transition management into four types of activity. Frantzeskaki *et al.* (2012: 26) describe these categories as:

1 *Strategic:* activities at the level of a societal system that take into account a long time horizon, relate to structuring a complex societal problem and creating alternative futures often through opinion making, visioning and politics.

2 *Tactical:* activities at the level of sub-systems that relate to build-up and break-down of system structures (institutions, regulation, physical infrastructures, financial infrastructures and so on), often through negotiation, collaboration and lobbying.

3 *Operational:* activities that relate to short-term and everyday decisions and action. At this level actors either recreate or change system structures.

4 *Reflexive:* activities that relate to the evaluation of the existing situation at various levels and their interrelation or misfit. Through debate, structured evaluation, assessment and research, societal issues are continuously structured, reframed and dealt with.

E-mobility transition management

Understanding the structure and dynamic nature of governance in the transport system is a topical area of study, likely motivated by strategic importance of this sector. Considering the operation of governance to pursue the sustainability agenda in transport, Marsden and Rye (2010) note that the complex arrangement of formal governance institutions in the UK, which exist across different spatial jurisdictions, generates confusion regarding institution responsibility and leads to a lack of commitment to the management of transport demand. Schwanen *et al.* (2011) offer additional insight on this issue and suggest that the *governmentality* approach of UK transport policy, which is based on the principles of ecological modernism where the goals of economic growth and environmental sustainability coalesce in a green economy, contextualises the current orientation towards the application of technical innovations and economic instruments in the transport sector. This perspective is attuned to the focus on promoting a transition to e-mobility, primarily serviced through the provision of EVs, which allows the system of automobility to be retained and for green growth to be promoted through the manufacture of low carbon high-value technologies.

Of particular relevance to the focus of this chapter, the ways in which the governance system can take an active role in fostering a transition towards e-mobility has also received focused attention (Nilson *et al.*, 2012). Using the automobility system as a case study, Schot *et al.* (1994) discuss three principal strategies which could be useful in stimulating socio-technical transitions. These strategies involve the modification of the selection environment, such as through implementing new regulations or altering taxation policy, the creation of a technological nexus, where new agent networks are established, and the development of alternative variations through technical innovations. This final strategy is often referred to as Strategic Niche Management (Kemp *et al.*, 1998), which aims to improve the under-utilisation of technologies by the establishment of protected spaces in which niche innovations can be experimented with and further developed in order to address prominent transition barriers.

Considering the barriers which are restricting an e-mobility transition, Steinhilber *et al.* (2013) conducted an in-depth assessment of the testimonies offered by key stakeholders in the EV sector, with their analysis suggesting that two issues related to e-mobility governance require focused attention. First, governance has the opportunity to steer developments in vehicle technologies, ancillary systems (such as energy and information communication technology) and vehicle production processes to enhance the technical utility of EVs. Second, governance can foster the introduction of novel business models to improve the attractiveness of EVs to private citizens and corporate fleets. Most recently, Mazur *et al.* (2015) assessed the policies employed by the UK Government in order to promote a transition to EVs. Their evaluation was based on the transition pathways of the MLP outlined by Geels and Schot (2007) and involved an analysis of the existing mix of policies which are aimed at supporting the EV transition and the expressed future vision for vehicle transport. They argue that the UK's transition policy for EVs holds parallels with the reconfiguration pathway, which spans significant alterations in the socio-technical regime's architecture and can lead to incumbent regime actors (such as mainstream automotive manufacturers) being displaced by emerging niche agents (such as e-mobility start-ups).

The Scottish context

The distinctive nature of Scotland's transport policy since devolution has already attracted academic attention, with Shaw *et al.* (2009) noting that whilst high level strategic transport objectives across the devolved administrations of the UK (partially illustrated in the left image of Figure 11.2) are relatively synchronised, the implementation of specific policies to pursue these objectives have somewhat diverged. This policy divergence is likely motivated by the unique properties of Scotland's transport system (partially illustrated in the right image of Figure 11.2), which is required to respond to varied demands ranging from those of highly congested urban centres (located in Scotland's central belt) to those of isolated rural communities such as the highlands and islands (located towards the north and west of Scotland). Indeed, it is the unique characteristics of Scotland's transport system and the constrained level of authority held by the Scottish Government in its management of the system which offers an interesting case study for the e-mobility transition.

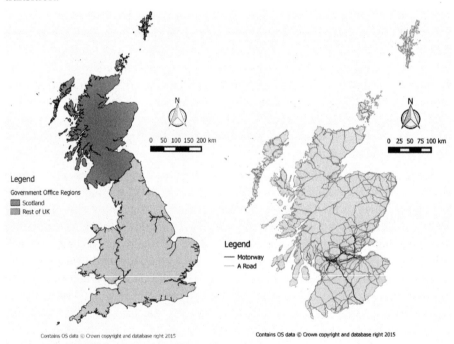

Figure 11.2: [left] Map of Scotland in situ with the rest of the United Kingdom. [right] Internal map of Scotland depicting road configuration.

As previously noted by Smith *et al.* (2005), the application of governance to manage transitions often faces constraints concerning the activities which can be pursued. With this in mind, acknowledging the presence of such constraints and understanding the limitations they impose will likely represent an important step in the development of a successful transition management framework. A number of the constraints faced by the Scottish Government concerning the e-mobility transition stem from the specific conditions surrounding the authority granted to it in terms of transport policy since devolution. As concisely outlined by Butcher (2015), certain powers have been transferred to the Scottish Government (such as the management of the strategic road network), whilst others have been reserved by the UK Parliament (such as the taxation of vehicles and fuels). The reservation of some powers is justified by the argument that a certain degree of harmony is required between the transport systems in Scotland and the rest of the UK. This implies that, for certain aspects of transport policy, the Scottish Government has to comply with the legislation enacted by the UK Parliament. A similar situation is present concerning the regulation of car technical attributes, with the European Commission setting the legislation which certifies if a particular vehicle model meets the required standards to be sold within the EU through the European Community Whole Vehicle Type Approval process (European Commission, 2007).

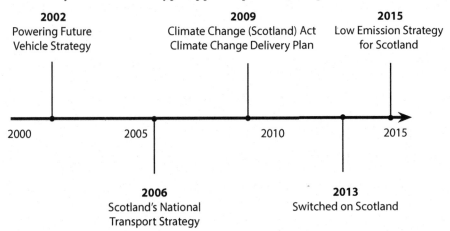

Figure 11.3: Timeline detailing the main policy documents concerning Electric Vehicle policy in Scotland.

Whilst the Scottish Government's power to govern the transition towards e-mobility is constrained in particular areas, enough agency exists for a unique e-mobility policy to be developed. Figure 11.3 details some of the key policy documents which have discussed EVs, commencing with the UK Government's Powering Future Vehicle Strategy (Department for Transport, 2002) which represents the first articulation of a desire to support alternatively fuelled vehicles, through to the Scottish Government's most recent consultation relating to how e-mobility coalesces with Scotland's low emission strategy (Scottish Government,

2015). Of particular importance is the document *Switched on Scotland* (Transport Scotland, 2013), which acts as an integrated transition strategy aimed at achieving the widespread electrification of road transport.

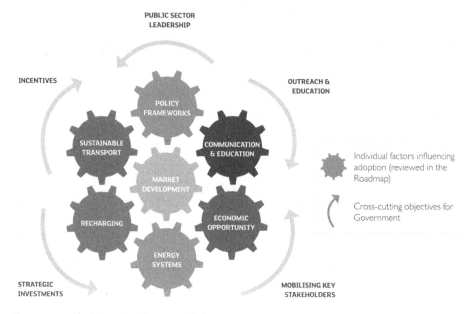

Figure 11.4: The Transition Framework for promoting electric mobility in Scotland with seven key policy areas. Source: Transport Scotland (2013).

The development of this transition strategy was the product of a series of collaborative workshops which engaged with stakeholders from a wide range of backgrounds in order to generate a comprehensive inventory of opinion concerning e-mobility. The assessment of this inventory followed an exploratory road-mapping approach (Beeton *et al.*, 2008) which led to the establishment of a Transition Framework that details a group of interlinked components displayed in Figure 11.4. The framework components are represented as cogs in order to illustrate how progress in the transition towards e-mobility will require synchronised activity, with the framework only rotating as quickly as the slowest cog. Around the circumference of the framework are a series of cross cutting objectives that cover areas which the Scottish Government has the ability to influence and assist in guiding governance activity.

The remainder of this chapter focuses on this Transition Framework and makes use of the governance framework developed by Loorbach (2010) in order to analyse how the Scottish Government has established its governance approach to fostering a transition towards e-mobility, the key elements which this approach contains and some of the constraints the application of governance faces.

Strategic transition activities

The development of the e-mobility transition strategy was motivated by the require-ment for the transport sector to contribute towards Scotland's strategic objective of a greener society (Scottish Government, 2011) and Scotland's ambition to achieve substantial reductions in its greenhouse gas emissions inventory (Climate Change (Scotland) Act, 2009). This alignment between the transition strategy and high-level policy objectives provides credibility to the strategy but necessitates that its outcomes are assessed though their ability to deliver tangible benefits to these objec-tives. With the e-mobility transition likely to require significant levels of investment in the short-term and with sales of EVs expected to remain niche until the medium-term, this can create a certain degree of tension between the transition strategy and the strategic objectives. Thus, establishing a widely accepted long-term *Strategic Vision* for the e-mobility transition, which clearly articulates the desired pathway and sets out a series of logical steps to achieving this pathway, may alleviate some tension.

Early in the development process, a strategic board was convened to assist in guiding the production of the Strategic Vision for e-mobility in Scotland. This stra-tegic board was comprised of a varied set of representatives, covering individuals working in local government, private sector energy companies, charities, auto-motive manufacturers and e-mobility supply chain companies. This mix of partici-pants helped to unlock diverse perspectives on the topics to be considered and for the Strategic Vision to be formed out of a participatory policy process. However, this diversity also introduces challenges for policy formation, as managing the perspec-tives and expectations of different actors who are engaged with the e-mobility transition can prove difficult when views are divergent. Disparities concerning what should and should not be included and the priorities assigned to different issues require sensitive navigation. Thus, the creation of a Strategic Vision for the transition can prove to be a contentious issue, requiring negotiation between the government agencies managing the transition and the associated actor network.

In an effort to visualise the transformational changes which will take place in Scotland's car fleet resulting from the e-mobility transition, a *Market Outlook* was estimated as part of the strategic visioning. This Outlook is displayed in Figure 11.5 and illustrates the anticipated rate at which EV propulsion systems may diffusion into the mainstream car market and provides a quantitative basis through which to consider the Strategic Vision of the transition strategy. The outputs of technological horizon scanning methods, from which the Outlook was developed, generally become vaguer as you move further into the future, which leads to increasing levels of uncertainty surrounding market structures in the medium to long-term. Conse-quently, transition governance can face constraints which stem from the inherent uncertainties surroundingmedium and long term system developments (Morton *et al.*, 2014). Whilst the establishment of strategic visions can be useful in illustrating the desired development of a particular transition, these visions require embedded flexibility to allow them to adapt to emerging developments. To this end, the Market

Outlook attempts to strike a balance between providing some clarity concerning the potential shape of the e-mobility transition in terms of objective figures whilst understanding that a spectrum of futures for e-mobility are possible.

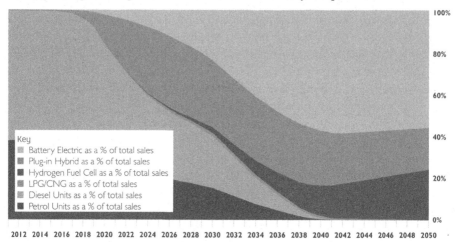

Figure 11.5: Market Outlook for the potential diffusion of Electric Vehicle propulsion systems throughout Scotland's car fleet. Source: Transport Scotland (2013).

Tactical transition activities

The Strategic Vision for the e-mobility transition set out in Switched on Scotland represents an aspiration which will require transformational changes in car fleet composition and the structure of ancillary systems. To bridge the gap between ambition and realism, the transition strategy sets a series of *Enabling Measures* which are associated with the different components of the Transition Framework (Figure 11.4). These measures concentrate on the issues for which the Scottish Government has the means to act, to allow effort to be focused on delivering achievable outcomes, and are temporally synced to the Market Outlook.

With the Scottish Government representing one of the largest car fleet operators in the country, one of the Enabling Measures is assigned to utilising public procurement policies to promote the deployment of EVs in the early stages of the market. Regulations aimed at increasing the visibility of the benefits stemming from the purchase of an EV and to guide procurement decisions have been produced (Transport Scotland, 2014). The installation of such regulations displays public sector leadership in the shift towards e-mobility, assists in demonstrating the functionality of EVs to the general populace and provides confidence to private sector firms to invest in the market.

Whilst the Scottish Government has the ability to regulate purchasing behaviour within its own fleet, its legislative authority concerning the management of the entire car fleet in Scotland is constrained in two areas which may limit its ability to stimulate the early market for EVs. First, the UK Government has reserved the power to set fiscal policy concerning transport fuel duty and vehicle registration and circulation tax rates (Butcher, 2015). This restricts the Scottish Government's ability to stimulate EV adoption through alterations to the taxation policy surrounding the vehicle market. An example of such an alteration is Green Fiscal Reform (Ekins *et al.*, 2009), whereby tax rates on environmentally damaging activities (such as the purchase and operation of vehicles with high emissions levels) are increased whilst tax rates on activities viewed as public goods (such as employment) are reduced to produce a revenue neutral outcome. The second constraint is associated with the powers reserved by the European Union to set vehicle fuel efficiency and emissions regulations, with one of the current targets stipulating a requirement for automotive manufacturers to have an average emissions factor for the cars they sell within the union to be no greater than 95 grams of carbon dioxide per kilometre by 2021 (European Commission, 2014). The ability of the Scottish Government to put in place more stringent targets or to alter the approach to setting targets in this area is thus restricted to its ability to influence the legislation set concerning this issue at the European level.

Operational transition activities

The Enabling Measures of the transition strategy detailed in Switched on Scotland tend to cover intermediate objectives which are aimed at realising the Strategic Vision for an e-mobility transition. To generate a link between the Enabling Measures which are required to promote EV adoption and the immediate activities of governance, a set of *Actions* have been developed. These Actions cover more tangible activities with clearly defined outcomes intended to direct day-to-day operations. A number of these Actions involve identifying niche markets for EVs to deploy in, which provides an opportunity for EV performance to be evaluated and acts as a platform for EVs to enter the mainstream market. With the car market expected to see the proliferation of innovative business models over the next decade, the potential to connect the diffusion of EVs with the promotion of alternative vehicle access solutions represents a clear opportunity for niche market deployment (Shaheen & Chan, 2015). Linking the e-mobility transition strategy to policies aimed at developed car club operations in Scotland offers dual benefits in promoting sustainable mobility by reducing the need to own private vehicles and encouraging the use of EVs. A wider interpretation of this is that understanding how the Actions associated with a specific transition strategy can feed into and receive input from tangential government operations may assist in identifying prospects for joint initiatives.

Associated with the procurement regulations aimed at promoting EV uptake amongst public sector fleets, a £3.6 million fund has been made available to Scotland's local authorities which aims to bridge the purchase price differential between an EV and a conventionally fuelled vehicle (Transport Scotland, 2010). Adoption of EVs amongst local authority fleets provides both a niche market for EV deployment and allows for this technology to be evaluated across a range of different conditions and circumstances. This example illustrates the cooperation which is often necessary between national government, that has the capacities necessary to develop transition strategies, and local government, which has control over much of the transport systems throughout Scotland's settlements. This control covers a number of areas which could be of use in promoting EV diffusion such as parking regulations, the installation of EV charging infrastructures alongside the potential to introduce low emission zones. Thus, with a transition strategy being set at the national level but the ability to perform actions to promote EV adoption being held in part by local authorities, there is the potential for a disconnection to emerge between national strategy and local activity if coordination in transition activities is not pursued.

Reflexive transition activities

The topic of e-mobility transitions alongside the market potential of EVs has seen significant levels of attention over the past decade leading to rapid developments in the understanding of sector conditions. This pace of change leads to a situation where any established transition strategy will quickly become outdated if it is not reviewed and amended to account for new developments. To ensure that Switched on Scotland benefits from emerging insights, two mechanisms have been installed into the transition strategy to allow for reflection and adaptation.

The first mechanism involves arranging regular events with stakeholders in order to provide forums for the discussion of recent developments and gather opinions on points of interest. In order to link the events to the existing structure of the transition strategy, each of the forums is connected to one of the components of the Transition Framework (Figure 11.4) which acts as a focus point for the forum's discussion. These forums follow a regular format, whereby external speakers who are engaged with the e-mobility transition are invited to share their insights followed by open discussions surrounding the particular topic of focus. Through these discussions, emerging issues are identified and the potential consequences for the transition strategy are considered. The second of these mechanisms relates to scheduled appraisals of the transition strategy, which formally review the progress made to date and considers if amendments to the structure of the strategy are required to either account for changes in sector conditions or to improve the strategy's effectiveness.

Conclusions

The use of governance to steer socio-technical transitions in key systems onto sustainable trajectories through the development and deployment of transition strategies is becoming an important means through which to generate desirable futures which are harmonious to societal objectives. Using the transition towards e-mobility as a case study, this chapter investigates the activities of governance in Scotland in an effort to demonstrate how transition management operates across different timeframes which range from long-term strategic visioning to short-term actions. Through the evaluation of the transition strategy developed by the Scottish

Government, it is apparent that not all options are on the table, with the activities of governance being constrained by a mixture of different issues. A number of these constraints have been described in this chapter and reflect the restricted authority of the Scottish Government to manage the transport system alongside the situational context of Scotland as a nation. However, governance constraints can also extend beyond these issues to incorporate considerations such as the political acceptability of transition activities, the allocation of resources to support transition activities and the experience levels of managers assigned to develop and deploy transition strategies.

Understanding the constraints which governance faces will likely represent an important step in producing an effective transition strategy for two principal reasons. First, charting the presence and extent of the constraints which restrict transition management activities will be of benefit in the short-term by allowing effort to be directed at issues over which governance has an adequate degree of control. The issues which can be affected by governance represent areas where governance agency should be directed so that resources are allocated efficiently. Additionally, charting the governance constraints which are present can assist in understanding when the authority to affect a specific issue is held at either a different level of governance or with a different transition actor. An appreciation of how governance authority can be spread across a range of different actors, institutions and levels of governance can prove useful in perceiving where the establishment of strategic partnerships could allow for the agency of a transition strategy to be extended.

Second, with socio-technical transitions generally occurring over an extended period of time, the identification of constraints which are restricting governance at the start of the transition process does not necessarily mean that these constraints are fixed for the duration of the transition process. Constraints may become flexible in the medium to long-term due to emerging conditions which either affect the particular issue being constrained or the ability of governance to exert influence over the particular issue. An example of such a situation might be the further devolution of taxation authority to Scotland from the UK parliament, granting the Scottish Government the ability to set different rates for vehicle registration and circulation taxes in order to encourage the adoption of EVs. With this in mind, governance should not consider constrained issues as representing closed books in transition management, but rather take the opportunity to evaluate what may alleviate the restrictions imposed by these constraints and formulate potential strategies to deploy if alleviation occurs.

Acknowledgements

The research presented in this chapter has been made possible due to a research grant provided by the ClimateXChange Centre in Scotland. The author's are grateful for the access granted by the Scottish Government concerning their policy formation processes regarding the e-mobility transition strategy.

References

ACEA, (2015). The automobile industry pocket guide. Available at: http://www.acea.be/uploads/publications/POCKET_GUIDE_2015-2016.pdf. Accessed 1 Feb. 2016.

Beeton, D. A., Phaal, R. & Probert, D. R. (2008). Exploratory roadmapping for foresight. *International Journal of Technology Intelligence and Planning*, **4**(4), 398-412.

Butcher, L. (2015). Transport in Scotland. Available at: http://researchbriefings.parliament.uk/ResearchBriefing/Summary/SN03192. Accessed 1 Feb. 2016.

Climate Change (Scotland) Act, (2009). Available at: http://www.legislation.gov.uk/asp/2009/12/contents. Accessed 1 Feb. 2016.

Cohen, M. J. (2012). The future of automobile society: a socio-technical transitions perspective. *Technology Analysis & Strategic Management*, **24**(4), 377–390.

Department for Transport, (2002). Powering future vehicles strategy. Available at: http://www.lowcvp.org.uk/assets/reports/DfT%20Powering%20Future%20Vehicles%20Strategy%20-%20July%202002.pdf. Accessed 1 Feb. 2016.

Dijk, M., Orsato, R. J. & Kemp, R. (2013). The emergence of an electric mobility trajectory. *Energy Policy*, **52**, 135–145.

Ekins, P., Dresner, S., Potter, S., Shaw, B. & Speck, S. (2009). The case for green fiscal reform: Final report of the UK Green Fiscal Commission. Available at: http://www.greenfiscalcommission.org.uk/images/uploads/GFC_FinalReport.pdf. Accessed 1 Feb. 2016.

European Commission, (2007). Directive 2007/46/EC – Establishing a framework for the approval of motor vehicles. Available at: http://eur-lex.europa.eu/legal-content/EN/TXT/PDF/?uri=CELEX:32007L0046&from=EN. Accessed 1 Feb. 2016.

European Commission, (2014). Regulation 443/2009 – Setting emission performance standards for new passenger cars. Available at: http://eur-lex.europa.eu/legal-content/EN/TXT/PDF/?uri=CELEX:02009R0443-20140408. Accessed 1 Feb. 2016.

Eurostat, (2015). Transport Theme: Table – Modal split of passenger transport. Available at: http://ec.europa.eu/eurostat/en/data/database. Accessed 1 Feb. 2016.

Foxon, T. J., Hammond, G. P. & Pearson, P. J. G. (2010). Developing transition pathways for a low carbon electricity system in the UK. *Technological Forecasting and Social Change*, **77**(8), 1203–1213.

Frantzeskaki, N., Loorbach, D. & Meadowcroft, J. (2012). Governing societal transitions to sustainability. *International Journal of Sustainable Development*, **15**(1/2), 19–36.

Garcia, M. L. & Bray, O. H. (1997). Fundamentals of technology roadmapping. Available at: http://prod.sandia.gov/techlib/access-control.cgi/1997/970665.pdf. Accessed 1 Feb. 2016.

Geels, F. W. (2002). Technological transitions as evolutionary reconfiguration processes: a multi-level perspective and a case-study. *Research Policy*, **31**(8-9), 1257–1274.

Geels, F. W. (2005). The dynamics of transitions in socio-technical systems: A multi-level analysis of the transition pathway from horse-drawn carriages to automobiles (1860–1930). *Technology Analysis & Strategic Management*, **17**(4), 445–476.

Geels, F. W. & Schot, J. (2007). Typology of sociotechnical transition pathways. *Research Policy*, **36**(3), 399–417.

Graham-Rowe, E., Skippon, S., Gardner, B. & Abraham, C. (2011). Can we reduce car use and, if so, how? A review of available evidence. *Transportation Research Part A: Policy and Practice*, **45**(5), 401–418.

Kemp, R., Schot, J. & Hoogma, R. (1998). Regime shifts to sustainability through processes of niche formation: The approach of strategic niche management. *Technology Analysis & Strategic Management*, **10**(2), 175–198.

King, J. E. (2007). The King Review of Low Carbon Cars Part One: The potential for CO2 reduction. Available at: www.lowcvp.org.uk/assets/presentations/Julia%20King.pdf. Accessed 1 Feb. 2016.

King, J. E. (2008). The King Review of Low Carbon Cars Part Two: Recommendations for action. Available at: http://www.climatesolver.org/sites/default/files/pdf/bud08_king_1080.pdf. Accessed 1 Feb. 2016.

Loorbach, D. (2010). Transition Management for Sustainable Development: A Prescriptive, Complexity-Based Governance Framework. *Governance*, **23**(1), 161–183.

Markard, J., Raven, R. & Truffer, B. (2012). Sustainability transitions: An emerging field of research and its prospects. *Research Policy*, **41**(6), 955–967.

Marsden, G. & Rye, T. (2010). The governance of transport and climate change. *Journal of Transport Geography*, **18**(6), 669–678.

Mazur, C., Contestabile, M., Offer, G. J. & Brandon, N. P. (2015). Assessing and comparing German and UK transition policies for electric mobility. *Environmental Innovation and Societal Transitions*, **14**, 84–100.

Meadowcroft, J. (2009). What about the politics? Sustainable development, transition management, and long term energy transitions. *Policy Sciences*, 42(4), 323–340.

Morton, C., Anable, J. & Brand, C. (2014). Policy making under uncertainty in electric vehicle demand. *Proceedings of the ICE - Energy*, **167**(3), 125–138.

Nillson, M., Hillman, K., Rickne, A. & Magnusson, T. (2012). *Paving the Road to Sustainable Transport: Governance and innovation in low carbon vehicles*. Oxford: Routledge.

Offer, G. J., Howey, D., Contestabile, M., Clague, R. & Brandon, N. P. (2010). Comparative analysis of battery electric, hydrogen fuel cell and hybrid vehicles in a future sustainable road transport system. *Energy Policy*, **38**(1), 24–29.

Santos, G., Behrendt, H. & Teytelboym, A. (2010). Part II: Policy instruments for sustainable road transport. *Research in Transportation Economics*, **28**(1), 46–91.

Schot, J., Hoogma, R. & Elzen, B. (1994). Strategies for shifting technological systems: The case of the automobile system. *Futures*, **26**(10), 1060–1076.

Schwanen, T., Banister, D. & Anable, J. (2011). Scientific research about climate change mitigation in transport: A critical review. *Transportation Research Part A: Policy and Practice*, **45**(10), 993–1006.

Scottish Government (2011). National performance framework. Available at: http://www.gov.scot/Resource/Doc/933/0124202.pdf. Accessed 1 Feb. 2016.

Scottish Government (2015). Low emission strategy for Scotland. Available at: http://www.gov.scot/Publications/2015/01/3287. Accessed 1 Feb. 2016.

Shaheen, S. & Chan, N. D. (2015). Evolution of e-mobility in carsharing business models. In Beeton, D. & Meyer, G. (eds.). *Electric vehicle business models: Global perspectives*. London: Springer.

Shaw, J., MacKinnon, D. & Docherty, I. (2009). Divergence or Convergence? Devolution and Transport Policy in the United Kingdom. *Environment and Planning C: Government and Policy*, **27**(3), 546–567.

Smith, A., Stirling, A. & Berkhout, F. (2005). The governance of sustainable socio-technical transitions. *Research Policy*, **34**(10), 1491–1510.

Steinhilber, S., Wells, P. & Thankappan, S. (2013). Socio-technical inertia: Understanding the barriers to electric vehicles. *Energy Policy*, **60**, 531–539.

The Committee on Climate Change (2015). Sectoral scenarios for the fifth carbon budget – Technical report. Available at: https://www.theccc.org.uk/publication/sectoral-scenarios-for-the-fifth-carbon-budget-technical-report/. Accessed 1 Feb. 2016.

Transport Scotland (2010). Low carbon vehicle procurement support scheme. Available at: http://www.gov.scot/Resource/Doc/935/0103593.pdf. Accessed 1 Feb. 2016.

Transport Scotland (2013). Switched on Scotland: A roadmap to widespread adoption of plug-in vehicles. Available at: http://www.transport.gov.scot/report/j272736-00.htm. Accessed 1 Feb. 2016.

Transport Scotland (2014). Guidance on the implementation of The Cleaner Road Transport Vehicles (Scotland) Regulations 2010 SSI 2010/390. Available at: http://www.transport.gov.scot/report/guidance-implementation-cleaner-road-transport-vehicles-scotland-regulations-2010-ssi-2010390. Accessed 1 Feb. 2016.

Wells, P. & Nieuwenhuis, P. (2012). Transition failure: Understanding continuity in the automotive industry. *Technological Forecasting and Social Change*, **79**(9), 1681–1692.

12 Innovations to Transform Personal Mobility

Tim Schwanen

Transport Studies Unit, School of Geography and the Environment, University of Oxford, UK.

Introduction

After decades of expanding automobility – the practices, landscapes, institutions, knowledges and cultural representations centred on the privately owned car – across the global North, a new era has dawned. Use and private ownership of the car seem to have peaked (Goodwin & Van Dender, 2013) and a renaissance of urban rail and cycling is taking place. Some commentators have announced the end of automobile dependence (Newman & Kenworthy, 2015), but others are more cautious. The latter point out the numerous path dependencies in terms of land use, policy and governance, finance, expertise and embodied sensations and emotions that trap the western world into continued reliance on the private car (Dennis & Urry, 2009; Kent, 2015); and the fact that car ownership, driving licensing and car use are increasing rapidly elsewhere and more than ever before at the global scale (Schwanen, 2015a).

The geographical complexities of peak car and the renaissance of rail and bike suggest both the importance of, and need for, innovation in the mobility of people, goods and information. The causes for peak car are varied, complex and hotly debated in the academic literature but innovations – novel technologies, institutional arrangements and user practices, such as public transport smartcards, urban light rail, car sharing and all kinds of cycling training schemes – should be listed as relevant factors. At the same time, the relentless global expansion of automobility implies that new innovations will have to emerge and existing ones diffused more widely if CO_2 emissions from transport, air quality problems, obesity levels and all kinds of social inequalities are to be reduced significantly. It is for these reasons that I will examine innovation processes more closely, discussing specifically how innovations in personal mobility in urban areas can be understood.

In this chapter, I argue that innovation processes in personal mobility are social and geographical in nature and therefore require the bringing together of thinking from innovation studies, such as the work on socio-technical transitions, with theorising from geography and urban studies. I will first introduce the thinking on socio-technical transitions and then explore geographers' responses to this approach. Throughout I will selectively refer to my own empirical research into innovation processes in personal mobility in several UK cities – Oxford, Brighton, Liverpool and London. This research relies on document analysis; interviews with local entrepreneurs, policymakers, politicians and activists; and limited mobile ethnography (Schwanen, 2015b). It recognises that 'innovation' is a polysemic, value-laden term and uses the deliberatively broad description of a configuration of heterogeneous elements – technical artefacts, designs, practices of consumption, business models, etcetera – that is new(ish) to an arbitrarily defined area. Thus, electric vehicle charging infrastructure can be as much an innovation as, say, personalised travel planning offered by local government or a smartphone application to encourage low carbon mobility in a specific city.

Understanding innovation

Innovation has long remained a black box in transport and mobility studies. Insofar as new technologies, institutional arrangements and user practices were considered, the emphasis was usually on predicting the (potential) impacts they might have on transport systems, congestion, economic growth, CO_2 emissions, air quality, obesity, etcetera. This orientation reflects that the historical *raison d'être* of academic transport research lay in offering decision support to policymakers and other stakeholders in the transport sector. However, since the late 1990s innovation processes have gradually been unpacked by innovation scholars for whom transport is one domain among others in which sustainability transitions are both needed and gradually unfolding.

These scholars have tended to draw on two theoretical frameworks – the innovation systems (IS) and the socio-technical transitions (STT) approaches. Both approaches suggest that innovation is a systemic process involving many different actors rather than a single individual or company; they differ in how that systemic process is understood. The IS approach examines *'all important economic, social, political, organisational, and other factors that influence the development, diffusion, and use of innovations'* (Edquist, 1997: 14) in order to derive policy recommendations (Markard *et al.*, 2015). The focus is typically on technological innovations, such as alternative fuels in the transport context (e.g. Suurs *et al.*, 2010). Because of its technology focus, the framework is less suitable to understanding other types of innovations in urban mobility. The remainder of this chapter therefore concentrates on the STT approach, which has been used to study a wide range of innovations. Examples include electric and hydrogen vehicles, park and ride schemes, travel information provision and car sharing (Hoogma *et al.*, 2002; Nykvist & Whitmarsh, 2008; Geels *et al.*, 2012; Schwanen, 2015b).

Socio-technical transitions

The multi-level perspective (MLP) (Rip & Kemp, 1998; Geels, 2012) holds that innovations can only durably reconfigure existing mobility systems if developments in what are known as socio-technical niches, regimes and landscape are somehow aligned and reinforcing each other. A mobility system is understood here as a socio-technical system – a conglomerate of technologies, infrastructures, markets, regulation and policy, cultural values, user practices and various forms of knowledge that fulfil the societal function of transport. This system is held together and enacted by social practices that are conditioned by – and simultaneously reproduce – all kinds of rules, including cognitive routines, shared beliefs, social norms and conventions, regulations, industry standards, protocols, contracts and laws. Collectively these rules constitute the socio-technical regime. This regime is dynamically stable; innovations are usually incremental, led by incumbent actors and therefore with few implications for existing power relations. Typical examples include fuel economy improvements in the regime of automobility, which do little to challenge vested interests or its dominance in mobility provision, and are therefore relatively popular among incumbent actors like the car industry (Penna & Geels, 2015).

In contrast, more disruptive or radical forms of innovation that potentially challenge prevailing sets of rules need the protection of socio-technical niches – spaces in which actors at the fringe of the existing regime can experiment with innovations. In niches, innovations are shielded from regime pressures, nurtured and empowered (Smith & Raven, 2010). This is because, as the strategic niche management (SNM) and transition management (TM) literatures have demonstrated, it is in niches that the social networks supporting a given innovation are expanded; interests and expectations of various stakeholders are aligned through the articulation of collective visions; and learning about design, regulation and user experience takes place (Kemp *et al.*, 1998, 2007; Schot & Geels, 2008). For Geels and Raven (2006), niche development entails the formation of local/global interactions. They submit that the embodied, local knowledge generated in individual experiments and R&D projects is aggregated into more formalised agendas, models and theories shared by a growing network of actors. This more global knowledge helps to shape and frame subsequent localised experiments, which extend and refine the more generic learning and network formation, thereby strengthening the niche's momentum.

All of this will enable diffusion and competition or symbiosis with the prevailing regime(s). Whether diffusion and regime change happens, in which ways and at what pace depends on the pressure the socio-technical landscape exerts on the existing regime. The landscape is here effectively a residual category that gathers all the wider contexts and developments over which regime actors have little influence, including anthropogenic climate change, economic crisis, demographic shifts and the rise of the Information Age. It is from the interactions between niches, regime and landscape that a transition emerges (Geels, 2012).

Concerns and refinements

As the dominant perspectives on socio-technical transitions, the MLP and SNM/ TM have been criticised extensively (Smith *et al.*, 2005; Shove & Walker, 2007, 2010; Genus & Coles, 2008; Lawhon & Murphy, 2012; Bulkeley *et al.*, 2014; Affolderbach & Schulz, 2016). Providing an exhaustive overview is beyond this chapter; suffice it to say that the following concerns are most relevant for understanding innovation processes in urban mobility:

- Technological innovations, such as alternatively fuelled vehicles, are commonly privileged over innovations in the other elements that constitute socio-technical systems.

- Prevailing accounts of the activities needed to shield, nurture and empower niche-innovations have been considered technocratic and managerialist. The politics and power dynamics of innovation processes – and socio-technical transitions more widely – have remained underexposed and underconceptualised. Taking these arguments further, one might rather provokingly assert that the MLP and SNM are symptomatic of a wider 'post-political' condition according to which anthropogenic climate change can only be governed by accepting capitalism, the neoliberal logic of the market and expert management as given and by supplanting ideological contestation by consensus (Swyngedouw, 2010).

- Insufficient attention has been directed towards the social distribution of the effects of niche-innovations and socio-technical transitions: Who gains? Who loses? In what ways?

- The focus tends to be on actor networks and institutional structures rather than individual actors or small groups of individuals whose biographies, motivations and visions may play a key role in the emergence and early development of a particular innovation.

- The people who make use of socio-technical systems tend to be assigned rather passive subject positions: they are often imagined as (non-)adopters and (non-)users of innovations rather than as active and political subjects. Moreover, the heterogeneity in needs, preferences, capabilities and experiences of '(non-)users' is seldom recognised.

- The understandings of space (see below) and time on which STT thinking is premised can be developed further. Whilst imagining the world as in flux and intrinsically dynamic, SNM and the MLP are also committed to a linear understanding of time: the interest is both in the growth and diffusion of niche-innovations and in the transition from one socio-technical system to another.

STT scholars have responded generously to these – and other – concerns and gone to great lengths to address their critics. Most of the above points have been addressed in some way or other in STT research (Geels, 2011, 2014; Raven *et al.*, 2012), although it is an open question whether the responses have satisfied those critics. As space is limited, this chapter concentrates on concerns over politics and space in STT thinking.

For instance, Avelino and Rotmans (2009) and Geels (2014) have sought to address the recurring point that STT thinking has paid too little attention to how politics and power mediate innovation processes. Geels (2014) introduces power and politics into the MLP by using various political economy approaches to elaborate the interactions between policymakers and incumbent firms in theoretical terms. He proposes that niche-innovations are often slowed down or otherwise frustrated by those actors *'forming a core alliance at the regime level, oriented towards maintaining the status quo'* (p. 26). Alliances of this kind are common because the neo-liberalisation of policy over the past decades has made networking and close contact – often mediated by the cultural capital (Bourdieu, 1986) cultivated in specific higher education programmes and institutions – between policymakers and business actors both important and frequent.

Geels also borrows from Avelino and Rotmans (2009) by proposing that it is the aforementioned regime-level alliances that resist niche-innovations through the mobilisation of multiple forms of power:

- *Instrumental*: when resources such as money, expertise and access to the media are used to advance causes and objectives that are in policymakers' and incumbent firms' interests – examples in relation to passenger mobility in a large urban area in Western Europe would be reducing road congestion, strengthening economic competitiveness, maintaining the market share of conventional public transport providers, and discouraging difficult-to-regulate mobility services like peer-to-peer, smartphone application-enabled car sharing;

- *Discursive*: when meanings are inscribed onto innovations, and wider issues and agendas are set in ways that may be promulgated by the media and internalised by individuals seeking to fulfil their mobility needs – when, for instance, cycling is positioned as dangerous and inappropriate for children without adult supervision and/or as requiring the wearing of a helmet and high-visibility clothing;

- *Material*: when financial resources and technical capabilities are used to advance end-of-pipe innovations – when, for instance, in UK cities like Brighton and Oxford the time and expertise of civil servants is used to obtain national level subsidies for the purchase of plug-in-hybrid and battery-electric buses by incumbent bus companies (Schwanen, 2015b); and

- *Institutional*: when the wider culture of governing mobility privileges particular actions and forms of innovation – as when, in the UK, rules regarding the physical design and the dominance of articulating the value of innovations in economic, cost-to-benefit terms (*ibid.*).

As the above examples attest, my research into innovation processes in urban mobility in UK cities highlights the important role that various forms of power play in shaping innovation processes, and the valuable contribution Geels (2014) makes to understanding the politics of socio-technical transitions. However, my research also suggests that the thinking on the politics of innovation processes in urban mobility needs to be developed further. Politics is not limited to resistance and power generates more effects than funnelling innovation processes into particular directions. Politics and power operate through and on space in innovation processes, whilst simultaneously being refracted and conditioned by space.

Geographies of innovation

It took a while for geographers to engage with the STT literature but they have, predictably, been the first to critique the 'geographical naïveté' (Lawhon & Murphy, 2012: 362) of the MLP and SNM/TM. Insofar as geography was considered at all, regimes were typically situated at the national scale and landscapes at the supranational scale (see also Raven *et al.*, 2012). Niches were positioned at the sub-national – typically urban – scale when specific projects and experiments were concerned and at the national scale as far as the emerging knowledge and actor networks were considered (Sengers & Raven, 2015). This meant that the MLP's levels were further reified by cementing them in stable, nested spatial scales. Underpinning this geographical imagination were absolute notions of space as a passive, neutral container in which events and processes unfold. At best, space was understood in terms of contiguous, clearly delimited areas – territories – associated with and controlled by particular actor configurations such as a municipality, a national lobby organisation or the European Commission. These imaginings have been re-developed in various ways in recent years.

Spatialising socio-technical transitions

The first point geographers made was that innovation processes, niche formation and regime pressures are geographically uneven (Hodson and Marvin, 2010; Coenen *et al.*, 2012). Building on wider debates in their sub-discipline, economic geographers have argued that successful niche innovation depends not only on the institutional embeddedness that STT scholars have highlighted but also on socio-spatial embeddedness (Truffer & Coenen, 2012). Thus, it has been argued that radical innovations are more likely to emerge and flourish in places offering 'institutional thickness' – a localised capacity to support innovation resulting from formal and informal institutions, such as grant schemes or knowledge brokers funded by local government, as well as place-specific cultural norms, values, worldviews and networks (Coenen *et al.*, 2012; Longhurst, 2015). Institutional thickness enables spatial proximity between various actors to facilitate and reinforce knowledge formation (cognitive proximity), networking across and within organisations (organisational proximity), the building of trust and friendships (social proximity) (cf. Boshma, 2005).

My own research into innovation processes in urban mobility in UK cities confirms the relevance of institutional thickness. Much has happened around cycling since 2005 in Brighton, from street retrofitting to the construction of a cycle hub adjacent to the main train station, the creation of a cycling monitoring system, the establishment of cycle training in schools and emergence a string of regular cycling awareness events (Schwanen, 2015b). This level of activity is in no small part the consequence of local government financially and otherwise supporting community-led and private-sector initiatives to encourage cycling, consulting and collaborating with local stakeholders extensively, and cultivating good relationships with all constituencies within the city. Recent initiatives deemed successful have reinforced and solidified a place-specific culture of knowledge sharing, support, trust among actors, and respect for diversity of viewpoints and values.

Yet, my research also indicates that the socio-spatial embeddedness of cycling-related innovations in Brighton is not simply locally produced as a range of supra-local events, and processes have also been critically important. Examples of the latter are the local council's repeated success in obtaining funding from the national government's Department for Transport (DfT), good personal relationships between local council and DfT staff, and the significant input that national charity Sustrans has had in cycling-related initiatives in Brighton. In fact, what has happened in Brighton cannot be understood without due appreciation for the scalar restructuring of UK transport policy, which has long been strongly centralised and determined from Whitehall (MacKinnon et al., 2010; Schwanen, 2015b). National government have reconciled calls for more local autonomy over transport policy-making, greater national and international economic competitiveness of city-regions, and reduced government spending by increasingly awarding funding via competitive bidding to local authorities or regional consortia of public and private sector bodies. The result has been significant divergence in transport policy, institutional arrangements and powers across territories within the UK (MacKinnon et al., 2010), of which cycling in Brighton has benefited unusually (and other territories much less so).

The case of cycling in Brighton demonstrates that world cities like London are not the only places where scalar transformations mediate innovation and transition processes in urban mobility (cf. Hodson & Marvin, 2010). My research in Brighton, Oxford and Liverpool indicates how innovations in technology and other elements of socio-technical systems – cycling and electric vehicle charging infrastructures, alternatively fuelled buses, smart traffic management systems, et cetera – have become co-opted by a neoliberal discourse of cities as the focal points of global economic competitiveness across the urban hierarchy, at least in the UK. This, however, does not mean that the national scale has become much less important. As Mans (2014) also suggests with reference to clean technology, national policies and formal and informal institutions continue to play critical roles in shaping the development trajectories of innovations in urban mobility.

Relational reworkings

The above reflections have almost imperceptibly morphed into a discussion of relational geography perspectives on transitions. Scholarship in this vein holds that space is no container but arises from the relations between objects. Much of it is critical of the MLP because (Affolderbach & Schulz, 2016: 1952):

> [a] relational perspective questions the hierarchies and logics of the multi-level perspective where innovations are clearly situated within contained niches ...
> [and] dissolves the clear boundaries of niches and regimes, changes the relationship between different levels and disconnects the alignment and hierarchy between distinct levels and spatial scales. Even further, if transition processes are understood as assembled or simultaneously co-produced by agents at multiple scales, we need to question the origin of innovations and inherently the role of 'niches' as test beds.

Several relational reworkings have been proposed recently, including Bulkeley *et al.*'s (2014) political economy/ecology perspective on urban experimentation and Murphy's (2015) relational place-making approach. Both share important similarities with Affolderbach and Schulz's rapprochement of STT thinking and policy mobilities. The latter is a geographical critique of the policy transfer literature in political science (Peck, 2011; McCann & Ward, 2013). It starts from the observations that public policy formation can no longer be viewed through the lens of national bounded systems and nested scalar hierarchies (Cochrane & Ward, 2012), and that urbanism itself has been mobilised (McCann & Ward, 2011). Cities are increasingly interwoven in each others' constitution through the movements of policies and hence of:

- *Knowledge* – in particular forms of expert knowledge;
- *People* – especially technocrats and consultants;
- *Materials* – such as reports, statistics and stylised depictions; and
- *Politics* – here understood as ideological contests over appropriate forms and functions of the state (Temenos *et al.*, in press).

Evidently, policies do not move unscathed from A to B but mutate when they are first de-territorialised through processes of abstraction – simplification, selection, exclusion – and then re-territorialised and made to fit historically emerged places elsewhere. Movement is also uneven and shaped by politics and power (Peck, 2011; Wood, 2015). Moreover, the territories involved are remade as much as the policies themselves; co-evolution is the rule rather than the exception (McCann and Ward, 2011). The implication is that cities as well as innovations become 'assemblages' (Deleuze & Guattari, 1987) – continuously emergent yet history-dependent (re)-aligning 'bits-and-bobs' that transcend and defy conventional binaries (global/local, mobile/fixed, etc.) and wider classifications (culture, economy, politics, etc.).

Despite challenging crisp definitions of socio-technical systems and indeed innovations, the policy mobilities perspective has considerable purchase for understanding innovations that may transform personal mobility. First, it accommodates the empirical observation that hardly any of the initiatives in my research in UK cities are genuinely original in the sense of being the first manifestation anywhere (Schwanen, 2015b). Innovations in urban mobility, such as the Oxford and Liverpool bike-sharing schemes, are typically assemblages of elements from elsewhere with place-specific physical structures, funding opportunities, institutional particularities, etc. In both cities urban inter-referencing (Bunnell, 2015) has been critical to visioning, resource mobilisation and legitimisation. In Liverpool, the system that has been set up by the city council, CityBike, is inspired by London's scheme and often referred to as Liverpool's own Boris Bikes, after the former London mayor, Boris Johnson, under whose administration the bike-sharing scheme became operational. Moreover, CityBike is operated by a subsidiary of an international company that manages bike sharing schemes in other UK localities, including Oxford and Reading, as well as other countries in Europe and the Middle East. Interviews suggest that its design and governance are clearly informed by experiences the operators have gained elsewhere but are also distinctively re-territorialised, for instance in the cost structure of bike hires which is supposed to encourage longer-term subscriptions and use by city residents. There is also a second, separate scheme that is not unique to Liverpool, Bike & Go. This is run by a train operator that is a subsidiary of the Dutch railway company behind the highly successful *OV-fiets* (public transport bike) that is currently available at more than 270 train and metro stations in the Netherlands. Knowledge, individuals and materials that have been key to the early success of the *OV-fiets* are also at the heart of the Bike & Go scheme, which is rapidly diffusing across North, East and South-East England and Scotland.

Second, Affolderbach and Schulz (2016) suggest that the policy mobilities approach complements the MLP and SNM/TM by drawing attention to the role of key individuals in processes of change and innovation. My empirical research reinforces this point: building social networks and capital across different constituencies is important for the nurturing and empowerment of innovations, but so too is the leadership by 'champions' – a term I heard repeatedly in interviews to denote individuals who are strongly committed to particular innovations. Many of the examined cases, including Bike & Go in Liverpool and the aforementioned cycle hub next to Brighton's train station, suggest that understanding the biography, embodied values and knowledge, (career) ambitions, and social skills and other competencies of such individuals is essential to understanding the development trajectory of specific innovations.

Moreover, it is through engagement with champions and other mid-ranking policy-makers, politicians, entrepreneurs and activists through interviews and ethnography that the spatialised effects of instrumental, discursive, material and institutional power (Avelino & Rotmans, 2009) on innovation processes can be fully grasped. For instance, interviews were essential to my understanding of how the practices, techniques, regulations, logics and worldviews – the *dispositif* (Foucault, 1980) – through which DfT enable and constrain financial and other support for innovations in urban mobility that are territorialised in Oxford, Brighton and

Liverpool. Likewise, in her study of bus rapid transport in South Africa, interviews and ethnography allowed Wood (2015) to conclude that policymakers looked to learn from Bogota's *Transmileno* system rather than the systems in Lagos or Ahmedabad, which were arguably more compatible with South African contexts, because learning was equated *'with value: there is little economic, political, social benefit to building relationships across African and Indian cities'* (pp.1071-1072). The general sentiment was to turn towards more affluent cities because policymakers and politicians in South African cities saw themselves as also belonging to the global community of such cities.

Finally, analytical perspectives such as policy mobilities help researchers interested in innovations in urban mobility to better understand and negotiate the limitations imposed by the MLP's distinction between niche and regime. Protection as imagined by Smith and Raven (2010) – in particular, financial support (shielding), social network formation (nurturing) and the creation of enticing narratives for diversified constituencies (empowerment) – is essential to initiatives like Liverpool's Citybike and Brighton's cycle hub. However, such protection hinges critically upon active participation of regime actors and entanglement with prevailing mobility regimes from early onwards in a particular innovation's life-course. Identification of different levels from each other foregrounds protection but also risks expelling interconnections between niches and regimes into invisibility. The thinking on policy mobilities allows a different take on protection by encouraging researchers to trace how protection is continuously assembled and reassembled out of myriad relations and connections between longer existing – but still changing – constellations that fulfil the societal function of personal mobility and more recent, emerging ones.

Conclusions

Academic research into innovations in personal mobility is recent and burgeoning. It is nevertheless abundantly clear that innovations in personal mobility cannot – and should not – be understood in a technologically deterministic or economistic manner. Such innovations need to be imagined as social processes where 'social' is used in the Latourian sense as the outcome of the creation of connections between heterogeneous elements and not as 'a thing among other things' like the technological, the political, the cultural, etc. (Latour, 2005: 5). Protagonists of the STT approach have begun to think about innovations as social processes, even if they routinely use the word 'social' in its commonsense manner as a specific phenomenon. They have also responded generously to critics by re-assembling their concepts, categories and logics. As a result, they now have even more compelling stories to tell and policy recommendations to give than around the turn of the millennium, when the challenges of electric vehicle diffusion acted as one of the catalysts for the development of SNM and also the MLP. Key strengths of the STT approach are its comprehensive definition of socio-technical systems, its emphasis on path dependency and on the interweaving of long and short term dynamics, and its focus on the protection of innovations. Empirical research on all kinds of new technologies, institutional arrangements and user practices in personal mobility attest to these strengths.

Yet, every approach is fallible, partial and situated. It is therefore desirable that the migration of STT thinking across the boundaries of disciplines and epistemic communities has induced new rounds of critique and reworking (Hodson & Marvin, 2010; Truffer & Coenen, 2012; Lawhon & Murphy, 2012). Understanding of innovations in personal mobility can benefit substantially from geographers' critiques and reworkings. This is not merely because personal mobility is intrinsically spatial and geographical in nature, or because individuals' trip-making is concentrated in urban areas. It is also because in countries, such as the UK, state restructuring and the concomitant re-alignment of geographical scales is profoundly re-shaping transport governance. It is, finally, because the vast majority of innovations in personal mobility are transnational and to a lesser or greater degree assembled from materials, knowledge, visions, etc. from many different sites across the world. If understanding the implications of scalar dynamics and the transnational character of innovations in personal mobility means that some of the parsimoniousness and elegance of STT thinking has to be sacrificed, then this is a price worth paying. Given the many adverse environmental and social effects caused by personal mobility across the planet, there is an urgent need for policy and governance that genuinely encourages and supports innovations in clean and socially just forms of mobility.

Acknowledgements

The research described in this paper has been supported by the EPSCR (EP/KO11790/1). The patience of the editors, and their comments on an earlier version of the chapter, are gratefully acknowledged.

References

Affolderbach, J. & Schulz, C. (2016). Mobile transitions: exploring synergies for urban sustainability research, *Urban Studies*, **53**, 1942-1957.

Avelino, F. & Rotmans, J. (2009). Power in transition: an interdisciplinary framework to study power in relation to structural change, *European Journal of Social Theory*, **12**, 543-569.

Boschma, R.A. (2005). Proximity and innovation: a critical assessment, *Regional Studies*, **39**, 61-73.

Bourdieu, P. (1986). The forms of capital, in J. Richardson, J. (ed.) *Handbook of Theory and Research for the Sociology of Education*, New York: Greenwood, 241-258.

Bulkeley, H., Castán Broto, V. & Maassen, A. (2014). Low carbon transitions and the reconfiguration of urban infrastructure, *Urban Studies*, **51**, 1471-1486.

Bunnell, T. (2015). Antecedent cities and inter-referencing effects: learning from and extending beyond critiques of neoliberalisation, *Urban Studies*, **52**, 1983-2000.

Cochrane, A. & Ward, K. (2012). Researching the geographies of policy mobility: confronting the methodological challenges, *Environment and Planning A*, **44**, 5-12.

Coenen, L., Benneworth, P. & Truffer, B. (2012) .Toward a spatial perspective on sustainability transitions, *Research Policy*, **41**, 968-979.

Deleuze, G. & Guattari, F. (1987). *A Thousand Plateaus: Capitalism and Schizophrenia*, London: Continuum.

Dennis, K. & Urry, J. (2009). *After the Car*, Cambridge: Polity.

Edquist C. (1997). Systems of innovation approaches - their emergence and characteristics, in C. Edquist (ed.) *Systems of Innovation: Technologies, Institutions and Organisations*, London: Pinter/Cassell, pp. 1-35.

Foucault, M. (1980). *Power/Knowledge: Selected Interviews and Other Writings, 1972-1977*, New York: Pantheon Books.

Geels, F.W. (2011). The multi-level perspective on sustainability transitions: responses to seven criticisms, *Environmental Innovation and Societal Transitions*, **1**, 24-40.

Geels, F.W. (2012). A socio-technical analysis of low carbon transitions: Introducing the multi-level perspective into transport studies, *Journal of Transport Geography*, **24**, 471-482.

Geels, F.W. (2014). Regime resistance against low carbon transitions: Introducing politics and power into the multi-level perspective, *Theory, Culture & Society*, **31**, 21-40.

Geels, F.W., Kemp. R. , Dudley, G. & Lyons, G. (2012). *Automobility in Transition? A Socio-Technical Study of Sustainable Transport*, New York: Routledge.

Geels. F.W. & Raven, R. (2006). Non-linearity and expectations in niche-development trajectories: ups and downs in Dutch biogas development (1973-2003), *Technology Analysis & Strategic Management*, **18**, 375-391.

Genus, A. & Coles, A.M. (2008). Rethinking the multi-level perspective of technological transitions, *Research Policy*, **37**, 1436-1445.

Goodwin, P. & Van Dender, K. (2013). 'Peak car' – theme and issues, *Transport Reviews*, **33**, 243-254.

Hodson, M. & Marvin, S. (2010). Can cities shape socio-technical transitions and how would we know if they were?, *Research Policy*, **39**, 477-485.

Hoogma, R., Kemp, R., Schot, J. & Truffer, B. (2002). *Experimenting for Sustainable Transport: The Approach of Strategic Niche Management*, London: Spon Press.

Kemp, R., Schot, J. & Hoogma, R. (1998). Regime shifts to sustainability through processes of niche formation: The approach of strategic niche management, *Technology Analysis & Strategic Management*, **10**, 175-198.

Kemp, R., Loorbach, D. & Rotmans, J. (2007). Transition management as a model for managing processes of co-evolution towards sustainable development, *International Journal of Sustainable Development & World Ecology*, **14**, 1-15.

Kent, J.L. (2015). Still feeling the car–the role of comfort in sustaining private car use, *Mobilities*, **10**, 726-747.

Latour, B. (2005). *Reassembling the Social: An Introduction to Actor-Network-Theory*, Oxford: Oxford University Press.

Lawhon, M. & Murphy, J. (2012). Socio-technical regimes and sustainability transitions: insights from political ecology. *Progress in Human Geography*, **36**, 354-378.

Longhurst, N. (2015). Towards an 'alternative' geography of innovation: alternative milieu, socio-cognitive protection and sustainable experimentation, *Environmental Innovation and Societal Transitions*, **17**, 183-198.

MacKinnon, D., Shaw, J. & Docherty, I. (2010). Devolution as process: institutional structures, state personally and transport policy in the United Kingdom, *Space and Polity*, **3**, 271-287.

Mans, U. (2014). Tracking geographies of sustainability transitions: relational and territorial aspects of urban policies in Casablanca and Cape Town, *Geoforum*, **57**, 150-161.

Markard, J., Hekkert, M. & Jacobsson, S. (2015). The technological innovation systems framework: Response to six criticisms, *Environmental Innovation and Societal Transitions*, **16**, 76-86.

McCann, E. & Ward, K. (Eds.) (2011). *Mobile Urbanism: Cities and Policymaking in the Global Age*, Minneapolis, MN: University of Minnesota Press.

McCann, E. & Ward, K. (2013). Policy assemblages, mobilities and mutations, *Political Studies Review*, **10**, 325-332.

Murphy, J.T. (2015). Human geography and socio-technical transition studies: promising intersections, *Environmental Innovation and Societal Transitions*, **17**, 73-91.

Newman, P. & Kenworthy, J. (2015). *The End of Automobile Dependence: How Cities are Moving Beyond Car-Based Planning*, Washington, D.C.: Island Press.

Peck, J. (2011). Geographies of policy: from transfer-diffusion to mobility-mutation, *Progress in Human Geography*, **35**, 773-797.

Penna, C.R.C. & Geels, F.W. (2015). Climate change and the slow reorientation of the American car industry (1979–2012): An application and extension of the Dialectic Issue LifeCycle (DILC) model, *Research Policy*, **44**, 1029-1048.

Raven, R., Schot, J. & Berkhout, F. (2012). Space and scale in socio-technical transitions, *Environmental Innovation and Societal Transitions*, **4**, 63-78.

Rip, A. & Kemp, R. (1998). Technological change in S. Rayner and E.L. Malone (eds.) *Human Change and Climate Change – Resources and Technology, Volume 2*, Columbus, OH: Batelle, 327-399.

Schot, J. & Geels, F.W. (2008). Strategic niche management and sustainable innovation journeys: theory, findings, research agenda, and policy, *Technology Analysis & Strategic Management*, **20**, 537-554.

Schwanen, T. (2015a). Automobility in J.D. Wright (ed.) *International Encyclopedia of the Social and Behavioural Sciences, Second Edition, Volume 2*, Oxford: Elsevier, pp. 303-308.

Schwanen, T. (2015b). The bumpy road toward low-energy mobility: case studies from two UK cities, *Sustainability*, **7**, 7086-7111.

Sengers, F. & Raven, R. (2015). Toward a spatial perspective on niche development: The case of Bus Rapid Transit, *Environmental Innovation and Societal Transitions*, **17**, 166-182.

Shove, E. & Walker, G. (2007). CAUTION! Transitions ahead: politics, practice and sustainable transition management, *Environment and Planning A*, **39**, 763-770.

Shove, E. & Walker, G. (2010). Governing transitions in the sustainability of everyday life, *Research Policy*, **39**, 471-476.

Smith, A. & Raven, R. (2010). What is protective space? Reconsidering niches in transitions to sustainability, *Research Policy*, **41**, 1025-1036.

Smith, A., Stirling, A. & Berkhout, F. (2005). The governance of sustainable socio-technical transitions, *Research Policy*, **34**, 1491-1510.

Suurs, R.A.A., Hekkert, M.P., Kieboom, S. & Smits, R.E.H.M. (2010). Understanding the formative stage of technological innovation system development: The case of natural gas as an automotive fuel, *Energy Policy*, **38**, 419-431.

Swyngedouw, E. (2010). Apocalypse forever? Post-political populism and the spectre of climate change, *Theory, Culture and Society*, **27**, 213-232.

Temenos, C., Baker, T. & Cook, I.R. (in press) Inside mobile urbanism: cities and policy mobilities, in: T. Schwanen and R. van Kempen (Eds.) *Handbook of Urban Geography*, Cheltenham: Edward Elgar.

Truffer, B. & Coenen, L. (2012). Environmental innovation and sustainability transitions in regional studies, *Regional Studies*, **46**, 1-21.

Wood, A. (2015). The politics of policy circulation: unpacking the relationship between South African and South American cities in the adoption of Bus Rapid Transit, *Antipode*, **47**, 1062-1079.

13 Interrelationships of Internet Technologies and Transport Behaviour

Stefan Gössling

School of Business and Economics, Linnaeus University, Sweden and Western Norway Research Institute, Sogndal, Norway.

Introduction

The widespread introduction and uptake of information technologies (IT) including Internet, apps, and social media platforms has significant and complex implications for transportation and mobilities. This chapter discusses how IT influences mobility patterns, and how different IT innovations foster or substitute transport demand, concluding that IT may currently increase transport demand. The chapter highlights the complexity of interrelationships, and discusses three changes in transport demand growth in more detail, including the importance of apps for shared or public forms of mobility in urban contexts; competitive mobilities involving the use of social media; and automotive cultures fostered through the Internet. Trends and developments are discussed with regard to their implications for low carbon mobility transitions.

IT-transport interrelationships

Over the past decade, the Internet, social media, and specifically apps have come to be increasingly interwoven with our daily lives. The scale and growth in IT use and its implications for transport systems may be illustrated based on the example of Uber, a peer-to-peer taxi service founded in 2009. The platform originally organised private transport services by citizens using their own cars, charging lower prices than traditional taxi services. After six years, the company had expanded to 70 countries in the world, and was valued in January 2016 at US$62 billion (Newcomer, 2015). Not only did the company organise close to an estimated one million rides per day at this point, providing employment to tens of thousands of drivers, it also caused fundamental disruptions in taxi markets in those countries were the app was introduced. In the context of this chapter, the key question is, however, whether this fundamental change in the provision of transport services supports low carbon transport futures. Are convenient and quick ride-sharing services a means of reducing traffic, as they make car-ownership redundant? Does Uber's offer of shared rides between multiple people (Uberpool) lead to a significant reduction in transport volumes (and hence emissions), as it increases the load factor of cars? Or does Uber lead to growth in traffic, because the reduced cost of person-alised transport services makes these more attractive, perhaps also increasing the demand in luxurious car rides offered by the company? The purpose of this chapter is to discuss these issues, based on a general overview of IT-transport interrelation-ships and a more detailed consideration of three IT innovations with potentially significant repercussions for the decline or growth of transport demand.

As shown in Figure 13.1, the importance of IT innovations in the context of low carbon mobilities essentially addresses two dimensions: a) the choice of transport modes, which may be more sustainable (bicycle, bus, train/tram/subway) or less sustainable (motorcycle, car, aircraft); and b) overall transport demand, i.e. the distances travelled by individuals (which may increase or decline). Theoretically, a third dimension, i.e. the carbon intensity of the fuels used, is also of relevance, but this complexity is considered in the respective transport mode's carbon intensity (Figure 13.1). Importantly, transport mode choice and transport demand are inter-dependent, as they influence each other: someone favouring a bicycle over a car is likely to cover shorter distances on average, given that the maximum range for bicycling is shorter than for transport powered by combustion engines. Whether a given change in IT results in the growth or decline of emissions of greenhouse gases is thus an outcome of overall distances covered by a traffic participant, multiplied by the weighted average of the carbon intensity of the transport modes used.

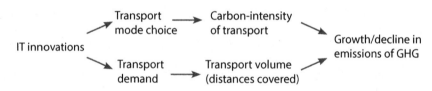

Figure 13.1: Interrelationships of IT and emissions of greenhouse gases from transport. Source: Author.

Notably, the role of IT in these interrelationships is potentially self-reinforcing or neutralising: for example, a person may choose to bicycle to work more often rather than to take the car, and as result, the overall distance travelled may also decline (as bicycling is more time consuming, and likely to involve shorter 'detours' – drive somewhere for lunch, picking up the laundry – than those made by car). As both carbon intensity and transport volume decline, the overall impact is even more favourable from a sustainability viewpoint, leading to a more significant decline in emissions. In comparison, someone changing from bicycle to car may contribute to growing emissions both because of the transport mode change and the greater distances travelled. Mode change effects can neutralise each other when less carbon intense transport is used, but transport volumes increase. This is known, for instance, in the case of purchases of smaller and less-energy consuming cars, which are driven considerably more: Studies of such 'rebound effects' indicate that about one fifth of potential savings are eroded by additional driving (Stapleton *et al.*, 2016). A very notable change in transport behaviour is also apparent in Generation Y and Z (those born after 1990), as these generations are less interested in driving licences (i.e., opportunities to drive themselves; Delbosc & Currie, 2014, see Chapter 3), but potentially considerably more 'aeromobile' than previous generations (Gössling & Stavrinidi, 2016).

In light of these complexities, how does IT affect transport behaviour, and, importantly, does it on balance increase or decrease transport volumes and emissions of greenhouse gases? This question has been controversially discussed over the past three decades, beginning with Salomon's (1986) linking of telecommunication opportunities to transport demand growth. Various publications have subsequently discussed these relationships (e.g. Banister & Stead, 2004; van den Berg *et al.*, 2013; Nobis & Lenz, 2009), though all authors concluded that the assessment of the outcomes of IT innovations was difficult. Yet, the consensus was that it was more likely that IT innovations increased overall transport demand. An important issue with these assessments is, perhaps, that authors investigating the implications of IT for transport behaviour have not been able to foresee the rapid change in available technologies that would occur in the future – most recently, this included apps – and the wide range of implications these technologies would have for transport behaviour (Gössling, 2016). There can be little doubt that each technological innovation has increased the degree of complexity with regard to IT's implications for transport demand: to assess the outcome of various technologies for low carbon transport futures has consequently become increasingly difficult.

This growing complexity of IT-transport interrelationships is illustrated in Figure 13.2, which shows that many of the digital devices and their functions now taken for granted by hundreds of millions of users were introduced only recently. The personal computer saw its mass-market breakthrough in the early 1990s. The mobile phone was introduced to larger markets in the mid-1990s, followed by transportable computers (notebooks), smartphones and tablets. Smartphones with touchscreens for direct finger use became known to mass-markets only in the late 2000s; this is, after the introduction of the iPhone and the platform Android for other phone brands. Even more recent were many software-based innovations. Web 2.0, the Internet characterised by interactivity and opportunities for users to generate content, was introduced in 2003. Social media were introduced soon after, with the most recent developments including mobile applications and chat services. This timeline illustrates the rapid changes in opportunities to use technologies – in particular the smart phone – and their even more rapid mass-market uptake as well as the difficulty in anticipating the outcome of these innovations for transport demand.

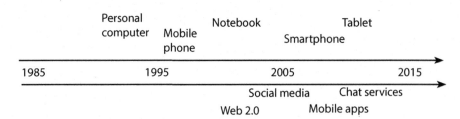

Figure 13.2: Approximate mass-market introduction of telecommunications innovations. Source: Author.

Implications of IT for transport mode choice and demand

In recent years, a wide range of IT innovations have become relevant for transport use. These have been summarised in Table 13.1, along with an assessment of their implications for transport mode choices (more/less sustainable) and transport demand (growing/declining). As indicated, IT is now relevant with regard to travel information, planning and routing; sharing; distance work; price comparison; safety; convenience; distribution of traffic; health; and mobilities (Gössling, 2016). These have interrelationships with transport mode choice and demand, with major changes often being introduced by individual IT sites or apps. For a more detailed discussion of the complexity of interdependencies see Gössling (2016).

A general analysis would suggest that IT innovations can work in two directions; that is, they can increase or reduce emissions. However, implications are not always comparable. As an example, convenience applications such as parking apps of different types are likely to increase emissions, as they make car driving more efficient. Depending on location, this may be a considerable advantage for drivers, as up to 8% of all traffic in urban contexts in the USA may be related to searches for parking space (Shoup, 2006). However, outside the USA, these apps may be less relevant. As another example, apps helping to monitor physical activity are likely to lead to more active lifestyles; yet their contribution to transport mode change (e.g. car to bicycle) or transport demand (number of kilometres cycled). In comparison to these examples, the most powerful changes are related to mobilities, which refer to demand changes linked to the very nature of travel motives. In other words, glamorisation of corporeal mobility (Cohen & Gössling, 2015), as well as travel visualisation on maps linked to competitive mobilities are of potentially great importance for transport volume growth, because they are interrelated with social status and personal identities, thus constituting mechanisms with potentially very important repercussions for transport demand growth. The following sections will discuss the three changes in more detail that are likely to have the greatest implications for transport mode change and transport demand growth, including the implications of IT for urban transport behaviour, competitive mobilities and car cultures. While the first of these has the potential to reduce transport emissions, the latter two are likely to increase emissions from transport systems.

Table 13.1: IT innovations and their implications. Source: adapted from Gössling (2016).

Change dimension	Emission growth	Example
Travel information, planning		
Public transport	↓	Moovit, Moovel
Alternative transport	↑↓	Uber, Mytaxi, car2go
Car	↑	Google maps, Waze
Bicycle	↓	BeeLine, GraphHopper
Sharing		
Bicycle sharing	↓	Spinlister, Bicimad
Car sharing (rental)	↑↓	Europcar
Car sharing (own)	↓	Car next door
Ride pooling, shared commuting	↓	Go2gether
Park sharing/renting	↑	Ez-Park / Lyft
Ride shares	↑	ParkFlyRent
Taxi services	↑↓	Hailo
Boat sharing	↑	Boathound
Distance work		
Content sharing	↓	Buffer
Chat services	↓	Hipchat
Video chat rooms	↓	Sqwiggle
Videoconferencing	↓	GoToMeeting
Price comparison		
Comparison of cost	↑↓	Moovel
Last minute deals	↑	Skyscanner, LTM
Safety		
Traffic safety improvement	↓	Velodossier
Participatory transport system development	↓	Givetpraj
Safety perceptions	↑↓	Metrocosm
Convenience		
Parking space reservation	↑	Justpark
Private parking space renting	↑	Park2Gether
Parking space payment	↑	Parku
Park time reminders	↑	Parker
Park location reminders	↑	Findmycar
Crowdedness indicator	↑	Xtra
Distribution		
Efficient use of existing capacities	↑↓	Transit app, Waze
Health		
Physical activity	↓	Pedometer, Fitbit
Energy 'burnt' (calories)	↓	Move
Air quality	↑↓	Moovel
Pathogen exposure	↑	PathoMap
Mobilities		
Virtual travel	↑	TripAdvisor, YouTube
Travel visualization	↑	Amcharts, maploco, mappable
Co-presence	↑↓	Whatsapp
Social status	↑	Facebook
Car cultures	↑	YouTube

↑Growth in greenhouse gas emissions; ↓Decline in emissions; ↑↓ Relationship uncertain

In Figure 13.1 the implications of IT innovations in terms of emission growth or decline are indicated by arrows. Where arrows point upwards, this implies growth in emissions; where they point downward, there is a potential reduction in emissions. Arrows in both directions indicate unclear relationships: these IT innovations may lead to an overall growth or decline in emissions.

Three major changes in IT and their implications for transport demand

Urban transport and non-ownership of cars

In recent years, a number of apps have been developed which offer the integration of a wide range of transport modes, such as busses, trams, trains, subways, as well as car rentals, car sharing or bicycle sharing (e.g. Moovel). Other apps (Beeline, Move) allow finding ideal directions, for instance for walking, bicycling, car use or public transport, also providing 'calories burnt' estimates (Figure 13.3), and thus encouraging physical activity.

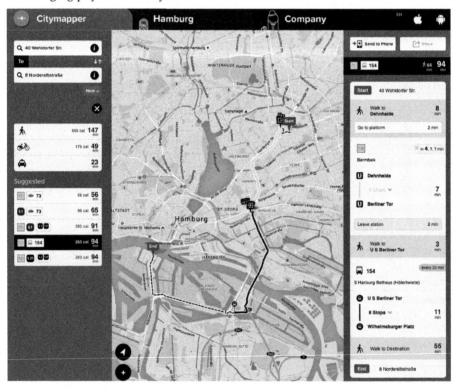

Figure 13.3: Screenshot from Citymapper website. Reproduced with permission.

These apps significantly improve connectivity, while also increasing interest in physical activity. Their importance for transport demand is thus twofold: they make public or shared forms of transport more attractive, while at the same time providing an efficient and cost-effective alternative to individual motorised mobility. Given that car sharing systems now make it possible to book a specific car by app within a few seconds, and often only a few minutes' walk from one's current location, car ownership is increasingly becoming inconvenient – it is more expensive, unless driving patterns involve high use – and requires various services (vehicle registration, insurance, maintenance and repairs, inspections and insurance) that are included for members of car sharing organisations. Even more convenient is to 'order' a driver through apps including Uber, Lyft or Carma. Because of these innovations, transport opportunities have diversified and become increasingly and more easily available, specifically in urban contexts. Notably, the exactness of departures/arrivals, either in terms of pick-up times or delays, is an increasingly prominent feature of these technology developments.

Largely as a result of these developments, several trends in cities are notable: there is a decline in driver licensure among younger people, a decline in car-ownership, and growth in shared forms of mobility, including bike rentals. Both the declines in driver licensure (Delbosc & Currie, 2014) and car ownership have been linked to car sharing opportunities (Belgiawan *et al.*, 2014), and both are likely to affect travel intensities, in the sense that transport demand declines (the importance of 'non-ownership' of cars has been discussed by e.g. Gilbert & Perl, 2008). Reduced demand in motorised vehicles has also been linked to the existence of bike rental platforms (Fishman *et al.* 2014; Martin *et al.*, 2010). There is still uncertainty as to whether these developments will lead to an overall decline in transport demand – the convenience of taxi services, for instance, may also lead to growing transport volumes – but there is evidence that at least a share of transport demand will be covered by more sustainable transport modes, i.e. bicycles, public transport or taxi services. Overall, apps thus have great potential to reduce transport demand, and to facilitate low carbon transportation, specifically in urban settings.

Competitive mobilities

Social media has significant influence on travel behaviour, as these create competitive mobilities, i.e. movement patterns that are based on comparison. Ultimately, these sites thus address the attractiveness of social status acquired through one's travelness (Urry, 2011). Examples of the impact of social media in this direction are now manifold. As an example, Facebook, as the largest social media site, offers visualisation of travel patterns. Guiding questions such as *'What are you doing?'* and *'Where are you?'*, encourage people to 'check in'; that is, to georeference one's travel patterns, with visited destinations automatically being visualised on world maps. Some sites, for instance TripAdvisor, also calculate the share of the world travelled, in itself a mirror of the 'missing' parts. Intended as a means of encouraging users to write more reviews, this also becomes a mechanism rewarding more travel, as users understand that to have travelled only a fraction of the world incurs a low degree of travelness, and hence low social status.

One of the most explicit developments in this regard is perhaps Expedia's 2015 Facebook campaign 'Travel yourself interesting'. A reflection of the sentence suggests two things: first, the reader is not currently interesting, and second, travel is a way of overcoming this problem. To suggest to anyone that they are not interesting is not a small threat from a psychological viewpoint. Clearly, only 'being of interest' would be a signifier of social connectedness; without social networks, one is alone (Caccioppo & Williams, 2008). To be of interest should thus be of great relevance to anyone, as loneliness ultimately suggests that, given the enormous importance of sociality for humans, life is without meaning (James, 1890). The solution to this contrived 'problem' is to travel. At first sight, this is a paradox: movement is about distance, while social connectedness is about proximity. Yet, in the context of Expedia's campaign, movement can be transformed – via 'travel points' – into social status, at least in the network of fellow point collectors, and hence into social connectedness. To this end, Expedia also encourages travellers to 'Challenge your friends', i.e. to directly compare travel points with (known) peers. Through this mechanism, social status is transferred to one's own, rather than abstract networks.

Another example of the semiotics of travel frequency is 'MostTraveledPeople' (Figure 13.4), a site offering a ranking based on 'places visited'. Places includes 849 locations on Earth, i.e. a more evenly distributed grid of places than represented by countries, of which there are only about 200.

Figure 13.4: Screenshot from MostTraveledPeople, comparing countries and places visited. Source: Reproduced with permission from MostTraveledPeople.

By ranking top travellers, fellow tourists see their own status in terms of places visited, in comparison to others. However, as they are unlikely to have met those other travellers or to even communicate with them, social status in this ranking is abstract; it can only be transformed into social connectedness if there is a mechanism to communicate one's global travelness within one's own network. Not surprisingly, most websites illustrating or visualising the number of places visited by a person (e.g. Country-counter, Amcharts, Maploco, Mappable) thus offer opportunities to tweet or to link results to Facebook sites. In all cases, websites need to be seen as powerful means of encouraging travel, as they link one of any human's most essential needs, social connectedness, with movement. This largely contradicts ambitions to foster awareness of travel's implications for climate change. As Gössling and Stavrinidi (2016) conclude in a study of a large Facebook network, discussions of environmental impacts of travel are conspicuously absent in travel discourses.

Car cultures

The Internet fosters car cultures through websites dedicated to mobility, as well as social media and YouTube clips. Two examples of the attractiveness of car cultures fostered through the Internet are the movie franchise 'Fast and Furious' and the YouTube clip 'Nissan GTR 900hp: four girls reactions', the latter an example of a specific type of video clip of which there exist hundreds. The *Fast and Furious* Facebook site approached 58 million likes in February 2016, and the *Fast and Furious* movies are, according to Wikipedia's widely accessible description, '*a series of action films, which center around illegal street racing and heists*' (Wikipedia, 2016: np). In other words, the movies feature a community of peers engaged in criminal activity, for which they use fast cars. The movies weave together a wide range of aspects that may explain their popularity. First of all, fast driving and risk taking is clearly an aspect that does appeals to large audiences. It is notable, however, that the movies are also interwoven with specific views on loyalty and friendship. As repeatedly outlined by Dominic, the group leader in the franchise (starring actor Vin Diesel): '*I don't have friends, I only have family*'. To belong to this diverse ethnical group of racers is, in other words, more than a close relationship: family is both a social *and* a biological relationship, and in contrast to friendship, family bonds cannot be terminated. To be part of the group requires qualification, however: one must prove that one is a risk-taking, capable driver. In *Fast and Furious*, social connectedness in strong reciprocal relationships is thus ultimately achieved through aggressive driving. This may also be the understanding of fans of the franchise, and thus make fast driving desirable.

In comparison, the YouTube clip 'Nissan GTR 900hp: four girls reactions' had been downloaded more than 25 million times in February 2016. It represents a specific type of video, in which women are driven by men in powerful sports cars (Figure 13.5). These videos follow the same protocol: A usually scarcely clad woman, the main focus of the video, enters a sports car as a passenger, and is taken for a short ride during which the car's rapid acceleration becomes visible. The speedometer and rev counter are sometimes blended into the video to emphasise acceleration in technical terms. In all videos, the women react with awe, i.e. visible expressions of disbelief, happy smiles, admiration, and sometimes fear. Videos thus play on motives of gender, control, power, and ownership, i.e. the man is driver and in charge, and potentially also the owner of the expensive car, while the woman is a passenger, i.e. relying on the driver both for excitement and safety.

Nissan GTR 900hp: four girls reactions

Michael Berenis

Abonnieren   125.702

25.362.309

Figure 13.5: YouTube screenshot: man driving woman in sports car. Source: Reproduced with permission from Michael Berenis.

The implications of such Internet representations of maleness are complex. First of all, videos, as well as movies such as *Fast and Furious*, associate driving fast or aggressively with skill, which is reinforced as a masculine feature (Özkan & Lajunen, 2006). This reinforces stereotypes in spheres were masculinity is considered desirable, while simultaneously establishing role models where male power and dominance over women is seen as attractive, reducing women to *'objects to a man's sexual desires'* (Krahé, 2005: 540). At the same time, it confirms driver identities, i.e. personalities that include cars on definitions of self. Where individuals feel superior because of car-based identities, they may project this self-image through aggressive driving and poor images of other traffic participants (Ruvio & Shoham, 2011). Drivers who are attached to their cars do not only drive more (Nilsson & Küller, 2000), they are also likely to see driving as a right, becoming psychologically dependent on motorised mobility. Hence, they are less likely to accept measures that would curb car use due to interwoven man-machine identities. Car cultures fostered by the Internet are thus an example of a powerful cultural understanding of automobility that would make low carbon mobilities more difficult to achieve.

IT and low carbon transport futures: an outlook

Global passenger transportation is locked into powerful growth processes, including car ownership and a rapidly increasing interest in aeromobility (IEA, 2009). Both are underlying factors fostering emission growth. With regard to more sustainable mobility, trends of cycling can be observed in cities around the world (Pucher & Buehler, 2012), but they currently reflect a growing mobility demand for most transport modes, rather than social change with the potential to contribute to low carbon transport futures. In this situation, questions have been raised (Creutzig *et al.*, 2015; Cohen *et al.*, 2014) regarding innovations that may contribute to changes in transport system in terms of declining transport demand, the use of less energy-intense transport modes, or the development of low carbon fuels. IT innovations may be of relevance with regard to transport mode use as well as transport demand, as they interact with a wide range of aspects of importance for transport behaviour. Internet sites, social media and apps now provide a wide range of opportunities to obtain traffic information, to plan trips or to find routes; to share cars, bicycle or other transport; to work at-a-distance; to pay for transport or to compare prices; to improve safety and convenience; to control or distribute space and capacity; to contribute to better health; and with regard to mobilities (Gössling, 2016). Yet, to assess the outcome of these innovations for the sustainability of transport systems is difficult.

For this reason, three aspects have been discussed in greater detail in this chapter. This includes, the rapidly growing number of apps for shared mobility and the use of public transport in urban contexts, where apps hold considerable potential to reduce vehicle numbers, to initiate change towards more sustainable forms of transport, and – potentially – to lead to an overall decline in mobility demand (Gössling, 2016). In comparison, social media sites fostering competitive mobilities are likely to increase the global interest in travel, as sites compete on the basis of parameters including the countries or places visited; the number of transport modes used; the highest number of specific locations on Earth visited; as well as abstractions of these, as exemplified by Expedia's travel points. Comparative travel has a wide range of implications, the most fundamental being the transformation of 'movement' into a purpose of its own: to overcome distance has assumed importance in its own right. For frequent travellers, this has complex implications for perceptions of self, and may ultimately result in the assumption of liquid identities modeled on constant movement (Gössling & Stavrinidi 2016).

Notably, expressions of such liquidity in identities are now emerging in various forms, from Expedia's encouragement to '*Challenge your friends*' on the basis of their travelness, to a Pinterest user's confession '*I travel, therefore I am – Places I've lived, visited and want to go to… I love to travel, it has made me who I am*'. Where travel, and specifically air travel, becomes part of identity formation it will be increasingly difficult to change behaviour in favor of low carbon transport futures. Yet, companies such as UK airline EasyJet already invite young, urban, mobile travellers to become part of 'Generation Easyjet', i.e. offering social connectedness in a community of frequent fliers; while German airline Lufthansa has extended its 'Non-stop you' campaign (first launched in 2013) into its third year, suggesting that all that should matter to individuals is their own happiness. However, people only concerned with themselves can be assumed to be less willing to accept measures that would curb their own activities in favor of the welfare of others. This, however, is a key issue with climate change, where contributions to climate change and the impacts of climate change are unevenly distributed, and where those making the greatest contributions to global warming are best equipped to adapt, given their financial resources (Gössling, 2010).

Finally, the chapter has discussed the consequences of the empowerment of automotive cultures through the Internet, as the car is the biggest barrier to sustainable transportation in most urban and rural contexts. Not only is automobility a major contributor to direct emissions of greenhouse gases (Creutzig *et al.*, 2015), it also contributes to 1.2 million fatal accidents every year (WHO, 2013), with an even greater number of people dying annually from automotive air pollution (Brauer *et al.*, 2013, Künzli *et al.*, 2000). Cars also occupy considerable space in cities, and to make room for more sustainable transport modes will require a reduction in car levels (e.g. Vasconcellos, 2001). In short: to overcome car cultures is a major objective of low carbon transport futures. Yet, this is difficult where cars are glamorised as desirable objects, and where these are interlinked with specific lifestyles or semiotics of dominance and power (Krahé & Fenske, 2002).

Overall, these examples show that the assessment of outcomes of IT for low carbon transport futures is complex, and in all likelihood to the detriment of sustainable transport systems (Gössling, 2016). While there is potential for many apps to improve public transport use and to make shared or public forms of transportation more desirable, more powerful social changes are currently initiated by social media and the Internet in opposite directions. To resolve this situation will be fraught with immense political and social challenges.

References

Banister, D. & Stead, D. (2004). Impact of information and communications technology on transport. *Transport Reviews*, **24**(5), 611-632.

Belgiawan, P. F., Schmöcker, J. D., Abou-Zeid, M., Walker, J., Lee, T. C., Ettema, D. F. & Fujii, S. (2014). Car ownership motivations among undergraduate students in China, Indonesia, Japan, Lebanon, Netherlands, Taiwan, and USA. *Transportation*, **41**(6), 1227-1244.

Brauer, M., Reynolds, C. & Hystad, P. (2013). Traffic-related air pollution and health in Canada. *Canadian Medical Association Journal*, **185**(18), 1557–1558.

Cacioppo, J.T. & William P. (2008). *Loneliness. Human Nature and the Need for Social Connection*. New York: W.W. Norton.

Cohen, S. & Gössling, S. (2015). A darker side of hypermobility. *Environment and Planning A*, **47**(8), 166-1679.

Cohen, S. A., Higham, J. E., Stefan, G. & Peeters, P. (2014). *Understanding and Governing Sustainable Tourism Mobility: Psychological and behavioural approaches*. London: Routledge.

Creutzig, F., Jochem, P., Edelenbosch, O.Y., Mattauch, L., van Vuuren, D.P., McCollum, D. & Minx, J. (2015). Transport: A road block to climate change mitigation? *Science*, **350**(6263), 911-912.

Delbosc, A. & Currie, G. (2014). Changing demographics and young adult driver license decline in Melbourne, Australia (1994–2009). *Transportation*, **41**(3), 529-542.

Fishman, E., Washington, S. & Haworth, N. (2014). Bike share's impact on car use: evidence from the United States, Great Britain, and Australia. *Transportation Research Part D: Transport and Environment*, **31**, 13-20.

Gilbert, R. & Perl, A. (2008). *Transport Revolutions: Moving People and Freight Without Oil*. Earthscan.

Gössling, S. (2010). *Carbon Management in Tourism: Mitigating the Impacts on Climate Change*. London: Routledge.

Gössling, S. (2016). Are information technologies leading to a growth or decline in transport demand? *International Journal of Sustainable Transportation*, submitted.

Gössling, S. & Stavrinidi, I. (2016). Social networking, mobility, and the rise of liquid identities. *Mobilities*, DOI: 10.1080/17450101.2015.1034453.

IEA (International Energy Agency) (2009). *Transport, Energy and CO_2: Moving Towards Sustainability*. Paris: International Energy Agency.

James, W. (1950 [1890]). *The Principles of Psychology, 3rd ed*. New York: Dover Publications Inc.

Krahé, B. & Fenske, I. (2002). Predicting aggressive driving behaviour: The role of macho personality, age, and power of car. *Aggressive Behaviour*, **28**, 21–29.

Künzli, N., Kaiser, R., Medina, S., Studnicka, M., Chanel, O., Filliger, P., Herry, M., Horak, F., Puybonnieux-Texier, V., Quénel, P., Schneider, J., Seethaler, R.,Vergnaud, J-C. & Sommer, H., (2000). Public-health impact of outdoor and traffic-related air pollution: a European assessment. *The Lancet*, **356**(9232), 795-801.

Martin, E., Shaheen, S. & Lidicker, J. (2010). Impact of carsharing on household vehicle holdings: Results from North American shared-use vehicle survey. *Transportation Research Record: Journal of the Transportation Research Board*, (2143), 150-158.

Newcomer, E. (2015). Uber Raises Funding at $62.5 Billion Valuation – The ride-hailing company is said to seek $2.1 billion in a new funding round. Available: http://www.bloomberg.com/news/articles/2015-12-03/uber-raises-funding-at-62-5-valuation. Accessed 5 Dec 2015.

Nilsson, M. & Küller, R. (2000). Travel behaviour and environmental concern. *Transportation Research Part D*, **5**, 211–234.

Nobis, C. & Lenz, B. (2009). Communication and mobility behaviour–a trend and panel analysis of the correlation between mobile phone use and mobility. *Journal of Transport Geography*, **17**(2), 93-103.

Özkan, T. & Lajunen, T. (2006). What causes the differences in driving between young men and women? The effects of gender roles and sex on young drivers' driving behaviour and self-assessment of skills. *Transportation Research Part F*, **9**, 269–277.

Pucher, J. & Buehler, R. (2012). *City Cycling*. Cambridge: MIT Press.

Ruvio, A. A. & Shoham, A. (2011). Aggressive driving: A consumption experience. *Psychology and Marketing*, **28**(11), 1089–1114.

Salomon, I. (1986). Telecommunications and travel relationships: a review. *Transportation Research A*, **20A** (3), 223–238.

Shoup, D. C. (2006). Cruising for parking. *Transport Policy*, **13**(6), 479-486.

Stapleton, L., Sorrell, S. & Schwanen, T. (2016). Estimating direct rebound effects for personal automotive travel in Great Britain. *Energy Economics*. doi:10.1016/j.eneco.2015.12.012

Urry, J. (2011). Social networks, mobile lives and social inequalities. *Journal of Transport Geography*, **21**, 24-30.

van den Berg, P., Arentze, T. & Timmermans, H. (2013). A path analysis of social networks, telecommunication and social activity–travel patterns. *Transportation Research Part C: Emerging Technologies*, **26**, 256-268.

Vasconcellos, E. A. (2014). *Urban Transport Environment and Equity: The case for developing countries*. London: Routledge.

World Health Organisation (2009). Global status report on road safety. http://whqlibdoc.who.int/publications/2009/9789241563840_eng.pdf. Accessed 06 July 2015.

14 Aeromobilities in Transition: From quick and dirty to slow and sexy

Rob Bongaerts, Jeroen Nawijn, Eke Eijgelaar and Paul Peeters

Centre for Sustainable Tourism and Transport of NHTV Breda University of Applied Sciences, the Netherlands.

Introduction

Air transport has become an important transport mode for holidays and business travel. Its growth since the 1950s has been aided by government support (e.g., infrastructure, funding) and technological innovations allowing for increases in capacity, speed and distance (Schäfer *et al.*, 2009). The reduction of the real cost of flying has been another strong driver of the growth of air travel. In the US, for instance, real costs per passenger kilometre declined by 90% between 1925 and 1975 (Mowery & Rosenberg, 1981). The cost of air travel per revenue passenger-mile reduced almost continuously from $0.2692 (constant 1978 US$) in 1937 to $0.0512 in 2000 (U.S. Census Bureau, 2010), a reduction of 81%.

Aviation has grown rapidly, and remained relatively unaffected by crises in the long term. Global revenue passenger kilometres (RPK) have increased by approximately 4.5% per year and reached more than 6 trillion RPK in 2014, having doubled since 2000. Air travel now exceeds 3 billion passengers per year, with particularly rapid growth outside of Europe and North America, with RPK growth rates of 11% for the Middle East and 8% for Asia and the Pacific (ICAO, 2015). The International Civil Aviation Organisation (ICAO) expects another doubling of RPK, to 12 trillion, in 2030 (ICAO, 2015).

The term 'aeromobility' has been adopted to describe the increasing use and importance of airplanes (Høyer, 2000). Air transport already plays a key role in international tourism trips with a 51% share of arrivals in 2010, growing from 38% in 1980 (UNWTO, 2011). The International Air Transport Association (IATA) is anticipating air transport capacity to be five times bigger in 2050 compared to the year 2000 (IATA, 2013). In terms of all passenger kilometres travelled worldwide,

Schäfer *et al.* (2009) expect the share of high-speed transportation (i.e. mainly air) to increase from less than 10% in 2005 to nearly 40% in 2050. In international tourism, aviation's share is expected to stabilise at approximately 52% of arrivals in 2030, yet with a doubling of arrivals compared to 2010 (UNWTO, 2011).

This rapid growth, coupled with the increasing distances travelled (Peeters, 2013), has made aviation a key contributor to travel-related carbon dioxide (CO_2) emissions. Aviation was found to contribute 40% of all global tourism CO_2 emissions in 2005, which in turn made up about 5% of all anthropogenic emissions (UNWTO-UNEP-WMO, 2008). Other assessments have international and domestic civil aviation accounting for 2.1% of global CO_2 emissions in 2012 (Cames *et al.*, 2015). While this chapter is limited to carbon emissions, it is important to acknowledge that the contribution of aviation to radiative forcing is possibly far greater. For tourism it is estimated to be between 5.2% and 12.5% (Scott, Peeters, & Gössling, 2010), due to the non-CO_2 atmospheric impacts of aviation (see Lee *et al.*, 2010). Of all transport modes, aviation emissions are growing fastest (Creutzig *et al.*, 2015) and this is likely to continue into the future. Aviation's share in tourism emissions is estimated to grow to over 50% by 2035 (UNWTO-UNEP-WMO, 2008).

These forecasts are not compatible with sustainable international emission pathways, as proposed by the Intergovernmental Panel on Climate Change (IPCC, 2014a). In its Fifth Assessment Report (AR5), the IPCC concluded that climate impacts are already observed globally, that anthropogenic drivers have been the dominant cause of warming, and that current emission trends will lead to severe and irreversible impacts for people and ecosystems (IPCC, 2014b). Avoiding climate change is generally associated with restricting the warming of global average temperatures to no more than 2°C compared to the pre-industrial era, a limit that was also adopted at the United Nations Framework Convention on Climate Change (UNFCCC) 21st Conference of Parties (COP21) in Paris (UNFCCC, 2015).

In order to fit with a low carbon pathway, Cames *et al.* (2015) calculate that aviation should not exceed 39% growth by 2030 compared to 2005 emission levels, and should be –41% compared to 2005 levels in 2050. They emphasise that more stringent targets are needed to account for non-CO_2 impacts.

Tourism demand

Cognitive dissonance

Tourism demand typically ignores travel related carbon emissions (Hares, Dickinson, & Wilkes, 2010; McKercher *et al.*, 2010). Even those tourists who hold positive attitudes towards environmental protection and engage in environmentally friendly behaviour at home are generally reluctant to change their travel behaviour (Juvan & Dolnicar, 2014). This gap, between attitudes and intention on the one hand and behaviour on the other, is generally explained through cognitive dissonance theory (Festinger, 1957) and construal-level theory (Trope & Liberman, 2010). Construal-level theory posits that events are represented at different levels of mental abstraction. High-level construal refers to more distant choices, whereas low-level construal refers to more proximate choices. These choices can be in conflict with each other and cause dissonance. This dissonance creates tension which results in feelings of guilt among tourists who have high carbon footprints (e.g., Cohen, Higham, & Cavaliere, 2011). However, this guilt has yet to affect behaviour change and it remains largely unclear as to why environmentally minded tourists refuse to make behavioural changes. We use the word 'largely' because it is obvious that individuals take holidays to de-stress, to experience pleasure, for novelty reasons, to learn something, and to have memorable experiences (e.g., Goossens, 2000; Nawijn, 2011; Tung & Ritchie, 2011). However, there is no research that indicates that, to achieve these goals, it would be necessary to take high carbon vacations.

One reason to explain why the intention-behaviour gap exists is put forward by Eijgelaar *et al.* (2016), who assume that because the effect of vacationing on carbon emissions is not made visible at time of booking, for example through a carbon label – unlike attributes such as price, length of stay and destination – tourists do not take this aspect into account. The current use of eco labels or carbon labels is often ineffective, largely due to poor communication (Gössling & Buckley, 2016).

Another line of reasoning draws from literatures on addiction, and argues of flying addicts (Cohen *et al.*, 2011), similar to addictions to alcohol or drugs. Ram *et al.* (2013) offer reasons for this addiction, namely that there is an appeal in exotic destinations, which are assumed to generate greater happiness and potentially satisfy an ongoing search for novelty. Although explanations of the observed gap between intention and behaviour have their merit, these offer no solutions from the consumer side (cf. Antimova *et al.*, 2012; Young *et al.*, 2014).

Tourism supply

The tourism and aviation industries are facing serious challenges in reducing future carbon emissions, as it is very likely that a greater number of people will travel more, further and more frequently in the future (UNWTO, 2016). Although IATA has the ambition to keep carbon emissions at 2020 levels, the likelihood of success is low. To date, efficiency gains have been offset by the increase in volume (IATA, 2013; Peeters *et al.*, 2016). Thus there is an urgent challenge to modify current trends and projections in such a way to avoid more, and ultimately reduce total emissions. The next section discusses three mechanisms for change: technological and operational, price, and behavioural mechanisms.

Technological and operational mechanisms

Industry bodies present a combined strategy of technology investments, more efficient operations, more effective infrastructure and positive economic measures for mitigating aviation emissions (e.g. ATAG, 2015; IATA, 2013). Technological measures that ultimately reduce emissions can be divided into two categories. The first category is related to the aircraft itself: weight, fuel efficiency and better use of the aircraft. The second is related to type of fuel being used. There have been many improvements in the first category, but according to IATA, more radical technological improvements can be expected by 2050 (IATA, 2013). However, Peeters et al. (2016), argue that the promise of future improvements will not succeed in achieving the necessary changes to offset the increased carbon emissions of air transport.

The second category seems more promising: the use of alternative biofuels, particularly from algae, to reduce carbon emissions. However, the success of these developments is uncertain for the mid-term, due to issues such as high associated water and/or land use, economics, and the potential for higher lifecycle GHG emissions than kerosene (Dray et al., 2012; Peeters et al., 2016). Improved operations, infrastructure, and economic measures (e.g. carbon offsets and global emissions trading) are a less important, but still serve a necessary contributing role in the industry mitigation schemes mentioned above. Yet, several studies have concluded that no combination of technological, operational and market-based measures would be sufficient to meet carbon-neutral growth or stronger reduction targets (e.g. Lee et al., 2013; Mayor & Tol, 2010). We reason that technological and operational improvements alone will not achieve low carbon aeromobility.

Price mechanisms

Direct carbon charge

Between 1990 and 2006, European carbon emissions from aviation increased by 87% (European Union, 2006). This was mainly due to decreasing air fares, because of low cost carriers entering the market. According to normal economic rules, a price decrease leads to an increase in demand. Therefore, in order to stop the growth of air travel, a price increase could result in lower demand. A logical step would be to internalise the external costs of aviation. Griffin and Steele (1986) explain that external costs occur when private benefits or costs differs from society's benefits or costs. Carbon emissions from air transport lead to external costs because the damages associated with aviation are borne by society instead of reflected in ticket prices. To internalise these costs we first need to know the volume of the externalised costs. Future carbon prices are very likely to increase. The US-Environmental Protection Agency estimated prices for 2015 to range from €9 to € 83 (IWGSCC, 2015), while Moore and Diaz (2015) consider prices up to €167 in their study. Consequently, it is difficult to define a price. Korzhenevych et al. (2014) estimate the climate cost of 1 litre of kerosene at €0.26, which is based on IPCC emissions factors and a carbon price of €90 per ton. When we use this price to calculate the total climate related social costs of the airline industry emissions of 705 million tons in 2013 (ATAG, 2016), we come to €6.3 billion.

Taking the IATA growth scenario and the increasing carbon prices into account, this amount will increase greatly in the near future. The costs can, however, be reduced by increasing airfares significantly in order to reduce or even reverse growth of the number of miles flown. In 2015, the International Council of Clean Transportation (ICTT) calculated fuel efficiency for the transatlantic sector and found that airlines on average carried 32 passenger-kilometres per litre of kerosene (Kwan & Rutherford, 2015), resulting in 900-1000 kg of carbon per person. As a consequence, a transatlantic ticket price increase of €90 to €100 would be necessary to include all external costs; the amount would probably have to be much higher if a radical reduction of the total kilometres flown is the goal. This price increase should be introduced globally by ICAO to avoid problems with a level playing field. As a result, the global aviation industry would be smaller in the future than it is currently.

Peeters and Dubois (2010) show that the 2005 share of air transport of 17% of all trips, should decline to between 2% and 7% in 2050, which means an air transport volume comparable to the 1970s and 2000s. The additional cost would be paid through a carbon tax and this could either be used to mitigate emissions in aviation, transport or elsewhere, but also to compensate for damages caused by climate change in the poorest countries of the world.

Taxes

In theory, consumer taxes are imposed to collect money to finance public utilities and to influence consumer behaviour. Corporate taxes are imposed to pay for any damage caused by the production of the product and that are not included in the price of the product. In practice, this process fails for the greater part of international air travel. The reason is that, currently, international travel is not taxed. There is no value added tax (VAT) imposed on kerosene nor on international tickets, as opposed to diesel and gasoline, which are subject to VAT and excise duties. Some states do, however, charge VAT on domestic air travel.

In most tax regimes, essential goods and exports are exempted from VAT. The exemption for air travel and kerosene is a result from the Chicago Convention dating to 1944, with the goal of stimulating the airline industry. To achieve a low carbon mobility future it is logical to introduce such taxes.

Price mechanism effects

In theory, increasing the prices of international air travel leads to lower demand for air travel and reduced carbon emissions. However, it is difficult to calculate the extent to which this will happen. Many variables including gross domestic product (GDP), disposable income and price elasticities will affect the outcome. According to Wit et al. (2002), the effect of charging €50 per ton CO_2, would lead to a decrease of 4.9% in travel demand. This decrease is not sufficient to realise a low carbon mobility future. Olsthoorn (2001) reported greater effects, using a price of €1,500 per ton CO_2, resulting in a reduction of air travel demand of 90%. This may be an environmentally desired effect, but questions remain on the social equity and economic impacts. To achieve real effects, it might be necessary to combine increased prices for carbon and introducing kerosene VAT taxes with a personal climate budget. WBGU (2009) estimated that an annual budget of 2,300 kg per person would prevent global temperatures to rise with more 2°C. More about these possibilities are discussed in the final section of this chapter.

Behavioural mechanisms

According to the Air Transport Action Group (ATAG), 80% of aviation carbon emissions result from flights of over 1,500 kilometres, for which there is often little alternative in terms of mode of transport (ATAG, 2016). This, along with industry-favoured technocratic measures, means the only way to achieve absolute emission reduction is to effect a change in travel behaviour (see also Lee *et al.*, 2013; Scott *et al.*, 2010). Peeters and Dubois (2010) show that in order to achieve substantial tourism emission reductions in 2050 compared to 2005 figures, a reduction in travel distances and a shift from long-haul to short-haul travel is required.

From long haul to short haul

Over the last few decades, demand for long haul travel has increased at a faster rate than demand for short haul travel. Between 1999 and 2008, global international scheduled air transport (RPK) increased by 4.7%, while, generally less distant, global scheduled domestic air transport increased only 0.4% in the same period (IATA, 2009). One of the main causes is the vast increase of travel by airlines registered in the Middle East (12.9% growth in 2008) and Latin America (8%) (IATA, 2009). Moreover, increasing disposable income levels lead to increasing demand for tourism products. It is very unlikely that this behaviour will change without governmental measures (Cohen *et al.*, 2014). If price mechanisms alone do not work, one could try to limit the numbers of tourists. The Kingdom Of Bhutan has successfully limited the number of tourists. This has led to a relatively low number of arrivals, but a high margin sustainable business model with few negative social and environmental impacts (Holden, 2009). Large scale global introduction of this model is one way to reduce carbon emissions.

De-marketing, a measure for demotivating consumers (Kotler & Levy, 1971), is another effective option. De-marketing has been deployed in various tourism contexts (Beeton & Benfield, 2002; Hall, 2014). By promoting regional tourism rather than the number of long haul arrivals, tourist flows could shift from long haul to short haul. Such a strategy would require a per carbon footprint assessment as for instance done for the Netherlands (Pels *et al.*, 2014b). Using personal carbon budgets or other measures, governments could restrict air transport. Such a measure is often viewed as unethical, as it would in turn restrict tourism's development potential for developing countries.

Out of the plane and onto the train

As people become more affluent, they will travel further and faster (Schäfer *et al.*, 2009). Therefore, limiting the numbers of long haul holidays, as suggested previously, should be combined with measures that stimulate short to medium haul transport by low carbon modes. Gössling (2015) showed that a majority of Germans who were planning a trip to New Zealand would take a train to Spain if the New Zealand trip was not available. Substitution on both destination and transport resulted in a decrease of emissions from 4,050 kg for a flight to New Zealand to only 300 kg for a train trip to Spain. These are necessary changes that are needed to establish low carbon tourism (Peeters *et al.*, 2009). In an example for Dutch outbound holidays, those taken by train have 41% lower carbon emissions than the average carbon footprint of Dutch holidays per day, whereas intercontinental long haul holidays emit 187% more than average (Pels *et al.*, 2014a).

To see is to do

Eijgelaar *et al.* (2016) assume that visualising the carbon emissions of travel, at time of booking, will cause the environmentally friendly intentions of tourists to influence decision-making, to some extent. In doing so, it is key to refer to low carbon trips as higher quality products (Gössling & Buckley, 2016), to label high carbon trips as bad (Van Dam & De Jonge, 2015), and to trigger empathic reactions rather than causing guilt and denial in consumers (Araña & León, 2016). It is important that this mechanism is extensively tested, as current scientific evidence for this assumption is limited in tourism. If successful, it could be included in environmental policies posed by, for instance, the United Nations World Tourism Organisation (UNWTO).

Future tourism transport scenarios

In order to achieve a low carbon aeromobility transition, it is likely that a combination of the aforementioned measures will be required and have to be introduced on a global scale. As technological optimism and self-regulation of the industry should be approached with caution (Cohen *et al.*, 2016), we focus our consideration of low carbon aviation transition scenarios on price mechanisms combined with behavioural mechanisms enforced by policymakers. Here we present three overarching scenarios, discuss how innovative low aeromobility and low carbon solutions can be achieved and consider which key stakeholders should be taking the lead on implementation of such scenarios.

Name and shame

Most labels in tourism, as in other sectors, are used as proof of 'good' behaviour. The intention-behaviour gap (Antimova *et al.*, 2012) and recent work on eco labels (Van Dam & De Jonge, 2015) and carbon labels (Eijgelaar *et al.*, 2016) suggest that this approach is not effective. It is likely to be more effective when 'bad' behaviour is labelled accordingly (Eijgelaar *et al.*, 2016; Van Dam & De Jonge, 2015). In general, voluntary positive certification has been shown to only work if it coincides with mandatory negative labelling (Van Dam & De Jonge, 2015) on a large scale (Zotz, 2010). In the context of flying, this labelling could be based on the performance of airlines, with the disadvantage that such an approach makes differentiating between different distance classes impossible and just affects the choice of the airline, which can still significantly modify the carbon footprint for a specific trip. Another approach might be to label tour packages in a way that the true carbon footprint is identified.

The polluter pays

Aviation receives an unfair competitive advantage in terms of pricing, due to a lack of taxes and excise duties. Taxes of €1,500 per ton CO_2 or higher are likely to have an effect on consumer flying behaviour. Candidates for introducing such taxes are national governments, international political bodies (e.g. EU), or international sector organisations, like the UNWTO. In its Davos declaration, the UNWTO agreed that *'the tourism sector must rapidly respond to climate change [...] and progressively reduce its Greenhouse Gas (GHG) contribution'* (UNWTO-UNEP-WMO, 2007: 2), which is a strong argument to lobby for such taxes. Yet UNWTO's aims to make travel available to as many people as possible worldwide and support developing countries are incompatible with advocating for CO_2 taxes. In any case, the UNWTO will need to take a more credible stance, when issuing statements like those in Davos, and when aiming to contribute to Sustainable Development Goals, including tackling climate change (UNWTO, 2015). A more realistic option would be, as in our previous scenario, for the EU to take the initiative. The EU is already developing initiatives to reduce the climate change impacts of aviation, in cooperation with ICAO and in extending the EU Emissions Trading System (EU-ETS) to domestic aviation in the first instance. These aim to stabilise net CO_2 emissions from international aviation at 2020 levels. However, more should be done to achieve substantial reductions in CO_2 emissions to avoid disruptive climate change.

Slow is sexy

Our final scenario is grounded in the mechanisms behind construal-level theory (Trope & Liberman, 2010) and is based on the ideas presented by Van Dam and Fischer (2015). The study by Van Dam and Fischer (2015) finds that a sustainable identity leads to more sustainable purchases and could serve as an intrinsic motivator to behave more sustainably in a tourism context. We believe the Destination Marketing Association International (DMAI), which is the global trade association for destination marketing organisations (DMOs) could play a key role in this scenario. The DMAI should introduce carbon management and eco-efficiency with respect to climate change as an element of the normal strategy and marketing of DMOs. DMOs should try to both aim at low carbon tourism and include such sustainable identities in their marketing campaigns. This can be accomplished by adopting carbon footprint assessment of the main market-product combinations through tools like the Carmacal issued recently by the Dutch tour operator branch organisation ANVR (see http://www.cstt.nl/carmacal). Depending on the kind of destination and its geographical position, the DMO may apply carbon management by choosing the most efficient airlines, improving high carbon footprint accommodations, developing non-air and/or short haul markets, increasing the length of stay for a given number of nights and improving revenues per night (as proposed by Peeters *et al.*, 2009). Nevertheless, many DMOs seem to be biased towards international markets (e.g. NBTC, 2009).

Conclusion

In this chapter we identified the need for behavioural change coupled with techno-logical efficiencies and policy measures, to make tourist travel more environmen-tally sustainable and contribute to a systemic low carbon mobility transition.

To understand the impact of demand, we need to understand the choice behav-iour of tourists with respect to the impact of their travels on climate change. The main finding here is that the gap between attitude – *'climate change is important'* – and behaviour – *'but I am not going to change my travel plans because of greenhouse gas emissions'* – rules out that consumers will voluntarily change their travel behaviour at the scale required for dramatic emissions reductions.

It seems that the continuous strong reduction of the real cost of flying combined with the strong increase of travel speed of air transport has played a major role in its fast and continued growth. Therefore, we explored the opportunities and effects of a carbon levy, taxes, and price mechanisms as well as labelling and slow travel and found very large price incentives will be needed to achieve the changes necessary.

There are three dominant behavioural paths: from 'long to short haul' from 'plane to train' and 'to see is to do'. The change from long to short (or medium) haul seems mainly a responsibility for the supply side (destinations, but also inbound and outbound tour operators). Changing from plane to train has a very large carbon reduction potential per trip as it shifts both from high carbon intensity travel to low carbon intensity and from long to short distances. Not only tour operators and destinations, but also rail companies and national governments should play a major role in this shift. 'To see is to do' comprises carbon footprint communicated to potential travellers at the moment of choosing destinations and transport modes. Several eco-labels exist in tourism, which all are positive labels, only applied to products that have a superior (low) carbon footprint compared to the ordinary travel product. However, recent research shows that negative labels, shaming and blaming, may be more effective.

A tourism sector further increasing its dependence on kerosene and thus a high carbon footprint, will face a grave future. New challenges and opportunities will inevitably arise, and will need to be, and can be, confronted and addressed, in the new world of low carbon tourism. This future may be difficult for parts of the tourism sector, including the air transport industry, but there will certainly be opportunities for other transport providers, which may include the railway industry.

References

Antimova, R., Nawijn, J. & Peeters, P. (2012). The Awareness/attitude-gap in Sustainable Tourism: A Theoretical Perspective. *Tourism Review*, **67**(3), 7-16.

Araña, J. E. & León, C. J. (2016). Are tourists animal spirits? Evidence from a field experiment exploring the use of non-market based interventions advocating sustainable tourism. *Journal of Sustainable Tourism*, **24**(3), 430-445.

ATAG. (2015). *Climate Action Takes Flight: The aviation sector's climate action framework*. Geneva, Switzerland: Air Transport Action Group.

ATAG. (2016). Facts and Figures. Retrieved 18-03-2016, from http://www.atag.org/facts-and-figures.html

Babiker, M. H., Metcalf, G. E. & Reilly, J. (2003). Tax distortions and global climate policy. *Journal of Environmental Economics and Management*, **46**(2), 269-287.

Beeton, S. & Benfield, R. (2002). Demand control: The case for demarketing as a visitor and environmental management tool. *Journal of Sustainable Tourism*, **10**(6), 497-513.

Boeing. (2015). *Current Market Outlook 2015 -2034*. Seattle, USA: Boeing.

Cames, M., Graichen, J., Siemons, A. & Cook, V. (2015). *Emission Reduction Targets for International Aviation and Shipping*. Brussels, Belgium: European Parliament, DG Internal Policies, Policy Department A: Economic and Scientific Policy.

Cohen, S. A., Higham, J., Gössling, S., Peeters, P. & Eijgelaar, E. (2016). Finding effective pathways to sustainable mobility: bridging the science–policy gap. *Journal of Sustainable Tourism*, **24**(3), 317-334.

Cohen, S. A., Higham, J. E. S. & Cavaliere, C. T. (2011). Binge flying: Behavioural addiction and climate change. *Annals of Tourism Research*, **38**(3), 1070-1089.

Cohen, S. A., Higham, J. E. S., Peeters, P. & Gössling, S. (2014). Why tourism mobility behaviours must change. In S. A. Cohen, J. E. S. Higham, P. Peeters & S. Gössling (Eds.), *Understanding and Governing Sustainable Tourism Mobility: Psychological and behavioural approaches* (pp. 1-12). Abingdon, UK: Routledge.

Creutzig, F., Jochem, P., Edelenbosch, O. Y., Mattauch, L., Vuuren, D. P. v., McCollum, D. & Minx, J., (2015). Transport: A roadblock to climate change mitigation? *Science*, **350**(6263), 911-912.

Dray, L. M., Schäfer, A. & Ben-Akiva, M. E. (2012). Technology limits for reducing EU transport sector CO_2 Emissions. *Environmental Science & Technology*, **46**(9), 4734-4741.

Eijgelaar, E., Nawijn, J., Barten, C., Okuhn, L. & Dijkstra, L. (2016). Consumer preferences on holiday carbon footprint information. *Journal of Sustainable Tourism*, **24**(3), 398-411.

European Union. (2006). Climate change: Commission proposes bringing air transport into EU Emissions Trading Scheme. Retrieved 4-3-2016 from http://europa.eu/rapid/press-release_IP-06-1862_en.htm.

Festinger, L. (1957). *A Theory of Cognitive Dissonance*. Evanston, Ill: Row Peterson.

Goossens, C. (2000). Tourism information and pleasure motivation. *Annals of Tourism Research*, **27**(2), 301-321.

Gössling, S. (2015). Low carbon and post-carbon travel and destinations. In C. M. Hall, S. Gössling & D. Scott (Eds.), *The Routledge Handbook of Tourism and Sustainability* (pp. 472-481). Milton Park, Abingdon: Routledge.

Gössling, S. & Buckley, R. (2016). Carbon labels in tourism: persuasive communication? *Journal of Cleaner Production,* **111**(Part B), 358-369.

Gössling, S., Peeters, P. M., Ceron, J. P., Dubois, G., Patterson, T. & Richardson, R. B. (2005). The eco-efficiency of tourism. *Ecological Economics,* **54**(4), 417– 434.

Griffin, J. M. & Steele, H. B. (1986). *Energy Economics and Policy.* Orlando, USA: Academic Press College Divison.

Hall, C. M. (2014). *Tourism and Social Marketing.* Abingdon, UK: Routledge.

Hares, A., Dickinson, J. & Wilkes, K. (2010). Climate change and the air travel decisions of UK tourists. *Journal of Transport Geography,* **18**(3), 466-473.

Holden, A. (2009). The environment-tourism nexus: Influence of Market Ethics. *Annals of Tourism Research,* **36**(3), 373-389.

Høyer, K. G. (2000). Sustainable tourism or sustainable mobility? The Norwegian case. *Journal of Sustainable Tourism,* **8**(2), 147-160.

IATA. (2009). *World Air Transport Statistics* (53rd ed.). Montreal-Geneva-London: International Air transport Association.

IATA. (2013). *IATA 2013 Technology Roadmap.* Geneva, Switzerland: IATA.

ICAO. (2015). *Air Transport in Figures.* Montreal, Canada: ICAO.

IPCC. (2014a). *Climate Change 2014: Mitigation of Climate Change. Contribution of Working Group III to the Fifth Assessment Report of the Intergovernmental Panel on Climate Change* [Edenhofer, O., R. Pichs-Madruga, Y. Sokona, E. Farahani, S. Kadner, K. Seyboth, A. Adler, I. Baum, S. Brunner, P. Eickemeier, B. Kriemann, J. Savolainen, S. Schlömer, C. von Stechow, T. Zwickel & J.C. Minx (eds.)]. Cambridge, UK and New York, NY, USA: Cambridge University Press.

IPCC. (2014b). *Climate Change 2014: Synthesis Report. Contribution of Working Groups I, II and III to the Fifth Assessment Report of the Intergovernmental Panel on Climate Change* [Core writing team, R.K. Pachauri & L.A. Meyer (eds.)]. Geneva, Switzerland: IPCC.

IWGSCC. (2015). *Technical Update of the Social Cost of Carbon for Regulatory Impact Analysis - Under Executive Order 12866.* Washington D.C: Interagency Working Group on Social Cost of Carbon, United States Government

Juvan, E. & Dolnicar, S. (2014). The attitude–behaviour gap in sustainable tourism. *Annals of Tourism Research,* **48**, 76-95.

Korzhenevych, A., Dehnen, N., Bröcker, J., Holtkamp, M., Henning, M., Gibson, G., Varma, A. & Cox, V., (2014). *Update of the handbook on external costs of transport.* Oxfordshire, UK: RICARDO-AEA.

Kotler, P. & Levy, S. J. (1971). Demarketing? Yes, demarketing! *Harvard Business Review,* **49**(6), 74-80.

Kwan, I. & Rutherford, D. (2015). *Transatlantic Airline Fuel Efficiency Ranking, 2014.* Washington DC, USA: The International Council on Clean Transportation.

Lee, D. S., Lim, L. L. & Owen, B. (2013). *Bridging The Aviation CO_2 Emissions Gap: Why emissions trading is needed.* Manchester, UK: Manchester Metropolitan University.

Lee, D. S., Pitari, G., Grewe, V., Gierens, K., Penner, J. E., Petzold, A., Prather, M. J., Schumann, U., Bais, A., Berntsen, T., Iachetti, D., Lim, L. L. & Sausen, R. (2010). Transport impacts on atmosphere and climate: Aviation. *Atmospheric Environment*, **44**(37), 4678-4734.

Mayor, K. & Tol, R. S. J. (2010). Scenarios of carbon dioxide emissions from aviation. *Global Environmental Change*, **20**(1), 65-73.

McKercher, B., Prideaux, B., Cheung, C. & Law, R. (2010). Achieving voluntary reductions in the carbon footprint of tourism and climate change. *Journal of Sustainable Tourism*, **18**(3), 297 - 317.

Moore, F. C. & Diaz, D. B. (2015). Temperature impacts on economic growth warrant stringent mitigation policy. *Nature Climate Change*, **5**, 127-131.

Mowery, D. C. & Rosenberg, N. (1981). Technical change in the commercial aircraft industry, 1925–1975. *Technological Forecasting and Social Change*, **20**(4), 347-358.

Nawijn, J. (2011). Determinants of daily happiness on vacation. *Journal of Travel Research*, **50**(5), 559-566.

NBTC. (2009). *Focus on the Incoming Tourist. Inbound Tourism research 2009*. Voorburg: NBTC Holland Marketing.

Olsthoorn, A. A. (2001). Carbon dioxide emissions from international aviation: 1950-2050. *Journal of Air Transport Management*, **7**, 87-93.

Peeters, P. (2013). Developing a long-term global tourism transport model using a behavioural approach: implications for sustainable tourism policy making. *Journal of Sustainable Tourism*, **21**(7), 1049-1069.

Peeters, P. & Dubois, G. (2010). Tourism travel under climate change mitigation constraints. *Journal of Transport Geography*, **18**(3), 447-457.

Peeters, P. & Eijgelaar, E. (2014). Tourism's climate mitigation dilemma: flying between rich and poor countries. *Tourism Management*, **40**, 15-26.

Peeters, P., Gössling, S. & Lane, B. (2009). Moving towards low carbon tourism. New opportunities for destinations and tour operators. In S. Gössling, C. M. Hall & D. B. Weaver (Eds.), *Sustainable Tourism Futures. Perspectives on Systems, Restructuring and Innovations* (Vol. 15, pp. 240-257). New York: Routledge.

Peeters, P., Higham, J., Kutzner, D., Cohen, S. & Gössling, S. (2016). Are technology myths stalling aviation climate policy? *Transportation Research Part D: Transport and Environment*, **44**, 30-42.

Pels, J., Eijgelaar, E., de Bruijn, K., Dirven, R. & Peeters, P. (2014a). *Travelling Large in 2013: The carbon footprint of Dutch holidaymakers in 2013 and the development since 2002*. Breda, Netherlands: NHTV Breda University of Applied Sciences.

Pels, J., Eijgelaar, E., Peeters, P., Landré, M., Nelemans, R. & Dirven, R. (2014b). *Travelling Large in 2009 'Inbound tourism'. The carbon footprint of inbound tourism to the Netherlands in 2009*. Breda: NHTV Center for Sustainable tourism & transport.

Ram, Y., Nawijn, J. & Peeters, P. (2013). Happiness and limits to sustainable tourism mobility: A new conceptual model. *Journal of Sustainable Tourism*, **21**(7), 1017-1035.

Schäfer, A., Heywood, J. B., Jacoby, H. D. & Waitz, I. A. (2009). *Transportation in a Climate-Constrained World*. Cambridge, MA, USA: MIT Press.

Scott, D., Peeters, P. & Gössling, S. (2010). Can tourism deliver its 'aspirational' greenhouse gas emission reduction targets? *Journal of Sustainable Tourism,* **18**(3), 393-408.

Stoknes, P. E. (2015). *What We Think About When We Try Not To Think About Global Warming: Toward a New Psychology of Climate Action:* Chelsea Green Publishing.

Trope, Y. & Liberman, N. (2010). Construal-level theory of psychological distance. *Psychological Review,* **117**(2), 440-463.

Tung, V. W. S. & Ritchie, J. R. B. (2011). Exploring the essence of memorable tourism experiences. *Annals of Tourism Research,* **38**(4), 1367-1386.

U.S. Census Bureau. (2010). Transportation indicators for motor vehicles and airlines: 1900 to 2001. *The 2010 Statistical Abstract: Historical Statistics* Retrieved 11-08-2010, 2010, from http://www.census.gov/statab/hist/HS-41.pdf

UNFCCC. (2015). *Adoption of the Paris Agreement. Proposal by the president.* Geneva, Switzerland: UNFCCC.

UNWTO. (2011). *Tourism Towards 2030 / Global Overview - Advance edition presented at UNWTO 19th General Assembly.* Madrid, Spain: UNWTO.

UNWTO. (2015). *Tourism and the Sustainable Development Goals.* Madrid, Spain: UNWTO.

UNWTO. (2016). *Tourism 2020 Vision.* Retrieved 02 March, 2016, from http://www. unwto.org/facts/eng/vision.htm

UNWTO-UNEP-WMO. (2007). *Davos Declaration. Climate Change and Tourism Responding to Global Challenges.* Davos, Switzerland: UNWTO/UNEP/WMO.

UNWTO-UNEP-WMO. (2008). *Climate Change and Tourism: Responding to Global Challenges.* Madrid, Spain: UNWTO-UNEP.

Van Dam, Y. K. & De Jonge, J. (2015). The positive side of negative labelling. *Journal of Consumer Policy,* **38**(1), 19-38.

Van Dam, Y. K. & Fischer, A. R. H. (2015). Buying green without being seen. *Environment and Behaviour,* **47**(3), 328-356.

WBGU. (2009). *Solving the Climate Dilemma: The budget approach.* Berlin, Germany: German Advisory Council on Global Change.

Wit, R. C. N., Dings, J. M. W., Mendes de Leon, P., Thwaites, L., Peeters, P., Greenwood, D. & Doganis, R. (2002). *Economic Incentives To Mitigate Greenhouse Gas Emissions From Air Transport in Europe.* Delft, Netherlands: CE.

Young, M., Higham, J. & Reis, A. C. (2014). 'Up in the Air': A conceptual critique of flying addiction. *Annals of Tourism Research,* **49**, 51-64.

Zotz, A. (2010). *Compulsory Carbon Footprint Labelling for Tourism and Travel Services?* Vienna, Austria: respect – Institute for Integrative Tourism and Development.

Case Study 5: Low carbon mobility transitions in China

David Tyfield

Centre for Mobilities Research, Lancaster University, UK.

Dennis Zuev

Centre for Mobilities Research, Lancaster University, UK and CIES-ISCTE, Portugal.

Introduction

China represents a test-case of global significance regarding the challenges of urban mobility transition. On the one hand, China is globally central to 'greening' mobility as the world's largest car market (Tyfield, 2014), and with significant further growth predicted (ibid.). On the other hand, the growth of a (fossil-fuelled) urban mobility system has been a central feature of the immense changes that have occurred since 1978 in China. Yet in both respects the need for an urban mobility transition is increasingly urgent, as manifest in issues of emissions and air pollution, urban gridlock and its social costs, and intensifying unrest around urban mobility issues. China, however, is also the site of significant government and corporate innovation efforts focused on opportunities for 'catch-up' in a key industry of the 21st century around the electric vehicle (EV) (Howell *et al.*, 2014). At the same time, the much lower-technology electric two-wheeler (E2W) has emerged as a global market entirely dominated by small Chinese firms and their Chinese customers (Tyfield *et al.*, 2015).

Despite the disappointment to date regarding EVs (low sales and low adoption for private use), the evidence shows a highly dynamic and geographically diverse situation in China. In particular, we highlight how the prospects regarding e-mobility system transition hinge on the uncertain assemblage of a diverse set of niches around China and the capacity of the EV and E2W to move down- and up-market respectively. This involves e-mobility becoming credibly associated in the public's imagination and experience with a new consumer-attractive, middle class urban-status and modern mobility system, including integration with the latest and most consumer-attractive digital and app economy. Prospects of mobility transition in China thus hinge primarily on issues beyond the current policy-dominating focus of high-technology EVs, such as the generational shifts towards prioritizing quality of life issues, together with associated openings for non-automotive sectors, notably in China's internet and telecom giants. In this case study, we offer an introduction to the multiple dimensions of low carbon mobility transitions currently happening in the key global case study of China, focusing on four cases: electric vehicles (EVs), low-speed EVs, electric two wheelers (E2Ws) and vehicle sharing.

Politics of low carbon mobility transition in China

China is the largest absolute GHG emission producer in the world, since 2007 (Tyfield *et al.*, 2014), and with rapidly increasing car ownership – growing approximately 20-fold from 200 people/vehicle in 1990 to 12 in 2012 – and plans for further urbanisation, it is already facing serious environmental problems caused (in part) by city traffic. By 2014, eight big Chinese cities had implemented restrictions on the purchase and travel of vehicles[1], and many other cities are following this example.

Figure 1: Map of China. Major cities highlighted in bold, provinces in bold italics.

Various measures to reduce car ownership and the use of private vehicles (e.g. licence plate lotteries, auctions and day-of-the-week restrictions), however, have neither improved air quality nor solved congestion problems in major cities. At the same time, private car ownership is in a phase characteristic of many post-socialist countries (Burrell & Hoerschelmann, 2014), where for a long period private car ownership was not possible. The automobile has become an important goal for consumers but now is slowly shifting from a status symbol to a family investment. This urge for a (large, foreign) car as a material and symbolic possession that has long been unattainable, remains very significant in China, complicating large-scale purchase of 'green' vehicles in the foreseeable future.

---

1 Beijing, Shanghai, Guangzhou, Tianjin, Guiyang, Shijiazhuang, Hangzhou, Shenzhen (December 2014)

At the same time, car-based urban transportation is deeply rooted in the interests of the configurations of fossil fuel-based economic, political, cultural and military power of 'carbon capital' (Urry, 2013). In China, this takes the form of powerful state-owned enterprises (SOEs), including in the automobile industry, which is considered a national 'pillar industry'. The government thus faces the dilemma of increasing production outputs and keeping consumption levels high, while at the same time, managing the social and environmental challenges of urban pollution and urban gridlock.

The solution chosen by policy, that will supposedly satisfy both of these goals, is wide adoption of electric vehicles, for public and private use. The Chinese case of EV promotion can be characterised by a strong degree of government involvement and financial support, but enduring low degree of EV sales, especially in the private sector. The national government has introduced several mechanisms to support adoption of electric vehicles: significant financial subsidies for private purchase and replacement of ICE vehicles to EVs (Liu, 2015); free license plates (in some cities, also for PHEVs); inclusion of EVs in public transport (notably in Shenzhen (Li *et al.*, 2015); and some EV-car-sharing schemes. These policies aim to capitalise on the opportunity for EV transition to allow China to 'overtake around the corner' in the (auto) mobility sector, as potentially a new niche for indigenous innovation. Various cities (such as Shenzhen) have also actively promoted transition from ICE vehicles to EVs, for instance, in the taxi fleet and government-used passenger cars by providing subsidies for replacement (ibid.). A total of approximately RMB30 billion (US$4.56 billion) was claimed as subsidies in 2015.

These subsidies pushed China's EV car market to grow prodigiously to over 330,000 vehicles; the world's largest EV market (Lu, 2016). Yet this remains only 2% at most of total car sales (let alone actual vehicles on the road) and is still significantly behind government targets. Pure electric vehicles are still not widely accepted due to a number of issues including: safety concerns regarding batteries; inadequate charging infrastructure and associated range anxiety; and consumer appeal. Moreover, these sales figures have been brought into serious question, since widespread subsidy fraud, selling 'ghost' vehicles, has emerged (Lu, 2016). Furthermore, notwithstanding all these subsidies, the most visible EV on China's roads (if not necessarily in the sales figures) remains an elite and foreign vehicle, the Tesla – a car that is out-of-reach for all but a tiny fraction of Chinese consumers (Want China Times 2014). The success of an EV transition thus seems to depend to a great extent on shifting EV demand down market to the emerging middle class(es).

As such, though, a low carbon mobility transition in China may be of even greater societal and political importance and difficulty than is recognised by the high-tech focused policy orthodoxy. Moreover, the current landscape of low carbon mobility transition in China is complex and is comprised of multiple geographical strongholds where particular forms of low carbon mobility innovation dominate. For instance, Shenzhen, in the Pearl River Delta, is a city where an EV taxi fleet has been actively promoted by the local government as a part of the high-tech city self-presentation. Shenzhen is the home of the most successful national EV maker, BYD, and a whole range of battery manufacturing companies, but also now global ICT brands, such as Huawei, Tencent and ZTE. At the same time, Hangzhou in Zhejiang province, renowned for its bottom-up entrepreneurialism, is a stronghold for vehicle sharing, having the largest bike-sharing scheme in the world and several successful car-sharing ventures. The less prosperous province of Shandong, meanwhile, is characterised by the production and use of low-speed (*disu*) electric vehicles (LSEVs) with its major brand being Shifeng (Wang & Kimble, 2013). Finally, Shanghai, as the world's largest city by population and the home of arguably China's strongest 'carbon capital' SOEs, is also visibly a city where two-wheelers occupy a very prominent position, as city centre congestion makes electric scooters and bicycles the most efficient mode of transportation.

The question of future e-mobility in China thus involves how negotiation, competition and combination across these niches takes place. We consider three examples of this, in brief.

Low-speed EVs (micro EVs)

LSEVs are small vehicles in diverse forms that are limited to around 80 km/h and are relatively inexpensive. If we take into account the number of LSEVs produced, sold and owned, China has already become the largest EV country in the world: 400,000 LSEVs were sold in 2014, and the sales are projected to reach 3 million by 2020 (Perkowski, 2015). As such, LSEVs are already a visible part of e-mobility transition in a few northern and less wealthy provinces, such as Shandong, and neighbouring inland provinces Henan and Hebei. Yet the problem for this growing industry is that LSEVs have not been officially approved by government, leaving them in a regulatory and political grey zone that unsettles their progress. However, decreasing GDP figures recently have prompted the Chinese government to seek for new niches of increasing industrial output.

In this context, it is significant that while conventional EVs and even plug-in hybrid sales targets have had to be lowered, LSEV sales figures are likely to rise (Perkowski, 2015). It is possible, therefore, that the political and regulatory positions of LSEVs will be clarified soon, which could, in turn, stimulate their growth further. This is certainly the hope and expectation amongst LSEV manufacturers, who are currently just waiting for such clarification to emerge. Indeed, it is significant that the 2015 national *New Energy Vehicle Yearbook* (2015) in China contains an article on LSEVs for the first time in three years, since this is indicative of growing governmental interest in this sector. Finally, it must be noted that the term of 'low speed' EV is increasingly rejected not only by the industry itself but also by consumers and observers, since increasing technological sophistication of some of these vehicles means that they can reach top speeds of up to 80 km/h. This remains slower than a conventional car, and is significant in that it excludes the vehicles from highways. But increasingly (re-) branded as 'micro' EVs rather than 'slow-speed', these vehicles may well become ever-more attractive to middle-class urban Chinese buyers, especially as second vehicles for short journeys.

Vehicle sharing: bikes and cars

Meanwhile, for high-tech conventional electric vehicles, car-sharing has emerged as a promising mechanism of promotion (Jung 2014), possibly mitigating the enduringly high economic costs of batteries. Car-sharing is also seen as possibly an effective way to transform the mind-set of the Chinese consumers, particularly regarding strong associations of automobility with private car ownership, by instead introducing them to a novel and different experience of (auto)mobility as accessible service.

China has seen an immense growth of EV car-sharing operators in recent years, with schemes launched officially in four pilot cities in 2014 (Wu, 2015). However, their scale remains small due to a number of issues. Among the most critical is the lack of parking space (and landlord intransigence in this regard), which is crucial for installation of EV chargers. Hence even among large car-leasing operators, such as *eHi*, EVs are still only a small fraction of the fleet (10%). Nonetheless, all major cities now have several car-sharing initiatives (Jung, 2015). In some cases these schemes serve a particular district (e.g. Jiading in Shanghai), or they are used for other goals than providing actual mobility solutions, such as advertising or testing software and cars, e.g. Shanghai Auto's scheme called *Chexiang*. Hangzhou, however, is home to amongst the most prominent EV car-sharing scene (Jung, 2014). Here a local, private producer with significant support of the local government (Kandi) uses its EVs for operations with high demand amongst locals and the many tourists coming to the city for its famous West Lake.

China has also regained its former status as a cycling nation, currently being the leader in public bike-share schemes both in terms of vehicle numbers and service stations (Lohry & Yiu, 2015). China now has 64% of the world bike-sharing fleet (Larsen, 2013). These schemes are both much cheaper than those in Europe and utilise bicycle infrastructure that remains from when the bicycle was vehicle of choice. Both government-run bike-share schemes and public-private partnerships (PPP) exist though the former are proving more effective. This is perhaps because these government-run schemes are intended as a viable public transportation option under direct control of the local government bodies and not a profit-making business (Lohry & Yiu, 2015). Hangzhou again features in this regard. Its government-run scheme has flourished, growing from 2,800 bikes and 61 service points in 2008 to 70,800 and 3,131 service points in 2014 (Wu, 2015). Wuhan, meanwhile, briefly boasted the largest ever bike-sharing scheme, but this PPP initiative failed due to mismanagement of invested resources (Tyfield & Zuev, 2015). The growth of bicycle to regime-challenging status, however, is limited by the increasing speed, rhythm and sprawl of contemporary Chinese cities, creating demand for a cheap and more convenient vehicle than the bicycle. This could include the electric two-wheeler.

Electric two-wheelers

The situation with E2Ws in China and their role in a low carbon transition is still not clear (Ling *et al.*, 2016). E2Ws are currently the most visible element of a Chinese low carbon mobility transition, even in big cities. Manufacturing E2Ws is also a growing, although highly fragmented, domestic industrial sector – the largest e-bike industry in the world – with over 200 million on China's roads, though growth is forecast to slow down (Navigant Research, 2015). There have been few studies, limited to a few cities, on the role of E2Ws in mobility transition, yet some of these studies suggest that E2Ws are often used together with a car (Ben Dror, 2014) or can be a stepping stone to a car purchase (Fishman & Cherry, 2016) rather that its long-term replacement. Importantly, however, E2Ws have significantly changed the traffic landscape of the Chinese cities and have provided increased mobility for the lower income populations as well as rising middle classes (Cherry *et al.*, 2016). But in China a car is still seen as the second-most important family investment (after the house) and E2Ws are often associated with low *suzhi* (personal quality) population (i.e. associated with the status (display) of low income, uneducated, rural migrants or workers).

As one interviewee during fieldwork in Shekou district of Shenzhen noted: *'this area (Shekou) is of the people with low suzhi, low education, low level of culture, they don't understand what is 'huanbao'², and for them electric bike is the most convenient and cheapest way of getting around, going to work and sending kids to school'.* As such, the broader impact of the E2W depends to a great extent on its capacity to move up-market and challenge these social associations. In this respect, fragmentation and specialisation of the E2W market with emerging up-market brands of e-scooters like *Niu* – what one of the e-bike dealers in Shenzhen called a 'little Tesla' – may yet challenge this association of E2Ws with low-salaried delivery workers, transforming the profile of demand.

In the meantime, the E2W is proving highly resilient. Regulation of electric two-wheelers has undergone attempts to ban them in several cities, since they are seen as dangerous and unruly. Yet many of those bans have been lifted given the importance of E2W-based mobility for continued economic development; for example, given long-distance commutes to the newly built residential areas. E2Ws are also commonly used for short trips – to work and for delivering and picking up children from school – even by parents who have cars, as they offer more convenient mobility escaping congestion. E2Ws have also provided an essential tool for many services in big cities, being now the mainstay of delivery companies, including fast food (such as *Ele.me*, promoted by Chinese e-commerce giant Alibaba) and express deliveries.

---

2 环保 – huanbao, environmental protection

With the growth of the Internet and online consumption in China, the fleet of electric two wheelers used for this sort of deliveries is only likely to grow. In the context of costly parking provisions and aggravating congestion, it seems likely that E2Ws will remain a preferred mode of transportation in the city centres.

There are questions, however, regarding E2Ws' low carbon status and environmental impact. One of the main issues related to questioning the low carbon status of E2Ws (vs. EVs), however, is battery use and recycling, since currently most of the E2Ws use a lead-acid battery. Li-ion battery is becoming more popular and cheaper, however, and this also makes the E2W lighter, thereby opening up new (and higher status) markets as a complementary tool for the solution of the 'last mile' problem, especially for the daily commuters who use cars or subways. Other objections concerning the GHGs emitted from the electricity generation are also less significant for E2Ws than for EVs, being lighter vehicles. Yet from a transitions perspective it also represents a popular individual mobility option with demand that is unlikely to decrease, even if it changes in form, in the near future. Moreover, the E2W has substituted motorcycles in the case of most large urban centres and has therefore led to improvement of air quality and reduction of noise pollution (Wells & Lin, 2015).

As such, E2Ws, along with and in competition with LSEVs, are a potential niche for developing and strengthening Chinese low carbon innovation capacity. Their widespread use in China provides multiple companies with an excellent testing ground and revenue to develop their R&D departments and expansion into other world markets (Tyfield et al., 2015). Indeed, some of the Chinese E2W manufacturers already demonstrate their priority markets in Europe rather than China, evidencing a differentiation and strengthening of the sector.

Prospects and futures

In this case study we cannot possibly do justice to all the dimensions of low carbon mobility transition in China or the potential pathways for this transition. The Chinese government has realised that EV adoption is not a single fix to the transportation problem and the programmed targets of EV sales for the forthcoming years have been lowered. The Government is also committed to implement other low carbon transport policies and a strategy to encourage walking, cycling and public transport – including via building new, high-profile satellite car-free cities such as Chenggong, near Chengdu. The first ever national urbanisation plan, announced in 2014, also proclaimed the need for human-oriented cities, where walking and cycling may occupy a significant share of transportation (Chan, 2014).

How all these trends interact and come together remains uncertain. But with continuing fast urbanisation and large growth in transport demand in second and third tier cities there is growing demand for affordable and individualised mobility. The combination of new vehicle forms, car-sharing initiatives and electrification presents China as a potential global leader in urban e-mobility, despite the challenges and disappointments to date regarding the conventional electric car and, indeed, perhaps in large part *because* of the intensity of contemporary challenges of the environment and congestion.

References

Ben Dror, M. (2014). E-bikes bring individual and sustainable transport to China. *TheCityFix*. February 27. Available at: http://thecityfix.com/blog/e-bikes-bring-individual-sustainable-transport-china-maya-ben-dror/. Accessed 24 Jan. 2016.

Burrell, K. & Hoerschelmann, K. (eds.) (2014). *Mobilities in Socialist and Post-Socialist States. Societies on the Move*. Palgrave McMillan: London.

Chan, K.W. (2014). China's urbanization 2020: a new blueprint and direction. *Eurasian Geography and Economics*, **55**(1), 1-9.

Cherry, C., Yang, H., Jones, L. R. & He, M. (2016). Dynamics of electric bike ownership and use in Kunming, China. *Transport Policy*, **45**, 127-135.

Fang, H. & Zhu, Y. (2015). *Development trend survey of low-speed EV. in Blue Book of New Energy vehicle. Annual report on NEV industry in China*. 239-256. Social Sciences Academic Press. 低速电动汽车行业发展形势 调查。中国新能源汽车产业发展报告。

Fishman E. & Cherry, C. (2016). E-bikes in the mainstream: reviewing a decade of research. *Transport Reviews*, **36**(1), 72-91.

Howell, S., Lee, H. & Heal, A. (2014). Leapfrogging or stalling out? Electric vehicles in China. *Faculty Research Working Papers*. RWP-14-035. Harvard Kennedy School.

Jung, A. (2014). *Carsharing in China – A Contribution to Sustainable Urban Transport?* GIZ: Bonn.

Jung, A. (2015). Fewer cars, more mobility Can carsharing work in China? *International Transportation*, **67**(1), 26-29.

Larsen, J. (2013). Bike-sharing programs hit the streets in over 500 cities worldwide. Available at: http://www.earth-policy.org/plan_b_updates/2013/update112. Accessed 24 Jan. 2016.

Li, C., Zhan, C., DeJong, M. & Lukszo, Z. (2015). Business innovation and government regulation for the promotion of electric vehicle use: lessons from Shenzhen, China. *Journal of Cleaner Production*.

Ling, Z., Cherry C., Yang, H. & Jones, L. R. (2015). From e-bike to car: a study on factors influencing motorization of e-bike users in China. *Transportation Research. Part D. Transport and Environment*, **41**, 50-63

Liu, J. (2015). Electric Scooters in China: an alternative pathway to transport electrification. Available at: http://ees-magazine.com/electric-scooters-in-china-an-alternative-pathway-to-transport-electrification. Accessed 24 Jan. 2016.

Lohry, G. F. & Yiu, A. (2015). Bikeshare in China as a public service: Comparing government-run and public-private partnership operation models. *Natural Resources Forum*, **39**(1), 41–52.

Lu, A. (2016). Green jaded: Plug-in auto industry suffers a black eye. *Shanghai Daily*. January 27. Available at: http://www.shanghaidaily.com/business/auto/Green-jaded-plugin-auto-industry-suffers-a-black-eye/shdaily.shtml.

Navigant Research (2015). Electric motorcycles and scooters. Market drivers and barriers, technology issues, key industry players, and global demand forecasts. Available at: www.navigantresearch.com/research/electric-motorcycles -and-scooters.

Perkowski, J. (2015). China's other electric vehicle industry. *Forbes*. April 8. http://www. forbes.com/sites/jackperkowski/2015/04/08/chinas-other-electric-vehicle-industry/ #240d00c42f9b.

Tyfield, D. (2014). Putting the power in 'socio-technical regimes': E-mobility transition in China as political process, *Mobilities* 9(4), 585–603.

Tyfield, D., Zuev, D., Li., P & Urry, J. (2015). Low carbon innovation in Chinese urban mobility: Prospects, politics and practices. *STEPS Working Paper* 71, Brighton: STEPS Centre. 2014.

Tyfield, D. & Zuev, D. (2015). Bringing vehicle sharing to China. 9 October. Available at: http://steps-centre.org/2015/blog/bringing-vehicle-sharing-to-china/.

Urry, J. (2013). *Societies Beyond Oil*. Zed Books: London.

Wang, H. & Kimble, C. (2013). Innovation and leapfrogging in the Chinese automobile industry: Examples from Geely, BYD, and Shifeng. *Global Business and Organisational Excellence*. September-October.

Want China Times (2014.) The who's who of new Tesla owners in Shanghai, 26 April, Available at: www.wantchinatimes.com/news-subclass-cnt.aspx?id=20140426000003 &cid=1206. Accessed 15 Jan. 2016.

Wells, P. & Lin, X. (2015). Spontaneous emergence versus technology management in sustainable mobility transitions: Electric bicycles in China. *Transportation Research Part A: Policy and Practice*, **78**, 371–383.

Wu, X., Yang, X. & Shi, H. (2015). Innovative practice of EV-carsharing in China for urban E-mobility. Presentation at EVS28, Kintex, Korea, May 3-6. Available at: http://www.a3ps.at/site/sites/default/files/downloads/evs28/papers/C1-01.pdf.

Case Study 6: Achieving a low carbon transition in Japan: The role of motor vehicle lifetime

Shigemi Kagawa, Daisuke Nishijima and Yuya Nakamoto

Faculty of Economics, Kyushu University, Japan.

Introduction

In order to achieve climate change mitigation goals, reducing greenhouse gas (GHG) emissions from Japan's household sector is critical. These emissions, arising from household heating and cooling, and transport, increased by 60% from 1990 to 2012 (Ministry of the Environment, 2014). In light of this sharp increase in GHG emissions, attention has turned to the production and consumption of durable goods (e.g. passenger vehicles, air conditioners, and refrigerators) that consume large amounts of energy. Accomplishing a transition to low carbon and energy efficient consumer goods is particularly valuable as a policy tool for reducing emissions in the residential sector. In this case study, we present an analysis of the lifetime of personal vehicles in Japan, and consider the optimal scenario in terms of retention and disposal, specifically as it relates to GHG emissions.

As a policy measure to reduce the carbon dioxide (CO_2) emissions originating from the transport sector, the Japanese government introduced a vehicle replacement scheme (April 10, 2009 to September 30, 2010) which provided a subsidy of ¥250,000 (approximately 2,300 US$) to vehicle owners, to incentivise the replacement of older vehicles with more fuel-efficient new vehicles (e.g., hybrid passenger cars with high energy efficiency more than 35km per litre). As a result of this policy, ownership of hybrid passenger vehicles increased by 233% in the four years between 2010 and 2014, reaching 4.7 million hybrid vehicles (Next Generation Vehicle Promotion Centre, 2016). The scheme aimed to curb driving-related CO_2 emissions by increasing the fuel-efficiency of motor vehicles. However, the market expansion of fuel-efficient vehicles could contribute to increased environmental impacts through CO_2 emissions occurring in production and pre-consumer phases.

As the lifetime of passenger vehicles increases (i.e. the average vehicle age rises), the number of newly registered vehicles generally decreases (Kagawa *et al.*, 2011), resulting in fewer new vehicle sales, which has an adverse economic impact (Kagawa *et al.*, 2009). On the other hand, a decrease in vehicle production and sales will reduce embedded energy and the associated GHG emissions of the industrial activities. However, fuel consumption for the residential sector is affected by a range of factors including changes in fuel economy and distance travelled (see Greening *et al.*, 2000), a higher number of older vehicles, which often have a relatively poorer fuel economy than newer vehicles, which can increase fuel consumption and GHG emissions for the residential sector (Kagawa *et al.*, 2011).

By retaining private vehicles for longer, consumers will not need to purchase new vehicles and are therefore likely to respond in one of two ways: (1) Save the money, or (2) spend the money on other goods and services. Any money spent will stimulate the production and consumption of other goods and services, which, depending on the specific goods or services, will indirectly increase secondary energy consumption (Kagawa *et al.*, 2008). The production and consumption of goods is of particular interest to this case study, since the consumption profile is of critical importance to a low carbon mobility transition and the ownership of private motor vehicles. Thus, changes in the lifetime of durable goods have interesting and important impacts on the environment, and a clear significance for Japan's transportation industry and its ability to achieve GHG emission reductions (Kagawa *et al.*, 2011).

The production and consumption of motor vehicles in Japan

The production of motor vehicles in Japan increased rapidly from 1950 to 1990, with peak annual production reaching approximately 10 million vehicles in the year 1990, due to Japan's so-called 'bubble economy' (Figure 1) (Japan Automobile Manufacturers Association [JAMA], 2016). After the Japanese asset price bubble burst in early 1992 (Horioka, 2006), Japanese car production declined sharply to 1995 before increasing again from 1996 to 2008 (JAMA, 2016). Figure 1 depicts the impact of the global financial crisis on Japanese car production, with a strong decline in 2009. A similar trend can also be seen in the net exports of new passenger cars from Japan (JAMA, 2016).

Figure 2 shows the evolution of passenger vehicle ownership in Japan between 1950 and 2014. During the period between 1975 and 2014, an average of 4 million new passenger cars per year entered the Japanese vehicle fleet, whereas an average of 3 million old cars per year left the vehicle fleet. The stock addition of new passenger cars reached 5 million vehicles in 1990 (Figure 2). Between 2011 and 2014, new vehicle sales increased, and consequently the total number of passenger vehicles has grown to 60.7 million (JAMA, 2016). If we divide this number by 52 million, the approximate number of Japanese households in 2014, the national average vehicle ownership rate is estimated to be 1.17 per household, an average of at least one car for each household. The vehicle ownership per 100 people in 2005 and 2014 were 44.7 and 47.7, respectively compared to other countries the national average vehicle ownership rate of Japan is similar to Belgium (46.9), Norway (44.1), and Netherlands (43.4) (OECD, 2009). Thus Japan's vehicle ownership per capita is relatively high and car ownership contributes to increasing CO_2 emissions through the life-cycle of passenger cars during pre-consumer and driving phases.

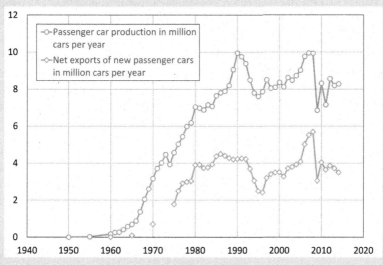

Figure 1: Evolution of productions (left axis) and net exports of new passenger cars (right axis) in Japan (1950-2014). Source: Author's diagram using data from Japan Automobile Manufacturers Association (2015).

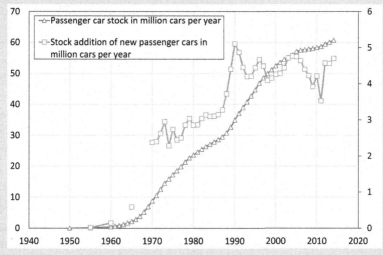

Figure 2: Evolution of passenger car ownership and stock addition of new passenger cars (right axis) in Japan (1950–2014). Source: Author's diagram using data from Japan Automobile Manufacturers Association (2015).

Methodology

Stock and flow of passenger vehicles

The lifetime of a specific durable goods, such as motor vehicles, is affected primarily by mechanical failure (e.g., McCool, 2012). The generalised gamma distribution is widely used for mechanical failure analysis in the field of reliability engineering (see e.g., Cohen *et al.*, 1988; McCool, 2012). In the spirit of reliability engineering, we start by assuming that the disposal of a passenger vehicle can be modelled as a generalised gamma distribution including three parameters, α, β and ρ (see, e.g., Cohen *et al.*, 1988; McCool, 2012). The cumulative disposal ratio of a specific passenger vehicle over time is obtainable from the specified generalised gamma distribution. As time (i.e., lifetime) approaches infinity, the cumulative disposal ratio approaches 1. In other words, when car lifetime is long, almost 100 per cent of passenger vehicles are discarded as end-of-life vehicles. The cumulative car survival ratio of a specific passenger vehicle is easily calculable as 1–cumulative disposal ratio.

Therefore the number of retained passenger vehicles (i.e., the current stock of passenger vehicles) over time can be estimated by multiplying the number of passenger vehicles registered as new in registration year by the cumulative survival ratio (e.g., Kagawa *et al.*, 2011). The lifetime distribution also gives the disposal ratio for passenger cars after some years have passed since registration year, so that the proportion of passenger cars registered as new in registration year that are disposed as end-of-life vehicles at specific year is obtainable. The number of end-of-life vehicles over time can be estimated by multiplying the number of new passenger cars in registration year by the disposal ratio.

Final demand for passenger vehicles

For the purposes of this study, we assume that the number of new vehicles that consumers purchase in a given year is equal to the total number of passenger vehicles disposed of in that year. Based on this assumption, we can determine the final demand for new vehicles by multiplying the sale of new vehicles by the producer's price of a vehicle. As in Kagawa *et al.* (2008), we assumed that the final demand for new vehicles has a proportional influence on commercial margins (e.g., automobile sales dealerships) and transportation margins (e.g., road transport services from automobile production plants to sales dealers).

Final demand for fuel consumed by passenger vehicles

By using the number of retained passenger vehicles, which is obtained from the lifetime distribution of passenger vehicles, it is possible to estimate the consumption of gasoline fuel needed for driving the vehicles. The yearly gasoline consumption of a specific passenger vehicle (litres) can be determined simply by dividing the total distance travelled by the vehicle in a year (km) by the fuel economy of the vehicle (km/L).

However, it is very difficult to calculate useful figures for individual passenger vehicles, and it would be virtually impossible to aggregate all such individual values to determine the total gasoline consumption for all passenger vehicles. As such, the total gasoline consumption for passenger vehicles is generally estimated by dividing the total distance travelled in a year, obtained by multiplying the total number of retained passenger vehicles, by an estimate of the average distance travelled per vehicle each year, and then dividing the obtained value by an estimate of the average fuel economy of vehicles (see Kudoh et al., 2004, for a detailed discussion of the methods of gasoline consumption estimation).

By multiplying the total number of vehicles sold by the average yearly distance travelled by number of new vehicles, we can calculate the distance travelled each year by vehicles (i.e., total distance of new vehicles). If this annual distance is divided by the average fuel economy, then we can obtain the gasoline consumption for vehicles sold in a given year. Also, if we divide the yearly distance travelled by the average fuel economy for vintage vehicles, we can calculate the gasoline consumption for vintage vehicles sold before a given year. Consequently, the total gasoline consumption (litres) for vehicles sold in or before a given year and retained until a given year can be obtained by summing up the physical gasoline consumptions (litres) of new and vintage vehicles.

The final demand for gasoline consumption can be obtained multiplying the physical gasoline consumption by the annual average gasoline price (yen per litre). As in the final demand of new passenger cars, this fuel demand affects commercial services (e.g., gasoline supply service at gasoline services stations) and transport services (e.g., transport services between gasoline refineries and gasoline service stations), and we estimated the commercial and transport margins for gasoline demand.

Life-cycle CO_2 emissions associated with final demand

We here use the top-down type life-cycle input-output analysis (see, e.g., Suh, 2009). The input-output analysis can be easily conducted based on a national input-output table made by many developed and developing countries (Tukker & Dietzenbacher, 2013). The national input-output table records the amount of intermediate inputs of commodity i required for production of commodity j, the amount of final demand of commodities sold to final consumers such as household, government, and so forth, value added such as labour income, and commodity outputs (Miller & Blair, 2009).

Dividing the required intermediate commodity input by commodity output yields the intermediate inputs of commodity i required for a unit of production of commodity j. The matrix $\mathbf{A}=(a_{ij})$ is called the 'technical coefficient matrix' in the input-output analysis (Miller & Blair, 2009). Importantly, it is well-known that the matrix

(I–A)$^{-1}$ represents the direct and indirect requirement matrix, the (i, j) elements of which represent the direct and indirect inputs for commodity i required to produce a unit of commodity j (Miller & Blair, 2009). Here **I** is the identity matrix.

Multiplying the direct and indirect requirement matrix by the final demand of new passenger cars and gasoline yields commodity productions associated with those final demand. Furthermore, if we multiply the calculated commodity productions by CO_2 intensities showing the direct CO_2 emissions per unit of commodity output, we can estimate the life-cycle CO_2 emissions associated with the final demand for new passenger vehicles and gasoline. This is the life-cycle input-output method (see Kagawa et al., 2008, 2011 for further details).

Passenger vehicle lifetime analysis

Kagawa et al. (2011) applied this method and discussed the role of passenger vehicle lifetime change in CO_2 emission reduction policy. In this section, we explain their analysis and major findings and discuss problems that were not addressed by them. As in Kagawa et al. (2011), we focus here on an ordinary passenger car with an internal-combustion engine larger than 661 cc. The three parameters of the generalised gamma distribution for ordinary passenger cars are presented in Table 1 (see Kagawa et al., 2011 for the parameters estimation).

Table 1: Three parameters of generalised gamma distributions for ordinary passenger cars. Source: Kagawa et al., (2011).

Newly registered year	Scale parameter $\hat{\alpha}$	Scale parameter $\hat{\beta}$	Scale parameter $\hat{\rho}$	Mean: average lifetime $\bar{y}$
1990	1.34	0.97	8.03	11.36
1991	3.98	1.34	4.26	11.54
1992	11.09	2.56	1.37	11.49
1993	12.51	2.93	1.07	11.52
1994	15.22	4.99	0.53	11.41
1995	15.41	4.96	0.55	11.66

Using the parameters provided in Table 1, we can specify the lifetime distributions for cars newly registered from 1990 to 1995. In addition, Kagawa et al. (2011) assumed that the lifetime distributions for cars newly registered from 1996 to 2000 were the same as for those that were newly registered in 1995. The environmentally extended input-output table for 2000 in Japan (National Institute for Environmental Studies, Japan, 2009) was used to estimate the life-cycle CO_2 emissions due to passenger vehicle lifetime changes. Next, we explain the previously reported scenario analysis used to assess the environmental impact that would occur if the average lifetime were to continue to increase or decrease over the 10-year period from 1990 to 2000.

Figure 3 shows the effects of changes in the average lifetime of ordinary passenger cars newly registered between 1990 and 2000 on CO_2 emissions in 2000.

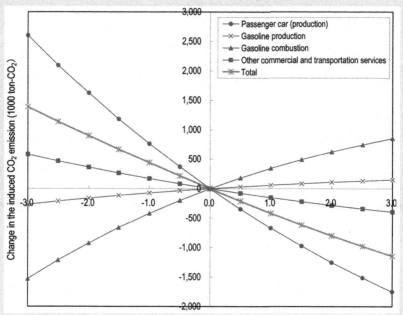

Figure 3: Effects of changes in the average lifetime of ordinary passenger cars that were newly registered between 1990 and 2000 on CO_2 emissions in 2000. Source: Kagawa *et al*. (2011).

The vertical axis in Figure 3 shows how the amount of CO_2 emissions associated with automobile and gasoline final demand in 2000 (baseline emissions: 73 million tons-CO_2 eq.) is influenced by a change in average car lifetime (see Figure 4 for the baseline emissions associated with automobile and gasoline final demand). A positive value on the vertical axis indicates that a change in lifetime leads to an increase in CO_2 emissions, with a negative value indicating a decrease in CO_2 emissions.

We also find that the CO_2 emissions associated with motor vehicle production substantially decrease due to an extension in car lifetime, even though CO_2 emissions associated with gasoline combustions increase (Figure 3). The reason for this is that an extension in motor vehicle lifetime contributes to reducing the number of new motor vehicles sold; thereby it has an impact of reducing the number of motor vehicles produced and the amount of CO_2 emissions associated with motor vehicle production (Kagawa *et al*., 2011).

On the other hand, an extension in car lifetime increases the number of old and less fuel-efficient vehicles still in service and consequently increases the CO_2 emissions from the vehicle fleet on the road (Kagawa *et al*., 2011). A crucial observation here is that total induced CO_2 emissions, (i.e. the combined emissions from motor vehicle production, gasoline refining, gasoline combustion, and other services [see 'Total' in Figure 3]), decrease due to an extension in motor vehicle lifetime. This finding implies that the product lifetime extension scenario would contribute to a reduction in carbon emissions (Kagawa *et al.*, 2011). Thus we find that extension of car lifetime can play a crucial role in mitigating climate change through a reduction in life-cycle emissions attributable to the transport sector.

Kagawa *et al.* (2011) reported that the net environmental benefit of both reducing the passenger vehicle lifetime and further improving the fuel economy of new passenger cars is positive. An important finding is that if the fuel economy of all ordinary passenger cars improves to the same level as that of the hybrid passenger vehicles with higher fuel efficiency of 35 km per litre, life-cycle CO_2 emissions can be reduced by 3.2% under the baseline automobile lifetime scenario. However, it should be noted that the environmental benefit of 3.2% is actually considered to be a decrease, because the CO_2 emissions associated with manufacturing hybrid vehicles with greater fuel efficiency is much higher than manufacturing conventional gasoline-powered vehicles (Kagawa *et al.*, 2013).

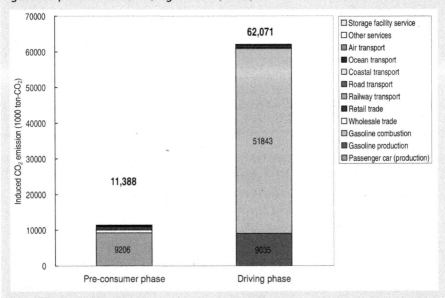

Figure 4: CO_2 emissions associated with motor vehicle production and driving in 2000. Source: Kagawa *et al.* (2011).

When a vehicle lifetime reduction policy, such as the vehicle replacement scheme of Japan, is introduced (see, the report by the Japan Automobile Manufacturers Association (2009) for the Japanese scheme) and the market share for vehicles targeted in the replacement scheme is expanded, significant attention should be paid to the additional materials and parts that are required for producing the target vehicles (e.g. hybrid vehicles with greater fuel efficiency) and how their additional inputs will affect the environment through their productions.

Extending the lifetime of passenger vehicles can bring about considerable environmental benefits (i.e., reduction in CO_2 emissions) through the entire economy (Kagawa *et al.*, 2011). In contrast to the vehicle lifetime reduction policy, we propose a vehicle lifetime extension policy to combat climate change. Specifically, the automotive industry and/or governments can offer incentives to owners of older 'green' vehicles that have better fuel economy to retain and use these vehicles for a longer time. One such effective measure could be a subsidy provided by the government to owners of older vehicles with a poor fuel economy, to incentivise the replacement of their vehicles with second hand vehicles with a higher fuel economy. This measure could maximise the environmental benefit compared to the previously introduced vehicle replacement schemes that focus on new vehicles.

Conclusions and further research

In this case study, we have outlined a method for estimating how changes in passenger vehicle lifetime affect CO_2 emissions. From the viewpoint of life cycle analysis, the method presented here is still incomplete because the analysis framework does not include the recycling processes for end-of-life vehicles that have been disposed of and waste treatment processes for secondary materials from the end-of-life vehicles. As shown in Kagawa *et al.* (2015), the framework can be extended to waste input-output analysis, as developed by Nakamura and Kondo (2002). A number of environmental and resource policy studies, using a wide variety of the analysis frameworks, are expected to be conducted in the future.

The lifetime of used cars has not been well modelled in previous studies (Kagawa *et al.*, 2008, 2009, 2011, 2013). Used cars dominate the car market in many developed countries, so it is very important to include the lifetime distribution functions for used cars in the systems analysis. By doing so, the effects of increasing the lifetime of used cars and expanding their market share for CO_2 emissions can be estimated, the effectiveness of current policies can be assessed, and effective emission-reduction policies that focus on used cars can be proposed.

The analysis framework can be extended to a multi-regional input-output analysis (see Miller & Blair, 2009). This would enable the modelling of intra- and inter-regional trade associated with the final demand for durable goods (passenger vehicles in the present study) and CO_2 emissions induced by this trade. An effective policy may involve importing new or used passenger vehicles with higher fuel economy from a specific country while replacing vehicles with higher fuel economy with older passenger vehicles with lower fuel economy in another country.

In conclusion, using data from Japan we have shown the critical importance of including whole-of-life energy and carbon calculations when assessing the contributions that new technologies can make towards low carbon mobility transitions. While energy-efficiency gains are important, replacing technologies can overlook the energy and carbon embedded in the production phase. Without this perspective, policy designed to reduce GHG emissions may result in increased emissions and further exacerbate global climate change.

Acknowledgements

The present study was supported by Grants-in-Aid for Research (No. 20353534 and No. 25281065) from the Ministry of Education, Culture, Sports, Science and Technology in Japan. We thank the editors, Debbie Hopkins and James Higham for helpful comments. All errors are our own.

References

Cohen, C. & Whitten, B.J. (1988). *Parameter Estimation in Reliability and Life Span Models*, Marcel Dekker, Inc.

Greening, L.A., Greene, D.L. & Difiglio, C. (2000). Energy efficiency and consumption – the rebound effect – a survey, *Energy Policy*, **28**(6-7), 389–401.

Horioka, C.Y. (2006). The causes of Japan's 'Lost Decade': The role of household consumption, *Japan and the World Economy*, **18**(4), 378–400.

Japan Automobile Dealers Association (2016). www.jada.or.jp/contents/data/index. html. Accessed 31 March 2016.

Japan Automobile Manufacturers Association (2009). Japan's measures to withstand impact of global crisis on its automotive industry - JAMA shares at the 4th Indonesia International Automotive Conference. http://www.jama-english.jp/asia/news/2009/vol36/index.html. Accessed March 4, 2016.

Japan Automobile Manufacturers Association (2016). Motor Vehicle Statistics of Japan. http://www.jama-english.jp/publications/MVS2015.pdf. Accessed March 4, 2016.

Kagawa, S., Kudoh, Y., Nansai, K. & Tasaki, T. (2008). The economic and environmental consequences of automobile lifetime extension and fuel economy improvement: Japan's case, *Economic Systems Research*, **20**(1), 3–28.

Kagawa, S., Nansai, K. & Kudoh, Y. (2009). Does product lifetime extension increase our income at the expense of energy consumption? *Energy Economics*, **31**(2), 197–210.

Kagawa, S., Nansai, K., Kondo, Y., Hubacek, K., Suh, S., Minx, J., Kudoh, Y., Tasaki, T., & Nakamura, S. (2011). Role of motor vehicle lifetime extension in climate change policy, *Environmental Science & Technology*, **45**(4), 1184–1191.

Kagawa, S., Hubacek, K., Nansai, K., Kataoka, M., Managi, S., Suh, S. & Kudoh, Y. (2013). Better cars or older cars?: Assessing co_2 emission reduction potential of passenger vehicle replacement programs, *Global Environmental Change*, **23**(6), 1807–1818.

Kagawa, S., Nakamura, S., Kondo, Y., Matsubae, K & Nagasaka, T. (2015). Forecasting replacement demand of durable goods and the induced secondary material flows: a case study of automobiles, *Journal of Industrial Ecology*, **19**(1), 10–19.

Kudoh, Y., Kondo, Y., Matsuhashi, K., Kobayashi, S. & Moriguchi, Y. (2004). Current Status of Actual Fuel Consumption of Petrol Fuelled Passenger Vehicles in Japan, *Applied Energy*, **79**(3), 291–308.

McCool, J. I. (2012). *Using the Weibull Distribution: Reliability, Modeling and Inference*, John Wiley & Sons, Inc., New Jersey, USA.

Miller, R.E. & Blair, P.D. (2009). *Input-Output Analysis: Foundations and Extensions 2nd Edition*, Cambridge University Press, New York, USA.

National Institute for Environmental Studies, Japan (2009). Embodied Energy and Emission Intensity Data for Japan Using Input–Output Tables, http://www.cger. nies.go.jp/publications/report/d031/eng/index_e.htm. Accessed 16 May 2016.

Next Generation Vehicle Promotion Center (2016). http://www.cev- c.or.jp/tokei/hanbai. html. Accessed 31 March 2016.

Ministry of the Environment, Japan (2014). *Japan's Climate Change Policies*, 1–74.

Nakamura, S. & Kondo, Y. (2002). Input-output analysis of waste management, *Journal of Industrial Ecology*, **6**(1), 39–64.

OECD (2009). Environment: Private vehicle ownership, in *OECD Regions at a Glance 2009*, OECD Publishing. http://dx.doi.org/10.1787/reg_glance-2009-34-en.

Suh, S. (Ed.) (2009). *Handbook of Input-Output Economics in Industrial Ecology*, Springer, New York, NY, USA.

Tukker, A. & Dietzenbacher, E. (2013). Global multiregional input–output frameworks: an introduction and outlook, *Economic Systems Research*, **25**(1), 1–19.

Conclusions

15 Low Carbon Mobility: Urgent futures and radical transitions

James Higham

Department of Tourism, University of Otago, New Zealand & University of Stavanger, Norway.

Debbie Hopkins

Transport Studies Unit, School of Geography and the Environment, University of Oxford, UK.

Introduction

More people than ever before are moving more frequently and at accelerating speeds, often for shorter periods of time (Creutzig *et al.*, 2015). These mobilities are largely dependent on unsustainable high-carbon technologies (IEA, 2015). Continuing technical innovations have enhanced the energy efficiency of some transportation technologies. However, efficiency gains and other technical breakthroughs tend to reduce the cost and increase the uptake of transportation, rather than reduce absolute transport-related carbon emissions (Vivanco *et al.*, 2015). Demand for high carbon transportation is growing and is forecast to continue to grow rapidly over the course of the next three decades to 2050 (Creutzig *et al.*, 2015; Peeters & Dubois, 2010). High demand for personal mobility in the developed world, which is now greater than ever, is compounded by a rapidly developing appetite for high-carbon forms of transportation in the emerging economies of the world. Transportation now accounts for 23% of anthropogenic CO_2 and is growing in both relative and absolute terms (Creutzig *et al.*, 2015).

State of the Climate

The State of the Climate is a continuing series of annual summary reports on the global climate system produced by the National Ocean and Atmospheric Administration (NOAA) and published in the *Bulletin of the American Meteorological Society*. The 2015 State of the Climate Report (NOAA, 2016) draws together the '...*contributions from more than 450 scientists from 62 countries, drawing on tens of thousands of measurements of Earth's climate*' (Milman, 2016). NOAA (2016) reports that 2015 was the hottest year on record, exceeding the previous hottest year (2014) by 0.1°C and pre-industrial temperatures by 1°C. This is attributed almost entirely to the continued emission of greenhouse gases. Meanwhile the United Nations agency, the World Meteorological Organisation (WMO, 2016), reports that in the first six months of 2016 temperature data confirms a 1.3°C increase upon the late 19th century pre-industrial baseline.

> '*Global temperatures for the first six months of this year shattered yet more records... Two separate reports from the U.S National Oceanic and Atmospheric Administration and NASA's Goddard Institute for Space Studies (NASA GISS) both highlighted the dramatic and sweeping changes in the state of the climate. June 2016 marked the 14th consecutive month of record heat for land and oceans. It marked the 378th consecutive month with temperatures above the 20th century average. The last month with temperatures below the 20th century average was December 1984*' (WMO, 2016).

These temperature increases should be considered alongside the fact that 3.5°C above pre-industrial levels has been described as the 'extinction event' (Denayer, 2016). Rapid changes in climate are a consequence of concentrations of CO_2 that reached 399.4ppm in 2015 (NOAA, 2016). The oceans of the world have absorbed much of the CO_2 that has been released into the atmosphere over the course of the last century. Global sea levels are 70mm higher than when satellite measurement began in 1993, increasing at an average annual rate of 3.3mm due to glacier melt and thermal expansion of the world's oceans (NOAA, 2016).

Paris 2015

The Paris Climate Agreement (December 2015) came about following intense negotiations at the 21st Conference of the Parties (COP) to the United Nations Framework Convention on Climate Change (UNFCCC). It embodies the commitment of 196 countries (Parties to the Agreement) to the goal of stabilising global average temperatures below +2°C relative to pre-industrial levels (UNFCCC, 2015), with many Parties to the Agreement indicating a commitment to stay within a 1.5°C target. The *State of the Climate* (NOAA, 2016) reports leaves absolutely no doubt about how difficult this will be. Signatories must now develop policies that align with 2030 emission reduction goals as expressed in Intended National Determined Contributions (INDCs) (UNFCCC, 2015). Given the failure of earlier climate negotiations (Vidal *et al.*, 2009), the Paris Agreement has been described as one of the '*world's greatest diplomatic success*' (Harvey, 2015 online) and as a '*remarkable international consensus*' (Scott, Hall & Gössling, 2016:1). Clearly the success of Paris lies in the execution of 2030 INDCs (Clémençon, 2016). The meeting of 2030 INDCs will determine the extent to which anthropogenic climate change, already in train (NOAA, 2016; WMO, 2016), can be mitigated and the most severe consequences of climate change avoided (Scott *et al.*, 2016; Bailey & Jackson Inderberg, 2016).

It is both in the extent of the INDCs and the likelihood of achieving Paris INDCs that doubts arise. Some consider the Paris Agreement likely to only slow the rate at which GHG emissions are *increasing*, rather than achieve the radical emission reductions that are required to achieve a low carbon energy system, and that a zero net increase in atmospheric CO_2 and other GHGs by 2050 will be insufficient to avert the most severe consequences of climate change. The absence of specific targets for international aviation and maritime transport (European Federation for Transport and Environment, 2016) in the Paris Climate Agreement has also been highlighted as a cause of considerable doubt. The absence of international transport emissions from national GHG inventories is a longstanding challenge that continues to confound efforts to mitigate transportation emissions (Smith & Rodger, 2009).

Transportation and climate change

The links between transportation and climate change are well established. Transport accounts for just under a quarter (23%) of total global energy-related CO_2 emissions, and transport emissions are projected to double by 2050 (Creutzig *et al.*, 2015). The Intergovernmental Panel on Climate Change [IPCC] 5th Assessment Report (AR5) notes that transport emissions must be addressed as part of the challenge of achieving a low carbon energy system in order to stabilise the global climate. A special issue of *Transportation Research Part D: Transport and Environment* on Climate Change and Transport (Volume 45, June 2016) explores this relationship in detail. In this special issue, transportation is recognised as the second largest source of anthropogenic CO_2 emissions (Jochem *et al.*, 2016), but growing fast and likely to soon exceed emissions from electricity generation (IEA, 2015).

The continued and accelerating growth of transportation emissions is attributed to changing mobility patterns among the high emitters of hypermobile developed societies, combined with the rapid development of high carbon intensity transport systems in emerging economies (Jochem *et al.*, 2016). The level of decarbonisation required to align regional and global transportation systems with the agreed targets of the Paris Climate Agreement (2015) has proved to be a particularly acute challenge. Mitigation of transport emissions remains largely absent from the political agenda, despite growing recognition of the urgent need to address transportation emissions, because it is fundamentally incompatible with neoliberal ideals (Harvey, 2011; Young *et al.*, 2014). The political risk of addressing transportation emissions arises from the relationship between economic growth and cheap transportation (Creutzig *et al.*, 2015).

Notwithstanding the political risks of confronting transportation emissions, it is critical that transportation emissions are accommodated in the INDCs of the Paris Climate Agreement, and that international aviation and maritime transportation emissions are addressed. These challenges will require that transitions are embraced, both in terms of policies relating to the socio-technical transportation system and the practices of contemporary mobility (Sheller & Urry, 2006). Such transitions extend to systems of transport infrastructure (Geels, 2004; Schwanen, 2013), the adoption of low carbon transportation innovations, where and how people live and work (Lohrey & Creutzig, 2016), and how people engage in leisure and tourism mobilities (Scott *et al.*, 2016).

The challenges that such transitions present cannot be overstated. High-carbon mobility practices are deeply embedded in political, economic, infrastructural and behavioural practices (Barr & Prillwitz, 2014). These practices are reflected in path dependencies that present considerable barriers to system-wide sustainability transitions (Kemp *et al.*, 2012). Our socio-technical transportation systems and mobility practices are embedded in elements of technology, infrastructure, policies and regulations, markets, cultural meanings (Rees *et al.*, 2016) and in contemporary practices of production, consumption and lifestyle (Hall, 2004). Large-scale and widespread transitions in such complex systems must embrace behavioural, policy and technical approaches to address transportation systems and mobility practices systematically rather than as independent system elements (Schwanen, 2013).

Reflecting a system-wide approach, the structure of this book addressed three key aspects of low carbon mobility transitions in three separate parts: *People and Place, Structures in Transition*, and *Innovations for Low Carbon Mobility*.

Part 1: People and Place called for new forms of engagement between policy makers (and academics) and publics, and for new approaches to changing social practices, highlighting the need for deep and contextually rich insights into what are now cast as problematic transportation behaviours and mobility practices (Chapter 2: Barr). The treatment of people and place in this book then explored generational mobilities (Chapter 3: Delbosc), examining the relationship between automobility and life course in terms of such things as work, education, psychological wellbeing and social exclusion. Here the changing roles of cars in society were explored in terms of generation effects, noting that millennials may view cars from utilitarian rather than aspirational perspectives to the extent that alternatives to car use may offer significant new opportunities to reduce car dependence.

Part 1 also underscored the importance of considering mobility practices through a public health lens, which draws attention to the need to consider the benefits of mobility against the negative impacts of different transport systems in terms of health, wellbeing and equity. These negative impacts must be thoroughly understood in relation to scale of analysis, ranging from local impacts such as air pollution, road traffic injuries and reduced levels of daily exercise, to the global impacts associated with transportation emissions and climate change. In Chapter 4 (McMillan and Mackie) a strong case was made for the full suite of equity and wellbeing outcomes to be embraced in transport planning, to move beyond business-as-usual systems that give priority to road infrastructure and volume. The business and leisure lifestyles of the hypermobile elite, the high emitters that have proved unwilling or unable to modify their aeromobility practices, provide other challenges in moving towards low carbon mobility practices. Chapter 5 (Cohen) highlighted that while corporeal mobility may be central to the performance of identity, making established practices particularly intractable, the less glamorous or 'darker' sides of hypermobile lifestyles and frequent business travel offers insights into the wellbeing consequences of hypermobility, which play a part in the transition to low carbon mobility systems.

The case of the Chinese migrant communities in Sydney, (Case Study 1: Kerr, Klocker and Waitt) highlighted the lower rates of car ownership and use among minority migrant groups, challenging dominant narratives of car dependence and providing fascinating insights into the co-existence of diverse automobility practices within societies. This case highlighted the profound importance of recognising the benefits of alternative practices, which are often rendered invisible due to the dominant paradigm of high car dependence. This paradigm must be questioned, and policy makers must better recognise and support the practices of groups (ethnic or otherwise) who are already engaged in the low carbon transport practices that are urgently needed. The co-evolution of Cape Town's urban transport systems (Case Study 2: Seeliger and Kane) provided further insights into unique aspects of people and place. It examined the move towards opening Cape Town streets in order to address the city's apartheid spatial form and reduce reliance on private vehicle use, which has traditionally only served the interests of the affluent members of society. Evolving urban transport systems in the interest of inclusiveness and equity offers a pathway towards a low carbon urban transport future. Contextually rich and in depth understandings of people and place are critically important to local low carbon transitions that are, in turn, critical to the global climate footprint of transportation systems.

Transition requires that fundamental changes in society occur over a concentrated timeframe in order to move from existing to new systems of equilibrium. Within this context, low carbon mobility transitions are particularly challenging because of transportation path dependencies (Schwanen, 2013). Mobility transitions are problematic because they require high levels of investment to change transport infrastructures combined with the difficulties involved in changing existing mobility practices. These challenges were addressed in *Part 2: Structures in Transition* where in Chapter 6, Michael Hall noted that transport policies overlap with and, therefore, do not function in isolation from other policy fields, including urban design, energy policy, business and economic development and tourism. Changes to policy regimes and structures of transport provision are further challenged by the debates surrounding local, regional and national policies and where responsibility lies for low carbon transitions that play out across a range of local-global spatial scales. The interdependence of policy paradigms and socio-technical regimes was highlighted in Chapter 6; however it was also observed that regions, while set within national and supranational institutional frameworks, can and must act upon sustainability transitions, to then function as 'cells of development' within a wider unsustainable system.

Path dependence informed Chapter 7 (Imran and Pearce) which further highlighted the importance or local/regional political leadership, to influence and inform national policies that must integrate the efforts of different policy fields (e.g., business and employment, industry and innovation, housing, land use and transportation) to support local/regional low carbon transitions. Similar challenges of path dependence exist in transport systems such as in India (Chapter 8: Joshi, Joseph and Chandran), where in the last decade a rapid *high* carbon mobility transition has unfolded. Driven by high rates of economic development and rising household incomes, the tradition of low energy transport systems in Indian cities (e.g., walking, cycling) has given way to carbon intensive transport systems. Reversing this process of transition will require a transport planning paradigm shift away from affluence and speed, to give renewed priority to public and non-motorised modes to transport. The important roles of institutions and governance, at both the metropolitan and national levels, to drive system change is also evident in Finland (Chapter 9: Kivimaa and Temmes) where the initial steps have been taken along a pathway towards low carbon mobility. These insights demonstrate that mobility structural change challenges the foundations of economies.

Newman (Chapter 10) observed that the end of structural oil dependence, including automobile dependence, is critical to the transition away from fossil fuel economies, despite the fact that decarbonisation of the global energy system requires fundamental changes in economic policy. As Bows and Anderson (2007) note, efforts to reduce aviation emissions are challenged by a climate change 'policy clash' given the critical role that aviation serves in regional and national economies, in terms of the mobility of commerce, people (tourism) and high value freight (Smith & Rodger, 2009; Hopkins & McCarthy, 2016). Here the case is made that mobility structures must be addressed at the supranational level (IEA, 2015) to continue and entrench emerging trends towards lower car dependence in some societies, peak car (including the transition to electric and automated vehicles), the decoupling of wealth and auto- and aero-mobility, and re-urbanisation driven by new tech- nologies and the knowledge economy. Of course these trends are not universal and contrast the case of Brazil (Case Study 3) which Kuhnimhof and Weiss described as being on an auto-oriented path and, as such, must seek efficiency gains and alternative low carbon or emission free energy sources to achieve low carbon auto-mobility. Case Study 4 (Stroebel) adopted a neo-Gramscian perspective to highlight that the legitimacy of the tourism industry is not yet under threat, but pre-emptive strategies to secure the future legitimacy of the tourism in a low carbon economy, requires that low carbon leisure and tourism transitions are actively pursued without delay.

Technical solutions and innovation for low carbon mobility (*Part 3: Innovations for Low Carbon Mobility*) offer their own unique challenges and opportunities. Technical solutions, such as the promise offered by electric vehicles (EVs) with zero tailpipe emissions, offers much potential but governance is critical to meeting that potential. This is clearly evident in the case of Scotland (Chapter 11: Morton and Beeton) where the devolution of taxation authority from the UK Parliament may extend the capacity of the government of Scotland to set rates for vehicle registration and taxation that encourage the adoption of electric vehicles; a strategy that has proved to be very effective in fostering automotive fleet replacement and uptake of EVs in Norway. The importance of governance was underlined by Schwanen (Chapter 12) who adopted a socio-technical transitions approach to address innovations to transform personal mobility. Schwanen noted the importance of a multi-level perspective which recognises that innovations can only reconfigure mobility systems if socio-technical niches, regimes and landscapes are aligned and mutually reinforcing. This is critically important given that the socio-technical system represents a highly complex assemblage of technologies, infrastructures, markets, policies and regulations, cultural values and user practices. The system, according to Schwanen, is bound together by social practices as expressed in cognitive routines, shared beliefs, social norms, industry standards and laws. Such complexity requires that policy and governance supports innovations that allow socio-technical transitions to low carbon mobility systems.

The technologies and user practices that underpin the socio-technical system include complex Internet technology (IT) – transportation interrelationships that were explored by Gössling (Chapter 13). This chapter drew the attention of the reader to apps that facilitate shared mobility and the use of public transport, and which offer the potential to reduce independent car use and overall mobility demand. Social media platforms, conversely, may foster competitive mobilities. Internet platforms encourage foster automotive cultures that glamorise cars as desirable objects that are linked to desirable lifestyles. Challenges remain, and opportunities exist, to understand and harness the role of IT in the transformation of mobilities.

Operational innovations and technical efficiency gains in jet aviation have been the subject of intense debate in relation to low carbon transitions (Peeters *et al.*, 2016). Global passenger demand for air travel continues to grow at 5-6% per annum (Bows-Larkin *et al.*, 2016). While aviation fuel efficiency gains have been presented as a solution to the high emissions of aviation, those gains have consistently fallen short of the 1.5% per annum (2009-2020) target set by ICAO (EFTE, 2016). Even the most optimistic technology forecasts do not offset current and expected growth in demand for aviation (ICAO, 2016, Mayor & Tol, 2010; Peeters *et al.*, 2016). The aviation growth trajectory is incompatible with the low carbon transitions as expressed in the Paris Climate Agreement. As such Bongaerts, Nawijn, Eijgelaar and Peeters (Chapter 14) called for a transformation in air travel behaviour from long to short haul and from short haul to rail. Herein lies considerable potential for the reduction in aviation emissions, which should be combined with clear and confronting aviation carbon footprint communications.

The importance of political will in supporting low carbon innovations was evident in Case Study 5 (Tyfield and Zuev). China is the world's largest car market and urban mobility transition in China is critical to the dual challenges of reducing global carbon emissions and restoring local air quality. The planning of car-free satellite cities and human-centred cities that give priority to walking and cycling may form part of the response, alongside an urban e-mobility transition that is driven by the intensity of current urban congestion and associated environmental issues. By way of further contrast, in Japan (Case Study 6: Kagawa, Nishijima and Nakamoto) a subsidised vehicle replacement scheme aims to support the uptake of new generation fuel efficient vehicles. The scheme has resulted in an increase in hybrid passenger vehicle ownership of 233% (2010-2014) or 4.7 million hybrid vehicles. In Case Study 6, consideration was given to the life course of used vehicles, highlighting the need to appreciate whole-of-life energy and carbon calculations when assessing new technologies that require fleet replacement as part of low carbon transitions. Clearly energy efficiency gains are important, but so too is the need to accommodate the energy and carbon consequences of fleet replacement.

Concluding statement

We are living in times of urgent transition to low carbon societies and economies. Neither the challenge nor the urgency of these processes of transition can be overstated. The Paris Climate Agreement (2015) articulates a widely held commitment to addressing the continued rapid growth in GHG emissions and confronting the dramatic social and ecological consequences of a changing global climate (IPCC, 2014; NOAA, 2016; WMO, 2016). This commitment recognises that radical and system-wide transitions toward low carbon mobility are urgently required. In this book, we drew upon 'socio-technical' perspectives, which refer to the co-evolution of social and technological relationships. Socio-technical transitions highlight the dynamics by which fundamental change in these relationships occur. *Low Carbon Mobility Transitions* examined the flows of people in private daily transport, commuting, business, leisure and tourism travel. It also focused on climate change mitigation, and pathways to reduce the carbon-intensity of current systems of mobility.

The policy response in most cases has been slow. Transport is a difficult sector in which to reduce energy demand (Anable *et al.*, 2012; IEA, 2008). Command-and-control, market-based and soft policy measures are available to transport policy makers (Friman *et al.*, 2013; Sterner, 2007) but social and infrastructural lock-in has been a barrier to action implementation (Banister & Hickman, 2013; Randles & Mander, 2009). In light of systemic challenges and political risk aversion, governments have been content to leave accountability for transportation emissions to consumers, by relying on behaviour change towards lower carbon lifestyles (Barr *et al.*, 2011). It is abundantly clear that radical system transitions are required to address *aggregate* transportation emissions, rather than leaving consumers to assume responsibility for their *individual* transportation emissions (Schwanen *et al.*, 2011).

Low Carbon Mobility Transitions has critically explored the wide-ranging and diverse regional contexts in which a low carbon transition has, is being, or can be achieved. In doing so, it has highlighted the place-specific, geopolitical and cultural sensitivities of low carbon transitions at national, regional and local (metropolitan) scales. The mutually-informing and overlapping roles of behaviour change, transportation policy and technical innovation were critically examined in this book, and it makes clear the need for transportation policies, infrastructure investments and planning for sustainable mobility practices to be integrated (Barr & Prillwitz, 2014; Lohrey & Creutzig, 2016).

In this book we have brought together the theoretical and empirical contributions of scholars from a range of disciplines to provide a critical treatment of low carbon mobility transitions. Insights were drawn from transportation, travel and tourism and mobilities research to explore the prospects for low carbon mobility transitions across the full spectrum of local/regional, national and global scales of analysis. It is critically important that the varied social, cultural and geographic contexts of low carbon mobility transitions that were identified in this book are taken up and acted upon to inform the low carbon mobility transformations that are so obviously and urgently required. These insights must inform efforts to ensure the full accountability of transportation emissions, and to ensure that the INDCs that are outlined in the Paris Climate Agreement (2015) are upheld and achieved in full measure.

References

Anable, J., Brand, C., Tran, M. & Eyre, N. (2012). Modelling transport energy demand: a socio-technical approach. *Energy Policy* **41**, 125-138.

Bailey, I. & Jackson Inderberg, T.H (2016). New Zealand and Climate Change: What are the stakes and what can New Zealand do? *Policy Quarterly* **12**(2), 3-13.

Banister, D. & Hickman, R. (2013). Transport futures: thinking the unthinkable. *Transport Policy* **29**, 283-293.

Barr, S., Gilg, A. & Shaw, G. (2011). Helping people make better choices: Exploring the behaviour change agenda for environmental sustainability. *Applied Geography*, **31**(2), 712-720.

Barr, S. & Prillwitz, J. (2014). A smarter choice? Exploring the behaviour change agenda for environmentally sustainable mobility. *Environment and Planning C: government and policy*, **32**(1), 1-19.

Bows, A. & Anderson, K.L. (2007). Policy clash: can projected aviation growth be reconciled with the UK Government's 60% carbon-reduction target? *Transport Policy* **14** (2), 103-110.

Bows-Larkin, A., Mander, S.L., Traut, M.B., Anderson, K.L. & Wood, F.R. (2016). Aviation and Climate Change -The continuing challenge. In *Encyclopedia of Aerospace Engineering*, R. Blockley and W. Shyy (Eds), Chichester: John Wiley.

Clémençon, R. (2016). The two sides of the Paris climate agreement: Dismal failure or historic breakthrough? *Journal of Environment & Development* **25**(1), 3-24.

Creutzig, F., Jochem, P., Edelenbosch, O.Y., Mattauch, L., van Vuuren, D.P., McCollum, D. & Minx, J. (2015). Transport: A roadblock to climate change mitigation? *Science* **350**, 911.

Denayer, W. (2016). How climate change is rapidly taking the planet apart. Part 2: amplifying feedbacks, divestment. Retrieved 3 August 2016 from http://www.flassbeck-economics.com/how-climate-change-is-rapidly-taking-the-planet-apart-part-2-amplifying-feedbacks-divestment/.

European Federation for Transport and Environment (EFTE) (2016). Aviation emissions and the Paris Agreement: Europe and ICAO must ensure aviation makes a fair contribution to the Paris Agreement's goals. Retrieved 30 May 2016 from http://www.transportenvironment.org.

Geels, F.W. (2004). From sectoral systems of innovation to socio-technical systems: insights about dynamics and change from sociology and institutional theory, *Research Policy*, **33**, 897-920.

Hall, C.M. (2004). *Tourism: The Social Science of Mobility*. Melbourne: Pearson Education.

Harvey, F. (2015). Paris Climate Change Agreement: The world's greatest diplomatic success. *The Guardian*. Retrieved 31 May 2016 from https://www.theguardian.com/environment/2015/dec/13/paris-climate-deal-cop-diplomacy-developing-united-nations.

Hopkins, D. & McCarthy, A. (2016). Change trends in urban freight delivery: A qualitative inquiry, *Geoforum*, **74**, 158-170.

International Civil Aviation Organization (ICAO) (2016). Global Aviation CO_2 Emissions Projections to 2050. Retrieved 31 May 2016 from http://www.icao.int/environmental-protection/GIACC/Giacc-4/CENV_GIACC4_IP1_IP2%20IP3.pdf.

International Energy Agency (IEA) (2015). World Energy Outlook 2015. Paris. Retrieved 3 August 2016 from http://www.worldenergyoutlook.org.

Intergovernmental Panel on Climate Change (IPCC) (2014). Working Group III Contribution to the Fifth assessment report of the intergovernmental panel on climate change. In O. Edenhofer, R. Pichs-Madruga, Y. Sokona, E. Farahani, S. Kadner, K., Seyboth, J. Minx, Adler, A., Baum, I., Brunner, S., Eickemeier, P., Kriemann, B., Savolainen, J., Schlömer, S., von Stechow, C., Zwickelm T. (Eds.), *Climate change 2014: Mitigation of Climate Change. Fifth assessment report of the intergovernmental panel on climate change*. Cambridge: Cambridge University Press.

Jochem, P., Rothengatter, W., & Schade, W. (2014). Climate Change and Transport. *Transportation Research Part D: Transport and Environment.* **45**: 1-3.

Kemp, R., Geels, K.W. & Dudley, G. (2012). Introduction: Sustainability Transitions in the automobility regime and the need for a new perspective. In: F.W. Geels, R. Kemp, G. Dudley & G. Lyons (Eds.). *Automobility in Transition? A Socio-Technical Analysis of Sustainable Transport*. Abingdon: Routledge.

Lohrey, S., & Creutzig, F. (2016). A 'sustainability window' of urban form. *Transportation Research Part D: Transport and Environment*, **45**, 96-111.

Mayor, K. & Tol, R.S.J., (2010). Scenarios of carbon dioxide emissions from aviation. *Global Environmental Change* **20** (1), 65-73.

Milman, O. (2016). Environmental records shattered as climate change 'plays out before us'. Retrieved 3 August 2016 from https://www.theguardian.com/environment/2016/aug/02/environment-climate-change-records-broken-international-report

National Ocean and Atmospheric Administration (NOAA) (2016). *2015 State of the Climate*. Retrieved 3 August 2016 from https://www.climate.gov/news-features/features/2015-state-climate-highlights#wows1_3

Peeters, P.M. & Dubois, G. (2010). Tourism travel under climate change mitigation constraints. *Journal of Transport Geography* **18**, 447-457.

Peeters, P.M., Higham, J.E.S., Kutzner, D., Cohen, S. & Gössling, S. (2016). Are technology myths stalling aviation climate policy? *Transportation Research Part D: Transport and Environment* **44**, 30-42.

Randles, S. & Mander, S. (2009). Practice(s) and ratchet(s): a sociological examination of frequent flying. In: S. Gössling & P. Upham (Eds.), *Climate Change and Aviation: Issues, Challenges and Solutions.* Earthscan: London, pp. 245-271.

Rees, D., Stephenson, J., Hopkins, D. & Doering, A. (2016). Exploring stability and change in transport systems: combining Delphi and system dynamics approaches, *Transportation*, DOI: 10.1007/s11116-016-9677-7.

Schwanen, T. (2013). Sociotechnical transition in the transport system. In: M. Givoni, & D. Banister (Eds.). *Moving Towards Low Carbon Mobility*. Cheltenham: Edward Elgar.

Schwanen, T., Banister, D. & Anable, J. (2011). Scientific research about climate change mitigation in transport. *Transportation Research Part A: Policy and Practice.* **45** (10), 993-1006.

Scott, D., Hall, C.M. & Gössling, S. (2016). A review of the IPCC 5th assessment and implications for tourism sector climate resilience and decarbonization. *Journal of Sustainable Tourism*, **24**(1), 8-30.

Sheller, M. & Urry, J. (Eds.). (2006). *Mobile Technologies of the City*. Abingdon: Routledge.

Smith, I. J. & Rodger, C. J. (2009). Carbon offsets for aviation-generated emissions due to international travel to and from New Zealand. *Energy Policy*, **37**(9), 3438-3447.

Sterner, T. (2007). Fuel taxes: an important instrument for climate policy. *Energy Policy* **35** (6), 3194-3202.

UNFCCC (2015). Adoption of the Paris Agreement. Retrieved 31 May 2016 from https://unfccc.int/resource/docs/2015/cop21/eng/l09r01.pdf.

Vidal, J., Stratton, A. & Goldenberg, S. (2009). Low targets, goals dropped: Copenhagen ends in failure. Retrieved 31 May 2016 from http://www.theguardian.com/environment/2009/dec/18/copenhagen-deal.

Vivanco, D.F., Kemp, R. & van der Voet, E. (2015). The relativity of eco-innovation: environmental rebound effects from past transport innovations in Europe, *Journal of Cleaner Production*, **101**, 71-85.

World Meteorological Organisation (2016). Global climate breaks new records January to June 2016. Retrieved 3 August 2016 from http://public.wmo.int/en/media/press-release/global-climate-breaks-new-records-january-june-2016.

Young, M., Higham, J.E.S. & Reis, A. (2014). Up in the air: A conceptual critique of flying addiction. *Annals of Tourism Research.* **41**, 51-64.

Index

Printed in the United States
By Bookmasters